MORE PRAISE FOR *SOLITUDE* BY ROBERT KULL

"Unlike other memoirs, *Solitude* never reads like the author trying to hammer a lesson. Instead, Kull engages in a messy process of discovery, right there on the page, inviting us to share in the raw material of his struggle — and resulting in something far more real, intimate and wise."

— *Common Ground*

"This book represents a breakthrough. Analogies with Thoreau or Edward Abbey are not wrong in trying to identify the unique mix of wilderness survivalism with philosophical reflection, but those authors represent nineteenth and twentieth century themes respectively. Kull embarks on the cusp of a new century and strikes a post-modern tone. . . . Robert Kull is a unique voice pursuing the complexity of solitude and self. His book is a very welcome addition to the experience."

— www.hermitary.com

"This book will be enjoyed by those committed to better understanding their own spirituality and wilderness enthusiasts who hear the call of the wild."

— *Winnepeg Free Press*

"This enlightening book contains Kull's diary and a series of mind-stretching and soul-stirring interludes."

— www.spiritualityandpractice.com

"Writing this book has given Kull the opportunity to guide others to reflect on what it means to be alive, part of the greater whole, and to live with compassion and equanimity."

— *ForeWord*

"The year he spent in near-total isolation (his lone companion was a cat) resulted in this book which is part page-turning diary and part in-depth examination of the great outdoors all around him. A fascinating, if at times claustrophobic, chronicling of one man's attempt to reconnect with nature and find peace."

D1397061

"The book is written as starkly as the lifestyle Kull is crafting, and comprised largely of his daily logs: fishing, studying limpets, watching wildlife, each experience a chance to stoke enlightenment. 'It's interesting to try to pin down the borders of the colors,' he says after endless rains release a rainbow. 'I've never tracked these moving shafts of light before; have seen them only as a brief touch, rather than a lingering caress.' *Solitude* lacks the bravado one might expect from such a tale, and Kull's honesty allows the writing to flow far beyond the territory navigated by typical egotistical adventurers. 'These have been rough days psychospiritually,' he writes after one particularly trying set of storms. 'It's painful to feel I'm failing. When I leave here, I shouldn't say much to anyone about this year.' Thankfully, he changed his mind and published his moving story."

— *Audubon* magazine

"Bob Kull has done something relatively rare in the modern world: He has made a retreat/journey/pilgrimage that suits his own need and desire. He has learned essential lessons, and like a good spiritual adventurer, he is letting us in on the lessons he learned. Although his adventure is fascinating, it is his inner discoveries that appeal to me. It is worth everything for him to say that he is not a hero and his adventure is not heroic. That is just what we desperately need today: nonheroic adventures. This is an amazing story, worth reading and being inspired by. Bob is like a modern shaman, going out and coming back. And readers can take a good portion of Bob's experience into themselves and be changed by it."

— Thomas Moore, author of *Care of the Soul* and *Dark Nights of the Soul*

solitude

solitude

Seeking Wisdom in Extremes

Robert Kull

A YEAR ALONE IN THE PATAGONIA WILDERNESS

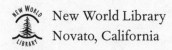
New World Library
Novato, California

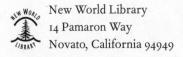 New World Library
14 Pamaron Way
Novato, California 94949

Copyright © 2008 by Robert Kull

All rights reserved. This book may not be reproduced in whole or in part, stored in a retrieval system, or transmitted in any form or by any means — electronic, mechanical, or other — without written permission from the publisher, except by a reviewer, who may quote brief passages in a review.

The poem by Rumi on page 63 appears by kind permission of Coleman Barks.

Text design by Tona Pearce Myers

Library of Congress Cataloging-in-Publication Data
Kull, F. Robert.
Solitude : seeking wisdom in extremes : a year alone in the Patagonia wilderness / Robert Kull.
    p.   cm.
Includes bibliographical references.
ISBN 978-1-57731-632-9 (hardcover : alk. paper)
1. Solitude. 2. Spiritual life. I. Title.
BJ1499.S65K85 2008
204.092—dc22
[B]   2008020886

First paperback printing, July 2009
ISBN 978-1-57731-674-9
Printed in Canada on 100% postconsumer-waste recycled paper

New World Library is a proud member of the Green Press Initiative.

10   9   8   7   6   5   4   3   2   1

For Patti and Cat
and for
the wind and rain of southern Chile

CONTENTS

PREFACE

On February 5, 2001, I went to live on a small, remote island on the Pacific coast of southern Chile, just west of the Andes Mountains and more than a hundred miles by water from the nearest small town. It was a wild, stormy, uninhabited region of rain and windswept islands and fjords, with no boats or airplanes and only the occasional faint sign of distant human activity.

I took all the equipment and supplies I would need to build a camp and stay, completely alone, for a year. The experience was exciting, difficult, and fascinating, often painful, and sometimes filled with wonder. Physical adventures and the challenges of survival counterpointed emotional exploration, philosophical reflection, and spiritual awakening.

Most stories have a beginning, middle, and end, and they draw us into some other time and place. This story is different; it's all middle — no clear beginning, no definite end — and it slips out of time and into the eternal *now*. It's a journey into one of the most remote places on the planet and into some of the darkest recesses and brightest openings of the human spirit.

Solitude has the power to catalyze shifts in consciousness, so rather than write *about* my year alone, I have let the voice of solitude speak *directly* through the words and silences of my edited wilderness journal. Paradoxically, the voice of solitude must, in some sense, remain silent. As soon as the solitary begins to speak, even if by writing to an imagined reader, he (or she) is no longer truly alone.

In places, I've set reflective "Interludes" between journal entries to add perspective. These were written afterward, and they step back from the immediate intensity of my experience in solitude to reflect on important ideas or aspects of the year. But the heart of the story beats within the hours, days, and months of the journal. There, I've tried to scrupulously tell my truth as I lived it — even painful parts I might prefer to keep private. Although I haven't included photographs here, many beautiful images can be found at www.bobkull.org.

In many cultures, solitude is recognized as an opportunity to journey inward; in our culture, spending time alone is often considered unhealthy because we tend to believe that meaning in life is found only through relationship with other people. But to be fully human, we need relationship not only with other people but with the nonhuman world, with our own inner depths — and with Something Greater. For me, that nonmaterial Presence is mysterious and sacred. It can be experienced, but not defined. And I've learned that in coming into a deeper relationship with my self, I develop the capacity to connect more deeply with others.

One of the challenges of solitude is that you have to face yourself. There are no easy escapes. During the year, I struggled with ongoing cycles of resistance and release. Each resolution gave rise to new tension, as storm and calm followed each other in succession. The fundamental tensions were emotional and spiritual, and the moments of resolution did not arise from changing the world, but from coming to accept the world and myself as we are.

My intention in writing this story is not just to describe my own year alone in the wilderness but to evoke the experience for others and guide them into solitude with me. Nestled within this tale of physical and spiritual adventure, there is also an invitation to reflect on our common life as we each struggle to live fully and face our daily challenges with compassion and equanimity. There are no sure answers in these pages, only the space to pause and listen to life calling to life; reminding us that we, too, belong here.

INTRODUCTION

THE CALL OF SOLITUDE

There are times when life seems to snatch us up and carry us toward an unknown destination. We hear something calling from deep within and suspect that if we don't respond, we will wither into a hollow shell. I heard such a call in the mid-1970s, and it changed my life. I was in my late twenties, working as a logger on the west coast of Canada's Vancouver Island, drinking in the local pub, and attempting to be a hard-ass macho. I began to feel a powerful need to be alone. I quit my job and watched myself — almost as a spectator — buy a canoe, purchase supplies for three months, and paddle into the backcountry of northern British Columbia.

I've always spent time alone in nature. My earliest memory is of sitting on a rock one hot dusty morning, cap gun in its holster at my hip, watching the clouds and buzzards drift across the southern California sky. There was tension in my family, and between us and the neighbors, so perhaps I disappeared into the woods and pastures seeking peace and a place where I could be myself. I doubt, though, that I knew then why I went; I still doubt I really know why I go. I can give plausible reasons, but finally, I just feel, from time to time, a mysterious urge to leave society behind.

Deep solitude is strange and powerful and can be frightening. During my teenage years and into my twenties, I often spent days alone in the wilderness, but three months was a radical leap I wasn't psychologically prepared for. I almost lost it out there in northern British Columbia. I almost didn't survive. After six or seven weeks, without other people to help me maintain my identity, the facade of autonomous self-sufficiency started to crumble. Fear crept in as I awoke to how small and vulnerable I was in the face of an enormous and threatening universe. My life felt frighteningly tenuous, and death always instantly possible.

Bears loomed large in my solitary mind. Each night was worse than the one before, as I crouched by the safety of my campfire, hiding from the dangers in the darkness beyond. Finally, I knew I had to either return to the distractions, and apparent safety, of civilization or face the darkness alone.

I left the fire and walked into the forest, edging my way through the dark. I lay down and waited. Time passed, and even the distant glimmer of the fire had died when I heard a bear coming toward me. As it snuffled closer and closer, terror struck. I could feel myself losing it and slipping over the edge into mindless panic. If I moved even a finger, I would be lost. Beyond reason and without reserve, I called for help.

In that moment of surrender, I felt lifted and found myself floating in a pool of clear light. Looking down, I sensed myself lying peacefully on the forest floor. The world was no longer a hostile alien place, but my home. No true separation remained between me and the world.

After that night of inner transformation, the whole world seemed vibrantly *alive*, and I lived for several weeks deeply integrated into the universe, glorying in the beauty of mountains, lake, and sky. There was also Something Else out there; Something nonphysical and beyond definition. I was part of that, too, and felt accepted and at peace. Those weeks were so filled with joy and wonder that I decided I would someday live alone in the wilderness for a whole year.

THE WORLD OF PEOPLE

But when I left the magic of the forest and returned to the chaos of the human world, I lost my way, and the clear inner light faded. I traveled to Mexico with my lover, and sat for long hours by the sea, but caught only brief glimpses of the joy and wonder I'd thought would always fill my life. I didn't know what I'd done wrong, but I felt I'd somehow failed an important spiritual test. I sank deeper and deeper into darkness, clinging to the dead memory of what had been a living flame. My lover tried to understand, but I couldn't explain what I was going through, and she finally left me.

Alone again, I drifted north to California, and lived for a while in a cave in Death Valley — sleeping long hours and attempting to interpret my dreams. During the day, I read the Bible and Carl Jung, trying to understand and accept what had happened to me in the wilderness, without getting sucked back into the fundamentalist Christian dogma I'd grown up with. The depression and the grief for what I'd lost eased only when I discovered Buddhist meditation practice and learned that peak spiritual experiences are inherently transient.

As my mind cleared, I began to remember something I'd thought about in the wilderness. When I was twenty, I'd left the United States to live in Canada rather than fight in the Vietnam War. It had been an ethical choice, but during the months in solitude I came to recognize that I'd avoided an important social responsibility: not to go to war but to contribute two years of my life to serve the community in a positive way.

A friend told me about an agency that sent volunteers to teach organic vegetable gardening in the Caribbean. I signed up to spend two years in the rural mountains of the Dominican Republic, beyond the reach of cars, electricity, and running water. A month after I arrived, the agency sent word that they had lost their funding and I should use my return ticket back to the States.

But I believed in the work and decided to stay. I built a small shack to live in, continued to cultivate the demonstration garden, practiced my Spanish, and traded vegetables for the staples I needed. I also did small carpentry jobs to earn the thirty dollars a month I learned to live on. After I'd been there for a year, Hurricane David swept through and wiped out the homes of many of the poorest people in the tiny village where I was living. I abandoned the garden and focused on bringing in relief supplies, doing first aid, and rebuilding houses.

Despite the political strife that sometimes caught me up, those years were magical. The deep connection I felt was as much with the people as with the land, and I was overwhelmed by how much I received from those I had gone to help. Even though we didn't share much intellectually, our heart connection was, and still is, strong.

Then I fell in love — with an American woman who was on the island filming the reconstruction effort. She returned to the States but came back to share my one-room shack. As a gift to her, I poured a layer of concrete over the dirt floor and replaced the dim oil lamp with a brighter propane light. We lived together in the mountains for two years before moving to the sea.

On the coast, I found a job running the water sports department in a resort hotel, where I learned and taught windsurfing and scuba diving. The party atmosphere of the Caribbean was very different from our quiet life in the mountain village. We began to each go our own way until our relationship broke, and I was alone again . . . except for a steady stream of tourist women. During the next four years, the inner light almost flickered out as I leapt jubilantly into sex, alcohol, and scuba diving. Then one morning, while I was riding my motorcycle across the island to go diving with humpback whales, a drunken farmer crashed his pickup into me. I was flown to Montreal, where the doctors in the Royal Victoria Hospital tried unsuccessfully to reattach my right foot, which had been ripped off in the crash. When I emerged from the hospital a year later with a prosthetic leg, I'd lost my dive business and could barely walk. My life in the Caribbean was over.

THE WORLD OF INTELLECT

It was hard to accept that my body was no longer what it had been, but rather than cling to what I'd lost, I focused on developing my mind instead. I decided to go back to school. I'd dropped out of the University of California at Berkeley when I was nineteen because I felt too restless to sit in a classroom. Rather than the nine-to-five office job I believed a university degree would lead to, I'd wanted a life of physical activity and adventure. Now at forty, I enrolled in McGill University to study biology and psychology. Studying science as a mature student was challenging and occasionally amusing. Sometimes, when I walked into a lecture hall on the first day of class, the other students would stop talking and sit up to attention . . . until I scrunched down into one of the desks among them. "Huh? He's not the professor? What's this old fart doing here?" It was often a lonely life.

I immersed myself in the intellectual world like a dry sponge soaking up a flood of new information. I'd always read on my own, but now I was studying in a directed and systematic way. I loved it at first, but slowly the academic approach began to pall, and by the time I graduated — with a fellowship to pursue a master's degree in biology — something vital was missing from my life. I felt as though I'd become a hollow shell filled with abstract facts and theories that seemed to have little connection to my heart or to my own actual experience. Once again I heard solitude calling and spent two months canoeing alone in northern Quebec. During that summer, the world came *alive* again. The sense of existing in a *living* universe was what had been missing in the university.

I decided against graduate school, worked for a year as a carpenter to earn money, and left for what I thought would be three months in Mexico. A year and a half later, after lingering in San Cristóbal de las Casas, Mexico, and Argentinean Tierra del Fuego, I found myself sailing up the remote wild coast of southern Chile. It was astonishingly beautiful, and during the three-day ferry ride, I began to imagine an exciting project that braided together two apparently disconnected threads of my life: I would use the money from the academic fellowship I'd been awarded to carry out a biological study, while living alone for a year in that pristine coastal wilderness.

I made my way back to Canada and enrolled in the master's degree program at the University of British Columbia in Vancouver, Canada, but the deeper I settled into graduate studies, the more I realized that biology was not my main interest. What I truly wanted to explore was the effect of deep wilderness solitude on a human being — in this case, on me. I would be both researcher and subject. I also wanted to examine my relationship with the nonhuman world and to learn how the direct experience of profound belonging in the universe might lead to changes in human behavior that would be less damaging to the Earth. I expected there to be resistance among conservative professors to this unorthodox approach, but I would risk it. I transferred to the Interdisciplinary Studies PhD program.

One of the most important, but often trivialized, tasks facing a new graduate student is selecting a research supervisor and supervisory committee. This is the group that will most directly support or hinder the PhD process. Especially when wishing to carry out nonconventional research, choosing individuals who are open-minded, ready for adventure, and with whom you can openly communicate is vital. I was very careful and selected such people. They were excited about my proposal to study myself as I lived for a year alone in the wilderness. But there were two strong caveats: they offered no additional funding, and they did not guarantee that I would actually be awarded a PhD for the adventure. I willingly accepted those conditions.

My relationship with the rest of the university was sometimes less positive. Mostly, I pursued my academic study on my own. I had friends among my peers, but no close associates. The faculty frequently treated me with amused tolerance rather than respect or disapproval. One professor told me I was too old for such a radical project, that such things were for younger people. I suspected his comment might apply to my graduate work in general. A fellow graduate student, who was also doing nontraditional research, said she was very glad I was in the department because my project made everyone else's seem fairly conventional.

I learned an important lesson at the university. Walls of resistance often turn into doorways if you lean steadily against them for a while. Once I was asked to give advice to a group of new graduate students, and I suggested that they take as long as possible to earn their degree. At first their supervisory committee would find many reasons why their dissertation was not acceptable; eventually the committee would just want to get rid of them and would support damn near anything. Of course the quality of the work must be excellent when you step outside the usual framework.

PREPARING TO STEP OFF THE EDGE

In early 1998, I received an email out of the blue from Patti Kuchinsky, a woman I'd met briefly twelve years earlier while I was living in a Buddhist community in New Hampshire. The community had recently published an email list of everyone linked to it, and Patti decided to write to me. Over time we became intimate spiritual friends and partners. Actually, we have never been able to clearly define our relationship, since it is mysterious and continues to unfold. During the years of academic study and logistic preparations for my journey into solitude, Patti was an invaluable counselor, editor, and emotional support. Today, although she lives in Texas and I in Canada, we remain in close and intimate contact, and nearly every year, we go canoe camping and fishing together for two or three weeks.

In the summer of 2000, I met and fell passionately "in love" with Susan. This was definitely *not* on the list of things I needed to do to get ready for a year alone in the wilderness. Our relationship made no rational sense to either of us, but we neither could nor really wanted to break it off. This has been a somewhat frequent pattern in my life: I become infatuated with someone, and for a time desire overwhelms my thoughts and feelings.

As I began my trip preparations, I pored over maps of the Chilean and Canadian coasts and imagined myself hidden away in some remote inlet. To find complete solitude, I knew I would need to go to an inhospitable locale, probably far from the equator. From experience, I also knew I would need to be at least a hundred miles from the nearest town in order to feel fully disengaged from civilization.

I wanted to be on the coast for three reasons: I love the sea; winter temperatures wouldn't be as extreme as they would be inland; because of my prosthetic leg, I would need to transport supplies and haul firewood by water. Since I'd be using a small inflatable boat for transportation, I had to be in an area of protected waterways where storms would be less dangerous.

As I soon learned, human activity is frequent along the coast of British Columbia all the way from Vancouver to Alaska: bush planes, logging and mining, commercial and sport fishing, sailboats, cruise ships, and kayakers. If I wanted to experience absolute solitude, British Columbia's coast was not remote enough. While it would be much cheaper and easier to stay in Canada than to ship my gear and travel to southern Chile, I would likely be disappointed with myself for not making the extra effort. I focused my gaze southward on the area I had seen from the ferry, and in doing so, cast my fate literally and metaphorically to the wind (see map, Tip of South America, on page 353). Punta Arenas, the only large town in southern

Chile, and the administration center for the region, would be my staging point.

THE LOGISTICS OF SOLITUDE

The logistics of preparing to live for a year in the wilderness without coming out for supplies are daunting. In the fall of 1999, I started making lists of everything I would need to build a camp and survive, adding items I might need if things went bad, and then tossing in some treats for physical and emotional comfort. I don't usually plan far ahead when I travel, but this time I knew that if I waited until it was nearly time to go before making supply lists, I would almost certainly forget something important. There were lists on scraps of papers all over my office. (For the final list of everything I brought with me, see the Appendix, beginning on page 333.)

In September 2000, I began the actual trip preparations. I'd intended to be gone long before then, and although I didn't realize it, others were speculating I might never actually go. But that possibility didn't seriously cross my mind. I consolidated the scattered lists I'd made and grouped items into categories: tools, building materials, camping and fishing, boat and motor, household, clothes and toiletries, electric and electronic, repair kits, first-aid, food.

Gathered together, the lists seemed endless. On previous trips alone into the wilderness, I'd taken only a small amount of gear: canoe, plastic and tent, sleeping pad and bag, fishing gear and a few tools, food, grill, a couple of pots, clothes and rain gear, basic first-aid kit, and several books. This time, though, I was going high-tech — partly as the result of planning to stay for a complete year and survive winter in an extreme climate. A tent would not be enough. I would need to build a more substantial shelter, and I would need more than an ax and a canoe to cut and haul firewood. A second reason for the complexity of the lists was that I'd agreed I would send out a short email message each month to let the university, my family, and Patti know I was still alive. This required that I take not only a laptop computer and satellite telephone, but also the means to keep their batteries charged. These main items required many other associated tools and materials.

I also created an email code system. The default was code green. That indicated all was okay. I planned to email this code on the first of each month, and if they didn't receive a message by the third of the month, they would come looking for me. If I felt myself to be at risk — either because of injury or sickness, or because I was going on an extended overnight boat trip away from camp — I would send a code yellow and explain the circumstances. I would also specify a date by which I would email again. If they didn't hear from me on the specified day, they would come looking for me. If I felt my life was immediately at risk due to serious injury or illness, I would send a code red describing my condition and specifying the time I would send the next message. If they didn't receive word from me at the stated time, they would come to rescue me — or retrieve my corpse.

The regular first-of-the-month email was more for peace of mind than anything else. If I were to have a serious accident and not be able to send out a message, chances are I'd be dead before they realized I wasn't sending the check-in message.

I already owned most of the tools, fishing gear, and camping equipment I would need, and I managed to purchase nearly all the other equipment second-hand. One stern necessity was to obtain everything as cheaply as possible because I was financing the project primarily with money I'd saved by working as a teaching assistant. At the last minute, the university unexpectedly kicked in $10,000.

During September, October, and November, I shopped, searched (rather unsuccessfully) for detailed information on my destination, applied for a Chilean visa, obtained shots, and took care of all the other details a year-and-a-half absence requires. In October, my mother, whose body and mind had been deteriorating for several years, died, and I went to California to be with her during her last days. But I was moving too fast for her death to really hit me.

Packing and shipping my gear to southern Chile was a major task. I had stuff squirreled away everywhere inside and outside the house, but somehow I squeezed it all into two crates, each measuring about three by three by five feet. I took the crates to a transport company, labeled them with my name and the Chilean National Parks Service (CONAF) address in Punta Arenas at the other end of the world, and drove away wondering if I would ever see them again. I had no money to replace the gear should the crates go missing.

Obtaining permission from the Chilean government to spend a year alone on the remote southern coast was an interesting and, at times, nerve-wracking process. In early 2000, I sent in my application forms and waited — unconcerned since I still had almost a year until my proposed departure. As months passed, I sent emails; CONAF did not reply. Slowly I became concerned.

Finally, in November, I told my friend Juan-Pablo Cerda, who used to work for the Chilean government, that I was up against the wall. We did what we should have done much sooner: he called a friend. His friend knew someone who worked in the CONAF office in Punta Arenas, and he asked her to help me obtain the permissions I needed.

Alejandra Silva should be in charge of CONAF for all of Chile! She is friendly, helpful, reliable, and very efficient. She emailed information about the southern coast and pointed out that the climate is extremely inhospitable, but said that if I was willing to sign a notarized form releasing CONAF from responsibility for damage to my equipment and injury or death to me, they had no problem with my proposed project. Within three weeks I had their written permission in hand and rushed to the Chilean Consulate in Vancouver.

It's easy to obtain a three-month tourist visa and also easy to renew such a visa, but to do so you must leave Chile, cross into Argentina, Bolivia, or Peru, and reenter Chile. Since I would be alone in the wilderness for a year, that wouldn't work, so I applied for a one-year residency permit. By that point, I was starting to feel tense. I'd shipped the crates of gear and purchased a nonrefundable airline ticket with a departure date only five days hence — and I had no visa.

The consul told me it would take only three or four days to obtain the visa, but his bureaucratic assistant was less sanguine. He pronounced the consul an unrealistic optimist and said the process would require at least two weeks. This was not good news, and my stress level ratcheted up. I hustled back and told the consul what his assistant had said. He replied that the man had a gloomy outlook on life, and he assured me there would be no problem. Happily, he was right. Three days later, I picked up my visa, and two days after that, on December 15, I was on a plane to Santiago de Chile. By the time I reached the Vancouver airport after that frantic final month, I was whipped.

THE ROAD SOUTH

A week later, I awoke to rain and to the fact that I was on a bus headed south away from the sun and warmth of Santiago — into clouds, wind, and cold. What had I done? Why had I chosen to go to southern Chile, despite warnings about the extreme weather? As is usual for my life's larger decisions, I had no rational answer — just an inner call. The steward (a civilized feature of express buses in Chile) came by with a breakfast of sorts: cheese sandwich, stale pastry, and nasty instant coffee that I slurped through a straw as we lurched along.

The bus trip lasted two days and nights — a mixture of the ordinary, the strange, and the semiconscious. Since the Chilean coast is far too fractured to permit a road down the Pacific side of the Andes, we crossed into Argentina and followed the same route I'd hitchhiked four years before on my way to Tierra del Fuego (see map, Tip of South America, on page 353). When I'd hitched, the trip had taken nine days. I'd carried a backpack, camped out, eaten wild blackberries while waiting for long hours beside the road, and gotten stuck for two days at the border crossing, until a long-haul trucker picked me up and carried me all the way.

This time, once my luggage was stowed, I didn't have a thing to worry about. I looked out the window or slept, and when it rained I was snug and dry. On and on, the bus rolled and dipped over the Patagonian grasslands — mile after endless mile of brown, green, gold, and silver, with occasional slashes of brilliant red or orange. And always the wind, which made me wonder about my own future on the sea, as I drifted deeper into South America and farther from my life in Canada.

FINAL PREPARATIONS

I arrived in Punta Arenas tired from the long ride but not too sore. A new stage in the journey was beginning, with new worries: Would the crates of gear arrive? How would I transport them 150 miles overland to Puerto Natales, a small town that is the departure point for boats traveling up the coast? (See map, Puerto Natales to Retreat Site, on page 354.) How would I find a boat to take me from there into the wilds? Where would I build a camp? I'd solved so many problems already with the aid of helping hands, it seems like I'd have learned some faith. At a deep level I did have faith or else I wouldn't have begun the journey, but on the surface I fretted.

The next day, I registered with the police and applied for an ID card. While reviewing my paperwork, the officer frowned and said there was a serious problem. I began to review my past sins, with a mental nod to Interpol and the FBI, but wisely didn't confess them. He pointed out that the name on my passport was Frank R. Kull, but that my visa was made out for Frank Robert Kull. Serious stuff, indeed! Muttering to myself about the gloomy (and possibly malevolent) bureaucrat in Vancouver, I explained that in Canada we use middle name or initial more or less interchangeably. He didn't seem convinced, so I repeated the assertion several more times — always a good tactic, I find. He finally decided I wasn't trying to con him and said he would contact Santiago to correct the discrepancy. As far as I can tell, he never heard back.

Then I presented myself to CONAF. They were very friendly but regarded me with some skepticism; they just couldn't imagine why anyone would be lunatic enough to spend a year alone. I was soon given the nickname Gringo Loco. They also gave me some bad news. I chose December because I assumed summer in southern Chile would be about the same as summer in northern British Columbia: warmish days and reasonably calm weather. Wrong. Summer down there is the windiest time of year, and I wouldn't be able to transport my gear in my small boat up the coast from Puerto Natales. CONAF said their ship could take me if I would pay $1,000

USD for fuel. That was far beyond my budget, and it was the first major glitch in my plan. They suggested I talk with German Coronado, captain of their boat and the official in charge of several huge national parks along the coast. Maybe we could work out a deal.

The next morning, I bused to Natales to talk with German about transport and to ask his advice about where would be a good place to set up my camp. German spends most of his time in Puerto Eden, a tiny fishing village thirty hours by boat further north, and he knows the coast well. We spread the marine chart, and he pointed to a small bay at the very end of a remote inlet, hidden in the foothills of the Andes and about a hundred miles by boat northwest of Puerto Natales. He said no one ever goes there, so I decided I would.

German told me I could catch a ride with them for much less than $1,000 if I was willing to wait until the end of January when they would make their regular patrol and pass within twenty-five miles of the inlet. I agreed; I was in no hurry now that I knew the weather would not get worse in the next couple of months. In any case, I still had to wait for my crates to arrive, and I needed to buy food, lumber, and other supplies that were too heavy to ship from Vancouver.

Punta Arenas is a nice place. The people are warm, open, and honest. From Vancouver, southern Chile seemed like the other side of nowhere, but after a while it felt like the center of the world. For the six weeks I was there, I rented a large room in a private home. I needed the space because by the time I was finally ready to go into solitude, I had a huge pile of supplies. Doña Mercedes, my landlady, was an excellent cook. She knew her own mind and wasn't afraid to speak it. Now and then, when her teetotaling son was out of the house, she'd sneak a quick glass of wine with me. I liked her a lot.

I'd already purchased a bunch of gear and supplies in Vancouver, but I continued to shop in Punta Arenas, finding, of course, plenty of nifty little items I hadn't thought about until I stumbled across them. I learned to always scan store windows as I walked by, since some held odd and fascinating collections of merchandise: an upscale women's clothing boutique displayed one small shelf of power tools; an auto parts center also sold homemade jam and watercolor paintings. Most of the things I needed were relatively easy to find, but some items eluded me. I never did find stovepipe to fit the wood-burning stove I'd shipped from Vancouver, and I had to have it custom-built.

My crates were supposed to arrive in Punta Arenas about the same time I did at the end of December, but they didn't. After anxiously checking at the port every few days to see whether anyone knew anything about them, I finally found the crates sitting on a dock in Valparaiso, far to the north. They took two more weeks to make their way south.

Eventually, CONAF told me German Coronado and their boat would not be traveling upcoast anytime soon. Another ride I tried to set up also fell through, and the uncertainty of the endlessly shifting situation was nerve-wracking. I tried to relax and just go with it, but over and over I got caught in my expectations of how I wanted things to be and how I thought they should be. I was almost ready to go, and I still had no idea how I might eventually make my way upcoast with all my gear. But I believed something would work out.

LAST EMAIL FROM TOWN

FEBRUARY 4, 2001, PUERTO NATALES

It's been an intense two days. Yesterday in Punta Arenas I went to the government warehouse to complete the paperwork so I could claim my crates of gear, which finally arrived from Valparaiso last week. The Regional Director of Customs thought my project interesting and signed a waiver that allowed me to import the gear without paying duty — as long as I take everything with me when I leave Chile. The whole process, including storage fees, cost only $25 USD. That was good news, since I'd heard rumors that some visiting scientists had been charged high import duty on their equipment.

Earlier in the week, the Chilean Navy had finally agreed to take me to the bay where I intend to build my camp, but yesterday when I met with the officers, I discovered they aren't willing to take me all the way. The area is so remote, marine charts don't show depth soundings, and they're concerned their ship might run aground on submerged rock. They'll leave me and my gear on a beach fourteen miles north of the bay, and I'll need to haul everything the rest of the way myself. The officers were polite, proper, and friendly. They feel responsible for my safety and want to be on my monthly check-in email list. They have a twenty-four-hour hotline I can call on my satellite phone if I get into serious trouble. It feels good to have a safety net.

The transport truck I'd hired to haul my stuff to Puerto Natales showed up on time and we went to the customs shed to pick up the crates of gear. I expected a hang-up of some sort, but amazingly everything proceeded without a hitch. Then we went back to my place and began to load. By the time the lumber, hardware, and food, etc., were in the truck it was crammed full. We agreed that he'd pick me up at 8 this morning for the trip to Natales.

Shortly after the driver left, a woman from CONAF called to say she had captured two kittens from the back patio for me. I hadn't planned to take a pet into solitude, since one of the joys of living alone is being free to follow the flow of the moment without considering the needs and desires of anyone else.

I don't claim this freedom is good or bad, only that in taking a cat the situation is altered.

CONAF strongly suggested I take a cat if I intend to eat shellfish. Southern Chile is troubled by frequent red tide that makes bivalves, such as clams and mussels, poisonous. The government has an extensive testing program for the commercial fishing fleet, but local people use cats as guinea pigs. If the cat pukes or dies after sampling suspect shellfish, they don't eat it themselves. I would need to do the same.

Exhausted, I headed back downtown on foot. The two kittens — wild, even savage — were loose in the woman's office. No one had spent time holding them, and they weren't eager to alter the arrangement. With difficulty, I captured one, a female who definitely did not want to go into the box. She snarled, clawed, and bit me. Then I snagged the other, a male. Hmm. In a year, this could lead to a bunch more cats. As I sat there considering, the female was still snarling inside the box and fighting to get out. I decided that if she really didn't want to go, I wouldn't force her. So now I have just the male.

The truck picked us up at 8:30 this rainy windy morning. The kitten didn't seem to like the drive and cried most of the way. We were heavily overloaded, and at one point the truck started to swerve back and forth across the road. It got worse and worse, and then the driver touched the brakes. I thought we would flip, and yelled, "No brakes, no brakes," and he finally got the truck under control.

Here in Natales two navy enlisted guys helped us unload. Then the driver and I went to the hardware store. Over the phone yesterday the store owner said I could pick up the two 55-gallon drums they were holding for me today, Sunday, even though they would be closed: the owner lives next to the store and would open up for me. But when I knocked, there was no answer. "Uh-oh," I thought, "this is where things start to fall apart." But the door finally opened and I purchased the drums (plus more nails, even though I think I already had plenty).

The manager of the propane company in P.A. had assured me I could pick up the three tanks he'd reserved for me in Natales at any time, but the propane station was locked when we arrived. The woman next door told me the manager was out of town. "Uh-huh, *here's* where things fall apart." But just then, amazingly, the assistant manager drove up.

"Yes, we have your tanks. Lucky you caught me. I'm about to go fishing." We loaded the propane and went to the gas station to fill the 55-gallon drums and six 5-gallon cans. Then back to the docks.

Over and over when I've tried to arrange things ahead of time I've had to either give up or have watched my plans fall apart. But over and over, too, things have worked out at the last minute in unexpected ways. Why do I still resist living by faith? I'm seriously stressing myself and it doesn't seem to do much good. But perhaps the last-minute miracles won't happen if I stop the preparatory work.

By then, four navy guys were working and had most of my gear on board their ship. We unpacked and inflated my boat, then loaded it, the gas drums, and propane tanks. It was very windy all day, but the rain held off until we finished. It still seems incredible that everything worked out and I'm ready to go. The crew offered me a cup of coffee, which turned out to be a huge steak dinner. They asked if I wanted to sleep on board, but with the kitten and my exhaustion I opted for a pension in town.

It's now after 10 PM and I've come to this internet café to send this last email before leaving for solitude at dawn tomorrow morning. Finally, it looks like preparations have completed themselves and I'm away. It's been a long haul and I'm worn out — ready to sit in my cabin and rest. All I need do first is ferry my gear from where the navy drops me to the bay and build the cabin. With luck it will take about three weeks. As it stands, this may be the last news you receive from me until next year — other than the brief monthly check-in emails — but it's also possible that I'll send reports of my life from time to time. I'll let things unfold as they do. I hope you all have a wonderful year in your different lives. Take good care. Thanks so much for your support and caring. It means a lot to me. — Bob

FEBRUARY 2001

SURVIVAL KIT

Food, Water, Stove, Pot, Cup,
Space-blanket, Blanket, Tarp,
Rope, Machete, Satphone, GPS,
Compass, Batteries, Jumpsuit,
Life-vest, Kayak, Foot-pumps,
Anchor, Oars, Paddle, Waders.

— Reminder to myself, taped to my cabin door

I left Puerto Natales yesterday at dawn on the Chilean Navy patrol boat, *La Yagan*. Looking back as we headed down the channel, I watched the town diminish into the landscape and realized that, if all goes well, it would be the last time I'd see a town for a year. The early sun glinted off the windows and tin roofs and shaped the still-snowy peaks beyond. A rainbow arced from land to sea, and I decided to take it as a sign of good things to come. Why not? Then I turned to look northwest toward the remote wilderness where I planned to build a camp and live alone for the coming year. There I saw storm skies and wind-chopped water.

It took us ten hours to travel the hundred miles to the tip of the peninsula where the navy had decided they would leave me. While part of the crew began to ferry my supplies to shore in their small Zodiac, the others lowered my own inflatable to the rough water. Once in the boat, slapped by wind-driven 40°F spray, I noticed the navy guys were all wearing survival suits — and I wasn't. Hmm. Not bringing one seems like a fairly important oversight in my planning. I can probably keep dry in chest waders and raincoat, but if I capsize or go over the side, I'll be in serious trouble.

The weather continued to deteriorate, and the captain decided it was too dangerous there for his crew and me in our small boats. He moved to calmer water to drop the rest of my supplies on this tiny island where I now sit writing. Unloading took a long time. The navy guys piled my gear high on the rocks, but knowing they were in a hurry I told them to just leave the lumber I'd brought to build a cabin on the beach. It was a tough grunt wrestling the two heavy crates I'd shipped from Vancouver and the 55-gallon drums of gasoline from the inflatables up into the bushes. We finally had all the supplies ashore as dark was falling. They immediately left to seek safe haven from the building storm.

The lower beach in this small cove is covered with rocks; further up, there is grass, dense brush, and trees. Working in the dark with my headlamp for light, I laid down a semilevel platform of 2×4s and plywood in the grassy area, set up my tent on the plywood, and then watched the tide come in . . . and in.

I'd assumed the grass would be above the high-tide line, but I was wrong. It turned out to be sea grass, and at 1 AM water started splashing against the underside of the platform. I jammed more 2×4s under there to raise the plywood, while cursing at and pleading with the tide to stop. Uh-huh. I finally moved my sleeping gear out of the tent and up to higher ground. By this time all the lumber was floating in a foot of water, so I waded over to heave it up into the bushes before it could drift away.

Just when it seemed the tide was at its peak, the wind picked up again and drove the sea back up to the bottom of the plywood. Exhausted, cold, hungry, and discouraged, I crouched in the dark on a tiny island in the middle of nowhere, pounded by wind-driven rain and far from other people. I felt pretty damned forlorn and started to wonder what I'm doing here. Crying in his cardboard box inside a plastic garbage bag, the kitten didn't seem too happy either. But the tide finally started to ebb and I put the gear back in the tent and slept. My body hurt everywhere.

It's been raining and blowing on and off all day today, but here in the lee of the trees only the strongest gusts can get to me — unless the wind shifts from northwest to southwest, then I'm screwed. The navy captain told me that seldom happens. I've moved the tent platform higher up the beach and raised it two feet above the ground. I'm glad to have stayed dry so far, but I'm a bit worried about all my food on the beach where we started to unload a mile from here. I hope they set everything above high tide, but until the wind drops I have no way to check.

FEBRUARY 7, 2001

Still blowing, and it may be tough to move my gear the fourteen miles south to the small bay where I want to go. I'm waiting for the wind to die and feeling frustrated even though it's very beautiful here. Across the channel to the west I can see more than thirty waterfalls cascading down the rock cliffs of

Staines Peninsula to the sea. In the other direction, when the clouds lift, the snowy peaks and glaciers of the southern Andes loom.

Maybe the weather is never calm here; this may be as good as it gets. The wind has eased, but it's still raining. A while ago I went to check my food and the propane tanks. Everything is still there, but the tanks had floated around and the food bags had been washed by the sea. I hope the waterproofing held, but won't know until I get a cabin built and have a dry place to unpack. I brought back the first-aid kit and a jar of peanut butter and moved everything else to higher ground.

I'm training the kitten to go outside to crap. A tent full of gear with sleeping pad and blankets on the floor is not the best place for the task. I've never had trouble with such training before, probably because I've had cats only in the tropics where it was warm and I cut a hole in the door for them to freely come and go. Here I need to unzip the tent flap to let the kitten in or out. He must have dumped a load in here half a dozen times, and cat shit is not my favorite smell. We have a new rule: "No! Outside." Then a small swat and a heave out of the tent. Also a thump to stay away from the camp stove when it's lit and away from my food. I get particularly upset when he claws at the tent's mosquito net to come back in. But for the most part I'm glad he's here with me. He sleeps curled up behind my knees or snuggled into my belly.

I'm trying to just *be here* rather than feeling prevented from going to the bay where I want to be. Waiting is part of the process, too. I don't control the world. During preparations for this journey, over and over I had to let go of my plans and let things happen as they did. It's the same here.

This is summer? I've been here five days and have seen the sun for a total of maybe twenty minutes. There's almost constant wind now, but supposedly there won't be in winter. Four dolphins (Chilean Dolphin or Peale's Dolphin) swam around in front of camp for a couple of hours this morning. I went out on the rocks to call and sing to them. In the afternoon, I took the boat five miles down the inlet toward the bay, then turned back because of rough water. It settled at times, but never really flattened out. I'm anxious to get going, but don't want to take foolish chances.

The GPS unit worked great the other day: located satellites with no problem, gave readings for location, direction of travel, and speed. Today it won't work at all. Damn! It's supposed to be waterproof but I suspect there's a bad seal. Luckily I brought a spare, but now that this one's broken, I have only one that works and no backup. I plan to make some long trips through this archipelago of islands, and if the remaining GPS dies while I'm out there somewhere, I could easily not find my way back to camp.

I'm keeping the down sleeping bag wrapped in plastic until the cabin is built, because if it gets damp it will lose its insulating capacity and be difficult to dry. Meanwhile I'm sleeping in long underwear, T-shirt, flannel shirt, wool vest, Hollofil vest, hooded sweatshirt, and a snowsuit. On top of that I have two blankets. I barely kept warm last night with the tent sealed up. The weather's so bitter raw and damp now in summer, what will winter be like? It's not easy here, that's for sure.

FEBRUARY 11, 2001

Today I stayed late in the tent — a small bubble of dry in the wet hugeness that surrounds me. I feel like an alien in this watery world. All the creatures here, except kitten and me, seem to be water beings. This morning, vague tendrils of terror crept through me. Alone. A tiny solitary speck completely vulnerable in the face of an infinite universe intent on my annihilation. Eventually I'll cease to exist, and death is possible at any moment — right now. Yet I know from other solitary retreats that there's light and peace beneath the terror.

In Buddhism, one takes refuge in the Buddha, the Dharma, and the Sangha. Who is my guide and inspiration; who do I lean on that has wandered this pathless land before? Yes, the Buddha. What is my Dharma, my source of knowledge and understanding? There are many: Buddhist teachings, the wisdom of Deneal Amos, the I Ching, Chuang Tsu, the Bible, and, most importantly, my own actual experience. Who is my Sangha, my community of fellow journeyers? Patti is primary now. I wonder if she always will be. Susan, not so much in terms of wisdom as for her love and respect. My supervisor and committee members, David, Lee, and Carl; my family; and my friends Pille, Diane, Madeleine, and Wil. There are many.

I've been here a week. In planning, I somehow never thought I might be stuck like this. I wonder if I really am. If I take half loads, I can probably make it to the bay without problem. It's the trip back against the wind, chop, and spray that concerns me. I'm trying to be patient and wait for the weather to improve, but in the back of my mind I question whether it ever will. The wind might quit for a day or two, but I'll need a week to move all my gear. Strange that I never asked anyone which month I should arrive. I just assumed that summer here, as on the coast of British Columbia, would be best. But this weather is exactly what I'd hoped to avoid until I get a cabin built. Always risky to extrapolate from what you do know to what you don't.

A while ago I tried the GPS again and it worked for a few seconds. I was pretty sure it had moisture inside, so — against all the warranty disclaimer warnings — I pried off the water seal, opened it up, and dried it over the stove for a few minutes. Closed and tried it. It worked! This is excellent news. From now on I'll keep it in a plastic bag when I use it in the rain.

NO ENTRY FOR FEBRUARY 12, 2001

FEBRUARY 13, 2001

Yesterday I did chores. I mixed two-cycle oil with gas for the chain saw and got it running, then assembled the mounting bracket for the backup outboard motor. I hope I never need it, but if the 15 hp outboard fails, the 4 hp should let me limp back to camp. I also cleaned up the tent and readjusted the tarps I've stretched over an A-frame structure I built to protect the plywood platform, tent, and area in front of tent where I usually cook and eat. And I put together a survival pack of food and other gear to take when I go out on the water in case it gets too rough to return before nightfall.

I'm more and more restless to move down to the bay so I can start building a cabin. I feel very vulnerable here, and on the map the bay looks much more protected from the wind. It's also more hidden and remote. Even though unlikely, it is possible that fishermen might come by here occasionally. German told me no one ever goes down there.

It's slightly warmer today and the black flies came out for the first time. Hungry buggers. Guess there's not much flesh around. Two dolphins came by for a while. Kitten is not crapping in the tent any longer, but he did get into my cheese. I discover I'm pretty impatient and violent in my castigation: not just "No!" but also a shake or a swat and at times a toss through the air. I've decided not to hit him anymore, or at least pause so the cuff is not in anger.

I've started to read about working with anxiety in *Seeking the Heart of Wisdom*, a book of Buddhist meditation instruction by Joseph Goldstein and Jack Kornfield. It presents a clear, pragmatic approach that I hope will help defuse my fear. But I sense that Buddhist philosophy and meditation will not be my only path here.

Finally a calm morning with some blue sky. I went to the bay but didn't find
a good building site. A couple of places are well protected from the wind, but
the hillside there is steep and wet with thick brush. On my way back, I stopped
to pick up the food and one propane tank from the beach where the navy
dropped them. This way I'll be ready tomorrow morning to head straight to
the bay. But as I returned to this tiny island, I realized I can just stay here if I
want to. There's no stream, but it's rained every day since I arrived. I plan to
collect rainwater from the roof of the cabin, so water shouldn't be a problem.
There are some standing dead trees in the forest nearby, and if they're not
rotten I could use them for firewood. I think the solar panels would work ok
except in June and July when the sun might dip behind the trees.

The view here is spectacular, and it feels much more open and wild than
down at the bay. Another lovely thing is that dolphins come by here, and I'm
not sure I'd see them in the bay. The biggest plus in staying here is that I
wouldn't need to move all my gear. The biggest potential problem is southwest wind; this spot isn't at all protected from that direction. I don't know
what to do, sleep on it I guess.

I set the clock for 7 AM. Rain. Went out to check the ocean. Not bad, but not
calm enough that I wanted to chance a trip to the bay with a loaded boat. I felt
very reluctant to start moving all this stuff with a small boat and unpredictable
wind. I imagined having half my gear at the bay and the weather turning foul
for weeks or getting stuck down there with tent and sleeping bag still here.
None of my imaginings were encouraging.

I guess I'm letting go of another preconceived ideal and accepting a gift
from life. This is where the navy dropped me, and it's probably the best all-
around spot I've seen. Maybe I've just stopped to really look at what I already
have instead of reaching for an imagined something better. I consulted the
I Ching to ask if I should stay here. The hexagram was "Wanderer" changing to "Retreat," which seems to support my decision to stay.

I unloaded the boat, carried everything up onto the rocks, and covered the
food sacks with a tarp. Checked a few and none seem to be wet inside. That's
very good news. Back in Punta Arenas a local outdoor guide told me that
considering the weather here, he strongly recommended I put all my food in
watertight barrels. I couldn't afford barrels, but I took his advice to heart and
sealed everything in a second layer of plastic and nylon sacks. Very glad I

did. Water has seeped through the rice sacks' outer layers. If I hadn't double-wrapped them, I'd have a serious problem with wet, probably moldy, rice.

One of the things I learned during logistic preparations was to really listen to other people's advice rather than pretend to already know everything. Many people have been generous with information and support, and listening to their suggestions has saved me a lot of grief.

As I unloaded the boat I felt light and happy for the first time since arriving here. It's been only ten days but feels like much longer. I've been stewing and fretting about the need to build a cabin while it's still summer, but now that I can start anytime, I'm in no hurry. Typical.

FEBRUARY 16, 2001

It was a wild night with wind and rain roaring in the trees. Sometimes, like a huge *presence*, the wind swooped howling down, and even here in this protected nook the tarps over the tent cracked and shuddered under the assault. I'm glad I took time yesterday to tie things down more securely. As far as I can tell, everything is still dry.

The cat and I were restless in the storm. He was in and out of the tent at least six times before I finally made him settle down. If he was in, I worried he might have to crap and let him out. If he was out and wanted in, he'd scratch the mosquito net, and that got me to open the flap immediately. I ate instant chicken soup for dinner, which gave me the runs. Since it was so nasty outside, I stayed in and used my improvised chamber pot. One hasn't lived until one has shit in a plastic bag. Very nice. Today I get to wash it out. Generally, I've been relieving myself on the beach at low tide. All in all, since I'm alone here, I think that's the best way to go until I dig a latrine among the trees. I haven't shaved since I arrived, haven't bathed, and have brushed my teeth only four or five times. Haven't felt the need. Just the way it is.

Yesterday I hooked up the two-burner stove to the large propane tank I fetched from where the navy dropped it off. I want to save the small butane stove and canisters to use if I go exploring. But heading out in this climate for overnight trips in a small open boat isn't especially inviting. Finding campsites will be difficult, since every place is rough and brushy or below the high-tide line. One option is to rig up a removable plastic shelter and sleep in the boat.

I knew I'd forget to bring at least one important item, and I have: plastic to line the inside of the cabin walls to create a dead-air space for insulation. On my building materials list, the inner-wall plastic was on the same line as the plastic for the outer walls. When I decided to use tarp instead of plastic on the outside, I crossed off all the plastic wall material without really thinking. Happily, I brought plenty of other plastic and will be able to make do.

I think I'll miss the rich variety of animals I'd likely see on the coast of Canada. There are only a few species of land mammals in southern Chile: huemul (a kind of deer), guanaco (llama), puma (cougar), foxes, and some small rodents. This tiny island probably has none at all. I won't, however, miss bears. One of the benefits of coming here rather than staying in Canada is that I won't have to build a bearproof food-storage cache or worry that bears will break into the cabin, tracking the smell of the fish I hope to catch.

I do have frogs, though — very vocal neighbors that produce an amazing repertoire of sounds. They're not like any frogs I've heard before. Their calls are a sort of cross between frog and cricket: an almost metallic or electronic clicking. And loud! Each seems to find a place to celebrate in a pool under a rock that acts as an echo chamber. I can't tell how many there are. Sometimes it seems like only one, and sometimes they sound like a New Age jazz ensemble riffing off each other. One will wind up with a series of clicks and trills while the others lie back and either keep silent or hold a sort of steady rhythm. Then another will join the lead and they intertwine their songs together. It's quite wonderful.

They're only about an inch in length. Elegant with yellow belly, spotted back, and long delicate toes. I saw one of them yesterday and stomped it. Not really, but when I was feeling anxious about moving my stuff to the bay and thought they might be some kind of insect keeping me awake half the night in a roaring storm, I admit that fantasies of extermination did cross my mind. They certainly like the rain. Just chirrup away when it starts coming down. I hope the cat doesn't eat them.

But now the rain has stopped for a while and there is another lovely rainbow. It's interesting to try to pin down the borders of the colors. High clouds are pierced by sunbeams that stroke the flanks of the hills and the face of the sea. I've never tracked these moving shafts of light before; have seen them only as a brief touch, rather than a lingering caress. But now I watch as they form and shift and fade again.

For visuals this place is a delight. Across the eastern channel, rock-rugged hills, and beyond, snow and glaciered mountains with sharp almost-needle peaks. A light breeze from the west brings the roar of waterfalls from rock walls a mile and a half away. All afternoon, the sea has been flat calm, and if I'd seen this two days ago, I might now be moving my stuff to the bay. But I've begun to build here and am glad to be getting on with it.

Work went well today. It rained hard all morning, and I lounged. When the rain eased about 1 PM, I decided to get started. I hacked an opening in the brush and laid out the cabin. The soil is soggy, with the water table only five inches below the surface, so as foundation posts I'm using the still-rooted stumps of four small trees I cut down. I'll also set in eleven more four-by-four-inch posts. One corner of the cabin will rest on the rock ridge that juts into the sea to form one side of this small cove. Another corner will rest on a length of log I laid in the mud. The rain is raining again, the cat just woke up, and the frog is calling. Coffee water is hot, and I'm away.

FEBRUARY 17, 2001

Perhaps I'll use the odd extra nail in the cabin. My intention has been to resist my usual tendency to overbuild, since I must take the cabin apart again in a year. But holy mother, what a storm last night. It made the one during the night before seem moderate. About 2 AM all hell broke loose. Rain hammered down, driven by the steadily roaring wind, and occasionally a ferocious blast would come shrieking over the trees behind me to batter the tent and tarp.

At one point I stuck my head out to check on things with the flashlight and saw the cat sitting out there in the pitch black night apparently enjoying it all. I suppose I'd have been doing the same if I hadn't been anxious that this shelter would come down or the anchor drag and the boat wash onto the rocks. The boat is still tied out in the cove between the anchor and a tree on shore because I haven't yet cleared enough rocks from the beach to pull it up above high tide. It was getting blown around but seemed ok, so I lay there in the tent and tried to copy the cat's example with both the inner and outer storms.

A whole universe of noise. Groans and roars, whistles and shrieks from the wind, surf pounding on the rocks and rain on the tarps. Occasionally, in a lull, I could hear a frog chirruping. Brave heart. I wonder if in his pool beneath the rock he was aware of the raging storm and of how his voice vanished in the tumult.

Finally about 3:30 AM the storm eased and I looked out again. The A-frame had shifted and the tarps were flapping loosely. I stripped naked but for rubber boots and raincoat and went out to adjust the A-frame, retie the tarps with stronger cord, and tighten the boat tether. As soon as the cat saw there was work to do, he came in the tent and went to sleep.

I can't remember ever being in such a gale. Thankfully everything weathered it without damage, but I won't skimp on nails in building the cabin. And it's protected here. What must it have been like out in the open? The other day at low tide I walked the beach to the exposed point a hundred yards from here and was almost blown over, even though there was just a breeze here around the tent. I can't imagine being on the water during last night's storm.

Now it's pissing down again. This weather makes Vancouver's climate seem stable, even benign. It's rained every day since I arrived. There's been almost continuous cloud cover with only two or three hours of partially blue sky in almost two weeks. But the quality and density of the clouds vary.

Sixty feet from the tent, my boat and motors float in the cove. I probably wouldn't be here without them or the stove, chain saw, solar panels, flashlight, etc. They are useful things that improve my life. But when I consider what their manufacture and maintenance implies — the resources consumed, the pollution produced, the living conditions for the factory workers who built them — I feel conflicted.

Perhaps the "tragedy of the commons" is our culture's overriding metaphor. We realize that collectively we are seriously damaging the Earth, but we feel the technology and consumer goods that are the main sources of environmental degradation improve our individual lives. Few of us want to personally do without these things, so we look for alternative solutions: recycle, down with big business, the illusion of sustainable development, and so on. But finally, I think we will need to renounce some of our material goods. Am I willing? This trip makes me wonder. How high-tech I've become compared to other wilderness retreats.

FEBRUARY 18, 2001

I hurt. My hands are cut, swollen, and sore, thumbs starting to split at the tips, which is always a problem in the wet and cold. My shoulders and arms ache, and phantom pains stab my amputated foot. I think I'm also getting absentminded. Outside the tent, I always wear neoprene chest waders or rubber boots with felt liners (actually only one felt liner, since my prosthetic foot doesn't get cold). The other day, I hopped from the tent platform into the ever-present puddle, only to realize I'd put on the liner but forgotten the boots. Amazing how quick a felt liner sucks up water and how long it's taken to dry. Today, when I put on the right boot it felt very loose. Oh . . . I'd forgotten to put on the leg and was slipping the boot onto my stump. I'd better take care; can't afford to space-out here.

It's been a beautiful day. Just a sprinkle of rain, and sometimes sunny with interesting clouds and a breeze. It was even warm enough to work in a T-shirt for a while. I'm more and more glad I was dropped off here and have decided to stay. What a gift. The mountains today are glorious. A day for photographs. The black flies were a bother, but it's cool now at 9 PM and they have gone.

Many of the birds here are unafraid and the cat is stalking them. When I see him I yell, "No!" He's learned what that means. Hunting is his natural urge, but the birds are too lovely to let him kill. A small one with spiky top-knot (Thorn-tailed Rayadito) landed on a branch above my head today. I held up a finger and he flew to it and paused there for a moment before continuing on his way. [Note: I didn't take a field guide for South American birds with me, so I made up names that described the birds I didn't recognize. In the journal I've retained these names, but also note the common names that I later determined from my notes, photographs, and memory. There were many birds I couldn't identify.]

Yesterday was a heavy workday. I dug holes eighteen inches down to bedrock for the foundation posts. The holes immediately filled with water and sloppy mud, so I carried bag after bag of rocks from the beach to pack around the posts. There will be about two feet of vertical space beneath most of the cabin, enough to store firewood — if I ever get any. I also nailed in the first of three horizontal support beams. Each will be twenty feet long and supported by five posts.

Construction went well with no major screwups or frustrations. I worked steadily but didn't rush. Of course I made a bunch of wrong-length cuts, but I just fixed them and didn't get angry with myself. It always startles me when I measure several times and then cut a board too short anyway. When I realize the mistake and try to figure out how I made it, I can't. It's very odd.

A layer of plastic over the beams will act as a vapor barrier and create dead airspace for insulation. On top of the plastic I'll nail the two-by-four-inch floor joists and then the plywood floor. This should be the heaviest part of the job. Attaching the wall tarps will be frustrating — especially if there's wind — but not as physically difficult. Everything I'm doing out here I've done before at some time in my life. I like this kind of living and I'm fairly good at it.

Today, I set in the rest of the posts and the other two beams, then carried up and cut to length the nine floor joists. The lumber is wet and heavy since it was sawn green just before I bought it and has been soaking in the rain since then. I'd hoped to get the joists in place today, and would have except...

I discovered another major flaw in my preparations. I'd planned to staple the tarp to the outside and the plastic to the inside of the cabin's wooden frame. It was a good plan. I brought a staple gun and two thousand staples for the job. Unfortunately, although I paid close attention to the length of the staples when I bought them, I never thought to check their width; none of the staples fit the gun. This is unbelievable. Arghhh! In the hectic rush to get everything ready in Vancouver, I just looked at the box, recognized the color, and grabbed them. Luckily I brought a pound of one-inch nails and can use those, but it will take a lot longer to hang the tarp and plastic.

FEBRUARY 19, 2001

Tired, sore, not in the mood to write. It's been a long day with intermittent rain all afternoon. At least the black flies went away, and I filled the containers with water running off the tarp above the tent. I'll put rice on for dinner when I finish my coffee. I have only one cup for measuring. I make lousy rice. Seems like a simple task, but somehow I always do it wrong. Cat on knee, frogs under the rock carrying on.

The mountains were super clear today and I put the binoculars on them. Finger glaciers from the Southern Patagonian Ice Field pour down between beautiful needle spires and jagged rock ridges. I haven't yet seen full sun on them or the flash of blue fire from the glaciers' compression ice. Perhaps one day I'll climb the hills that lie between here and the mountains. I won't chance a fall, though. Alone, the stakes are too high.

FEBRUARY 20, 2001

I feel quite vulnerable so near the sea. I'm often hammered by rain beating on the tarp overhead, but last night the new-moon storm tide pushed waves much further up under the tent than I'd expected. The platform was still eighteen inches above the highest surges, but when I shined the flashlight out into the dark to check the boat all I could see was moving water in every direction. I'll be glad to move into the cabin, which is twelve feet back and three feet higher than here. Hopefully using pressboard under tarp for the roof will muffle the sound of the rain.

I'm whipped again. The floor joists and floor, corner studs, and top plates that will support the roof are all in. Usually plywood walls stiffen a building, but since I'm making the walls from tarp, I've had to reinforce the corners with triangular bracing. They required a lot of angle cutting, which was a slow process. I built a stepladder to reach the roof from inside the cabin and a taller straight ladder for working from the outside. I also secured everything against the high water the tide tables predict for tonight.

There was another lovely rainbow today — with all the rain, they're common here — and through the mist and clouds I could sense, if not clearly see, the faint presence of distant hills. Ah, now I remember. This is so beautiful and I'm incredibly lucky to be here. Next time in the city, when I'm bemoaning not having a career or money, I must remember this.

Today has been cold with spitting rain. The wind must be from the northeast since the eastern channel, semiprotected when the predominant northwest wind is blowing, has been rough all day. There's another small island just behind this one, and beyond that, half a mile further north, a much larger and higher island that offers some protection to this area. In front of me, about two hundred yards south, is a third small island, and closer in, off to the southwest, a tiny islet. These two small islands and the islet form a semiprotected basin in front of my camp that is usually fairly calm. Large diving ducks and cormorants (Olivaceous Cormorant) fish there, and I plan to join them soon.

My boat is tied in a tiny cove about sixty feet wide and, depending on the tide, between six and fifty feet from the beach to its mouth. At low tide the boat nearly touches the bottom, and I can easily wade to it. At high tide it floats in about five or six feet of water, and to use it, I loosen the rope tied to shore and pull the boat across to the rocks on the far side of the cove. It works ok, but I want to figure out something that feels more secure and is easier to use.

I didn't start work on the cabin until after 1 PM today, but I'm usually a slow starter, and since it stays light until almost 10, I can work until after 8. Things are moving along with all the studs up and the three window holes framed. I hadn't intended to build so skookum, but every time I think, "That's good enough," my memory of the fierce storm the other night urges me to drive in another nail or two.

The sea is calming now, tide coming in; the rain has stopped and I can see hills but not mountains. And me? Feeling ok, I guess. There's too much physical stuff going on to pay much attention to anything else. It's been cold all day, but I've stayed dry. Or maybe I'm getting used to being damp. I hang sweaty socks and T-shirts on a line in the tent. Clothes that have gotten rainwet hang under the tarp outside. Considering there's no good way to dry clothes, I'm doing well. I had instant soup with macaroni, and rice with soy sauce, for dinner, plus a piece of chocolate for dessert. Yum. The kitten is cuddled in my lap. Things could be a whole lot worse.

A night of rain, pain, and dreams, and now another cold, grey, windy morning. What have I done coming here? I sense that something deep within called

me to such an extreme locale. My notion was to spend a lot of time outside —
to become woven into the natural world again. But I imagine this climate will
push me inward: into the cabin and into myself.

FEBRUARY 23, 2001

I'm building the cabin to be ten feet deep by sixteen feet wide, five of which
is a porch that's open on the southeast side facing the sea and mountains. The
front and rear walls are seven and a half and five feet high respectively. The
sidewalls slant down from front to back. I planned and built the cabin frame
to fit the tarps I bought in Vancouver. The tarps are white and will allow light
to pass, so the cabin should be fairly bright even on cloudy days in winter.
That and cost are the main reasons I'm not using plywood for the walls.

Today when I measured and cut the tarps to cover the walls, I discovered that one of them does not measure approx. 13´6″ as the package label
claims. No, it's actually 12´11″. Grrrr. If I were near a store, this would be
a minor inconvenience because I could just exchange the tarp. But here I'll
need to scab in another piece of tarp along the bottom of the walls to create a
watertight seal. I believe this would be valid grounds for a nasty letter of complaint to the manufacturer. Mutter, mutter.

It's a lovely, quiet evening. Cloudy, but there was pale orange in the sunset sky — the first color I've seen here. A while ago, just as I'd quit work for
the day and paused to look out over the sea, a large bird I hadn't seen before
swooped to perch on the top of the front wall just ten feet from me. Long,
slightly curved, pointed, black bill, stubby tail, grey body with white flecks,
grey-black legs and feet. It sat for a while then flew off.

FEBRUARY 24, 2001

Last night was another cold, uncomfortable one. My back and shoulders feel
like they're clenched into deep spasms, and my hands ache and burn. I take
painkillers, do stretches to loosen the knots, and try to accept and relax into
the pain, but nothing helps much. I sleep bundled up, and since it's not particularly cold I'm probably chilled because of the damp. I continue to wonder
what winter will be like. Already I'm ready for some warm, blue sunshine.
Imagine how I'll feel next year.

It's been flat calm all day with, at times, just a slight wind riffle from the
southeast. A change in weather? The light is different, too — more silver
than grey — the hills reflecting pale blue in the sea. I can see the snowy mountains, and it feels like a crisp fall day, but I don't know the weather here yet.
Ah, it just started to rain lightly. Good, that should settle the dust. This

twenty-four-hour dry spell has been rough. I have a new system for cooking rice. I put it on and let it cook until I smell it start to burn. Seems to work pretty well.

Long workday. I finished attaching the tarp walls and sealed the corners and seams with silicone. It looks tidy and I hope it will be wind- and rain-proof. Just need to spot-nail in a grid pattern over the whole outside to prevent flapping in the wind. Hanging the tarp would have gone a lot faster if I could have used the staple gun rather than pounding in nearly a thousand small nails with the hammer. I still shake my head over bringing the wrong-size staples. Perhaps this, too, deserves a stern letter of complaint. But I doubt the postal service would deliver it to me out here. I wonder if this calm will last or if another nasty storm is on the way. I guess a storm will come or not; in either case I'll be here.

FEBRUARY 25, 2001

NOON: I think the endless rain is getting to me. The tension I feel seems similar to the fear I've felt toward bears during wilderness retreats in Canada — as though something dangerous out there is coming to get me. But here there are no scary animals, just wind and rain. I suspect it's mostly my own dark feelings I'm afraid of. I've begun to meditate for thirty to forty minutes in the evening. As usual I spend more time lost in thought than simply remaining aware of physical sensations, emotions, and the process of thinking. My primary focus of attention is sound: rain and wind, waves on rock, frogs, birds. The sounds of water surround me.

As far as I can tell, it's rained lightly but steadily since last night. I've been working in front of the tent under the tarp, but it's time to climb into rain gear. It's also time, in the larger scheme, to walk the walk. I've often talked about surrender. In my preparations for coming here I was repeatedly confronted with the need to surrender my preconceived plans and adapt to what was actually going on. Now there's rain. The rain is. The rain is not going away, nor am I. If I don't begin to practice accepting life — including rain — as it is, I'm going to have a lousy time here.

The tide comes in and washes my shit away. Poof. Gone. It's so easy to understand how we have damaged sea and sky and rivers... and our hearts. Greed. To want just a little more. It makes perfect sense. What's the harm? I reach out to grab something, and the agitation of wanting and grabbing dissolves in the currents of my heart. Poof. Gone. Until slowly, little by little, my heart fills with greed, my life is polluted with this toxin, and I can no longer enjoy what actually is. Time to work. I want a cabin!

EVENING: Worked late. I cut and nailed the rafters in place, and with them overhead, the cabin got a lot smaller. Another six inches of height would be nice, but then the tarps wouldn't fit at all. I never expected to put the cabin together this securely, and I'm starting to run short of nails. Tomorrow I'll have to drag three sheets of pressboard for the roof out from under the tent. This game of musical materials is hard work. For the past several days I've been juggling 2×4s trying to find straight ones, and I had to replace the tarp that was over the tent with plastic so I could cover the cabin walls with the tarp. Hope I'm not hit with another big storm because the plastic might not hold. Same thing for dinner yet again, which won't make the cat happy. He doesn't seem to like macaroni and instant soup. Imagine that.

It was a splendid afternoon. Some blue sky for a short while, and even a direct ray of sun for about five minutes. The clouds lifted and the mountains loomed sharp and mysterious against the silver sky. A kingfisher (Ringed Kingfisher) flew by calling. Up on the ladder nailing down the rafters, I heard the dolphins blowing and looked out. The world seemed new from up there. Two of the dolphins were swimming as they usually do, but a third was going in circles and breathing heavy or even panting. Then he leapt from the water white belly up. I'm no dolphin expert, but it is late summer and something seems fishy. Good on them. As dark comes on there's an ominous feel in the air... or is it in my heart? The sea has begun to move, restlessly it seems. Does it portend an outer or an inner storm?

FEBRUARY 26, 2001

Sun! I'm actually sitting in it as I write. Oh. Well, I was a minute ago. Ah, yes, now again. And blue sky in places, too. Amazing. The sound of the sea gently lapping the rocks is lovely and peaceful when it's the only water sound on a dry morning. The clouds over the mountains are ragged — layered dark grey, silver, pale yellow — and moving fast. Sunlight slides across the rock cliffs to the west, flickering on waterfalls. A kingfisher just landed in the nearby tree: brilliant rusty-orange nestled among dark, dead, angular branches. When I heard no rain early this morning, I leapt up to empty the tent and pull out three sheets of pressboard from beneath it. Then everything went back in and still no rain. A miracle.

EVENING: The wind is up and out of the west. The boat is tugging at its leash, which always makes me uneasy, and the plastic over the tent is rattling and slapping. I hope it holds. It just started to sprinkle but held off until I got the roof on, so for the first time since I've been building the cabin I didn't have to wear rain gear. It would have been a much more difficult and unpleasant job in the rain, but even so, humping the pressboard up onto the rafters wasn't easy. At one point I fell off the ladder — or rather it went over and I jumped off. After that I started to tie it in place. Can't afford an injury.

The ladder also fell on my head today, and a few days ago a 2×2, which is now part of the ladder, fell on my head. Maybe it doesn't like me. I, on the other hand, am in love with my felt boot-liners. I wear one to work in (which gets a bit damp from sweat) and one to sleep in. I've yet to get a cold foot. Hmm, I think my perceptions of and attitudes toward supposedly inanimate objects might be starting to change. Solitude can do that. I've been here three weeks today. Doesn't seem like it, though.

Just caught a glimpse of what I think was a nutria as it disappeared around the corner of the cove. Looked a bit like an otter with a long tail. Jeez, the rocks are slippery here! I go around half the time like a crab on all fours.

FEBRUARY 27, 2001

It's wet out there. There was an hour of pretty good weather this morning, but now it's pissing down again. My dream has expanded from a whole day without rain to two nice days in a row, and then three, etc. Greed. If the rain and wind give me a chance, I'll stretch the large tarp over the roof later today. Day after tomorrow, I need to send the first monthly "I'm ok" email, and I should get the system working before then. The GPS is still misbehaving. Seems to work only when warm, so there's probably still moisture inside. A humming-bird (Green-back Firecrown) just came by. Perhaps I'll put out some sugar water. Oh, it's stopped raining. Maybe it will get warm and sunny. Uh-huh.

FEBRUARY 28, 2001

Cloudy but not raining. Woke early and I'm tired and cranky. Too much work, too many aches and pains, not enough sleep. But there's no reason to take the day off, since I find little comfort lying inside the tent reading. I don't miss sex or even chocolate ice cream that much, but a hot tub would sure be a treat; not just the heat, but the release from gravity. Back in Canada I had fantasies of building a tub here and solar-heating water to soak in, but I doubt there's enough sunlight. Actually, my real fantasy was to find an unknown hot spring and build my cabin beside it. In the meantime, I'll try to get the tarp on today and make sure the satphone is working so I can send a first-of-the-month check-in email tomorrow.

The cat is hunting birds. I yell, "No!" but instinct is too strong. I set down my oatmeal, put on my leg and rubber boots, and go to harass him. My allergies are kicking in as he gets older, and I don't think I'll let him into the cabin once it's built. It's ironic that after all my effort to stay away from cats in Vancouver, I bring one to sleep with me in the tent. Although he's often irritating, I've grown attached to him and doubt I'll actually use him to test shellfish for red tide toxicity. It would be kind of like coming home from work to find some suspect leftovers in the fridge and calling your kid or little brother over to sample them before eating them yourself.

EVENING: I spent all afternoon trying to get the satphone working. It took a long time to find a location for the antenna that would let me use the phone from the tent where it and the laptop are protected from the rain. Having the phone on for so long searching for a satellite killed its battery. So I had to drag out one of the 12-volt truck batteries, open the watertight storage barrel with all the electronic gear in it, and find the battery connector. What a hassle, and I started getting ready for tomorrow days ago.

Of course when I had the barrel open, stuff strewn everywhere, and was worried it would any minute start to rain on the electronic gear, Cat came over to get in the middle of what I was doing. I set him aside and he returned. I set him aside again and he came back. I tossed him into the mud and he decided to stay away. Cats are the most stubborn animals in the world!

But it was a glorious afternoon. There was a double rainbow, and three dolphins came by close to shore. They were definitely making love among the kelp beds. Two would roll over and swim on their backs while the third swam above one or the other. Then two would swim belly to belly on their sides. It was very erotic and surreal.

MARCH 2001

When listening for your heart song,
listen for us as well.

— Email from Patti, sent just before I left for Chile

It's a restless day, with the wind up, the ocean moving, and the mountains in view. I sent a check-in email this morning. At first I couldn't find a satellite, but finally connected with AORW FRANCE, located above Brazil, and one of two satellites available to me from here! Perfect. The communication system seemed to be working, which was a relief after all the hassle hooking it up, especially because I don't feel confident of my skill with such devices. This afternoon I checked for replies so I'd know for sure my message went through. Nothing. I sent the message again and I think that one made it ok. I did pick up an email Patti sent several days ago saying they've been a bit concerned since I'd promised to send my latitude and longitude coordinates as soon as I found a place to settle. With all that's been going on, I forgot to do it. But considering that they don't seem to be very worried and also how much hassle it is to send messages, I don't feel too bad.

Moved all my food into the cabin, and that frees up the tarps I need for the porch walls. I also emptied and dismantled one of the shipping crates to use for building shelves.

EVENING: It's storming again and I'll have to wait until the tide goes out to check the email. Wind is driving rain and spray across the sea in dense horizontal sheets. Even in my protected cove the water is roiling, and the boat yanking at its tether. Small waves break over my dangling feet as I sit on the platform in front of the tent. The water surging under me feels too close for comfort, and I'm ready to move to the cabin to put more distance between me and the sea. I'm glad this is happening in daylight. The mountains have disappeared. Ten minutes ago they loomed, forbidding to my eye, in misty silver light beneath a higher layer of solid grey. I saw a frog heading for higher pools a while ago, staying ahead of the incoming tide. Hope she made it. Hope I make it, too.

LATE NIGHT: God, what a storm out there. It's unbelievable. Slamming in from the southwest, and I'm unprotected from that direction. This is even worse than the last big one. The roaring and howling are overwhelming, and the savage force of the wind and rain beyond words. I've been lying in my small refuge, flooded with anxiety and trying to separate my fear from the auditory and tactile energy of the storm. Struggling to accept my death. So far, I haven't been very successful. *Wham!* The tent shudders in a brutal blast. I flick on the headlamp and peer out through the tent flap to check the boat, but can barely see through the swirling rain and spray. Oh shit! The boat is not where it should be. It's broken loose and is up against the rocks on the far side of the cove.

I rush to strip naked and pull on chest waders, boots, and raincoat, grab my knife, and hunch into the storm. Staggering over slippery rocks through the froth of the waves, half blinded by wind-driven spray, I make my way to the boat. The tether rope is still tied to the bow, but has broken free from where it was snubbed to shore. I get a hand on it and drag the boat away from the rocks and back to the middle of the cove. I knot the tether around a stout tree and hope it will hold until morning. I also hope the motor hasn't been damaged on the rocks. I hope . . . for so many things. Tomorrow I must find a way to haul the boat up the beach above the high tide. I don't want to leave it floating out there anymore.

Before shedding my soggy gear and climbing back into the tent, I check the plastic tarp for the tie-down loops I'd reinforced with duct tape. Miraculously, they're still holding. Even in this howling wind, the cabin sits on its base posts like a rock. Well, I wanted adventure.

MARCH 2, 2001

DAWN: The storm raged all night. I looked out several times to be sure the boat hadn't pulled loose again. It looked kind of strange, but I couldn't tell why in the dark. Now at first light I see the boat floating upside down, both motors submerged in the sea.

This feels like the end, the last straw, just too much to deal with. I'm exhausted from all the work and tension of the past months, and I've had enough. I was right to feel anxious about leaving the boat tied out in the water, but I never imagined it would flip.

I'm not hurt or stranded away from camp, but this is still a serious problem. Other than fire, submersion in saltwater is the worst that can happen to an outboard. I guess I can survive without the motors, but two of the propane tanks still sit on the beach a mile away, and the tank I have here won't last the year. Without the motors I have no way to gather firewood or go fishing and exploring. Looking ahead, this could be a long, hard year with no way to heat the cabin and not even enough gas to cook. Ah hell, the wind is coming up again.

NIGHT: Dinner is cooking and it's dark. I've only now quit working, and I'm too tired to write much. At first when I saw the flipped boat, I felt numb and just sat there in despair. I had no idea what to do, but knew I had to do something, so I stripped naked again, pulled on the chest waders, and waded out to the boat. The tide had ebbed and I salvaged the 4 hp motor from the bottom where it had landed when the boat flipped. Then I unclamped the 15 hp from the transom and carried it to shore.

I cleared enough rocks from the beach to open a rough landing strip and gouged a hole in the brush with the chain saw. Flipping the boat over and dragging it up above the high tide line was a slow grind.

Then I had to face the outboards. Over the years, I've tinkered with different kinds of motors, but I'm no mechanic. In this case I had no idea where to even start, but luckily, I brought a shop manual and some spare parts with me. I checked the table of contents to see if there might be a section at least partially relevant to my situation, and at the bottom of the page I found a gift from the universe: a section titled "Motors Submerged in Saltwater."

Following the instructions, I washed everything in freshwater, dried all the electrical connections I could reach, and used alcohol to absorb any remaining moisture. I squirted oil into the cylinders via the sparkplug holes, and also disassembled and cleaned the fuel lines, fuel pump, and carburetor. When I put everything back together, the fuel pump leaked. I took it apart again and managed to stop the leak. Then I dragged the boat back down to the water, clamped the outboard to it, and cranked it over. Nothing. But on the third pull, it caught and ran! What a huge sense of relief and gratitude. It doesn't sound as good as it did, but at least it runs.

Question is, will corrosion slowly destroy the electrical connections I couldn't clean? I forgot to bring a socket large enough to remove the flywheel, and some electronic components are hidden underneath. I brought a flywheel puller and spare components, but forgot the right size socket. Unbelievable. Anyway, the motor is working and I'm very, very thankful. I'll fetch the propane tanks the next calm day. I also worked on the 4 hp for a while, but it showed no sign of life, so now I have no backup motor.

MARCH 3, 2001

MORNING: First full night's sleep in a month. After yesterday I was worn out. I'd slept sporadically in the storm and woke to the flipped boat and submerged motors. I worked nonstop all day and didn't eat anything except some coffee in the morning. Last night I taped my split fingertips with duct tape to ease the pain, put in earplugs to dampen the sound of wind and water, and tucked the blankets close around me against the cold. I crashed about 10:30 and slept straight through until Cat woke me at 7 this morning. Then back to sleep for two more hours.

I woke to broken clouds with patches of blue here and there. The mountains are semiclear, and my pen casts a faint shadow. A light breeze from the northwest is moving the sea, so I won't be going for the propane tanks today. Yesterday, the weather went through radical changes, but rained and hailed only when I was in the cabin working on the motors.

Emails arrived from my contact teams in the north and from the Chilean Navy and National Parks Service. The parks official said he hoped the winds hadn't bothered me too much, so I guess these storms are unusual even for here. I wonder: have the winds really bothered me much? I guess it will depend on whether the outboard continues to function for the year I'll be here.

I want to explore the anxiety I so often feel. It's deep and poisons my life. I've seen over and over that things work out — not always as I'd planned, sometimes much better — yet still I look ahead with fear. Instead of relaxing into life, I'm often needlessly tense and worried. This last storm was an example. I worried that the cabin wouldn't hold together, that the plastic over the tent would tear loose, that the boat would break free, or that some other undefined bad thing would happen, but I hadn't thought at all about what actually did happen. Once faced with a real problem, I dealt with it. Even when things get really nasty — like my foot getting ripped off in the motorcycle crash — life continues. So why not let go of the worrying?

Last evening two beautiful birds (Kelp Goose) about the size of small geese landed on the rock out front. I fetched the field glasses and edged to within fifteen feet of them. One is completely white with yellow legs and black eyes and bill. I think he's the male but only because he's largest. The other has yellow legs, a ring around each eye, and a pale pink bill. Her breast is dark brown or black-barred with white. Belly and tail are white, and the wing tips show some iridescent blue green. In flight she is spectacular. A black line runs down the center of white wings. Her back and tail are white with two dark lines.

MARCH 4, 2001

Tomorrow I'll have been here a month, but I've been so busy that the effects of solitude aren't very noticeable — at least not consciously. I'm still mostly eating oatmeal, peanut butter, dehydrated soup with macaroni, rice with lentils, and instant coffee. My cooking and eating gear consists of two old pots I've had for years, a cup, small bowl, tablespoon, and teaspoon. I'll open the other foodstuffs and kitchenware once I move into the cabin where it's dry. For drinking and cooking I catch rainwater that pours from the plastic over the tent and store it in two 2½-gallon containers. My reserve supply is in the washtub that has filled on its own straight from the sky.

The cabin is closed in and the floor is drying. So far, I see no leaks. Today I attached some of the inside plastic wall lining and built the major shelves, which filled immediately. Tomorrow I'll put up the rest of the plastic. Then I can move in. I'm ready. I'd like to build a table and bed first, but the wood I need is under the tent.

Last night I woke to a nasty backache. I put a tennis ball under my shoulder and rotated my arm to massage the pressure point, which helped some. Patti taught me that. She is such a good friend, and I'm realizing more and more how much she's shared with me. So much of what I do is oriented toward what others will think. Over and over I wonder how Patti will see my work on the cabin if she comes to visit at the end of the year.

It's raining and blowing, and the tide is surging up in the gathering dark. I'm tense with anxiety, even dread, toward the wind and sea — or rather toward the raw natural world. *What if* . . . Another huge storm hits and this time my tent is blown apart? A rogue wave strikes and I'm washed away and drowned?

MARCH 5, 2001

A delicate grass grows in the intertidal zone. Tall, thin stalks topped with seed heads bend in graceful curves, and the slightest breeze sends them into swaying shivers. On calm days, the soft pulse of the sea rocks them gently back and forth, hour after hour. When it storms, waves rush in and flatten them almost horizontal, back and forth, hour after hour. How can something so delicate be so resilient?

I've moved into the cabin, even though it's a huge mess. Gear piled up, wood, sawdust, and tools everywhere. The bed and table are not built and no windows in yet, but this afternoon I had a sudden urge to move. I'll cook on the stepladder and sleep on the floor. I'm so accustomed to being outside that I keep going to the porch to see what's going on out there.

A while ago I went to the rock with the pint of deluxe ten-year-old whiskey Diane gave me as a gift for this journey and thanked Spirit for bringing me here; thanked all the people who have helped make this retreat possible; then thanked Diane for the hooch and knocked back the first drink since I arrived. I watched rain slanting against the rock cliffs to the west and heard the roar of a passing hailstorm drumming the surface of the sea.

MARCH 6, 2001

It's so noisy here especially at high tide. The sea crumples and rushes against the rocks, the wind roars in the trees, rain pounds on the roof, and the sound of distant waterfalls swells or fades depending on wind direction and runoff. Strange that way out here where there's supposed to be peace and quiet I sleep with earplugs at times. I think this resistance to noise is linked to my resistance to meditation — to just being with things as they are even though they sometimes seem unpleasant and intrusive. I'm sitting for only half an hour in the evening and then my back gets very painful. Yeah, and so what?

My moods shift as fast and furiously as the weather: joy, thankfulness, peace, anger, fear, frustration, calm steadiness. I try to stay with it all, to keep watching and waiting.

Cat and I have been at it again. He sure is willful. Gets into the middle of whatever I'm doing. Seems to give up only once he senses real anger or pain. I haven't hit him again, but a couple of times he's tried to claw me when I've squeezed him till he cried. Am I just getting his attention or am I mistreating him? He's still very affectionate, but I wonder. Last night he was after a large moth on the porch, which seemed fair since I won't let him hunt birds. But the moth fluttered against the porch roof and Cat clawed up the tarp wall trying to catch it. "No!" Won't take long for the tarp to leak at that rate.

I was warm last night for the first time since I've been here, but what a hassle tucking the blankets and sleeping bag around the sleeping pad. I'd taken off my prosthesis to meditate, and decided to just balance on one leg to make up the bed. Then the batteries in the headlamp died and left me working by touch in the dark. Only thing is, six of my fingertips are split and wrapped in duct tape so I couldn't feel anything. And of course right about then Cat jumped into the fray. But it was worth it to be warm.

Peaceful low-tide morning and I feel much safer with more exposed beach. Spacious and free. I imagine the tide will flood very high tonight. A while ago I walked to the far point to look at some dead trees, and they seem too rotten to burn. Finding firewood could be a problem and fires a luxury rather than a daily event.

Often when I tell people about going into solitude they ask, "But what do you do all day out there alone?" Sometimes time stretches on forever, usually when there is physical, emotional, or spiritual pain, otherwise the days zoom by. Yesterday I built a bed and designed shelves and sliding drawers for underneath. The cabin is small and I need to use the space efficiently. This morning I brought in the gear from the other crate and dismantled it to use for shelves. Now all my equipment and supplies, except the propane tanks on the other beach, are near the cabin and out of tide's reach. I got out more salt, and had to grin. I brought fifteen pounds of the stuff! That's over a pound a month. So far I've used maybe an ounce. What was I thinking?

I found the thermometer today and it read 45°F, which felt like about what it's been most days. Some summer. I'm getting very ready for a fire. The question of firewood looms. On the west coast of Canada there's a huge supply of driftwood logs and you can be picky about what kind of wood to burn. Maybe there's plenty here, too, and I just don't know how to find it yet, but I've seen very little driftwood, and the trees in the forest are wet or rotting.

Tonight, after dinner on the porch, I walked to the low-tide water's edge to watch the night. Moonbeams flared from behind dark clouds, dramatically lighting hills and sea. Then the full moon briefly showed through a ragged break. I bathed in the beauty and called to her. Imagine wanting to plant a flag there.

I've seriously injured the rotator cuff in my right shoulder and can barely move my arm. Christ, this shit never quits. All it took was a moment of inattention and I slipped and fell. The low-tide rocks here are treacherous, probably covered with microalgae, and other than glare ice I've never been on anything so slippery. Even when they look dry there's little traction except on rough patches. Because of my leg, I use lightweight rubber boots that don't have Vibram soles and so don't grip at all. A nutria was fishing near the water edge and I wanted a closer look, so I went out onto the rocks. I was half watching him — moving when he dove, freezing when he came back up — and only half watching my feet. I went down hard with no warning at all.

The pain comes and goes. As long as I keep the arm supported it's ok, but if I put any strain on it, oh fuck, it hurts. I can't immobilize it, though. I know from when I tore the same rotator cuff three years ago that I need to move it within the pain range as soon as I can. I imagine there will be some nasty nights ahead. For now I've filled the hot water bottle with cold rainwater and taken an anti-inflammatory. So much for finishing the cabin, setting up solar panels and wind generator, building an outhouse, and fetching firewood. This could lay me up for weeks as far as heavy work goes. I'm glad to have built and moved into the cabin.

I've had about enough of the active life for a while and might rather like to be intellectual again. By the time I'd finished my PhD qualifying exam, I was sick of books and ready to get on with this project. It's now been eight months of almost nonstop activity, and I'm fried. Would have preferred to get my camp completely set up before taking a break, though. Oh well, things are what they are. Now and then, usually in the middle of a storm in the night, I sense that in coming here I've maybe bitten off more than I can chew.

I guess if I had to bugger my shoulder, watching a nutria was a good way to do it. In Spanish, *nutria* means sea cat, and it's well named: the face definitely looks like a cat. Not sure what it was eating, but if shellfish, that means — according to German — there's no red tide here. It was diving repeatedly but not cracking anything open on the surface. When it saw me it stopped and stared. Me too. In a sense it was greed that caused the fall. I wanted to see how close I could get.

There were two ducks in the water when the nutria swam into the basin. Boy, did they get up on the rocks in a hurry. Didn't go back in until they were sure he had gone. I saw a condor (Andean Condor) earlier. Wheeling black and wild, high against the mottled sky.

MARCH 10, 2001

What's that sound? Have I heard it before? It's like a breeze bringing the roar of distant waterfalls, but not quite. A motor? Ah, the teakettle coming to a boil. I just got it out and I'm not used to its murmur yet.

The only place I feel safe walking here is on the narrow strip of beach I cleared for hauling up the boat. Interesting that I fell on the low-tide rocks. Just the other day I noted how peaceful and safe I feel at low tide and how vulnerable when the tide is high. Appearances.

Arm and shoulder still sore, but the cold water bottle helps. I kept it on

most of yesterday and again today. The only time my arm is really comfortable is when it's supported. Some movements are sort of ok, but if I forget and
reach out to pick something up — ouch! I need to start exercising it today. If
I wait even a few days the muscles will stiffen and start to atrophy. I can't afford to lose strength, there's still too much work to do.

This morning I checked the onions, garlic, and potatoes that were still in
plastic bags. Good thing I did; a few are starting to rot. So the injury has an
upside, since I probably wouldn't have checked them for a couple of weeks yet
and by then the rot would have spread. In finally cleaning up the cabin I found
the carpenter's level I'd been looking for all week. I also happened on the
mirror and saw myself for the first time. Grizzled look: shaggy hair and grey
beard. Eyes deep with pain. I'm tired of pain. Seems like I've had more than
my share over the years — physical and emotional. Or maybe other people
just shrug it off better than I do.

Songs keep running through my head. One repeats over and over, and
then another takes its place. For a while it was "Now I Walk in Beauty," the
Navajo prayer song, then it was the old pop tune "Up on the Roof," and after
that the country-western "She's a Good Hearted Woman in Love with a
Good Timing Man." The last was particularly tedious since those are the only
words I can remember and they may be wrong. Today I'm singing "Deep in
December It's Nice to Remember."

And that's the trick. Somehow in looking back, almost any situation
seems to have been ok. The challenge is to live that acceptance in the present,
not just in memory.

MARCH 11, 2001

62°F. It's been a glorious day, with sunlight and scattered clouds over the
mountains. *First day without rain.* Yet I'm still wearing thermal long underwear, two sweaters, a sweatshirt, and vest. Weird. Ah, the dolphins just
showed up, and hummingbirds are working the feeder three feet from my
head. They're still nervous when I'm sitting here but getting used to me. God,
what a place this is. I sit here and all these critters come by, living their lives.
There are kelp beds and shellfish in the shallow basin out front, so I guess it's
a good area to feed.

Exercise and the cold water bottle are helping. My shoulder is feeling
somewhat better, and I can use my arm for light tasks. I assembled the stove
(dreaming of a fire), decided where to put the outhouse, stretched damp
clothes out to dry, hung the onions and garlic in the open air. Just dubbing
around.

MARCH 12, 2001

I was convinced it never did this here. It's been sunny and warm all day with only a few scattered clouds in an otherwise clear blue sky. I wonder how many days in the year will be like this. For now, this one is enough. The sun inspired me to hook up the solar panels. I built wood frames to face north-northeast at 45 degrees from vertical and weighted the bases with heavy rocks to hold them firm in the wind. Eventually, when my shoulder heals, I'll move them to the point, but for the moment they're on the rock ridge in front of the cabin. If I cut down a couple of trees, the panels will get another three hours of sun each day, but I like the trees and they protect me from the wind.

I also took a sponge bath in the sun! Hadn't bathed since I arrived but didn't feel particularly dirty. I seldom sweat and there's no dust here. Winter temperatures will be a lot colder, and I'll need to find at least enough wood to have one good fire a week to warm up the cabin, bathe, and do laundry.

The only novel I brought to Chile is *Right Ho, Jeeves*, by P. G. Wodehouse. It tells a frivolous story that I've already read several times, but I love the language and can read it again and again. Getting lost in novels is an escape for me, and I decided against bringing any others because part of my reason for coming here is to remove myself from the easy escapes human culture so seductively offers. But on a back street in Punta Arenas I found a hole-in-the-wall used bookstore with one short shelf of dusty novels in English. I bought several to read in town and brought with me here the ones I hadn't finished. I've now read *Apropos of Dolores* by H. G. Wells, *The Perfect Storm* by Sebastian Junger (I'm not sure that was such a good choice considering my small boat and the weather. Kind of like taking *Jaws* on a scuba vacation.), and am in the middle of *The Family Moskat* by Isaac Singer. How different that world is from my present life.

Last night while meditating I opened my eyes to an orange moon glowing through the trees. I went carefully out to the rocks and soaked in the quiet beauty of it all. Now the mountains are shining with day's-end light. The sun is gone, but I've hooked up part of the electrical system and will have light to cook by. So I sit here with no dinner started and watch evening fall and the dolphins play in the basin. Looking out over this quiet evening, it's hard to imagine the weather I've seen these past five weeks.

MARCH 13, 2001

The rocks continue to do me in. I'm trying to be very careful, but I slipped and fell hard again today and reinjured my shoulder. It's very sore, and I have the cold water bottle on it. Cat is sniveling, and I'm not sure what his lament is. I fed him the same rice and black beans that I cooked for dinner. He doesn't like the beans and wants to eat only the rice, but he needs protein so I mash them together.

It's been a nice enough day. Not like yesterday, but pleasant. Just now a ministorm rolled through. Strong wind and rain. The solar panels didn't quiver, and all the water containers filled from the temporary gutter I rigged along the back edge of the cabin roof. This afternoon I finished the electrical system. The solar panels now charge two truck batteries that link directly to the satphone and a 12-volt light. An inverter, also connected to the batteries, converts the 12-volt direct current to 110-volt alternating current to charge the laptop and AA flashlight batteries. The cabin is still a huge mess, but I hung the door. Makes the place feel cozier.

The Simon and Garfunkel song "Cloudy" drifts through my head, bringing memories of New England colleges in the fall. Coeds, wearing boots and wrapped in scarves, move through swirling leaves on their way to private rendezvous. There's something mystical about them, a sense that they know the secret; not know as knowledge, but in the way they feel. Like they're where they should be, doing what they should be doing; comfortable and confident with themselves in the world.

MARCH 14, 2001

Time changed pace today and the clock slowed to a crawl. Not the second hand — the minutes are still moving along — but the hour hand. I feel I've been here a long, long time and that a year is forever. Two days ago I marveled at how fast the weeks had sped by. Now, yesterday seems to have crept into the past. I suspect this has to do with physical discomfort. I'm feeling old, achy, and worn out. Maybe now that I've slowed down because of my shoulder, the last frantic months are catching up with me. I'm also feeling lonely and miss Patti and Susan. Like the wind and the rain, these moods come and go.

MARCH 15, 2001

This calls for a celebration. Out comes Diane's whiskey. I also brought one bottle each of Scotch, Drambuie, and cheap brandy: enough for a small taste at night. But back to the cause for celebration. I'm sitting beside a fire! It's just a tiny test fire outside, but it is burning wood.

I haven't been out in the boat for a month, and have left this small beach only once. Today I walked the hundred yards to the point and — even though my shoulder seriously didn't like it — chopped some twigs and branches off a dead tree. They've caught fire easily. This doesn't mean finding firewood will be easy, but this particular wood does burn. I've worried about firewood since I talked to a man in Punta Arenas who used to dive for sea urchins along this coast. He said it never stops raining here and is so wet that clothes don't dry and wood won't burn. He was wrong on all counts. It rains a lot but not all day every day, clothes slowly dry, and this wood, at least, burns. How often I get caught in anxiety or hope based on false information!

I measured the distance from the cabin to the point, and the electrical wire I brought should just reach. A second cause for celebration! I'll set up the solar panels, wind generator, and batteries down there where it's open to the wind and the panels will have sunlight all day, even in winter. They say there is no wind here in winter, but they may mean no raging storms. Tough to imagine not even a breeze.

I picked up and straightened all the bent nails and still have about 350 of various sizes. Hard to believe that of all the nails I brought, so few are left. Most of the building is finished, except the outhouse, entry porch, steps, and awnings, so if I'm frugal the nails should suffice. I've run out of small-dimension lumber and had to use the chain saw to rip two 2×4s into 1×2s for shelf framing.

I finally opened the cheese and meat, and as expected the cheese was covered with mold. Scraped it off and gave Cat the scrapings. The smoked meat is fine, but the bacon shows some light mold in places. It's probably ok, though. When I go camping I often eat salami that's getting pretty odd. Washed it in hot brine and hung it to dry. The only perishables left to deal with are the potatoes, and except for a few moldy ones they're in good shape. Little by little, things are coming together.

It rained earlier, but now the sun is glowing through the clouds. There's a breeze and the ocean is on the move. Ah, the dolphins just came by. One of them leapt out of the water and swam on his back, beating the surface with his tail, so apparently they're still in courtship mode. Or perhaps he was saying hello to me. I wonder if they know what humans are. I wonder if I do.

MARCH 16, 2001

53°F. Spitting rain. Breeze and whitecaps, mountains half visible. The two small windows are in. With luck, they won't leak. My shoulder is sore, but at least it's working. Writing is especially painful. I saw a mosquito in the cabin today and killed it without remorse. I like the door open and lots of bugs come in, but they usually stay against the translucent walls and don't bother me.

43°F. What a hailstorm. I saw an opaque white wall coming across the water, and then it was on me. Stones the size of small marbles are hammering the ground and filling me with anxiety. Will the porch roof hold? Sometimes I'd rather be in a cabin with wood walls and roof, but the tarp covering definitely puts me in closer contact with the weather. Cranky night with my shoulder, but the chill in the air today makes the water bottle colder, which helps. What a blessing to be pain-free for a while.

I hung most of the ceiling plastic yesterday. I knew the job would be maddening, and it was. I had to separate a thousand staples with side-cutters, then drive them in one by one with the hammer. I was working overhead, which caused my shoulder to hurt, trying to keep the plastic stretched tight so it wouldn't sag, and at the same time holding the tiny staples in place with my duct-taped fingers.

Everything went wrong. I kept smacking myself with the hammer, or dropping the staples, or losing my grip on the plastic. The process provided an excellent opportunity to test the limits of my patience and the creative range of my profanity. There I was, an enraged lunatic perched alone in the middle of nowhere, cussing at an innocent piece of plastic — the peaceful afternoon shattered by bellowed profanity rolling down the waterways and echoing off the rock walls of Staines Peninsula. I decided to quit for the day.

Later, as I prepared to meditate, the physical world was against me again. I slipped the water bottle under my six layers of clothing, but it refused to stay on my shoulder. Then the blanket I wrap around me fell to the floor, and when I reached for it, the pillow I rest my arm on slid from my lap. When I reached for that, the water bottle shifted, and when I repositioned it, the blanket fell to the floor again. Of course pain was a background constant. I finally had to stop and laugh. Afterward I went out to see the stars, and even the Milky Way was shining.

Strong gusting winds, but everything seems solid. Dead calm and then, wham, the whole cabin vibrates. The bookshelves are built and the books put up. I look so intellectual now. Already I scratch my head at some of the titles I brought with me, but who knows where my mind will itch in six months? I don't know if I'm worn out and working slowly or it was just a fiddly task, but the shelves took much longer than expected. I'm not feeling well and suspect it's a physical symptom of the anxiety I link to the wind. It would be useful to have a barometer to track whether feeling poorly is correlated with barometric pressure. Too bad the one Patti sent from Texas didn't arrive in Puerto Natales before I left.

Cat is crying and repeatedly coming into the cabin even though he knows he's not allowed. A while ago I heard strange noises and saw his box shaking. I hope it's just dreams of adolescent disquiet and not some physical ailment.

I've been looking at how my frustration and anger affect me inwardly and how I express it toward myself, Cat, and my work. I miss so much and bring so much unhappiness to myself and those around me by being prickly and judgmental rather than content with the world as it is. Never mind the root causes, it's just a habit to feed and express the anger. If I can come out of this year with a softer aspect and more patience, the journey will have been worth it.

MARCH 19, 2001

53°F. Calm and cloudy with some blue sky.

I mounted transom wheels on the boat to make it easier to drag up above the high-tide line, and I saw a small rock on the beach that looked like flint and sparked when I smacked it with a steel file. Triggered memories of being a twelve-year-old Boy Scout. One day I'll try to start a fire with it.

Fwap, fwap, fwap. The tranquil evening is shattered by wings and feet slapping glassy water; a scattered flock of cormorants just now takes off, black backs and white bellies glowing in the evening light. A hawk flies by down low, and two eagles (Crested Caracara) circle higher up. A seagull swoops, calling, and Cat tries to stalk it.

All of a sudden the two resident nonflying ducks with pale yellow bellies and bright orange bills (Flightless Steamer-duck) start to frantically run flapping and squawking across the basin. A nutria in hot pursuit chases them for a long way out into the channel. She pops up for a breath and then back down, swimming fast beneath the surface. At one point she strikes a shoal of rocks, scrambles up, races across, then leaps back into the sea. The ducks finally escape, but that animal is a serious predator. Cat better be careful near the water's edge. I wonder if the nutria would come up on land to rob my bacon. Better hang it high just in case.

MARCH 20, 2001

MORNING: 44°F and quiet but for the distant murmur of waterfalls. If the calm holds, I'll go for the propane tanks. I long for silence, and hope there will be more still days in winter. The wind is often a huge oppressive *presence* in my mind. Planning boat trips in advance is impossible since I can't predict the wind and it can so quickly turn on me.

EVENING: But today was joyful, a time to give thanks. The sky remained sunny and the sea glassy calm, I discovered the outboard still works, I now have enough propane for the year, and I began to gather a supply of firewood! The challenge, of course, is to give thanks no matter what the circumstance, but sometimes that's not so easy to do.

This morning I assembled the survival kit and wheeled the boat down to the water. The outboard was difficult to start because I'm still not sure how much choke to give it. I went for the propane, and since the two-hundred-pound tanks float, I just tied them on and towed them, rather than wrestle them into the boat.

On the beach not far from the tanks I found three large driftwood logs! Can't believe I didn't notice them before. Maybe the recent storms washed them in. I cut and hauled twenty small rounds of light dry wood from one log that should burn well for kindling and twelve bigger rounds from another that are solid and heavy, not as dry, and will be more difficult to split. From the butt of that log I sliced two skookum chopping blocks. The tide was down, and moving the rounds over the slippery rocks to the boat was a nasty task, but I wanted to take advantage of the calm sea. Humping the rounds up the beach here was also a grunt. The wheels helped for dragging the boat up, but it still wasn't easy. I'm sore and not sure I'll be able to sleep tonight or move tomorrow. I took a Tylenol 3 and wish I'd brought a hundred of them instead of only fifty.

It's so still now I can see stars reflected in the sea. Two of them — large and low over the eastern mountains — twinkle from red to greenish blue, and far to the south I can see what I take to be the Southern Cross. I hear Diane's whiskey calling.

MARCH 21, 2001

I think of all the wind and rain these past six weeks, and now this. The mountain crest cuts a sharp purple line across the pale blue sky. The early sun just shows through the trees and has yet to touch the western face of the mountains. But in the hollow of their shadowed mass, a single jewel is shining. I put the glasses on it to see a tiny wisp of cloud caught by a slanting sun ray.

Now the sun pierces from behind the scattered kelp leaves floating in the basin and sparkles in the frosted grass on shore. A large black moth clings to the white wall of my cabin. To the west, the rock cliffs glow in the golden light, and waterfalls shimmer to the sea. Further out there's a light wind riffle, but here the water lies glassy calm. Seabirds call their foghorn honk, hummingbirds are feeding; Cat's asleep, and I'm writing these notes.

I woke before 8, stiff and sore, but felt better after stretching. I'd intended to try fishing and bring in another load of firewood, but if the wind doesn't blow up, this is a perfect day to cross the east channel and explore an inlet that leads into the mountains. I could use some rest and a treat, but my work ethic grumbles that I should take advantage of the calm to fetch more wood. For now I'll finish coffee, prepare the boat, and rejoice.

EVENING: 44°F and still flat calm. It's been clear all day, but now wisps of cloud drift over the mountains. I followed the inlet for five miles to its far end where a crystal river pours into the sea. Along the way I saw some pretty places and kept thinking, "I could have built here," but on such a day as this, everywhere is alluring. It's when the storms roll through. . . . I wandered for a while along the first sand beach I've seen, and it was delightful to stroll blithely with no risk of falling. The motor worked fine, but the wheel mountings caused water to splash into the boat, which added weight and decreased top speed to only 11 mph.

Back here I went west to Staines Peninsula and found a driftwood log. Cut and brought home twenty medium rounds that need to dry because the log has been under water at high tide. On the way home, I stopped to sunbathe on another delightful beach. I was wearing thermal underwear and full rain gear, but I sunbathed nonetheless. This morning before I left, I put an extra container of gas in the boat even though sure I wouldn't need it. But the load of wood radically increased gas consumption, and the main tank ran dry a mile from home. Sometimes I'm damn glad I'm anal about this "just in case" thing.

It felt great to be on the water. Now it feels good to be back in camp. I'm ready to settle in and read by the fire. The cabin is a mess and I'm more and more eager that it be organized and tidy, but if the weather holds, cleaning up will have to wait.

MARCH 22, 2001

Arms and shoulders ached this morning, but I went for wood anyway. Cutting and hauling has already been a lot of work and I'll need much more for the year. When I eventually light fires in the stove, I'll need to take off layers of clothes. Does this make sense? Why not just keep on the thermal underwear, sweaters, snowsuit, toque, and mitts? It's like Thoreau's realization at Walden that using a horse to plow a field requires more land to feed the horse and more work to clear the land, etc.

I was motoring slowly back with a load of rounds when several dolphins appeared and started playing with the boat. They swam just underneath, spun and cut back past the bow so close I could feel their wakes. Then they roared off toward shore forty meters away, skidded into a tight turn against the rock wall, and, sometimes three abreast, race back toward me. The last instant before contact they dove and swooped just beneath the bow again. They did this over and over, and I think part of the game was to see how close they could come without actually brushing the boat. I got bumped a couple of times and could almost hear the others jeering at the clumsy one. If I hadn't known they were dolphins and playing it might have been frightening.

During my first three-month wilderness retreat in British Columbia twenty-five years ago, I discovered something profound I couldn't put into words. Now, I'm fairly good with words but don't feel I'm learning or writing anything new. These journal entries contain descriptions of land and sea, weather, and daily life, but no deep shifts in consciousness or perception. In one sense this is ok, even perfect. If beauty and wonder are all there is, if there is no other manifestation of Spirit or God, so be it. This is more than enough. But I also feel I ought to have something to share when I go back. As Patti said before I left, "When listening for your heart song, listen for us as well."

I guess things will work out. The Bob Marley song "Three Little Birds" is drifting through my heart and mind. "Don't worry about a thing, cause every little thing going to be all right." I have no idea where the Zen activity of "gathering wood and carrying water" (or in my case, carrying wood and gathering water) will lead me, but slowly I'm beginning to learn to trust the process.

I saw jet contrails for the first time yesterday far away over the mountains, but it didn't seem to affect me. I don't have a sense of super solitude here a hundred miles from the nearest town and the world of other people. I'm just here. It's where I live now.

While looking for a place to build the outhouse, I discovered a small kingdom of delicate ferns and mosses; secret grottoes under the trees. I'm always facing the sea, the mountains, and the sky — the huge and awesome — but I'll turn inward, too, before long.

MARCH 23, 2001

I sure hope it rains tonight. What? Did I just say that? Yup. I need more water, even though I can still scrape by for a few days if I'm frugal. Who knew there'd be a four-day drought? Rain might also drown the black flies that savaged me outside today. I'm currently sitting on the porch, and while there are lots of black flies flying against the translucent tarp, none are around me. If I move three feet forward into the opening I'll get bit, but back here I'm left in peace. This is very weird, but I'm thankful. I discovered years ago that in a translucent enclosure black flies and mosquitoes stay near the walls and ceiling. Inside the cabin, too, they jitter against the windows and walls and leave me alone.

Fish for dinner! Tasty, but small and very bony. I fished a shallow kelp bed north of here in front of a beautiful rock wall, stained red in spots and naturally etched into abstract hieroglyphs. First time I've tried fishing and I did catch dinner, but they were hard to hook. I also cleaned up the first sign of humans I've seen: a large fishing float and some plastic bags washed in by the storms.

A breeze is blowing and the ocean lapping the beach. The stars seem super bright and I think I'll go bathe in them for a while. Often, as I go to bed deep in the night, I remember that it's still early evening where Patti and Susan live. Being up late here is different from in society. Once it's dark, it's dark, and 10 PM feels about the same as 3 AM.

MARCH 24, 2001

This is great. I'm looking out my three-by-four-foot Plexiglas window and the world comes straight in to me. Now I won't be able to hide from the enormity of the cosmos — unless I put up curtains. Perhaps curtains aren't primarily to prevent others from looking in, but to allow those inside to not see out.

55°F. Cloudy with bits of sun and blue; strong breeze, and sea on the move. March's weather has been much gentler than February's. That was one dog bitch of a month to arrive here and set up camp. I've been out in the boat for the past four days, and it's felt good to stay here today. I extended the rain gutter and caught a half gallon of a light sprinkle. Until it really rains again, I'll use the water trapped in rock pools for washing. Fish and potatoes for dinner. All fried in grease! Yum! Cat gets the heads and bones.

MARCH 25, 2001

MORNING: Happy day, it's raining! Am I losing my mind, saying that here? It's only sprinkling, but the sound of water falling into the bucket has changed from striking bare plastic to splashing in liquid. So there's at least enough for coffee and porridge.

"Worry Mind" is sure powerful. What if...? Because it's so cold and humid here, I need very little water. During the first week I just kept the large cook pot full of water I collected from a small area of the tarp over the tent.

Now I have about five gallons, which could last ten days, and a catchment system that collects water from half the cabin roof. Yet I run what-if scenarios in my mind: What will I do if the sea remains too rough to take the boat to the nearest creek? Should I start using part seawater to cook my porridge? Do I need to boil the water I might need to use from the rock pools?

This is loony. Basic survival requires a competent ego, but it has usurped control and is no longer a servant/friend of my whole being — which includes spirit, intuition, and love, and finds joy and peace through relaxing into the flow of existence. The ego wants to dominate, and in order to justify its overbearing presence, it creates looming illusory problems to solve.

TWILIGHT: The sea has calmed but is still restless in a light breeze; tide coming in, mountains hidden in cloud. A kingfisher calls from the island across the basin, two hundred yards to the south. It's been a lonesome day on and off. Not only do I miss Patti and Susan, but I miss being able to live harmoniously with anyone. Cat just jumped up for some loving. We're getting pretty attached, and I wonder what I'll do with him and where I'll go when I leave here.

The water-worry inspired me to hook up a real rain gutter. Nothing like a five-day drought to focus attention. First I criticize the ego's insurrection, and then let it do what it wants. All in a day's activity.

MARCH 26, 2001

Here's irony: unless I open the door when I cook, the windows fog up and I can't see out. After spending so much time, effort, and caulk to make the cabin completely watertight, I now need to build small openable windows for ventilation. The black flies are inactive so far today, but I imagine they'll be fierce later if the wind doesn't blow. I hope it's like Canada here and the flies are nasty for only about three weeks in fall and spring. Cat is dozing in the early sun. Ducks are in the basin. I'm glad to have them for neighbors and hope they stay all winter.

I wake each morning seriously stiff and sore, and feel I'll be stiff and sore forever. It's a challenge to live one day at a time and to meet physical pain with patience and compassion, rather than with fear and anger. Late last night I saw clearly that suffering results from holding on — physically, psychologically, emotionally, and spiritually. There are many ways to do it and many ways to talk about it, but basically I'm either holding on or letting go. Doubt, hate, certainty are ways of holding tight. Faith, love, wondering are open and loose. Yet aimless drifting can bring suffering, too. The trick is to stay open without clinging to the looseness.

EVENING: Even though it's fall, today was the first time it's felt like summer. 57°F with high light clouds and clear mountains. There was just enough breeze to keep the black flies down, and I lazed in the sun for a while. But it was too perfect a day for working to slack off for long, so I stretched electrical wire to the point instead. Struggling through the dense brush above the beach, I tied the wire to a tree every fifteen feet or so. Amazingly, I brought just enough to reach from the cabin to an area open to both sun and wind. I cleared a place for the solar panels in a small hollow and figured out where and how to erect the wind generator tower. Pain slows me down, and it's taking longer and longer to do each job. I also hung the bedding out to air for the first time and changed the mountings on the wheels so water won't splash into the boat.

A while ago I turned off the light to save juice and went down to the low-tide beach. The sky had been washed clean by the rain and was strewn with stars. I could hear dolphins breathing in the dark of the basin.

MARCH 27, 2001

So much for summer. It's wet, grey, cold, and windy. The ocean's up in arms. Arms up in shoulders, sore and achy. When I leave here, perhaps I'll head far north to the Atacama Desert to soak in the sun. Meanwhile, maybe I'll make a second cold water bottle from boat patching material and Shoe Goo.

A condor flew over a while ago and I had time to put the glasses on it. I've never seen one so close before. Long splayed wing tips and white head. He hovered low against the wind, then hooked a wing and was gone. A rainbow built against the western cliffs as morning sun shone on a patch of rolling swells and roaring whitecaps. Ah, a hummingbird just flew so close I could feel the breeze from his wings on my face. Maybe he saw his reflection in my glasses.

LATE AFTERNOON: Broken sky of grey and blue; the wind and rain have passed. An elegant gull swoops to steal the catch from three diving ducks. All four are stark contrasts in black and white. What can it mean? Why did the scene seem so peaceful when the ducks were diving for fish to kill, but lose that tranquil tone now that the gull is after them? Perhaps because I identify more closely with birds than with fish. Or because I can't see the underwater mayhem; out of sight is out of mind.

Longing and loneliness lie on me today, but it's not much different from the ache of eating alone in a city restaurant. What I really want is a double-scoop chocolate and pistachio ice cream cone. The fat has melted off out here and all my ribs are showing. I'm eating plenty, but with the cold and work I've probably lost nearly thirty pounds.

I'd thought perhaps the wind had gone until next spring, but it's back down to business today and the sea is ripping and roaring. The trees are shedding their leaves, and some are turning color. I wonder how intense the color change will be. I'll know within a month or two.

Hard to believe I've been here almost two months and I'm still not settled in. My shoulder has slowed me down, and once I moved into the cabin my drive to finish building lost some urgency, but now it's time to get it done. After organizing the food, I need to set up the stove, solar panels, and wind generator. I also need to hook up the water barrel and propane light, design a better system to haul up the boat, build an outhouse, entry porch, steps, and awnings, and get more firewood. The list goes on and on. Then, before I know it, it will be time for the huge sad job of tearing everything down again.

50°F. Grey and rainy, mountains hidden, strong breeze, sea neither calm nor super rough. Just another day. Now I remember, this is how it's been most of the time I've been here — except that short magic spell when there were blue skies and calm days.

How immediate and intense life can be: get up, deal with pain, drink coffee, cook and eat, write in journal, read, listen to rain on the roof, watch the tide come in and slip away, watch the ducks and hummingbirds, exercise, meditate, dream, defecate, grumble. After two nights of good sleep and two days of not too heavy work, I feel better.

I've been sorting and measuring food again today: dividing all items into four portions — one for each three-month period. Each item has a month written on it. From experience, I know I can go around and around trying to remember how much I can use each week. Things like powdered milk come in large cans, so I've calculated that a small can needs to last ten days. I've even drawn lines on the block of cheese with a Magic Marker to delineate how much I can eat each month. If I die here, people will probably think, "Wow, very organized. Too bad he died of a stroke, or drowned, or..."

Food consumption looks pretty good even though I hadn't figured Cat would eat almost 20 percent as much as I eat. The only thing I need to cut back on is oatmeal. Since I can't count on getting picked up just when I've been here a year, I'm setting aside a reserve to last an extra month. When I came I was so focused on getting here that I thought very little about leaving at the end of the year. I just figured that somehow I'd get back out with the navy boat or a fisherman, but it may not be so easy to make arrangements via email.

My staple meals are oatmeal in the morning and rice with lentils, black beans, pinto beans, or peas in the evening. I also have bouillon cubes and pasta to make soup, enough flour for a small piece of fry bread each day, and potatoes — a few of which are already starting to sprout. I expected to catch and eat fish regularly, but often the sea is too rough, so I'm glad I brought some bacon and other smoked meat. Along with these staples, I have condiments, plenty of good old-fashioned lard, and various treats: popcorn, dried fruit, honey, peanut butter and jam, chocolate, chocolate pudding, coffee, cocoa, sugar, powdered milk. I supplement this diet with multivitamins, vitamin C, potassium, calcium, and iron. Since I've been here I've drunk only instant coffee, but I have seven pounds of the real stuff for that first morning cup. And good news! I brought thirteen, not seven, bars of chocolate.

As I was folding the sacks where I've had the food stored since Punta Arenas, I started to feel like this is an ending rather than a beginning. So much has happened: spending six weeks in Punta Arenas and finding everything I needed to buy; packing and waterproofing all the gear and supplies; locating transport to Puerto Natales and then out to here; having my food on a beach a mile away during ten days of rain, wind, and storm tides; visiting the bay where I originally intended to settle and deciding to stay here; building the cabin; having the boat flip and repairing the outboard; injuring my shoulder; being constantly in the presence of incredible beauty.

Keeping company with the cat's-paws on the water, waves of loneliness and longing have swept over me all day. For whom or what? Susan, Patti, family, British Columbia and rainbow trout, Baja California and amberjack, sun and warmth? Perhaps the essence of longing is an awareness of the absence of people and places that have been important in my life; remembering the wonder I've been blessed to experience. I imagine I'll also long for here someday: grey skies, rain, wind, and whitecaps; hummingbirds at the feeder, Cat on my lap, heart in my chest — lub-dub. It is enough.

MARCH 30, 2001

53°F. Cloudy but no wind, sea restless, midtide and coming in. I wasn't in the mood to exercise my shoulder last night so I let it go, but remembering the way it feels now may put me in the mood next time I'm not. I'm going to make and start wearing a copper bracelet, which I hope will help the arthritic aching in my hands.

Anxiety has gripped me today. I feel myself tighten against it, but know that only by surrendering to my own suffering and death will the clenching fear dissolve; only by letting the world come in and by flowing out to meet it.

Of the teachings I've heard from meditation instructor Jack Kornfield, the need to acknowledge and accept anxiety has been most helpful. It's not *my* anxiety. Anxiety is part of our human condition, and we need to learn to treat it as an old friend, or least a familiar acquaintance. Many therapists say to do something to avoid anxiety, but in such endless activity much of our experience — joyful and painful — is lost. Seems like a hard bargain.

MARCH 31, 2001

The weather affects my mood so strongly. I awoke this morning to the sound of no-rain and have felt good all day. A light breeze from the east-southeast is pushing a slight swell through a fairly calm sea straight in toward me. The mountains are veiled down low in broken clouds with peaks just peeking through. A high cloud ring circles the sun so it might rain again soon, but for now the air feels light. Tomorrow is April 1 (equivalent of October 1 in the North) and time to hook up the stove for heat. I want to move the solar panels to the point and hope it will be calm the day after tomorrow. Uh-huh. Order it up!

Today has been productive. I hooked up the propane light, which works fine but is noisier than expected, collected a sack of sphagnum moss for storing the potatoes to prevent rot and more sprouting, and got the chimney through the cabin wall and braced on the outside. Had to climb on the roof to do it. That back corner is muddy, unlevel, and risky to work on. I still need to hook the stove to the pipe, but the tough job is done. Next big job is an outhouse. It will be a treat to shit in comfort sitting out of the rain. Before long, I want to fetch a boatload of gravel from somewhere. The soil here — a tangled mat of fine roots — holds a huge amount of water and turns into instant mud as soon as it's disturbed. Shoulder is, of course, painful.

I also built a tower for the satphone antenna close enough to the cabin that the cable just reaches and I can use the phone inside where it's dry. Very cool. There must be a small break in the trees across the cove in precisely the right direction, because I can link to a satellite from only that one spot. If I move the antenna eighteen inches in any direction, the reception fades. I'll write the "I'm ok" email in a while and leave it in queue to be sure everything is ready for tomorrow.

I saw two nutrias together a while ago, so perhaps it's mating time. If I hadn't looked just then, I'd have missed them. Maybe they come by every day but I don't happen to look when they pass.

INTERLUDE

ON JOURNALING AND STORYTELLING

Silence is the home of the word.
Silence gives strength and fruitfulness to the word.
We can even say that words are meant to disclose
the mystery of the silence from which they come.

—— HENRI NOUWEN

Years ago during my first long wilderness retreat, writing was not part of my daily activity. Only near the end of my time in solitude did I set down some short poems that seemed iconic of the experience. Later, I wished I'd written myself directions on how to return to the mysterious inner world of flowing *aliveness* I'd experienced. This time I wrote much more than I'd expected I would, and I eventually realized I wasn't simply describing my life in the wilderness, but was leaving a trail of crumbs to lead me back to the beauty and spacious wonder I often experienced.

THE MAGIC OF WORDS

Daily journaling was important to me during most of the year, but I also questioned its effect on my heart and mind. Writing, like thinking, is magical, but has a dark side. It's easy to get lost in the words. Since description and analysis require time, I could capture and understand an experience only once it was gone. Thus, writing tended to pull me out of the present moment and mute the intensity of experience — unless I remained clearly aware of the actual process of writing. Remaining silent was often preferable.

In fact, it was not actual journaling that became distracting, but thinking beforehand about what I would write and mentally describing to myself what I was seeing and feeling. When I did that I wasn't really in solitude, but in an imaginary future where someone else would be reading my descriptions. During those times I remained embedded in language and in my social identity, rather than free to experience my deeper identity as part of the universe.

But there was also a positive aspect to writing, and I'm glad I wrote as much as I did. At times putting an experience into words encouraged me to look more closely and reflect more deeply. And also, the journal now allows and invites me back into the days and months of solitude.

SHAPING A STORY

My original journal was almost nine hundred pages long, but during editing I haven't omitted any complete entries. If there's no entry for a particular day, there was none in the original. But I have had to choose which passages to exclude. This felt vaguely deceitful, until I remembered that the original entries themselves scooped only scattered dollops from the vast swirl of daily experience: they told one among many possible tales. I have, though, both in the original journal entries and in the editing process, tried to tell my truth as I lived it.

Although I've removed much of the repetition that was in the original journal, I haven't deleted anything — even painful and shameful passages — I believe to be important. I've been tempted to cut more of the descriptions of inner turmoil than I have, but to present only joyful events and meaningful insights would idealize and falsify the process of exploration and discovery. I've also tempered the profanity that peppered the original journal. Swearing was an important part of how I felt and how I recorded my feelings. There is risk and pain as well as satisfaction and joy in writing as nakedly as I have.

The weather, the challenge of survival, and the experience of physical and emotional pain were always important — sometimes overwhelmingly so. This physicality grounded my mind in my body and contextualized my psychological and spiritual explorations. Wanting to honor these rhythms as I recorded them, I have rarely moved passages from one day to another, but I have frequently rearranged and restructured paragraphs within any given day to smooth their flow.

In editing the original journal, I at first believed I should carve that mass using a single consistent narrative voice for the whole year. That dream slowly faded as I sat for months trying to develop a coherent plan. I finally gave up and let each paragraph emerge in its own way. Instead of one, there are many voices. Some are cultured and insightful, full of analytic critique and aesthetic caress. But there are also frightened, enraged, and uncivilized voices — howling from dark distant places. The different points of view, fluctuating emotions, and variable states of consciousness sometimes seem — and perhaps are — contradictory. The journal remains rough and irregular in places, not well-rounded or nicely squared at the corners. It's incomplete, full of unanswered questions.

I still fluctuate between experiencing myself primarily as a member of society and feeling myself to be a solitary embedded in the nonhuman world. The man shaping this essay in North America is not identical with the man writing in his journal far away in the remote reaches of southern Chile. This is why the different voices from solitude insist on being present in the journal and on contradicting the culturally accepted form of a structured narrative.

CULTURAL EXPECTATIONS

In the journal I can distinguish different stages during my year in solitude. The stages are not distinct or mutually exclusive, but they do reflect my shifting focus of attention as the months passed. At first I was dealing with surviving in the extreme environment, the challenge of building a camp and hauling firewood, and with physical pain. Once most of the heavy work was done and I had time to come back to myself during the long nights of winter, I sank into self-analysis. When spring sun began to stretch the days, restlessness urged me into books, adventure, and observation of the wildlife around me. As time passed and solitude gathered me in, I gave up reading and wandering the physical world, and settled more deeply into spiritual exploration.

While these stages loosely track changes in my inner and outer experience, they are also probably shaped by modernity's attachment to the notion of progress — to my belief that inner transformation would create a more dynamic personal story and signify a successful conclusion to the enterprise. In spite of questioning cultural norms, I was still vulnerable to their hidden power — in my actual experience, in my documentation of that experience, and during the process of editing.

The balance between inner dark and light shifts in the journal as the months pass. All through the year, inner and outer storms continued to pound, but my relationship to them changed. I also grew weary of recording the difficult times and began to notice how seldom I described the joyful ones. When settled into the moment, I seldom felt the urge to write about it, and so the original journal was unbalanced toward the painful.

LIFE SCRIPTS

When we are finally able to see (however dimly) the scripted story our family and culture have cast us in, what are our options? Must we either knuckle under or attempt to create a new persona/story and thereby alter our relationship with ourselves and our world? In the latter case, aren't we simply enmeshing ourselves in yet another cultural story — a story of reinvention? Any story we create — if we actually believe it and take it as our own — will limit our freedom to be *who we are not* in that new story. In *Thoughts Without a Thinker: Psychotherapy from a Buddhist Perspective*, Mark Epstein writes:

> The crumbling of the false self occurs through awareness of its manifestations, not through the substitution of some underlying "truer" personality. The ability to become aware of self-representations without creating new ones is, psychologically speaking, a great relief. It does not mean that we drop the everyday experience of ourselves as unique and, in some way, ongoing individuals, but it does mean that whenever we find ourselves entering narcissistic territory, we can recognize the terrain without searching immediately for an alternative.[1]

At times in solitude I was deeply concerned about the story I was telling myself, and imagined I would eventually tell others, about my experience and about who I am. But in times of peace and self-acceptance, the need for a coherent narrative seemed to fade. Just as scientific theories are likely stories about a world that is deeply mysterious, so are personal narratives about ourselves. When I slipped beyond words, I was simply a mysterious being existing in the present moment.

But personal stories often do seem indispensable as we wander through our days, and some stories align with our lived experience more closely than do others. The fit between our experience of ourselves in the world and the story we tell to make sense of that experience is crucial. When we recognize not only that we create stories to make sense of our experience but that the stories we tell also structure the experience, we have to acknowledge that our existence is very circular, indeed.

TALE OF THE HERO

In the journal, a saga of physical adventure and spiritual transformation runs parallel to and weaves through the drifting account of daily life — the autobiographical quest of the hero. This is a recognized, even expected, storytelling mode for someone spending a year alone in the wilderness, and I could have enhanced the heroic saga during editing. But instead I've allowed that tidy narrative to remain interrupted over and over by the unruly wildness of the "hero's" soul.

In the messier story, the hero's cultural ideals of personal success, social progress, and free will are questioned in view of the cyclic storms of depression, rage, fear, and doubt about his place in society and a felt lack of spiritual development. Despite differences in theology, moral orientation, and self-discipline, the man in that pedestrian tale may have more in common with St. Augustine and his surrender of personal agency to Divine Will than with the stereotypical self-oriented striving of modern culture's secular hero.

My goal in the wilderness was not to conquer either the external world or my own inner nature, but to give up the illusion of ownership and control and to experience myself as part of the ebb and flow of something greater than individual ego. But the goal of attaining enlightenment was elusive — except when it was not. Through a shift in consciousness, my quest came to an end as I realized there was nowhere to go and nothing to get. The notion of a holy grail out there — or even within — was illusory, and what I was seeking I always already had: I was not a special hero, but simply a speck of life like all other specks — unless I was not. Personal agency always reasserted itself, and these two aspects of my being struggled and then tentatively began to dance together.

Stories of spiritual seekers or solitaries in the wilderness are often portrayals of heroic adventure. It's difficult to not slip into this mode, but I've tried. We already have enough of such writing, and in its most blatant form it's little better than checkout-counter publications flaunting the amazing lives of superhuman "stars." To me this seems a disservice to us all. When I read such stories and compare them to my own actual life, I feel diminished. "That's not how my life is; what's wrong with me?" I'm also pulled out of my own actual life and into vicariously living the imaginary life of another. What I offer instead is a more human account so perhaps we can wander the spaces and silences of wilderness solitude together.

APRIL 2001

*Every little thing
gonna be all right.*

— BOB MARLEY

MORNING: Sun shines gold through floating kelp leaves and stirs them to leap from the water and remind me of swirling autumn leaves. Far out in the basin, the bodies of the grey back, creamy belly ducks blend with the sea, but their bright orange bills catch and throw sun rays in my direction. The mountains, half hidden in their misty negligee, fire my imagination.

A new month, time to send word that I'm ok. I tighten up when I must deal with the communication system. It takes my mind far away to other places and people, when I want to stay here with myself. And I'm still not certain the process will actually work. If the message doesn't go through, the navy might come to rescue me. That would be a major drag.

Damn, it's cold when the wind blows straight in like this! The sea's not really rough and I'd like to look for fish, but it would be a hassle to launch the boat against the wind. Maybe I'll wash clothes instead. I've been working and sleeping in the same two sets of thermal underwear, three shirts, two pairs of pants, sweater, sweatshirt, and vest for almost two months.

AFTERNOON: The emails went out and replies are back. Patti sent medical advice for my shoulder. Nothing I didn't already know, but it's comforting to hear it from a trained nurse. I cleared a space for an outhouse and dug a hole that immediately filled with water. When it really rains, my turds might still escape to the sea. Instead of chopping down bushes and disrupting the soil,

49

it might have been more ecologically friendly — but not nearly as comfy — to keep squatting in the rain on the low-tide beach.

Physical activity does dissolve (or cover up) anxiety, but one of the things I've come here to learn, or remember, is how to feel comfortable without losing myself in constant doing. Actually, I believe our whole culture needs to consider this if we want to survive and enjoy living. It isn't actually non-doing that generates anxiety, but rather fretting about doing or not doing. When I'm simply in the moment, without worrying about what I ought to be doing, my mind is at ease. It's when I try to microplan everything that my imagination runs amok — because I can't really know what will happen. Then after all the nutty speculation, things often fall into place naturally as the actual situation unfolds. But planning is useful, so the trick is to think about pending activity without becoming anxious.

EVENING: I'm on the windy point. The sun is dropping behind Staines Peninsula and the wind is from the west. Too bad so little direct sun falls on my cabin, but if it did, a lot more wind would strike it, too. I like it out here. It feels far from home.

I want to shift whom I'm writing to. For now, this journal is to someone else — Patti, perhaps. I need to write what I myself might like to read.

APRIL 2, 2001

EXQUISITE MORNING. 34°F. The blue sky is clouding over, and the sea lies flat with the tide on the make. Some black flies are already awake, but I hope the frost has thinned their ranks. I'm on the point for sunrise and coffee. I want to check the direction of the morning and afternoon light to determine how I'll angle the solar panels. As I wait for the sun to reach me, I'm reading Annie Dillard's *Teaching a Stone to Talk*. What a charming writer. Witty, sharp, and a very light touch. I like the hybrid combination of spirit and naturalist. She doesn't say anything new but says many valuable things in a new way.

EVENING: The weather stayed calm and I worked all day. Using a small metal bit in the woodworking brace, I opened guy-wire holes in the twenty-foot pipe I'll use as a wind-generator tower. Pipe steel is soft and the setup worked surprisingly well. Having to make do with the tools I have on hand is an interesting challenge. After pumping up the pontoon that's leaking, I loaded the boat with solar panels, batteries, pipe, ladder, wire, wood and tools, and motored to the beach near the point. I carefully carried everything over the slippery rocks and fell only once. Not bad. Mounting the panels and hooking them to the batteries took much longer than expected, but I wanted everything to be super secure since the point is completely exposed to the wind. I finished before dusk and decided to go fishing.

When I stopped to drop off the tools, change into warmer clothes, and fetch the fishing gear, I thought I'd be here for only a few minutes. I just dragged the boat up a little and didn't tie it to a rock. I've never done that before — and never will again. It took me longer to get ready than I'd expected, and when I happened to look out, I saw the boat drifting off on the rising tide. Shit! I raced down the beach, plunged into the sea, and just snagged the boat in waist-deep water. Another thirty seconds, I'd have had to swim for it, and the water is way too cold for swimming. Another two minutes, I'd have had to pump up the kayak and paddle after it. Lucky there was only a light breeze. I'm grateful and properly chastened.

By the time I put on dry clothes it was nearly dark, but I went fishing anyway. Stayed out for twenty minutes and caught eight that are so small I'm not sure how to prepare them. Cat, at least, will be happy.

I heard an airplane today beyond the hills to the east. Sounded like a big prop plane, maybe a military transport. Neither the noise nor the fact of a plane passing nearby bothered me at the time, but then I started thinking: What if they fly by every day? What if boats start to arrive? Ah yes, the world of *what if*. What if it doesn't rain soon? Madness! The outhouse hole has filled with clear water, so I can simply dig a shallow well anywhere if I need to. Or I can just take water from the outhouse hole — at least until I use it as an outhouse. This would, I believe, be considered multiple use of a resource.

APRIL 3, 2001

Weird. Cat had some sort of seizure. I saw his box shaking and figured he was having a dream. But he crawled out, froze up, and then became totally frantic and started to yowl. I thought he might be dying — perhaps from finding and eating toxic mussels — but he finally came out of it. As an aftereffect, he's started to wander into the cabin. I've taught him to stay on the porch even if the door is open, but just now he sauntered in like he has no idea he's not supposed to. Maybe some neural circuits got fried. Very odd. I wonder if cats suffer from epilepsy.

Maybe I'll hook up the stove today. I'm not sure why I haven't yet, especially considering that I've been here for two months and how cold and achy I am. Could I sense that once it's hooked up, I might want a fire all the time and need to collect firewood all the time, too? Better to not get in the habit. Or perhaps I realize that once the stove is working, I'll really be settled in, and psychologically I'm not ready for that. Huh? How ready do I need to be? It makes no sense, but seems to be the way I feel.

Behind the low clouds and morning rain the mountains have departed for an unknown destination, and even Staines Peninsula barely clings to corporeal existence. My *what if* worrying about the now-full water containers was a waste of time and energy.

My shoulder hurts, even though I'm doing the exercises I learned when I tore this same rotator cuff a few years ago. Amazing how quickly everything tightens up. I exercised for an hour before I went to sleep at 1 a.m., woke up stiff and sore at 3:30, got up and exercised, then went back to sleep. By 8 I was knotted up again. Ah, but this first cup of morning coffee.

Yesterday, I shielded the plastic walls and ceiling behind and above the propane lamp with tinfoil to protect them from the heat. A fire would be a serious problem. The lamp works so well I hardly need a stove. It puts out plenty of warm yellow light and raises the temperature in the upper middle of the cabin 10 degrees above outside. Last night it stormed again, but a feeling of snug comfort softened the anxiety. I'm beginning to trust the cabin.

I guess, at some deep level, I'm confident of my ability to cope with difficult situations, or I wouldn't be here. And on the surface, I carry a patina of self-reliance, even arrogance. But just beneath the surface, anxiety and doubt roil. Perhaps the deep confidence is not in myself, but in something greater. It's that Something I've come here to find, if I have the courage. Or perhaps that Something called me to communion and I responded.

For months I've busied myself with activity, and now it's hard to slow down. At times during the day I pause to just be, and these breaks, rather than formal sitting meditation, may be my natural spiritual practice. I suspect the scattered moments will stretch and join into a more continuous attitude of listening, watching, and waiting for wilderness solitude to have its way with me.

DUSK: A while ago two nutrias appeared on a rock a hundred feet away. Powerful black paws, strong tail, small stubby ears. One tried, without much enthusiasm, to snatch something from the other, and then they returned to the water. They dove repeatedly, and finally one surfaced with a fish it had to bite and chew. My, what big teeth they have.

The orange bill ducks were up on the rocks looking concerned, as they do when the nutrias are nearby. Earlier, the ducks were feeding in water too shallow for diving, but deep enough that they had to stretch to reach the

bottom. They were flipping themselves completely upside down — sort of
like stinkbugs — and thrashing fiercely with their orange feet to hold themselves in place. Tail feathers pointing straight up, creamy yellow belly and
butt bobbing high above the surface.

Still haven't hooked up the stove. Been doing electricity/electronics all
day. Charging the laptops presents a problem. Under load, only 11 volts
reaches the cabin, and the inverter keeps kicking out. I think the voltage drop
is caused by the long wire from the point. The batteries need to sit close to the
wind generator to receive full charge, but be near the laptops to charge them.
Grrrrr.

APRIL 5, 2001

51°F. Raining and fairly calm. Moon nearly full, and the tide way out. Soup's
on, and I've got to get unchilled. Still no stove installed. The ceiling is wet
over the door. I'll go up and patch the tarp on a nice day. I still have two rolls
of duct tape, one tube of caulk, and two tubes of Shoe Goo. I've long recognized the profound virtues of baling wire and duct tape, but I've only recently
added Shoe Goo to my list of vital wilderness survival materials.

I spent all day at the point. Cut down two dead trees that were casting
shadow on the solar panels. I'll use the wood to heat rocks for the sweat lodge
I plan to build down there. I hooked the inverter right to the batteries so 110
volts rather than 12 volts was running through the wires to the cabin. Fewer
amps, lower resistance, less drop in voltage, no problem charging laptops.
But the only lights I have use 12 volts, so I can either use the laptop or have
light. Dammit! It would have been so easy to bring a 110 volt to 12 volt con-
verter. Just wasn't thinking. I suppose I can walk back and forth to the point
and switch between charging computers and having light, but that would be
a major hassle on dark stormy high-tide nights. Feels like my whole life is
haywired.

APRIL 6, 2001

MORNING: A moment ago the eastern channel was flat grey-green and I was
sitting brain-dead. I knew it must be rough out there since surf is crashing on
the windward rocks and a swell runs in the basin. Then sun flashed through
the clouds, and the channel sparked with golden light and shining flecks of
white. Now the sun is gone again and the sea again flat grey.

Logic says the whitecaps are still out there and the golden vision still possible, in every moment. I sit — not even waiting — and watch the nearby
grass tremble in the same wind that whips those far-off flecks to white. The

distant light has gone, but so has the torpor from my eyes, and the grass comes shining through.

NOON: It's raining now. Sheeting across the sea; splattering rock pools into rippled turmoil; drumming on my roof and rattling against my ears to anchor me where I sit.

Cobra-headed diving ducks (King Cormorant) drift in the basin. Intense black back, neck, and top of head; white throat, breast, and belly. The line between is razor sharp, which gives the bird its look. Like branches capped with snow, they somehow reassure and lend a sense of peace. In the dark, their hooting calls ease my fears and carry me to the coast of Mexico and the mountains of the Dominican Republic. One honks its hollow note, and nearby another answers. Then, if you tune your ear, from down the channel you can hear a faint reply. Like roosters in a thousand distant pockets of the rural night.

But the black/white line of neck and head also looms from the low-slung body like the hooded threat of a cobra. It has that same visual — and, to small fish, possibly visceral — feel about it. In the boat the other day, I came upon a rock inhabited, temporarily, by fifteen or twenty of them. They swiveled at my approach, and then lifted off until I passed. They shoot like arrows through the air, all arc forgotten. Lean and linear, wings beating hard, bodies steady as airborne rocks.

AFTERNOON: I recall, as from a place and time far away and half forgotten, my grandiose intention in coming here: to explore, through living, the physical, psychological, emotional, and spiritual effects of deep wilderness solitude. Now my world has shrunk to this small beach and stretch of water; to what I'll eat for lunch; to hooking up the stove and rain barrel; to the pain in my shoulders, hands, and teeth. But still, my commitment to myself is to stay here for a year and experience whatever happens. If I have a stake — set expectations — I'm not truly open to discovery. I must trust not only the physical process, but the emotional and spiritual ones as well.

Still reading Annie Dillard. She is an inspiring wordsmith, seeking to see, then say, the world just as she wants it to sound; finding exactly the right one of a thousand words to do the job. Yet at times she irritates. A bit too consciously articulate. Too metaphoric and artistic. Too much made of each thing.

I, on the other hand, have no words for what I'm feeling. I could use a Buddhist term and call it emptiness, or emotional language and call it lonely longing sorrow. Perhaps it's purely physical — only wind and rain. No, not only — in either sense — but rather Wind and Rain in their full catalytic power to evoke.

Cat is acting like an asshole today. Moaning for no apparent reason and trying to climb on me. He seems to be this way when I am filled with loneliness and longing. Does he pick it up from me, or does some external influence affect us both? Is there some other hidden cause, or no cause at all? Maybe he's always like this, but it grates more sharply when I am feeling glum.

I was thinking — as I munched lard-fried potatoes — about not having many taste treats until I leave here. About the goodies waiting for me in town. How different if I was going to stay forever; if this was all there would ever be. Years ago, I used to think about leaving where I lived in the rural mountains of the Dominican Republic. My shack was as poor as any: tin roof, dirt floor, and wood-slat windows. Yet I could return to Canada at any time. I was free to leave, my neighbors were not.

But I'm learning the illusion of that belief. There is no way out. Ever. In each right now, I'm always right here. Sure, I can return to the land of ice cream and hot showers, but while eating my double scoop, I'll be right there. The only escape is unconsciousness, which seems too high a price to pay.

EVENING: The stove is in and looks good sitting there. I built a frame beneath to hold two inches of gravel for fire protection. Bits of kelp came mixed with the gravel, bringing in the smells of the sea. The outhouse base is also built. Next I need a seat and roof. The surrounding trees will protect me from the wind and rain, so it won't need walls. I'm glad. Shitting in a small stinky enclosure is an uncivilized thing to do. Full moon tomorrow and I could have a fire to celebrate. That's my carrot to finish the outhouse. Finally a fire. Will that change my world? Will I become a new man?

One of my teeth is bothering me and I'm rinsing it with warm saltwater. I considered having it pulled before coming here, but I wasn't ready to live with a big gap in front or go through the hassle of getting a bridge. I thought the tooth would be ok, but infection seems to be setting in. Hope it doesn't go really off; I've had enough pain for a while.

MIDNIGHT: Time for dinner. A while ago, an almost full moon shining through the trees caught my eye. I took the binoculars and walked to the point for a clearer view. The mountains and craters are visually interesting, but most wonderful are the small scattered bright spots connected by curved shining lines to a larger bright spot on the upper right. It's like a gob of brilliance smacked the moon and splattered, leaving streamers of light behind.

46°F. Calm and clear with clouds. Sunrise over the mountains was orange gold and glorious. The tide was so low I could have walked across the mussel beds to the small island beyond, and kelp lay strewn across the mud flats like orange fright wigs the morning after a juicy debauch. A silhouetted bird with long curved beak stood lean and upright on nonwebbed feet. Everything seems to be resting, but I'm going to work on the wind generator.

EVENING: A perfect day for the job: flat calm and no rain. The wind generator is up and looks good. The aluminum casing was poorly cast, and I had to file it down in spots before the rotor would spin freely without rubbing.

This morning a hummingbird flew into the cabin and got stuck trying to leave through the Plexiglas window. I tried to herd him toward the door but, like a bee or a fly, he kept banging frantically against the pane. I finally cupped him in my hands and released him outside. What a tiny gem. I would have liked to hold him longer, but thought he might have a stroke.

Tooth hurts and is worrisome.

Windy and wild, bright with moonlight and clouds, high tide, ocean up and snorting. Tooth feels better this evening. Saltwater rinse is magic. But other than that, I feel like I've been hit with a board. Shoulders, back, arms, and hands all ache. Seems like I've been working for days straight again in spite of my shoulder. I think I miss hot showers more than anything else. They always help to ease sore muscles.

I have zero personal experience with wind generators, and from what people told me, I'd been expecting a sort of mellow whump, whump, whump as the rotor turns. But holy mother, what a racket! The wind is blowing about 35 mph on the point and gusting to maybe 50, not unusual for here, and the generator is out there howling like a banshee. The sound starts as a low moan, changes to a rough growl, and then, when a gust blasts through, winds up and shrieks like it's left the Earth and joined the hounds of hell. Reminds me of an airplane climbing steeper and steeper until it stalls — which is exactly what the generator blades are designed to do when they twist in high wind to dump air and protect the rotor from overrevving. Ironic since this is the kind of noise I wanted to get away from. I finally couldn't stand it anymore and, as per the instruction manual, shorted the wires to slow the rotor. Of course now it's not charging the batteries. Maybe I'll email the guy I bought it from and ask for advice.

Crap. I just threw out more onions than I've eaten, and others are going moldy, too. Not removing them from the plastic bags sooner was a mistake. Oh well, I'll eat lots for the next few weeks and hope enough sound ones remain to flavor the beans for a while.

The outhouse seat is built and I've hung a woven nylon sack on the front side to prevent me from peeing in my boots when sitting there. Although I don't know what its original contents were, the sack is labeled "Product of Canada." Bathroom humor is alive, if not particularly well, even here. I still need to cut a hole in the seat. How big should it be? A truly metaphysical question that will require deep consideration.

I notice that I seldom pause to be fully conscious of living completely alone in the middle of nowhere. But when I do, I also sometimes think of the other people living in solitude around the world. I sense them to be my tribe even though we will never meet — unless we leave the circumstance that binds us. It feels good to know they are there, somewhere, as I am here, somewhere.

APRIL 9, 2001

The wind has been stomping and snorting on and off all day, cabin vibrating like it's sitting on Jell-O. I had my first genteel defecatory episode today, sitting comfortably out of the rain. Quite pleasant. I also hooked up the forty-gallon plastic rain barrel. Cut a hole in its side three inches from the top and cemented in a plastic pipe with just enough slope so water will run in. The pipe reaches out through the back porch wall and catches rainwater falling from the roof gutter. The far end of the pipe is open, and when the water level in the barrel comes up enough, rain will stop flowing in and run out onto the ground instead. An automatic shutoff valve with no moving parts that will prevent the barrel from overflowing and flooding the porch. Cool.

I split a round of firewood to see how my shoulder would do. Three weeks ago, when I tried to use the ax, the shoulder was very weak and painful. Today was better, but I wouldn't want to split too many quite yet. Have I been here only two months? Seems like forever. Maybe I'll take tomorrow off if I can stand it. I suspect I'm keeping some strong feelings at bay by staying busy.

APRIL 10, 2001

Didn't make it to bed as early as intended last night. Sitting comfortably in the outhouse, I looked up through the trees and was bushwhacked by the moon. What an enchanting time this full moon has been. I remember thinking, a few weeks ago, that I might never see the moon here. The weather has been great for the last while, but I bet serious rains are on the way.

I'm slowly feeling more relaxed, like pressure is lifting. I can at least look down the hours of the day without feeling I've got to get busy. Still plenty of small tasks to do, but the big jobs are done. I took it easy this morning. Sent emails asking for technical support with wind generator — which is, I suppose, breaking solitude, but it feels ok. This afternoon I organized the cabin and put stuff away. I finally feel moved in and settled. The rain catchment system works perfectly. The barrel fills to within three inches of top and then stops automatically. I'm good at solving these kinds of simple mechanical problems and might have been happier if I'd lived a hundred years ago.

How civilized. A fire in the stove, a small slice of cheese, two dried figs, and a drink of single malt Scotch in hand. The stove is working well, even though the wood is semiwet and needs coaxing to stay alight. It's evening and 40°F outside, but a toasty 65 in here. I've stripped down to thermal underwear, T-shirt, flannel shirt, wool vest, and Hollofil vest and pants. I feel almost naked.

I'm writing by the light of a candle I just found in the package Patti gave me to celebrate last Christmas. At the time, I was leaving Santiago for Punta Arenas and forgot to open it. This seems like a fine occasion. Patti is smart to understand how much treats like this can mean when you're alone, and she has a huge heart to prepare them. She sent gifts for last and next Christmas, one for my birthday in July, and a party package for next New Year's.

A while ago I smudged the cabin and myself with the sage I brought and with some needles from the small cypress tree growing out front. As I was smudging, I gave thanks for what I've been given and for all the people who helped make this journey possible. I gave thanks for my skills, too. Amazing to be here after so long. It's been twenty-five years since I first thought I'd like to spend a year in solitude. So far, my connection with nature has not deepened as it has in the past, but it will happen as it happens. I can only ask for the courage and patience to open myself and wait.

APRIL 11, 2001

Yum. First cup of real coffee since last December, and I can already feel the buzz. A fine morning it is for it, too. 41°F. Rainy, windy, and cold. I'm on the porch and not sure when I'll build a fire. I still think firewood — like food, booze, and painkillers — needs to be rationed. There's plenty out there, but gathering it is hard work. Then, too, when I light a fire, I go inside, close the door, and shut out the world — which is just what I want to stop doing. Maybe I'll save fires for when it's dark.

I want to take the boat and go exploring, especially to visit a glacier that comes right down to the sea. But a long trip seems unappealing at the moment. I can't count on the ocean to remain calm, and if I have to wait for storms to pass it will be difficult to find protected places to camp or to tie up and sleep in the boat.

My favorite little bird with the spiky topknot just came by. Dark brown back and a light grey breast that drifts to golden rusty brown on the sides of the belly. There are two bands of the same color over the head and spots of it along the back and wings. The tail looks like it has thorns sticking out from the sides of it. Maybe three inches tall and very quick. Insect feeder, I think. It roots around on the ground some, but often forages along the bark of trees. A new diving duck (White-tufted Grebe) is working the water edge of my front yard. Much smaller than the other divers I've seen; only seven or so inches tall. Grey-brown back darkens to charcoal on the top of the head. Small topknot. Cheeks are very distinctive: dirty white with a tracery of darker lines that look almost like tree branches.

I stepped on Cat a while ago, the third time in as many days. When he yowled, I didn't feel compassion for his pain or upset with myself for causing it, but rather annoyance with him for getting underfoot. He used to walk in front of me when I peed off the porch, and if I didn't notice and picked him up for some loving afterward, I got to pet a pissed-on cat. Most unpleasant. He's learned to not do that, and I imagine he'll also figure out to not get underfoot.

Now that I'm settled into the cabin, I wonder what will happen during these long stretches of dark grey time with no work to fill the hours. This is what I came for. All the preparation has been, in one sense, just that. Of course, from another point of view, it has not been preparation *for* anything at all, but just part of the total process of this retreat and of my life.

NOON: I got tired of being cold and lit a fire. So much for rationing firewood. Truly, this is sensual pleasure. I'm warm and drinking my second cup of real coffee, which tastes even better than the first. I'm also eating my first piece of fry bread with the last of the butter I brought. I've noticed before that after some time in the wilderness what I crave most is bread and butter.

Speaking of sensual pleasure. During my first long wilderness retreat twenty-five years ago, sexual desire, and even thoughts of sex, vanished so completely I didn't realize they had gone until I emerged, saw a woman, and was hit again by wanting. The absence of desire is not so absolute this time, but close. I've thought about masturbating a few times in the past two months, but decided to not go there, and the desire quickly passed. Maybe now, in a warm cabin, wearing fewer layers of clothing, more aware of my skin, and less tired from work, desire will arise.

4 PM: Another storm is raging, and the waterfalls on the Staines cliffs rush down in full flood. Wind-driven sea from the northeast swirls across the basin. I'm feeling fearful and lonely. What if the cabin starts to leak? What if I run out of firewood and can't find more? What if I feel like this forever? I wish Patti or Susan was here.

5:15 PM: Has it been only an hour? High tide surges up toward the boat, the woodpile, and me. Wind and rain batter my shelter. It seems like it has stormed and will storm forever. No matter what I tell myself about projection, anxiety and loneliness are viscerally linked to the weather. I know I will find the peace I long for only through surrender to death and to the immediate present. Easier said than done. Ah, for some companionship now.

5:50 PM: This anxiety is insidious. Since Vancouver, I've been worrying about one thing after another: my visa wouldn't arrive on time; the crates of gear I shipped from Canada to Chile would be lost or stolen; I wouldn't find transportation into the wilderness. The first night here I worried I would be washed away, then after I built a temporary shelter above high tide, that I would be blown away. I worried that the food we left a mile away would be soaked and ruined; after the boat flipped, that the motors wouldn't work; once I hurt my shoulder, that I wouldn't be able to finish the cabin; when it didn't rain for five days, that I would run out of water. All through those times, I held onto the expectation that once I had all my gear here, firewood in, water tank hooked up, stove working, *then* I would feel safe and secure. But here I am, warm, dry, and well-fed, still feeling anxiety and dread.

This is nuts! I'm creating needless suffering for myself and destroying my joy in living. But even though I can see it intellectually and have been through this before, the fear persists: tightly clenched shoulders and nausea; squinted eyes; a vague electric current pulsing through my body. There are only three things to do: I can take medication (which I have if I need it); run from or fight the feelings; learn to treat the anxiety as an old friend or at least a familiar acquaintance. I'm going out into the storm to give my imagination a rest.

7 PM: The tide peaked and is receding. The wind, at least for now, has dropped and is out of the northwest. Rain is still pouring down. Across the slate green western channel, the massive rock of Staines Peninsula is a paradox. It undulates north to south in alternating domes and hollows, from which

waterfalls crash to the sea. More immediately solid than the much larger Andes farther away to the east, Staines is massive, concrete, and unambiguous. Yet — half hidden in the raining mists that fill the hollows and drift across the cliffs — mysterious and phantasmal, too; only partially real.

Beyond, through, or within its physical presence, the rock evokes in me a world of experience that cannot be grasped, defined, or named. Swirling mists of feeling also veil half-hidden physiological states.

Medical science is comforting: certain of the world, much as orthodox religion is certain. To see the source of these dark feelings as chemical imbalance is less nebulous than to attribute them to unconscious personal neuroses or mysterious collective archetypes. Medicine has a point. The chemicals in my body are as real as the rock of Staines Peninsula. But there is more: ambiguous, paradoxical, lived experience. If I lose this, my life becomes flat and lifeless. Yet if I reject the solid foundation of the physical world, I wander rudderless and lost in solipsistic maunderings.

11:15 PM: But when the wind drops, the rain stops, and the tide ebbs away, then, with no effort at all, my belly loosens, my heart eases, and my spirit soars with love into the quiet night.

APRIL 12, 2001

Yesterday was the first day without painkillers since I've been here. I guess the warmth, lighter workload, and frequent stretching exercises are helping. Today I hung cheese and bacon on the porch out of Cat's reach. Each month I'll rewipe the cheese with vinegar. I'm amazed at how much I don't know. I've just read in a book that vinegar prevents mold. I had tried oil, thinking to cut off air, but that was the wrong direction. The requirement is acid, not base. I should have figured it out sooner because when I taught scuba diving in the Caribbean, I put vinegar in my ears to control the fungus. All things tie together if you let your mind range widely enough.

In *Desert Solitaire*, Edward Abbey claims that joy has evolutionary value. "Where there is no joy there can be no courage; and without courage all the other virtues are useless." Where is my joy? I'm exactly where I've chosen to be. I have enough food and supplies to last the year. I'm cold by choice and can light a fire anytime. I'm free to call and leave here when I choose. I'm loved, supported, and respected. Where is my joy, and where my "felt" courage? In the past I've thought that courage comes as a result of facing fear. But perhaps courage is somehow hidden beneath or within the fear itself and found by staying with it.

I can feel winter coming. Of course, I could feel it two and a half months ago in midsummer, too. Both my long wilderness retreats in Canada ended when winter closed in. But this time, if my courage and health hold, I'll be staying.

APRIL 13, 2001

Son of a bitch! I am so goddamned tired of falling down. Give me a break, world! I just slipped and fell again and I hurt everywhere. I think I've torn the rotator cuff in my left shoulder, too. I'm trying to be very careful, but one slightly off-balance step and down I go. The moss, mud, rock, and grass are all incredibly slippery under my prosthetic leg and rubber-soled boots.

I can't remember a time in my life without pain, but now it's getting worse and is more constant. In pain management they teach you to relax into the pain, visualize a place of peace and beauty, and go there in your mind. But here in this place of peace and beauty, where do I go now that I am filled with pain?

I think I'm starting to lose it. It doesn't feel safe to take a step or even stand anywhere, and I'm beginning to see the rock out front as actively malevolent — watching and waiting for the chance to harm me. So far I haven't cracked my head, but everything else just fucking aches and aches. I'm so tired of pain.

APRIL 14, 2001

Abbey's desert world is vast, his vision and explorations painted large and in detail. My world feels constricted and shallow: cabin, tiny beach, wind, rain, moods, pain. I'm too concerned with self, comfort, and survival, and sense I'm closing myself off from the world. This has happened before. On the other side — if I make it — there is joy and wonder. But why, over and over, must the passage be so hard and painful? Will the drama end once I'm truly tired of it and let it go?

AFTERNOON: The day is still overcast and not quite 50°F. The sea still grey-green and restless. A light wind rustles the trees. Nothing has changed; all is still in endless motion. Yet, I'm feeling peaceful. I will never be free of pain. It's part of the experience of living. What I can do, though, is loosen the grip of the self-pitying complaint "Why *me*?" and accept pain as part of the world — like the sun, rain, and endless movement of the sea.

NIGHT: The anxiety came back. Why? How? From where? I was building a ventilation hole in the cabin and noticed that the tranquil sound of the sea had become vaguely threatening. At random, I opened the book of Rumi poems that Susan gave me and read:

> *This being human is a guest house.*
> *Every morning a new arrival.*
> *A joy, a depression, a meanness,*
> *some momentary awareness comes*
> *as an unexpected visitor.*
> *Welcome and entertain them all!*
> *Even if they're a crowd of sorrows,*
> *who violently sweep your house*
> *empty of its furniture,*
> *still, treat each guest honorably.*
> *He may be clearing you out*
> *for some new delight.*
> *The dark thought, the shame, the malice,*
> *meet them at the door laughing,*
> *and invite them in.*
> *Be grateful for whoever comes*
> *because each has been sent*
> *as a guide from beyond.*[1]

Easy to agree with, hard to live by. But just what I needed to hear. I miss Susan badly now. I don't miss Patti in the same way; perhaps because she is so much with me here, or maybe this particular ache is yearning for sexual intimacy.

APRIL 15, 2001

52°F. Some wind, sea restless, high overcast, mountains shining sharp and clear all the way to the peaks. A while ago some animals swam by moving fast. Might have been nutrias, but they looked bigger.

I prepared for this retreat for so long; looking forward to immersion in the timeless wonder of Nature. And now I feel cut off, lonely, and frightened. Edging through the days and wondering if I'll make it. I need to commit myself to stop being unhappy and to stop sounding like a broken record. Life will be what it is.

APRIL 16, 2001

Wind and sea are moving, but not ferociously. Through broken clouds, sunshine touches the face of Staines. It was a tough night. I was up until 2 AM exercising my shoulders. My homemade chili pepper oil didn't work, and I had to use some of the commercial arthritis cream. What will I do when it's gone? Something else to worry about. I finally fell asleep but woke stiff and sore at 4. Up to exercise and apply the cold water bottle. Back to sleep until 7. Up to exercise, back to sleep till 9. This seems to be a pattern: exercise, sleep for a couple of hours, wake up cramped and sore, exercise again, sleep for two more hours. I dream of sleeping through a whole night. I think I've had only one such night in the past two and a half months. Maybe these aches and injuries are my body's reaction to finally coming out of high-stress mode. I often catch a cold or the flu as a comedown reaction, but out here there's no one to infect me.

A load of laundry is hanging on the line, a second load soaking, and water for a bath heating. First time I've washed clothes, and everything was filthy. It took all morning to do just a few light things. Now comes the heavy stuff: pants, shirts, vests, sweatshirt, and blankets. I remember the women in the Dominican Republic washing clothes together in the river. Doing it in community seemed to make their task lighter.

I cut my hair today, which, due to the weak power supply, was a slow and nasty process. It felt like the electric clippers cut halfway through each hair and then yanked on it until it broke off. Most unpleasant. I also shaved for the first time. I'm glad to be trimmed, although it was also ok before. I'm skinny and the skin under my chin and on my upper arms is loose. I'm no longer a boy. When did this happen? I've stopped wearing my watch, the ring that was Dad's, and the amulet I've worn for five years. Don't like the stuff on me.

It's time to let go of the macho "I can tough it out" attitude and start taking care of my body, emotions, mind, and spirit. In a sense I have been taking care of myself — but because I must to survive, not because I deserve the attention and care. I wonder — in the context of spiritual quest — why living has to be so hard. I wonder if everyone experiences life as hard.

Yesterday was Easter Sunday. Christ has risen. Spirit lives! The day passed unnoticed, and I feel sorry not to have celebrated. For me, the promise of the resurrection is that spirit can transform physical suffering. It's not about actual death, but that the physical body need not dominate consciousness.

Cat sits by the door quietly muttering and moaning. My first reaction is to tell him to shut up! But I do my complaining in these pages, and he has only his voice. So I bite my tongue, scratch his neck, and let him mumble.

APRIL 17, 2001

MORNING: 41°F. No wind. The sea shines silver-white to the east and dark green-brown where it reflects the southern island. Pale yellow clouds, with patches and bands of blue and grey, float high over the mountains; further south the wind has streaked them into curves. The sounds are soothing. An occasional goose's honk, and ripples from surfacing dolphins expanding out to caress the shore. I haven't missed reading the news these past two months. It's a relief to know nothing about the outside world. If I were up to it, this would be a perfect morning to collect firewood or go wandering, but it also feels good to stay quietly here.

There needs to be relationship. Without that, life is dead. My commitment here is to relationship with self, nature, and spirit. If I spend my time longing for relationship with Susan and fantasizing how it will be after this year, I'm wasting this precious opportunity. Then when I come out, I won't have done the necessary work that will allow me to be in real relationship with her. I don't feel this concern with Patti. Our lives are so deeply linked.

EVENING: This has been a gift of a day. (As I write these lines, I realize that for the past week I've been sunk in doubt and anxiety. How easily and unconsciously I lose faith.) For the first time, I took the kayak for a paddle. I discovered a small beach on the west side of the small island out front, took photos, drifted in the sun, collected some limpets for Cat, and did some fishing. Caught only four tiny ones. There must be bigger fish here since dolphins and nutrias spend time in the basin, but I don't know where they are or how to catch them.

This is what I envisioned: inflatable boat for longer trips, kayak for nearby. Probably won't paddle far since the wind comes up so unexpectedly and I can make no headway against it. From now on when I use the boat I'll take the kayak, too. With the 4 hp outboard not working, the kayak is my only backup in case the 15 hp dies. Come winter, I'll also be glad to paddle out to the sun. Now that it's moving into the northern sky behind the trees, my cabin is already mostly in shadow.

I'd hoped the dolphins would join me to get acquainted and play, but they came over, scoped out the kayak, and were gone. At one point I heard a sort of coughing scream from the east channel and saw a nutria (I think) leaping out in the deep water. I bet it was either in heat or rut or had just gotten laid.

APRIL 18, 2001

35°F. This could be lake country, far from the sea. A low mist covers the channel to the south, and the blue sky above is veiled and accentuated here and there with puffs and streaks of light, the sunrise clouds changing from rose to pale yellow. The sea is a mosaic of silver glass, clearly reflecting the mountains, and opaque velvet, made so by a delicate wind riffle. The stillness eases my heart. What would my experience be if I was spending this year in a warmer, drier place? The weather also brings restlessness. It's a day to be with a lover or on the move. Maybe I'll drag the boat to the water and go fishing to Staines.

Last night, a strange and ominous sound came from over there. A loud, almost motorlike vibration. It sent chills up my back, and I brought the chain saw and ax onto the porch. A nutria just came by, fishing. Hard to believe this is the same species as the creature I saw leaping out in the channel yesterday. That beast seemed at least three times as large as this one. Perhaps this is a youngster and that an old granddad.

APRIL 19, 2001

From what I've seen, this has been a sort of typical decent day. 51°F. Medium-high cloud layer, mountains semivisible except for the peaks, moderate wind, sea moving with whitecaps. I'm just back from fishing the basin in the cold dark rain. When I came in, Cat was on the porch, warm, dry, and eating fish. I'm thinking, "What's wrong with this picture?" I caught a dozen barely big enough to eat. Getting a system worked out: I stayed dry, took headlamp for when I need to see to tie on a hook, used pieces of fish from yesterday for bait, and prepared kindling before I went so the fire started easily. But I didn't take time to kill each fish as I caught it, and so they died slowly. I don't like doing that and will pause to kill them from now on.

Strange how my schedule has shifted to staying up so late. I often don't go to sleep until 2 or 3 AM. I'm also spending three to four hours a day just working on my body. Happily, I'm not so susceptible to the cold anymore, either because I'm warm for five or six hours in the evening or because I'm slowly adapting. Getting used to water and cat noises, too. Cat was sitting in the open doorway a while ago, sniveling quietly as usual, and I said, "Ssshhh." He looked up quite startled, eyes opened wide as if to say, "Oh, was I moaning again? I hadn't realized."

APRIL 20, 2001

And this would be a sort of typical bad day. 42°F. Not raging, but nasty; sky closed down in a low blanket of cloud, mountains and hills somewhere gone. The surface of the sea is streaked with wind-froth skirling away to the southeast, and sheets of rain drive horizontally across the water. Without sunlight to lift it up to dance and shine, the kelp floats sullen and soggy. A break in the cloud layer drifts over and faint blue glows, but soon it, too, follows a path to the southeast; grey slams shut again and blue is just a fading memory.

My world grows small: porch, Cat in his box, stack of firewood, thoughts of warmth. I can see only the midtide beach of rock and sea grass, moss climbing the stunted trees on the bluff to my left, and, in the far distance, the island lying heavy in its sodden bed two hundred yards away. I search the west and finally make out the faint silhouette of Staines Peninsula looming through the wet. Wind starts to move through the trees behind me, not roaring yet, and far from the demented howl of a full storm, but waking up again.

The lid begins to lift and light filters down less murkily. Southeast, the hills — as if by magic — slide back into being. Another patch of blue floats by. A ray of sun shines into a translucent silver drop that hangs from a twig in front of the cabin. A separate beam reveals the whitecaps previously hidden in the channel.

Three large boulders on the island across the basin leap up and shout, "We are here!" I've looked that way a thousand times while they have lain dormant and almost invisible, but now the slanting sun has stroked them into full tumescent existence. All around is opaque grey, but the three boulders, suddenly shaped and filled with color, bellow, "We are here!"

Southeast, the receding lines of hills are gone again. Just as well since I have no words for what I see when the mist thins. What are these lacks of color? Grey, black, and silver are not enough. A rich monochrome spectrum reaches out from that deep distance: close hills are dark and solid, and each line behind lighter in mass and tone.

Scratching through the mud and grass, a resident bird (Dark-bellied Cinclodes) hunts — apparently untroubled by the wind and rain. Wait. She has paused to plunge into a hollow in the rock and flutters there having a bath!

Now the storm moves in again with a crash, and wind slams my cabin walls. Even here in the lee of hill and forest, trees lean and sway in the gusts. Even here the sea churns through the narrow gap into the protected basin. Hooyah! Yet this is still mild compared to the February storms. As suddenly as the front rolled in, it's gone. Breaks in the cloud show blue. One leg of a rainbow arcs over the Staines rock and the sea laps softly on my tiny beach. Until the cycle repeats again.

EVENING: This would have been a good day to build a fire and hunker down inside. Instead I stayed out, opened my senses as wide as I could, and watched the weather moving through. I often had to choose between describing in words what I was seeing or photographing it. The changes came so fast it was impossible to do both.

APRIL 21, 2001

At Buddhist meditation retreats students are urged to sleep as little as possible to develop more continuous awareness. We often tend to escape from consciousness into sleep or into activity and substances. Here, I'm becoming clearer that there is no "away" where I can go. I would like to escape, but sleep isn't working and I don't have enough painkillers or booze to go that route. I begin to see more clearly the squirrel-race circles of my thoughts and to feel the results of that endless empty chatter. It's not that thinking is bad, but it becomes addictive and will not end my suffering as I expect it to.

I feel grief for Mom. Not because she's gone and I can no longer be with her, but for our time together when she was alive. Grief for all we couldn't share because so much stood in between. I guess we did the best we could, and maybe the union I longed for is always frustrated between mother and son. But there's a deep hurt in me that I was and am a loner — cut off from sharing love with anyone.

Two hummingbirds just flew into the cabin. One made it back out through the open door, but the other tried the Plexiglas shortcut. I rescued and held him for a while to caress his shimmering gold, rusty green, and iridescent magenta head, before I let him go.

APRIL 22, 2001

Physical weather is coming from the west-southwest; emotional weather from the north. Is what I feel loneliness for body warmth and smiling eyes, or longing for God, Spirit, my soul? I don't even know what these are. For the past few days I've cut back to two painkillers a day. I want to feel what there is to feel; to not hide from the pain, but find other ways to ease it. A while ago I went to the point to sense the wind, water, sun, and clouds with eyes, ears, skin and bones. Back here I was greeted by the rich smell of split firewood. Some smells vaguely like cat piss, but other pieces are as fragrant as a sun-drenched orchard in spring.

Today is Sunday, a day of rest. I may build a fire early and have a bath. I want to figure out how to keep the fire small to minimize wood consumption and keep the cabin warm, but not hot. I've already brought in the closest driftwood logs, and four or five months from now I'll have to scavenge further away for poorer quality wood. I prefer to be frugal now.

This daily writing feels like breaking solitude, as though I'm in conversation with someone and keeping myself tied to the verbal level of experience. Journaling might diffuse the intensity of immediate experience, but when I think of not writing, I'm hit with a wave of isolation, and loneliness. I may go there eventually, but it's not time yet.

TWILIGHT: 46°F. When I woke this morning, I saw the same sights I'm seeing now: mottled clouds and scattered rain, low tide, calm but moving sea. When the sky is overcast, it's hard to notice change in the direction of the light; this could be dawn.

It's been a fix-it day: I mended the long underwear and snowsuit, releveled the table, and drove nails into the floor where it was warping. I also emptied the rain barrel. The water had started to taste of creosote — not a pleasant flavor. Surprising that rain, merely falling through the drift of chimney smoke, picked up such a strong taste. This means I can't catch rain while the stove is lit. It's such a pleasure to have good water and fresh air. I sometimes long to be with people, but know that back in Puerto Natales there's cigarette smoke everywhere people gather.

I've begun to reread *Nature, Man and Woman* by Alan Watts. The book had a powerful impact on me when I first read it at nineteen, and I'm amazed at how much of what I now think I find in his writing. I don't know if I internalized his thoughts, or if I've discovered and continue to discover the same insights through my own inner explorations.

I've started sprouting lentils for greens to eat, and I've tasted and spit out some limpet a couple of times. Tomorrow, I'll swallow a bit. I assume they're nontoxic since they don't filter-feed and Cat is eating them without apparent problem.

At the moment he doesn't know where to turn. He's glutted with fish — belly tight as a drum — and he still has a mess of heads waiting to be eaten. He also has rice and beans in his dish, since I wouldn't want him to have an unbalanced diet. Hard to believe he was a wee kitten two and a half months ago. Happily, he's been crying less the past few days. He seems ok sleeping on the porch for now, especially since I spend a lot of time out here, too. In winter, I may change the arrangement.

Checked email again today. The wind generator help line answered my request for information by saying that not enough voltage will reach the batteries from one hundred yards away. I need to either move the generator and cabin closer together or learn to live in the dark. Some help. Guess I'll try bringing batteries back to the cabin. I also sent a message to the satphone company asking how to link with a satellite more efficiently.

Another fierce storm is shaking the cabin. I feel the tension of tightly clenched muscle in the deep layers of my body, emotions, and soul, and fear I will always be clenched into knots like this — cut off from love, peace, and participation with the world. I hear Cat playing on the porch, and every thump feels like a hammer stroke.

What is this core I'm knotted around? What painful wound am I protecting? I want nothing to touch me there — but rain, wind, cold, and Cat keep battering the walls I build. It may be shame that I'm weak or cowardly and not up to this experience. I feel I'm still in spiritual hiding, crouching out of the infinite eternal flow of existence; afraid to surrender to my fear and suffering, to vulnerability and death. And I'm also tight with fear not to. This long retreat into solitude could be my last opportunity: how far away can death be?

I sense I've seen all I'll see here — except perhaps for snow. No new animals or birds will appear, no different weather. What has been is what will be. The only surprises, likely unpleasant: people appearing, motor failing, getting caught on the sea in a storm, cabin falling apart, teeth giving out.

A while ago, I suited up and went into the pouring rain. I felt a sense of loss that Mom is no longer in this world. I can't visit her and know that no matter what, she loves me deeply and forever. Now there is no one to share the things I shared with only her. In the rain, I felt heartache and longing, and then tenderness and care for the animals and plants who live here. Often, I just hack them out of my way, but when I remember that this is their home and I am a guest, I'm happier and more peaceful.

FIRST SNOW: wet flakes mixed with rain. This feels like the beginning of winter, and I want a bigger supply of firewood. Buddhism teaches that craving pleasure creates suffering. Something in me cries that life without pleasure would not be worth living. The pleasures I crave are so innocent and sensible: a morning cup of coffee; a cabin snug and sturdy in the storms; the warmth of a fire; seeing a friend or hearing the clear words of a teacher; the absence of pain; peace and freedom from craving.

Each moment is a matrix of strong or faint cravings for or against something. How radical to think of being free from these. I doubt I know anyone who is seriously working to be free from all desire. Free from craving gross pleasures — lust, gluttony, hate — yes, but beauty? clarity? love? peace?

The low-slung snow on Staines Peninsula gives the cliffs a different shape and feel. From the point I see a face there for the first time. Stern and staring (but not malevolent) — one eye twisted — straight back at me. A mirror. I stand up straight and think, "Yes, I'm trying, but I'm the youngest child and only son, and that conditioning runs deep." Then, through a break in the clouds, blue sky and warm sun with no wind. How lovely and rare. Thank you.

Years ago, in wilderness solitude, a mystic light shone into my soul, and I believed I'd have a clear relationship with that light forever; I would follow wherever it led. Returning to the world of people, I lost sight of the light, and lost my way. That experience was, perhaps, the most painful of my life. It was like falling deeply in love and then, for some unknown reason, losing my lover. But worse. Now I think I'm terrified, not only of my need to surrender to love, but of the pain I'll feel when I leave here and am not strong enough to be true to that love and inner light. I ask for the courage to allow my heart to be broken open. What else can I do? I fear the unknown and my own vulnerability, but if I continue to guard myself, I'll die inside in any case. I've been through this before, and know that once I face my fear and surrender, I'll find joy and gratitude — and will wonder, yet again, why I resisted so strongly.

APRIL 27, 2001

The day stretches before me and I question how I'll fill my time and pass the hours. Will I be as fully present as I can be, or lazily wait for time to fly? How astonishing the mystery of existence. What are we doing here? Why something instead of nothing . . . or not even nothing? How strange to avoid *living* each moment fully.

APRIL 28, 2001

Yesterday I asked myself how I would fill my time — believing there was nothing new here for me anymore. After three months I'd seen all I would see until I leave. Today I went fishing. There were plenty of nibbles in the shallow kelp along the west side of my island, but no fish, so I paddled out to deeper water. The sea floor fell then leveled off at about 150 feet. I dropped my bait and soon my light trout rod bent double. I thought I'd snagged the bottom, until I felt the jerking. Using both hands, I slowly pumped the line in, all the while wondering what I could possibly have caught. Red snapper! What a treat after being here so long. Finally, real fish for dinner. I came back to fetch the ocean rod with stronger line, bigger hooks, and a heavier weight.

Back in deep water, I used a rock to anchor where I'd caught the first snapper, and caught nine more that each weighed about a pound. In this cool weather they should keep for several days, and who knows when the wind will let me fish again?

Floating silently in the kayak, I could have been living a thousand years ago. The gear would have been different, but that's peripheral to the process of asking for food with hook, line, and patience. Fishing links me deeply with land and sea; embeds me in the flow of the world. In receiving the gift of food, I feel profound gratitude for the Earth's generosity.

In some sense, purist catch-and-release fishermen don't get it. Fishing is not a sport; it's communion with the nonhuman world. To call fishing a sport is like calling gardening a pastime or church a social activity. On one level all three labels are accurate, but if it's nothing more to you, you've missed the heart of the matter — the place where you are no longer only you but part of something greater. Communion: take this bread and eat of My body, take this wine and drink of My blood; join in one body and one blood. Plant these seeds, eat of the fruit, and become one with the Earth. To catch and release fish is like planting a garden, tending the plants, and then turning the harvest under without eating it.

APRIL 29, 2001

Cat puked last night, and I worried that the heavy snapper bones had damaged his stomach. By now I would really miss him were he to die, but there was nothing I could do. This morning he has dragged another carcass from the bucket. I'm trying to teach him to gorge on his grisly load in one corner of the porch, rather than dragging it everywhere.

It occurs to me to wonder how it smells in here. I'm inured, but to someone else's nose it might seem pretty ripe and stink of wood smoke, firewood, glue, waterproof spray, bacon, creosote, me, and especially fish. If there were bears, I'd be in mortal terror — and with good reason.

No matter how I slice it, whether I consider God or an impersonal universe, terror is part of the equation. Many Christians, wishing to believe all is sweetness and light, have forgotten the God of the Old Testament who inspired Awe and Terror. And Christ on the Cross is the essence of pain. I, too, prefer the soft side of God — days like today that are calm, sunny, and safe. But in the night, when wind roars across the channel, that's God (or Nature), too.

While fishing yesterday, I wondered, yet again, how to leave fear behind and find peace in belonging to the universe. And then, again, I saw it. As long as I'm an individual human being, fear will be with me. I cannot find peace by getting rid of fear, but by making peace with it. I don't need to do anything special to be part of the universe, I cannot be otherwise. I simply need to be who I am, accept my place, and the depths will open.

Somewhere, I have a quote about love blossoming from a thousand times broken heart and about waiting without hope or expectation. I wanted to tape it to my door. While searching for it, I decided to take my passport, money, and ID cards from my knapsack and put them with the other important papers. Then I remembered that since leaping into the water nearly a month ago to catch the escaping boat, I haven't checked the goodies hidden in the hollow of my prosthetic leg. Everything was soggy, so now I have traveler's-check receipts, a photocopy of my passport, and a bunch of $20 and $50 bills clothespinned to the line behind the stove. I look like a miser admiring my hoard, and I must admit that when I counted the money and recorded the amount on the list with the food and other supplies, it gave me a sense of pleasure and security. Never did find the quote.

My emotions seem to cycle with the weather, as though there's no buffer between the world and me. When it's sunny, I feel happy and joyful. The wind comes up, I feel anxious. Grey and rainy, I'm glum. Even after years of meditation, I don't seem to have a stable place inside. And when I try to block out unwanted stimuli, it creates even more tension. I feel rebellious, but there's no one and nothing to rebel against, except the weather and my own pain. When I stop fighting and ease into the pain, it softens and sometimes disappears, so apparently I'm creating much of it by my own resistance.

Often, I project my pain and fear out onto the world so I can have the comforting illusion of possible escape. "If I go to a warm dry climate, the pain will stop. If the wind dies, so will my fear." But there will be other pain and other fear, and the need to escape will never end. My task here is to make peace with pain and fear and to realize that, finally, there is no possibility of escape because there is no real separation between the world and me.

Sometimes, I actually experience that there is no outside or inside, that the weather and my feelings are a continuum, that the world is not, cannot be, against me since there is no separation between us. I am the wind and rain. In those moments I feel peace and joy.

Tomorrow is May 1 and time to email that I'm ok. And in spite of the pain and uncertainty, I do think I'm ok. Cognitive, emotional, and spiritual ups and downs are all part of the journey. I wonder what else is still in store.

INTERLUDE

METHOD, SOLITUDE, AND MEDITATION

The intuitive mind is a sacred gift and the rational mind is a faithful servant.
We have created a society that honors the servant and has forgotten the gift.
—— ALBERT EINSTEIN

Theory is good, but it doesn't prevent something from existing.
—— JEAN-MARTIN CHARCOT

EXPLORING THE WORLD AND THE SELF

My explorations in solitude are a continuing process of personal transformation that opens me more directly to the mysterious unknown. In preparing for this retreat, I decided that instead of entering the wilderness with a set of structured goals and specific questions, as would be usual for academic research, I'd go with an open mind to see what would happen. Rather than trying to confirm an abstract theory about the effects of solitude, I intended to simply remain present to my own actual experience, whatever it turned out to be. I planned for the year to be a sort of hybrid cross between research project and spiritual retreat. I would start from where I was in myself and allow the process of exploration to develop naturally as the months passed.

This approach generated internal tension from both the academic and spiritual threads of my life. On the one hand I felt that in the larger picture I was wasting my time and an amazing opportunity by trying to contort the retreat to fit into an academically acceptable format. On the other hand I questioned whether such personal research was academically valid and what value it had for anyone else. What would it contribute to our common pool of knowledge?

Academic Validity

I also met with some skepticism from the academic community. The procedure of studying oneself is academically unconventional. I argued that I had to be both researcher and subject because I could see no alternative for an empirical study of the experience of solitude. If I were to merely read the writings of other solitaries, I would be studying their verbal reports, not their actual experience. On the other hand, if I were to spend time with a solitary to study his or her life, he or she would no longer be in solitude. Both these approaches are valuable, but to deeply explore the actual lived experience of solitude I had to go into the wilderness alone. I also argued that there are many valid approaches to research: One can do a broad survey of a large group of people, or study a few individuals in greater depth. Extending that, one can also do a very detailed study of a single person. Why, then, could that person not be oneself? Of course the issue of objectivity was always raised, but the notion of pure objectivity has long been questioned in many schools of social science.

A common question was: What is your working hypothesis and exact methodology? What is your critical measure? I didn't actually know what the latter meant, but I didn't like the sound of it, so I always responded that I didn't have one. This answer didn't necessarily satisfy everyone.

Another question frequently asked was: What three disciplines inform your work? One basic criterion for acceptance into UBC's Interdisciplinary Studies program is that the research cross departmental lines into at least three usually separate fields of study. Hence, people naturally wanted to know what my three disciplines were. But again, the question bothered me. The Interdisciplinary Studies program is based on the "overlapping circles" model, in which three circles are arranged in a triangle so they overlap slightly in the center. That overlap constitutes the common ground and the ways in which the individual disciplines connect to each other. To me, this mind-set seems static and constrained. In my thinking, I let the circles drift apart until they no longer overlap but remain in proximity. Interdisciplinarity is that ambiguous undefined space between them.

My intention was to study my own life and experience in solitude, and a life cannot be sensibly fractured into distinct domains of thought or practice. When I read a book that actually means something to me, I don't question whether it's psychology, philosophy, sociology, or spirituality. I'm simply one human being reading the thoughts of another human being.

Subjective, Qualitative, and Empirical

I didn't, however, enter solitude empty-handed. I have lived for more than fifty years in Western culture, and I carry with me an arsenal of ideas, beliefs, desires, fears, doubts, and especially memories and expectations from previous times in solitude, which I often use to hold the flowing present moment at bay. My ongoing and sometimes fearful struggle is always to lay down my arms.

My orientation (as much as I'm able) is to be a radical empiricist, willing to experience and value whatever mundane or unusual physical, emotional, psychological, and spiritual experiences I have. Living in deep wilderness solitude is an unusual situation that generates unusual experiences, but I believe even rare experiences should be accepted as part of our human potential. We are the sum of all the observations we make. When we refuse to acknowledge certain aspects of our lived experience simply because we cannot make rational sense of them, we impoverish our lives. Self-knowledge is vital to our understanding of the world and our place in it. The important question is not what aspects of experience should be accepted as valid, but rather what are the best methods and perspectives for exploring and understanding each experience.

To investigate solitude, my method is mindful observation layered with analytic introspection, while recording my observations and ruminations in a daily journal. Exploring and writing about such an intensely personal experience is vulnerable to criticism. It may seem hopelessly subjective and self-absorbed. Yet as philosopher Michael Polanyi and psychologist Abraham Maslow, among others, point out, all knowledge is fundamentally personal knowledge. Subjective experience can be transformed into valid public knowledge when one's perspective and method are explained, allowing others the opportunity to understand and examine them. Also, I'm not attempting to *prove* anything or to describe or define solitude in an abstract or objective way. My hope is that my personal experience will resonate with others and deepen our collective understanding of solitude.

In scholarly terms, I've chosen a qualitative, rather than a quantitative, research method.[1] Qualitative research often tends to be compared unfavorably with quantitative research — as though the former is just a sloppy, individualized instance of the latter in which personal descriptive words are substituted for precise numbers and repeatable results. But this is not the case. The difference between these methods does not lie in degrees of rigor. They are fundamentally different modes of explanation and reflect distinct ways of knowing the world.

In everyday life, we don't consider an event senseless because it cannot be explained quantitatively. Rather, an event seems senseless when we cannot fit it into the stories we tell to make sense of the world. When asked why we are doing something, we usually answer with a personal narrative, rather than a mathematical equation. However, quantitative knowledge is also important. It allows us to maintain perspective and to place our own immediate experience in a broader context of what others do and experience. One style of knowing and explanation is not better than the other; both are valid, and each complements the other.

THE PRACTICE OF MINDFULNESS

I practice a form of mindfulness meditation that is hybridized primarily from the Theravada teachings of Joseph Goldstein and Jack Kornfield, and from personal insight into my own mind/body process. This basic mix is seasoned with a sprinkling of Chuang Tsu, Krishnamurti, Pema Chödrön, Chögyam Trungpa, and Alan Watts.

Meditation is an important part of my attempt to put aside personal biases and anxious thoughts to become open to each moment and discover what solitude will bring. Very simply, the intention of the Buddhist meditation I practice is to reduce distractions and focus the mind in a nonjudgmental way on whatever is happening right here, right now: bodily sensations, emotions, feelings of pleasantness or unpleasantness, restlessness, sleepiness, doubt, the sense of volition, the process of thinking. Sometimes restlessness prevails; sometimes there is peace; sometimes insight. The objective is not to cultivate any particular experience, but to develop equanimity and compassion: to be with whatever arises; to release our habitual attachment to pleasant experience and avoidance of unpleasant experience; to release the desire to blame when we experience pain.

To meditate, one merely sits quietly and pays attention to the breath. No need to make adjustments. Breathe in and notice the breath, breathe out and notice the breath. Notice the shallow breaths and the deep breaths, just as they are. Notice the still moment between the in-breath and the out-breath. Almost immediately we realize how seldom we are actually present to ourselves and our environment. Watch a breath, watch a second breath, watch the beginning of a third and *fwoop*, the mind is gone. We are not even aware we were gone until we wake up seconds or long minutes later and realize we have been lost somewhere in planning or remembering, fantasy or analytical thought. Sometimes the mind shuts up for a while and simply notices the flow of experience without offering any commentary. Ahhh.

Use this simple — but definitely not easy — method to steady the mind and pay close attention to the here and now, and all else will follow naturally. Teachers can be important in guiding us over the rough patches and in suggesting avenues for exploration, but our truth is discovered in our own embodied existence in this moment, and this, and this. The practice is not limited to the meditation cushion; as mindfulness develops it carries over to everyday life.

Meditation and Thinking

Meditation is not an intellectual activity grounded in thinking. The source of understanding is insight arising from a still mind rather than from discursive analysis. The usual academic approach, from kindergarten to university, is to train the mind to memorize and (with luck) to think logically. Scientific exploration and discovery involve insight and intuition, as well as logical thinking, but I don't remember ever receiving training in school to develop these cognitive faculties.

In meditative traditions, constant thinking is seen as a symptom of an undisciplined mind. Analytical thinking is of course natural and useful, and is respected, but care must be taken to not become entranced by the thoughts and lose awareness of the thinking process itself.

When we pay attention to the arising of thoughts and bodily sensations, we may gain insight into the relationship between them. We may also gain insight into the relationship between questions and answers. So many questions arise in the mind: Does cultural and personal history determine my life? Do I have free will? Am I separate from the world? How solid are my opinions and the stories I tell about who I am and how the world works? What is enlightenment? Does language constrain experience? Must I live in language? All of these questions arise and dissolve in the mind/body flow, but intellectual speculation does not provide the answers. The questions go on and on until we begin to see through them and to realize that they are only words and may be no more answerable than the question: "Why isn't the moon made of green cheese?"

Meditation and Solitude

There are similarities between meditation and solitude. When sitting in silent meditation, even in a group, each person is alone. In meditation the mind slowly settles and we can see our mind/body processes more clearly. For me, this tends to happen in solitude. Daily I wake up to myself, live with myself, go to sleep with myself. In the absence of conversations with other people, my mind settles and clears, and I'm carried into more intense awareness of mental states, emotions, and bodily feelings.

There are also differences. Alone in the wilderness, I'm often immediately aware of transience, mortal danger, and death. During group meditation I'm not confronted as intensely with existential terror. In a structured meditation setting, a teacher can guide students through personal difficulties, but in solitude I have to face my fear alone, and there is the risk of panic.

Meditation and solitude fit well together. Meditation, for me, is a powerful means to stabilize the intense psychoemotional roller coaster that can develop in the absence of community. Because maintaining mindfulness in a social environment is difficult, solitude can be a powerful spiritual tool. I find that, with few distractions, my mind naturally slows and deepens even without strong self-discipline.

I'm interested not only in the workings of my mind but also in transforming my lived relationship with the nonhuman world. In solitude I'm released from the immediate tangle of the social web and free to explore other levels of existence. I have the opportunity to relax and experience myself as part of the rhythms of nature.

One challenging aspect of using mindfulness and solitude as method is the question of who is doing the exploring and who is being explored. As far as I can tell, these nodes of experience never hold still. In waiting and listening for insight into the nature of the mind/body process, the mind/body process changes. Neither the viewing scope nor what's under the scope holds still.

MAY 2001

NIGHT: 40°F. Calm and drizzling. The "I'm ok" email went out, and replies came back without problem. I wrote a short note to Patti because she said it means a lot to her. It's the first personal note I've sent, but I have sent several emails to request information on setting up the satellite phone and electrical system. I want to curtail these communication flurries; they're a distraction and an escape. My agreement with everyone is that I send one check-in email a month, but do not receive any news of the world unless Patti or a family member is deathly ill.

In reading about Big Mind in *Nature, Man and Woman*, I remember that the main reason I'm here is to immerse myself in a situation that encourages awareness of Big Mind. But by focusing so much on techno problems, I keep myself anchored in my small thinking mind. Everything is more or less working now, and it's time to let things be and relax into the now.

Watts writes that the term "Big Mind" was originally used by Shunryu Suzuki-roshi in his book *Zen Mind, Beginner's Mind*. For me, the term has many meanings, none of which can be clearly grasped conceptually, even though the shift from small to Big mind is experientially real. I hope during this year to learn how to more easily shift my consciousness to that open flowing space.

The fish weren't biting much this morning, and holy mother, the wind was cold out there. I finally noticed that the sea was covered in whitecaps. I figured that since I wouldn't go out in such conditions, I better not stay out either. When I got back to camp, I organized the next three-month supply of food. If last month is any indication, rice, milk, and oatmeal are the only items I might run short of.

High overcast, flat calm. The fire started easily for a change this evening. Good thing since I came in very chilled. Usually the stove is a hassle to light, and by the time I've split kindling and blown on the flames, I'm not cold anymore.

Spent almost all day fishing from the kayak. Still trying to get a sense of where and how to fish. At one point, I paddled to the small island just north of here. Above the rocky beach is a firm carpet of short grass where I could walk for a hundred paces without fear of falling. I did some fast laps to warm up and felt years younger. I've been feeling like a creaky old invalid creeping around, always watching my step to not slip and fall. There's been pleasure and joy on this journey, but very little lighthearted fun. It's mostly hard work. And when not physically active I'm still usually focused on spiritual/psychological exploration and on dealing with pain.

Something went splash in the afternoon light. I paddled over for a closer look, but the critter had gone. I think it was a nutria — mostly because I can't imagine what else it might have been. My Spanish dictionary says nutria is otter, but the ones here sure seem different from the otters in California. I've never seen an otter chase a fleeing bird, swim rapidly across an open channel, or make the kind of screeching growl I heard the other day.

Floating quietly in the kayak today, I started to think about my clothes: rubber boots I purchased new for this trip; pants from Goodwill in Vancouver; long underwear Patti bought me for our last camping trip together; T-shirt from Christmas with my family in California; flannel shirt from my years in Montreal; wool vest that was Dad's before he died; silk scarf from Susan; handwoven wool cap I found in Peru twenty-five years ago; leather belt and silver buckle from an old friend in Mexico; broad-brim hat I've worn constantly for the past seven years. A mosaic of my life and relationships.

MORNING: Strange to imagine that people in Canada are expanding into the longer days and warmer temperatures of summer, while I'm hunkering down into the dark belly of winter. I've never thought or read about the effect of alternate seasons on politicians from the northern and southern hemispheres trying to communicate with each other. They're never in sync psychologically.

I'm trying to be more aware of my body. I suspect I'm unconsciously clenching my muscles much of the time, and the only way to relax is to become aware of doing it. It's as though I'm always tensed up to reach for something or to ward off the blow I expect life to deliver. Living this way offers little relaxation and a lot of pain.

I also want to make a conscious effort to remember my dreams. Not that I plan to analyze or even write them down, but I suspect I've fallen into the habit of repression, and that might be one reason I wake up tense and sore.

Mom's death was the end of another kind of dream: that we would finally find communion without all the junk in between. The grief, in part, is because I believe it might never happen — with any woman. I'm beginning to see more clearly how I plague myself and the women in my life with the same criticism and heavy judgment Dad leveled at me. Both Mom and Dad are dead and gone, but I continue to act out the same scenarios in my present life.

I am — I guess I should admit — apparently afraid of commitment; perhaps because loss of freedom is involved. Or maybe it's not commitment I avoid, but breaking my promise. I see myself as inconstant in keeping long-term commitments, and since I value my word I avoid giving it. I hope my relationship with Patti is changing that. I've told her I won't disappear from her life, and she offers me the freedom to be who I am. There's no easy way out. Just steady day-to-day work to relax deep habits. Old, old stuff, but I need to keep seeing it and letting it go.

My lack of commitment to my own soul is even more serious. During my first long solitary retreat, I promised myself I would stay open to nature and to the inner light. During the twenty-five years since then, it feels like I've strayed far from that bond. I don't seem to have an inner pole star that guides me through the changing circumstances of my life. I hope (and fear) I'll find something here that will be a constant — something that will hold me, or something in me that is steady.

MIDNIGHT: It's been raining for hours, beating on my mind, even though I try to let it be and not resist. Feeling restless and lonely, at loose ends. Where will my life lead and with whom, or will I end up alone at the end? I've eaten every kind of treat I have — cheese, peanut butter, dried fruit, bread and honey, popcorn, chocolate, coffee, booze — and still I want something else. To go to a movie and drink a Coke, anything to escape for a while from the here and now. I got out my few photos of family, Patti, Susan, and myself. It gave me pleasure and comfort to look at them. I wanted to check for new emails, but didn't. Hunger for contact. The longing I feel for Susan will only get worse once I return north. I can't see any way we can be together, so I'll likely be more lonely back in Canada than I am now. Maybe I'll just stay here....

The rain stopped at dawn. It had been falling steadily since yesterday morning. Just thirty-nine more days and we'd have been biblical. I guess it sometimes rains like this in Vancouver, but I spend more time indoors there and don't really notice.

The blackflies were out in swarms today: at least a million on the porch, and since I had the cabin door open, nearly half a million in here. I lit the propane lamp to exterminate them, and my altar is now covered with sacrificial corpses. Luckily, the lamp, not me, gets the bad karma. I can see myself at Nirvana's pearly gates talking to a stern Buddha, holding a large illusory book. "Says here you murdered a bunch of blackflies on May 4, 2001." "No, no, it was the lamp that did it." "But you lit the lamp with blood on your mind." "Oh no, I only wanted to see the clear yellow light." "Uh-huh. Back you go as a flyswatter." I get a creepy feeling as I write that. I mean, what if ...?

I finally rigged up a fairly efficient boat-haul system. To pull the boat above the high-tide line, I set a five-foot-tall tripod about twenty feet ahead of the boat and tie it back to a tree. I attach the haul rope to the apex of the tripod, run it through one pulley on the front of the boat, back through a pulley attached to the apex, and back through a second pulley on the front of the boat. I must pull in four feet of rope to move the boat a foot, but exert only 25 percent of the force I would if dragging it without the pulleys. Transom wheels on the back and two plastic rollers under the front of the boat make the job easier, but it's still a strenuous process.

In the afternoon, I hooked up the solar panels on the point. I intend to use them on a regular basis and the wind generator only when the batteries get low. I figure that when the wind is blowing at least 30 mph, which it does a lot of the time, the generator will crank out 500 watts. If I lose 300 of them in the long wires coming to the cabin, 200 still arrive here. My lights each use 15 watts, so in one hour, the generator should replace fourteen hours of light-use. That means it would take about an hour and a half to recharge the batteries after using both lights three hours a day for three days. Probably none of these calculations has any relationship to what's actually going on in the physical world.

From the point I looked west across the channel toward Staines Peninsula and realized I'm getting hungry to go back over and fish where the waterfalls pour into the sea. Southeast I saw, more clearly than before, the exquisite mystic blue of the hanging glaciers. Nothing else I've ever seen shines with that tender and intense glacial blue. It slips through my eyes straight into my heart.

Tomorrow I'll have been here three months, a quarter of my stay. That matches the longest I've previously been alone. After that I'll be in new territory. What a silly idea. Each moment in life is always new territory, for everyone.

MAY 5, 2001

THREE-MONTH ANNIVERSARY: 49°F. Flat calm and cloudy all day. If this is typical winter weather, neither the wind generator nor solar panels will be much good.... One calm day and I'm away into fantasyland, but in general there is less wind now than there was before.

It's been a productive day. I was up early and got all the gear ready. Looked like I was taking off for a month instead of a few hours, but if the outboard dies or a storm prevents my return, I'll be marooned in semi-comfort. High tide made hauling firewood much easier, since I didn't need to carry it over slippery rocks. I had most of the log cut into rounds when the chain saw crapped out. It's probably a clogged gas filter. Sure glad it was the saw and not the outboard. I chopped the rest of the log in half with the ax and humped the two pieces into the boat. This load should replace the wood I've used so far.

At the base of a waterfall coming off Staines Peninsula, fishing was excellent. I caught ten before they quit biting and I headed north to explore the shoreline. Beautiful over there, especially where the rock face slams straight down to the sea.

Back here, I cut branches for the sweat lodge I'll build tomorrow. The trees here don't grow with straight or flexible branches, so it will look more like a small crooked tepee than a domed lodge. I celebrated this lovely day by toasting the world with a sip of Diane's fine old whiskey. Shoulders are sore, of course.

MAY 6, 2001

MORNING: 44°F. Calm and overcast, low tide coming in. It was a rough night. I woke up over and over from the pain in my shoulders. Exercised and took ibuprofen, used the cold water bottle, arthritis cream, and tennis ball. Nothing helped. I plan to sweat today and I need to collect fifteen stones before the tide covers them.

NO ENTRY FOR MAY 7, 2001

MAY 8, 2001

Glorious dawn. Though I'm filled with tales to tell, I'm also groggy from lack of sleep and too tired and sore to write. In any case, the book I'm reading, *Hermits* by Peter France, speaks of the value of silence. Much of what France writes about solitude is how it is for me. But even so, I resist accepting it. Negation of ego — the only path to real peace — is hard; hard, I say. For days I haven't been able to close my inner shutters, but that's why I'm here, so why complain now that it's intense and difficult? I feel so much love, gratitude, and pain here.

MAY 9, 2001

NIGHT: 42°F. Sea on the move. Rain and light wind all day, but now the sky is clearing and the breeze has dropped away. I haven't written in days, and still don't really want to, but I feel I ought to record this year in solitude. Until now, words have flowed easily, perhaps as a way to maintain a sense of contact with others. But *Hermits*, with its strong call to silence and humility, is touching me. Pouring all that happens into words — as though everything is of great importance — seems arrogant.

On my first long wilderness retreat I wrote nothing until the final week and then only some short poems. Perhaps that retreat was so powerful because I didn't anchor myself in language-based consciousness by writing.

And with that, I'm away. I was up soon after dawn on Sunday to gather stones and set up the sweat lodge near the point. I tied together the pole framework and covered it with the tarp that usually covers the boat — the same tarp I bought years ago for shade on the desert beaches in Baja California. I like the continuity of using things I got for a different purpose in another life.

I built a fire to heat the stones, and it was very uncooperative. I had to coax it for hours until the flames were blazing hot enough that I knew the damp wood was fully lit. Then it hiccuped and went out. Huh? Wait a minute, fires don't do that. They don't just go out once they're really burning. But apparently they do here. Very weird.

Late in the day, I finally decided the stones were as hot as they would get in the reluctant fire. I set a bucket of water inside the lodge and smudged each stone — which then became a Grandfather — with smoldering cypress needles as I moved it from fire to lodge. I stripped, smudged myself, entered the lodge, and pulled the flap door closed.

I sprinkled sage on the Grandfathers, introduced myself, and began my prayers. I asked for healing in my shoulders and for courage and strength to deal with the pain. I poured water and the sweat poured off of me. When the heat had gone I brought in the rest of the stones and repeated the process but with sweet grass this time. It felt good to sit there, wrapped in the dark wet heat. My sweat-lodge brothers and sisters in Vancouver, who taught me this practice, were praying together at the same time, and I joined their circle.

By the time I'd dressed and taken down the tarp, it was getting dark. The sky cleared and the full moon shone down as I sat soaking up the last warmth from the dying fire. I miss sitting by an open fire. Having the cabin here is different from previous retreats, during which I've camped out and been more exposed to the elements. But when the wind came up, I was happy to load the kayak and paddle to my refuge.

A hard night, and I was up until 4 AM. I tried everything, but nothing eased the ache in my shoulder. I didn't accept it with equanimity or grace; just sniveled and tried to escape any way I could. Pain woke me again at dawn. I tried to hide in sleep but couldn't, so I got up to a perfectly clear sky and mirrored sea. I checked the charts, got the survival kit together, lashed the kayak across the front of the boat, and headed north to explore the east channel, where I hadn't been before.

I tracked the far shore to look for firewood, and saw some driftwood logs, but most were four or five miles from camp. With heavy clothes, sun, and no wind, the 40°F temperature felt quite balmy.

East of the main channel, I motored into a long inlet that squeezes to a narrow neck halfway down its length. The water was opaque and strangely streaked with glacial silt, stirred by the strongly running tide. On the surface ahead, I saw something that looked like algae and wondered what it might be, but it didn't seem heavy enough to trouble me so I didn't try to avoid it. The crunching sound told me it was ice!

A strong current swept toward the bottleneck, and I pulled ashore to walk down for a look. Whooeee! The tidal bore was a churning rapid. The water dropped more than three feet on a run of seventy-five or so. I took photos, but the moving water will be blurred. All the camera's electronics, including light meter and speed settings, died some time ago, so I can shoot only at 1/90 second. Luckily I brought a spare light meter with me and can set the f-stop on the camera manually. Since I can't develop any film until I leave here, I have no idea if I'm getting usable photos. It's an act of faith to shoot in a vacuum for a year.

Back in the boat, I pushed off and pulled the starter cord. Nothing happened. I yanked again, still nothing. I was drifting uncomfortably close to the rapids when the motor finally caught. So far it's been reliable, but since it was submerged I know it could quit at any time.

Further north, I cut into a large bay fed by a river that looked enticing. Alone and far from camp, I decided it was too risky to go up — but then went anyway. The water was opaque with glacial silt and I worried I might hit rocks. Clunk. Yup, I hit rocks. Dumb. Why do I do these things? Luckily the prop wasn't damaged. I turned back to the bay, shut off the motor, and drifted in the afternoon quiet. A condor soared over the ridge of a looming glacier.

Coming home, I crossed to the west channel and Staines Peninsula by weaving along narrow passages with swirling current patterns that were created by the tide running through a cluster of small islets. I saw some plastic debris I'll clean up one day. I tried my luck in a snapper hole, and in half an hour caught enough for four or five days, then lingered to watch the sunset before coming back to camp.

Another night of pain and sniveling, and exercising my shoulder every two hours until first light yesterday. I wanted more sleep, but dawn was so exquisite I made coffee and stayed up to watch the day come on. Strange mysteriously dark reflections from the mountains rippled across the glassy water. And then colors began to shine.

I sharpened the chain, and found a wad of debris blocking the saw's secondary fuel filter. When I put it back together, it started easily. By the time I came back with a load of wood and dragged the boat up, I was toast. Meditating in the dark of the night, I heard a flock of birds running and flying across the water, and opened my eyes to a huge golden moon rising over the mountains.

It's a shame that after the wonderful gifts of the past days, I have so little acceptance of pain as part of the overall experience. I ask for help and try to relax into the pain, knowing intellectually that it's part of being alive. Meditation instruction teaches that a lot of what we experience as pain is actually the psychological tension of resisting strong physical sensation. But when my shoulders cramp up, I just want it to stop.

I feel so weak in the face of pain, especially when I read of spiritual warriors who realize that pain is not only inevitable but beneficial because it keeps us humble and open to help from a higher source. During these past four days, I've felt so blessed and grateful for all I've been given, but nights are different. My shoulders don't trouble me much while I'm active, but when I lie down they start to cramp and throb. During the day I can be philosophical about pain as part of life, but at night when I actually hurt, I have no reserve of stoic equanimity.

Perhaps tonight I can show a smidgen more grace in the face of the pain. I need to deal with my own mortality, and here is a good place to start. This is not abstract philosophical stuff, but immediate physical actuality.

MIDNIGHT: I've seen a lot of moonrises, but few like tonight's. One darkly sil-houetted mountain peak was haloed in misty light that spilled onto the sur-rounding ridges. I expected the moon momentarily, but the glow stretched through time and became brighter — and brighter. Finally, nearly full, the moon slid over the peak and cast a band of gold across the sea toward me. Out in the channel where the water was rumpled, the band was wide and dif-fuse, but as it slipped into still water, it focused into a narrow ribbon of smooth ripples. Closer still, the ribbon unraveled into distinct yellow threads, and each, riding its own ripple crest, was woven into the surrounding dark. Out came Diane's whiskey.

It's been another glorious day. Calm, cloudless, and blue. I woke re-freshed after almost eight hours of unbroken sleep and considered rushing out to explore, but decided to hang with the urge and stay here instead. The cabin now lies continually in shadow, so I took coffee to the sun at the point. What's with these damn blackflies? Don't they know that when frost comes, it's time for them to leave? I read for a while and walked some short laps on the small gravel patch. I miss walking.

I crossed to Staines to fish the afternoon high tide, and then motored north to a log I spotted a few days ago. I cut, carried, and loaded the rounds in less than two hours. Soon I'll have enough wood for the winter and can give my shoulders a chance to heal.

I cut myself for the first time since I've been here — while sharpening the chain saw, which happily wasn't running. I took it as a warning. But later, with the saw running, I also took a careless step, slipped, and almost sliced my leg. A seriously dumb and dangerous thing to do. A chain saw can instantly rip flesh to shreds. For the past week I've been very aware of the risk of cut-ting myself with the ax while splitting kindling, and have tried to be extra careful. Precognition of some sort?

God Bless you, Dr. Nelson. While she was writing the prescriptions for my medical kit, I asked for fifty Tylenol 3s; she suggested I take one hundred instead. I thought I'd declined since I didn't expect to need that many strong painkillers. Last night, my shoulder was so painful I decided to take one. The bottle seemed very full, so I checked the label. One hundred! Happy day. So far I've used only three or four because I've wanted to save them for an emergency, but now I feel freer to take one now and then when the pain gets nasty.

Pride may be one reason I force my shoulders to keep working, even though I've already cut and hauled enough firewood for several months. I do want the comfort of having plenty for the winter, but there is also the pride of having a strong resilient body that can suck it up and keep working. In *Hermits*, humility is pointed to again and again as the key to spiritual growth. Hard. Pride goes so deep. Once I stop thinking in terms of excessive pride, and begin to realize that *any* pride at all is a spiritual liability, whew. I expend so much effort trying to keep up a socially acceptable self-image. What a relief to let it go, even a little bit, for a short while.

This afternoon, the sea was so calm there were no ripples at all as the tide came in; just a slow steady rise in level. I watched the water creep up smooth rounded stones until its surface towered almost a quarter inch above their still-dry tops. Then one by one, these circular miniwalls of water would collapse with a rush. Did surface tension hold them up like that?

I also saw another nifty sight yesterday: small lavender blobs spinning in a quiet pool. Some sort of larval clusters, I suppose. Now and then a wee purple speck would whiz off and hook up with another spinning blob. Looked like a pretty frantic lifestyle to me, but I guess they like it.

The black and white geese have different vocalizations. The white one makes soft rapid cooing/chirping/clucking sounds, and the black-and-white one gives single resonant honks. The black-and-white one seems dominant and is probably the male, but I wonder.

MAY 12, 2001

MIDNIGHT: 28°F. Moon and stars in a cloudless sky. I woke this morning just after dawn to a shining sea and no trace of wind. Five miles south from here, on the far side of the east channel, a long hook of land juts out and forms a deep bay. Near the bottom of the bay, an inlet reaches east into the mountains. I wanted to explore the inlet and perhaps the lake that feeds it through a short stream.

I crossed the channel and headed south until I came level with the tip of the hook, now a mile west of me. Ahead I saw a smudge on the water that I recognized as ice. It made sense since the sun had just cleared the mountains enough to touch that side of the channel. I backtracked west, thinking to hug the sunny side, but a half-inch crust of ice covered the whole bay. I wondered if the temperature had dropped without my noticing, and worried I might get trapped by ice away from camp. But once out of the bay, the ice disappeared. Perhaps it freezes down there because so much freshwater melts in from the glaciers with little tidal exchange to wash it out.

This country is incredibly beautiful. I love the brown badlands feel to parts of it. I idled for a while in front of a giant amphitheater carved into a bare rock wall where scrub trees climbed the slopes and cliffs. Huge square boulders lay scattered here and there, and waterfalls ribboned into the sea. The sea itself was so calm today that half a mussel shell floated by, midchannel, caught in the tidal current.

It was quite warm in the sun this afternoon, but only 34 degrees here where my cabin sits in shadow on frosty ground. I've stuffed extra sacks around Cat's box for more insulation; with his thick fur, I doubt he gets cold.

According to the author of *Hermits*, the Desert Fathers clearly realized the need for obedience. At times I've also felt this need to obey — to surrender the ego's decision-making activity. But how? Not belonging to a religious order, whom do I obey? I think surrender and obedience — although not spoken of in those terms — are also central to Buddhist meditation practice. In remaining still, without grasping or aversion (nice dream), we are obedient to the moment, to how things actually are right now. In accepting things just as they are and not as we would like them to be, we surrender self-centered will. In keeping Suzuki-roshi's "beginner's mind," we remain humble in the face of the unknowable.

Ah, but... words. It's easy enough to grasp these ideas conceptually, what's hard is moment-by-moment practice. I can see that a year here won't be nearly enough, although five might make a difference in my life. In the meantime, tomorrow is another day, and tonight my heart is soft with love.

MAY 13, 2001

The night is dark and clear, the moon not yet risen. Today is Sunday, my chosen day of rest. I exercised just enough to loosen my shoulders and ease their ache, then took chair, coffee, and book to spend the day in the sun at the point. Cat, of course, went with me. I considered starting a fire and staying indoors, but didn't want to miss the windless blue-sky day. This weather can't last and I want to hoard it in my bones.

With closed eyes I lay on the rocks and listened to the water lapping the shore. The sound soothed my ears and heart. How different from the anxiety of three months ago when I felt the rain and surf beating incessantly against me. I was actually glad this morning to have a scatter of high cloud and a light breeze. It made the day softer and less crystalline brittle.

I read some excerpts from Thomas Merton in *Hermits*. He doesn't convince me. Too sure of himself. Too dogmatic in telling me about solitude — what is and is not healthy to do when living alone. The universal "You" slips too easily from his pen. And he never actually spent much time in solitude. For years, he petitioned the Catholic hierarchy to allow him to live as a hermit within the Trappist order, yet when he was finally granted the privilege, he received visitors all the time. His brother monks, trying to protect his privacy, turned people away, but Merton then told them about a back way into his cottage. Even sending an email and waiting for a reply alters the quality of my solitude, so it's hard to imagine that Merton, himself, traveled far into his own aloneness when he was so frequently with visitors and wrote and received so many letters.

What Merton writes makes sense to me, but I wonder how much is his own direct experience and how much he internalized from reading? He argues the need for silence to escape the incessant flow of language, but the man wrote over three hundred papers and thirty-seven books! And he died pretty young, too.

As I muttered and judged Merton's life, I noticed that the quiet spaciousness that had been growing in me all day began to fade. Discounting people as inauthentic is also what I do to myself and so stay bound to doubt and a sense of worthlessness. His life was what it was, full of contradiction — as is mine.

From below, I heard heavy breathing and looked down. A sea lion was working the kelp bed close to shore. Aha! This is what I saw from the kayak last week, what I've heard bellowing from over by Staines, and probably what I saw and heard in the east channel several weeks ago. It's nice when a bunch of separate mysteries coalesce into one larger mystery — which we call a sea lion. I now think the nutria is an otter. The creature I had come to think of as a nutria is a mythological beast; a hybrid cross of otter and sea lion.

I also watched one of the creamy-breasted ducks having a bath. It was dunking itself, then fluttering and flapping, and looked like it was actually turning somersaults in the water. The dolphins came by for a while, and a smallish hawk perched in the dead tree above me. I usually see more wildlife just sitting here than I do out in the boat or kayak.

I've been thinking about my response to blackflies. On the physical level it seems natural to be irritated by the bugs. After all, it's more pleasant to not get bit. But my psychological response makes less sense. I feel like my survival is on the line if a bug bites, and this is what causes me to react so strongly. Instead of just brushing the bug away or accepting a small bite, I freak out, wave my hands, and slap — causing myself much more pain than the bug would have caused.

It's this psychological reaction that also makes the pain in my shoulders so distressing. Yes, there's pain, and I can't do all I'd like to do, but I'm unlikely to die from it. In any case, if I want to be free of these angry responses, I need to give up my frantic psychological attachment to survival. Physically, of course, my biological drive is to survive. But beyond that, feeling anxious and angry about imagined threats to that survival is unhealthy and painful.

A while ago, I sponge-bathed and shaved and put in some long underwear to soak. Yuk, time to do laundry again already? Weeks have passed since the last time. For now, though, the fry bread is just ready to eat with hot chocolate.

MAY 14, 2001

40°F. A breeze from the southeast is pushing the sea directly toward me. The sky is clear, but not many stars. This morning I took the kayak to the windward point of the island just south of here to collect dead twigs for kindling. I climbed the headland there for the first time, and being fifty feet above sea level gave me a different perspective on the area. I paused to give thanks for this time in solitude. I seldom stop to really notice and appreciate that for the first and, perhaps, last time in my life I've been completely alone and undisturbed — day after day for months. Only occasional contrails far off over the Andes signal the world of people.

After unloading the boat, I split some wood, and Cat got in the way. He probably just wanted some contact after being alone all afternoon, but for me, he was in the way. I lost it and yelled at him, and as usual he disappeared under the house. A little later I called and he jumped into my lap, so I guess he doesn't take my yelling too seriously. I felt bad and explained that after I've been working all day, I'm just barely holding it together, and his added confusion sends me over the edge. I said I was sorry I had yelled, but I wonder. Why should I feel bad about yelling at him? What are acceptable ways to express anger? I often feel that giving the cat a swat or a gentle kick is not inappropriate. Animals often interact with each other using snarls, swats, and snaps.

MAY 15, 2001

38°F. Calm, dim stars. How nice, the fire caught easily tonight. I used some of the dry twigs I collected yesterday as kindling, then added small pieces of the wood I cut today across the east channel. There are several rocky beaches over there with plenty of semidry logs.

Finished reading *Hermits*. The last person the author writes about is writer/poet Robert Lax. Lax has been living hermitlike for most of his life, but within towns and cities. He doesn't see himself as a classical hermit because he isn't self-sufficient in his abilities. He believes a classical hermit must be able to chop wood. He tried it once without success, and doesn't think it's the sort of challenge he'd want to respond to if he didn't have to. How strange. What limitations we put on ourselves, as though chopping wood is some sort of extreme activity. But in one sense his intuition is right. He probably wouldn't like it out here. Chopping wood implies a constellation of other, more difficult, survival activities: finding, cutting, and hauling the wood; keeping the chain saw sharp and functioning; handling a boat; etc.

I've been meditating quite a bit in short snatches, rather than long stretches. Sending loving-kindness, being mindful of what I'm doing, exploring the tightness and pain in my back and shoulders.

MAY 16, 2001

41°F. Sea on the move beneath wind-blown rain. Ah yes, this is the anxiety-producing weather I'm familiar with. I walked to the point earlier this evening to feel and enjoy the fierce wind. Going there to visit it is very different from having the wind roar down on my cabin uninvited.

I siphoned gas from one of the 55-gallon drums into the 5-gallon containers I take in the boat; split wood, then cleaned up and organized the porch and under the cabin. It all looks tidier now. Before tucking the 4 hp outboard out of sight, I decided I'd try to start it. Whoa, spark in one plug! I'd been convinced for almost three months that it was dead, but maybe it was just wet before. The second plug had no spark at all. Weird.

One of my rubber boots split. This isn't good. I'll try to repair it with Shoe Goo. Before the year is over I'll probably be sorry I bought cheap boots instead of spending another $100 for good ones. Didn't imagine I'd be spending this much time in them. Still, the cheap ones are the lightest and easiest on my prosthetic leg.

I've been reading *Nature, Man and Woman* again. Most of what Watts says is based on Zen Buddhism and Taoism. Seeing through the illusion of self/ego is the only way to true peace and happiness. But if we claim that, then most Christian mystics were and are misguided, because they believe in an eternal individual soul that must surrender to God's Will. In both cases the key to peace, joy, and love is to give up a self-centered worldview.

Walking back from the point, I was reflecting again on writing these journal entries. It's not the writing, itself, that's the problem (if there is a problem), but thinking beforehand about what I'll write, and mentally describing to myself what I'm seeing and feeling. When I do that I'm not really here in solitude, but in an imaginary future where someone else (even if it's only a future me) is reading my descriptions. In this way, I cling to my social identity through interaction with other people, instead of seeking a deeper identity as part of the universe or in relationship with God.

It's been raining and blowing on and off all day. The ice on the puddles has melted, and it's nice to have it not so cold. This afternoon, one of the resident birds was gobbling up grains of rice just below the porch. Cat was sitting on the porch just far enough back from the edge that he didn't see the bird until it flew up right in front of his face. Really startled him, and he leapt back in alarm. The role reversal was pretty funny.

Phantom pains in my stump are going crazy tonight. Dammit! If it's not one thing it's another. What creates the experience of pain? It's clear that the same physical sensation is sometimes experienced as pleasure and at other times as pain. Context is key, but what aspect of context? I think, in part, it's whether I welcome the sensation or it comes against my will. A sensation I welcome is pleasurable, yet the same sensation feels painful if I don't want it. The trick is to learn to choose the pain and transform it into pleasure, or at least into a neutral sensation.

I've always placed great value on *insights*, but in some sense they're a dime a dozen. They come and they go. I long for understanding and wisdom, but no longer know what I'm seeking. If all is transient, including clarity and peace, then what is there to seek? I feel peace, love, and gratitude flowing over me at times, but no sense of a Supreme Being. And I still have no idea what my soul is. There are thoughts, emotions, physical sensations, and — though Buddhism says it's an illusion — a sense of I, but what is the soul? What does it look or feel like? How does it manifest itself to me?

Today is another day. A hummingbird just flew in and I cupped him in my hands, stroked his head lightly, and carried him back outside.

The phantom pains are back and I fear they will get worse. I look ahead and see a never-ending stream of pain in my life, and it's too much. Last night, for the first time, I felt overwhelmed and worn down to the point where I can't deal with any more physical discomfort, and maybe I'll just end it all. . . . It was a scary feeling.

It's not skillful to compare what's happening here to my first long

wilderness retreat, but I continue to do so. Back then I dealt with similar issues, but especially acute fear, rather than physical pain, anger, and resent-
ment. What scares me now is the remembered intensity of that experience,
how I was pushed to the edge of insanity before I let go of my defenses. I'm
not sure I still have the strength and courage to face such intensity, but if I
don't somehow surrender to my life the way it is, I'll have a desolate road
ahead. I feel I've been on this journey a very long time without reaping much
benefit, and now I'm not sure where to turn. No wonder I've been staying up
until 3 and 4 AM. Nights are difficult.

I saw clearly today that I have a strong goal in being here. And that —
in some sense — is just the problem. Goal-oriented behavior — the whole notion of progress and getting somewhere — is one of the things screwing up
our culture. Paradoxically, the place I'm trying to get to is right here: fully experiencing each day as meaningful in and of itself.

MAY 19, 2001

NOON: 40°F. Rain, light wind, sea on the move, mountains gone and hills
only faintly visible. I like daily sweeping as part of my morning ritual. There
is always a bunch of debris on the floor. The phantom pains have eased. I
wasn't using enough stump socks now that I've lost so much weight, and the
leg was loose and jamming the nerves. I'm still rinsing my tooth with saltwater morning and night to keep infection from exploding. After June 1,
I might start building fires during the day. So far it's been a kind of ascetic
practice to stay with the cold until evening: eight hours of ambient temperature, eight hours of warmth, eight hours in the sleeping bag.

I'm starting to see more clearly the interpretation I put on physical events,
like the weather. There is physical weather — sun, rain, wind — which just
is, and my emotional response — pleasure, peace, anger, anxiety — that I as-
sociate with the weather. If I can tease these aspects apart, and experience
weather as weather and emotional response as emotional response, my days
might be less dramatic and draining. This is so for pain, too. Woven into the
sensations is a cognitive/emotional component, which includes the belief that
the pain will last forever or become unbearable and that I'm being mistreated
or punished for something. This nonphysical aspect makes the pain much
more difficult to deal with.

Sitting on the porch a while ago, feeling, listening, and watching the dark
settle over mountains and sea, I finally surrendered and felt myself opening
into a peaceful space of stillness. Again I see how misguided are my efforts to
"get" somewhere. I'm already here. There is nowhere else to go. The *aliveness*

I seek is everywhere; I'm always in it and it in me, even though I often don't experience it consciously. Trying to get somewhere else psychologically only removes me further into a conceptual dreamland.

This morning, I took the sweat-lodge gear to the point in the kayak, built and tended a fire, and finally went into the lodge midafternoon. Wonderful to be hit with the moist heat, drip sweat, and be barely able to breathe. I asked for strength and guidance, prayed for many people in my life, and gave thanks for all I've been given. I wished there was someone to share it with.

Afterward, I sat by the sea to let my sweat dry before dressing. Dolphins and an eagle came by. As I sat naked, without leg or glasses, I thought, "Well, Spirit, this is all there is: missing a leg and a bunch of teeth; eyes not so hot; scars everywhere. Here I am." Then I thought of how I would appear to a woman. And my biggest fault is that I would expect her to be perfect.

40°F. Blue sky and clouds, some wind moving the sea. A morning of mild sorrow and despair. No way out. I'll never escape my life and fulfill my potential for joy and freedom. I've been over this ground so many times — hoping and believing that this time things will be different and I'll be saved from myself. Even realizing that there is no way out — and that surrendering to that fact really is the only way out — is illusion and manipulation. Perhaps reading *Nature, Man and Woman* brought on these feelings and thoughts. Almost all my hard-won insights are in the book. I might as well have simply read the book fifty times during the last thirty-five years and saved myself a load of grief, hard work, and pain.

Cold, grey, rain, and wind. The 4 hp outboard is working! I cleaned the electrical connections, sanded and adjusted the points, and voilà, spark in both plugs. Cranked it a few times and it fired up. This is very cool, but when I use the boat I'll continue to take the kayak so I can at least make it to land if both motors fail. I'm not confident in either of them since they were submerged.

I'm tempted to say I got the motor running, and in one sense that's so; but I also feel gratitude, as though it's a gift that it's running. It's like fishing. I go fishing and sometimes catch fish, but they are always a gift. My fishing skills make it possible to receive the gift, but my skills are also a gift.

I had the boat pumped up and gear loaded to go for wood when *wham*, the wind came snarling down the channel and clawed it into whitecaps. The weather here is like the rocks — dangerously seductive. The rocks look dry and safe, but are incredibly slippery. The sea was placid and, fifteen minutes later, savage.

One of the small birds with a spiky topknot just landed on my leg, then flew to the bacon hanging under the porch roof. She started to gobble down a bunch of dead blackflies stuck to it. Hope she comes back to finish the job.

I've put the booze away. It's become too important. Silly, since I sip only about a quarter ounce daily. Just a security addiction — like coffee and chocolate.

MAY 23, 2001

38°F. The stormy weather continues, and I remained land-bound today, going no further than the chopping block and the beach to pull the boat up higher.

Late last night, a luminous pool of crystal water, rippling over shining pebbles, opened deep inside, and I bathed in it. At times of late there have been moments of freedom from this straitjacket of self-criticism. Moments when I experience myself as just a man ... living alone in the wilderness of southern Chile. A fairly decent man doing the best he can.

I have a book written by Mark Epstein, who is a psychiatrist and a meditator. It points out the impossibility of fulfilling the ubiquitous human desire for perfection, and discusses the link between nonperfection and anxiety. It's useful to see my own experience in a more communal context.

This evening, an inner light shone up from within, and a voice called, "Come to me, trust me, depend on me. You cannot do it yourself. You're trapped where you are, and your struggling efforts to free yourself enmesh you more deeply. Come to me." "Yes," I answered, and surrendered. Yet my pride was soon fighting back. This is the work I came to do.

MAY 24, 2001

I woke in the dark to the patter of rain on the roof. It took me back to my years as a logger on the west coast of Vancouver Island. Feeling glum, I imagined living in some small town with a steady job, a committed relationship, and no plans to ever leave. Depression is often linked to certain kinds of thoughts I label "the future," and not to actual present conditions. Those thoughts have the quality of unchanging permanence, which is a central aspect of their oppressive quality. In the present, things don't happen that way. Everything is always changing.

I got up, exercised, and made coffee. My mood shifted and so did the weather. A storm front moved in and drove waves onto my beach. Feeling anxious as the cabin shook in the gusts, I waited for the very high tide that was on the way.

Some snow came down, but didn't stick, and now the storm has passed. The tide wet the bottom layer of the woodpiles. According to the tables, there will be still higher tides in June, July, and August, but during daylight hours. The February high tides came in the night when I couldn't see what was happening.

I wonder what tomorrow will bring. Hell, never mind tomorrow, how about the next few hours?

MAY 25, 2001

First real snow. Wet, but with flakes so huge that they swirled and drifted as though light and fluffy. Days — even in the cold — are easier than nights. In the day, there is the world to see and things to do. The pain is less intense. At night, the world closes in and my body grows large. Only rarely do I experience the sensations of my body as manifestations of the universe — like wind and rain.

So often I take the world personally, as though the wind and rain are directed against *Me*. It's insane to take them as a personal affront, and I sometimes smile at my antics as a sort of game. But it's such a deep habit that, often unconsciously, I take it seriously. Time to let this game go.

I spend a lot of time listening to the sounds of water, yet am just now listening to learn. A crack in the rock on the far side of the cove gurgles and whumps — each sound unique — and it seems to be the sea saying: "I am this, and this, and this." I close my eyes and follow the sound into the universe and feel myself float free. Then I hear the calm voice that calls, "Depend on me," whisper, "What about me?" My heart opens and I am flooded with peace and love. Yes. Clarity of mind is not enough without love.

The topknot bird that was eating bugs off the bacon flew into the cabin today and was trying to leave through the Plexiglas. She banged her head and fluttered onto the table, then noticed a dead fly lying there. "Oh, a fly, I'll just gobble this down before I continue to freak out." It was pretty comical. Eventually she found the door and left, but later returned, searching for this and that to eat. Now there are little gobs of shit all over.

As evening fell, I watched the creamy-breasted ducks — black against the snowy hills — patrol their grey-green turf. They seem especially territorial now that an intruding pair is skulking around. The resident land bird that feeds in my front yard chases another of its kind away. Their game of tag goes on and on. It's not as though one is the victor and the other driven permanently from the area. No, they both seem established here, and both spend a fair amount of time running instead of eating. To my eye, it doesn't seem to matter much who's running ahead and who behind. It's just what they do.

MAY 26, 2001

It's drizzling outside. I know, I was just out there puking in the dark. A couple of hours ago I ate some limpet. I chewed a little yesterday and spit it out. Tonight I swallowed a bit. As I chewed, I noticed a metallic taste and should have spit it out, but for some reason I swallowed instead. I doubt it's red tide poisoning, since no taste is associated with that toxin, and Cat ate some of the limpet and is fine. But I feel slightly odd and so decided to puke. Hope I'm ok. Should know in another few hours, I guess. I wish I knew why I do these things. My eyes are a little heavy, and I feel slightly feverish. It may be getting hard to breathe. My tongue, lips, and fingers feel tingly. Wow, wonder if I'm going to die. Wouldn't that suck?

I went fishing to Staines this afternoon. No fish, which is surprising since I've caught plenty every other time I've gone there. They may not bite when it's stormy like today. Heart is beating faster.

I put the 4 hp on the boat and ran it for half an hour. It worked perfectly and moves the boat along at just under 5 mph, which is better than I expected.

Cat's been having one of his snivel days. He started crying this morning and has been at it ever since. He seems to have two cries: one says, "I want," and the other says, "Poor me." Actually, that sounds a lot like me and it's probably all projection on my part.

I sliced my finger with the hatchet while splitting kindling today. Not a bad cut — just enough to remind me to be more careful — but it sure bled a lot. I still feel like something is very wrong and I'm going to lie down. If this is the last I write, good-bye, everyone. I love you all. This journey has definitely been worth it.

MAY 27, 2001

32°F. Calm, starry, beautiful. Well, I'm still alive. Last night got a little weird. I stayed awake until 3:30 AM to be sure I wouldn't die in my sleep. I'm still not sure if I actually poisoned myself, but doubt it since Cat ate most of the limpet and is fine. Probably just mind games. Such intense imagining is a risk in solitude. My shoulder was very sore last night and I took four ibuprofen. After not taking any for several days, I was aware of how drugged I felt. On the other hand, if I hadn't taken them, I might have been more upset about the possibility of dying. Silly stuff indeed.

Today is Sunday, theoretically my day of rest, but it didn't work out that way. I decided to cross to Staines. The 15 hp outboard is missing when I crank it wide open, and it feels good to have the 4 hp with me. Fishing was good. It seems like they bite only when the weather is clear and calm. How they sense this 150 feet below the surface is a mystery.

After fishing, I fetched the rest of a log I'd been cutting during the last stretch of good weather. I originally figured a dozen loads of wood would be enough for the year. I've now brought in eight loads and wonder if they will see me even through the winter. I'm glad to already have as much wood as I do, and want to cut all I think I'll need for November, December, and January before the summer winds return and I won't be able to cross the channel.

I've been reading some Buddhist teachings about restless mind in *Seeking the Heart of Wisdom*. Boredom and restlessness are two sides of the same coin. I'm coming to see that from a Buddhist perspective, the vast majority of our culture's activity is likely driven by boredom and restlessness. With my lifestyle, I'm the epitome of that. Not a cultural rebel at all, but right on the cutting edge.

MAY 28, 2001

35°F. No wind and the sea is calm. Socked in and snowing lightly. I can see no more than a hundred yards or so.

I caught myself thinking that I wish winter was already over. Yet the next three months may be the heart of this whole retreat. After that it will be spring, then summer, and I'll be looking ahead to leaving. It's time to stop telling myself I will start to *really* live in some imagined future time and circumstance. Once that imagined situation arrives, I dream up some other future. I know intellectually that here and now is all there ever is, and I'm working to actually stay in the present and live each day as it unfolds.

I've taken another vow to not yell at or hit Cat for crying. I get instantly furious when he whines, and instead of responding with compassion because he must feel out of sorts or he wouldn't be crying, I lash out. This is what I do to myself when I'm hurt or frightened. Instead of being gentle with myself, I get angry and push on through. If I can learn to be patient and kind with Cat, perhaps I will treat myself more gently, too.

Why do I accept whatever the ducks, eagles, and other birds do, but am offended by some of Cat's behaviors? I think it has to do with a sense of ownership. He is, in some sense (at least in my mind), mine and should do as I wish him to do. This is a problem in all my relationships. The most serious case is with myself. I feel I somehow *own* myself and have the right to control what I do and feel and what happens to me. From there it follows that the world is *mine* to do with as I wish. But I didn't make me, nor do I own me or the world. I'm just part of the flow of existence.

Quiet, sad, lonely afternoon . . . but lovely and tender, too. Still snowing, and it's sticking to the ground. I have a feeling there might be inches before morning. Makes me long for someone to be here with me.

MAY 29, 2001

A flock of black birds landed on the low-tide beach to feed together without territorial squabbling. After the hummingbirds and other territorial bullies, it did my heart good to see them hanging out together. I think they're some sort of corvid. Same black body shape, cocky movement, raucous communication, and beady intelligent eyes. They used their beaks to flip over rocks to search underneath for food: probably sand fleas or shrimp. When one found a good rock, others would scramble over to join the feed without apparent discord.

The small bird that's been cleaning bugs off the bacon landed on my shoulder today and then flew right into the cabin without concern. She's switched from bugs and is eating fat on the smoked meat. I keep telling Cat "NO" when he stalks her. I don't really expect him to stop since the urge is so primal, but maybe I can make him tense enough to throw off his timing when he pounces. Could this be the Church's plan with sex? It's not that they expect to actually stop unmarried folks from screwing, but maybe they hope to tense us up enough to throw off our timing so we don't really enjoy it.

I doubt I will ever again do formal science. Like most people, motivated by immediate personal concerns, I do casual science all the time. I hypothesize and test the hypotheses, about where, when, and how to catch fish; about what firewood works best and where to find it on the beach; about how different electrical hookups will work. But abstract theories don't attract me anymore. And as far as I can tell, I have no interest in trying to construct a mathematical model of what I'm seeing and feeling.

For me, the line separating lived experience and conceptual understanding is not as sharp as it used to be. In the past, when I was out like this, the world seemed to be a wonderful mystery — spontaneously *alive* and beyond all rational explanation. Now I live and also think about how the world might work. But I don't often have the strong sense of wonder and mystery I've had before, so perhaps the line is still sharp and I have merely mostly stayed on the near side.

Not much excitement now as I head into winter. Same old crap going round and round in my head and heart, with a small new insight now and then. But this is how I do my work: cover the same ground again and again, slowly seeing things from different angles. Today I caught myself secretly wishing that something exciting would happen — some sort of accident or disaster to deal with. This is truly scary. It's fairly suicidal if I set out to do risky things with the secret hope that I'll have problems and a juicy story to tell.

Years ago I heard about a rock-and-roll drummer always stoned on drugs and booze who cleaned himself up for a while. Then he went back to serious self-abuse. When asked why, he said that when sober he couldn't drum as well. Many of us seem to sacrifice our spiritual, emotional, and psychological health to be: a better scientist, politician, businessman, lover, soldier, environmentalist, spiritual seeker. Self-sacrifice for what we love is our cultural ideal, but I wonder. Is such behavior just ego-tripping and escape from existential angst?

Merton has gotten under my skin. I'm reading *Solitude: A Philosophical Encounter* by Philip Koch, and he quotes Merton at length: "The hermit's whole life is a life of silent adoration. His very solitude keeps him ever in the presence of God.... His whole day, in the silence of his cell, or his garden looking out upon the forest, is a prolonged communion."

This was written by a man who either had his head up his ass or was bullshitting the public. I've spent a lot of time in solitude, and have listened to and read many meditation teachings (meditation being a form of solitude), and nowhere does Merton's statement find support. On the contrary. The mind and heart are all over the place, from the most trivial, mundane, and negative to the joyful, peaceful, and sacred. Solitude is like the rest of life, only with less opportunity for escape into diversion. And where does Merton get off saying under which conditions one is or is not in the presence of God?

Or this: "Not all men are called to be hermits, but all men need enough silence and solitude in their lives to enable the deep inner voice of their own true self to be heard at least occasionally. When that inner voice is not heard, when a man cannot attain to the spiritual peace that comes from being perfectly at one with his true self, his life is always miserable and exhausting."

This is claptrap. I personally agree that we all need solitude, but who am I to say I'm right? Maybe others find their source of spiritual insight and peace though interaction with other people. Ah me, petty, petty, Bob. I think I got it out of my system for the moment. His writing is, though, well crafted and accessible. No wonder he's the most well-known and popular hermit in America.

Looking at the limpets on the low-tide rocks today, I wondered how much they move and if there is pattern to their movement. I thought of a simple way to find out. I could number their shells (with the nail polish I brought for just this sort of marking) to identify them as individuals. Then, each day at low tide, I could locate each limpet on the rock and record its position on graph paper. After a month I could connect the sequenced dots and have a track of their movements.

Funny how interested I've become in their movement when just yesterday I was thinking that I would probably never do formal science again. What intrigues me is to see them and the mussels apparently sedentary when all else is in motion. I picture a computer animation of their collective movements for the month. It might look like a slow-motion folk dance. Or perhaps they move only a quarter inch a day. I think I'll dab some nail polish on a shell or two to see if it sticks in the salt water.

I've started reading *Pedagogy of the Oppressed* by Paulo Freire. He writes about creating the future, and that triggered thoughts about whether self-directed personal growth is really possible or is an illusion. The duality I've set up may be part of my perfectionism. Absolutism. Either/or. As if there either is the possibility of change or there is not. Bam. But both these notions are only thoughts that run through my mind. Whichever I give energy to is more likely to manifest. At times it will seem like I'm stuck, have always been stuck, and always will be stuck. At other times I'll feel more space opening in my experience of being *alive*.

On my beach
ten thousand
broken mussel shells
slowly turn to sand.

Yesterday
each was
like me today
alive.

I crunch my way
among their corpses murmuring
brothers.

Down the channel
to the west
a fierce north wind
sends foaming whitecaps south.

And at my feet
the soft slosh of ebb tide
roars in my heart.

JUNE 2001

Our task is to see and accept the world
as it is, not as we would like it to be.

— S. N. GOENKA

MIDNIGHT: 34°F. Light snow on the ground, the wind blowing and the sea rough. Check-in went smoothly this morning and the process took only half an hour. This evening I picked up the replies. I spent most of the day building frames for the awnings that will go over the porch and main window. I had to cut heavy wire into short lengths to make nails. Incredible that from the thousands of nails I brought, I'm down to the last handful.

I measured food tonight and I'm set for another month. I'm eating hardly any pasta and not my full ration of rice, beans, or oatmeal, so I'll have plenty of staples to last. I sliced some smoked meat and found a nest of maggots inside. I cut them out and fried the rest of the meat. I was surprised how unpleasant I found the maggots, and hope the rest of the meat is not infested.

The two tamest birds come boldly onto the porch now; not only into Cat's territory, but also to eat his food. I think they've learned to come when I'm here, since I won't let him attack. He sits on my lap and watches them only a couple of feet away. He does twitch now and again, but mostly remains still. If he wants to hunt somewhere else that's fine, but not in front of me.

As I sat on the porch with Cat on my lap, I wanted to write a poem about the swirling snow, the quality of the light, and the birds black against the white; but I didn't want to move, and now the poem's gone.

I wonder if the people who told me there's no wind in winter actually believe it. This afternoon it howled down the beach to smite my cabin. I've always liked the wind, but now I often feel it's out to get me. In the cabin, I felt under attack, so I went to the point. Cat came along, and it was nice to have his company. Facing the wind and driving snow, I could see gusts writhing over the sea toward me, and heeded the warning to crouch and brace myself for the onslaught. I felt fine to be there — not anxious or threatened as I do in the cabin. There I go to meet the wind and can leave when I wish. Here I can do nothing but wait.

I sense that this deep anxiety is existential angst I project onto the wind. I feel threatened and want the security of certainty and safety even though I know it's an illusion. There is a potentially real danger hidden in this anxiety: in longing to be freed from fear, I might decide to "face it" and take the boat out into a storm. I might be projecting my anxiety onto the wind, but the wind does exist as a real physical force in the world.

In just three weeks the sun will start back to me. Winter solstice has never meant so much. If I didn't "know" the sun would return, I'd probably be terrified to see it disappear further into the north each day.

NO ENTRY FOR JUNE 2, 2001

JUNE 3, 2001

EVENING: 36°F. Grey and windy, sea churning. Winter wasted no time getting down to business, but last night the sky cleared and a nearly full moon shone on sea and snow. I had hopes for good weather today, but it's socked in tight. I got out the last of my winter clothes, and as I did a Simon and Garfunkel song drifted into my mind. I can't remember the name, but one of the verses is, "Then I'm laying out my winter clothes/And wishing I was gone/Going home/Where the New York City winters/Are not bleeding me/Leading me/Going home."

Today is Sunday. Yesterday, I looked forward to staying warm and relaxed by the fire all day, with no physical or psychological work to do. But today, without the strong stimuli to the senses I have outside, the hours stretch long and empty. I've been awake for nine hours and have another seven or eight until I can sleep again. I miss Cat and guess he's out on the porch missing me, too. I look out the misted window and see a grey world where now and then sunshine slants over the hills, until grey settles in again. Snow swirls by blocking the light and is gone, until it comes again. I could meditate and will tomorrow, but that's a disciplined activity, and for a long time I've looked forward to leisure.

I feel exhausted, as though I haven't stopped to really rest in years, because this sense of emptiness would overtake and swamp me. Each time I settle down somewhere, these feelings of unhappy meaninglessness arise, and off I go to escape them. Now there's nowhere to run, nowhere to hide, nothing to do. I've chosen these leisure hours to explore the feelings. It's not that I don't want to do things, but I'm tired of my activity being driven and joyless.

I guess I'll do something with the fire. It's getting chilly in here and dark out there. I'll bake bread and bathe, and then hang with the long heavy hours, as they stretch for months ahead of me.

JUNE 4, 2001

1:30 AM: One-day-shy-of-full-moon light pours onto untrodden snow. A black line on the beach marks where the recent high tide ended and the snow begins. To the west, the Staines rock face glows from within. Nearby, the sea is shining, too, and out further another dark line — analogue to the tide line here — marks where the wind riffle begins. Occasional cat's-paws skitter across the moonlit water.

Tonight Cat is asleep in his box, but last night he was out with me until late. Together we watched the black-and-white geese — phantoms in moonlight and shadow — feed on the low-tide rocks. Again and again, he began to stalk and I would softly call, "NO, NO, NO!" until I thought to simply call him to me. He's good about coming, and once on my lap, he traded the pleasure of two birds on the rock for a scratch under his chin.

Last night, too, I was gently released into the drift of the world, and sensed myself to be a manifestation of the One. Why do I resist this opening so? It feels — beforehand — like negation, like death, but once caught in the flow, there is the joy of belonging to and participating in the whole. Yesterday, I wrote about heavy hours of emptiness, and just a while later went outside and felt myself float free. I often feel such darkness and despair before release. It's just where I feel most fragile and vulnerable that the walls of my ego are weakest and can most easily dissolve. Just in the spaces I try to avoid. Just there.

Any self, no matter how healthy, is inherently unsatisfactory because it's cut off from the true pulse of living. But it should be possible to feel relatively good in this small I without becoming isolated inside. It seems twisted that the only reason I seek freedom is because it's unbearable in here. Once I float free, I feel "perfect" just the way I am, as all things are perfect, yet inside this small self I suffer. Is this suffering the path to freedom and so perfect, too, as the old Christian mystics claimed, and as it sometimes seems to me?

Sharing this experience of freedom with others is the only really worthwhile social contribution I can make. But not everyone will choose the solitary path I'm following. There needs to be a way people can work with what's already happening in their lives. Perhaps I can encourage others, if I ever learn myself, to welcome the darkness, difficulty, and fear. So far, I don't know how to find even my own way home, never mind showing the way to anyone else.

I spent most of today just being with the world and with myself in it. Then in the afternoon I felt a dark ominous *presence*, and tingled with fear as it approached. The fear was not my usual anxiety, but deeper and not associated with anything physical. I took refuge in the Buddha, in my Sangha, and in Christ — the light I sense within. Will this darkness come for me? Is it madness?

JUNE 5, 2001

MIDNIGHT: A breeze blows from the southeast, and the full moon is buried in falling snow. It's been a day of productive activity. I was up at 9:30 to a clear cold morning. Some light chop from the southeast, the cold temperature direction, ruffled an otherwise calm sea. A good day for fishing and fetching firewood. I had coffee and a dab of cold rice and beans, then forgot to eat again until tonight. I shoveled snow from the boat and went to Staines. It was slow and took work, but I have fish for most of a week now.

As I cruised the shore looking for wood, I spotted three sea lions on a ledge four feet above the water. Except for a pup tucked into a nook, they all dove in as I approached. I circled but not close enough to harass them. Perhaps they'll establish a colony there. I found a log on a gravel beach so smooth that I didn't even need to change from rubber boots to chest waders to cut and load the rounds.

It's definitely winter now. Low overcast sky, and everything covered in ice and snow. As I motored along, something seemed seriously out of whack, but I couldn't figure out what. Then I got it. The only other place I've spent time in inflatable boats was the warm sunny blue-water Caribbean, wearing a bathing suit and teaching scuba diving. So it seems odd to be bundled up in this snowy world. I felt that this is no place to be doing what I'm doing this time of year; then remembered there are guys in three-quarter-inch-thick wet suits diving for sea urchins not so far away.

JUNE 6, 2001

MIDNIGHT: It's been a day of harmonious rhythms. This morning, three eagles landed in the half-dead tree on the far side of my small cove. Trippy-looking birds: black crown; yellow-orange beak and throat; dark breast with a white fleck pattern; yellow legs and feet. One was young with immature plumage and had the disheveled look of a shag hairdo. Birds seem to like that tree. The kingfisher hangs out there, and hawks perch in the branches, too.

The eagles looked like they were hunting, but when one of the adults flew down to the beach, the small local birds continued to feed only three feet away. The adults eventually flew off, leaving the young one behind, and I heard them croaking from the other side of the trees — then silence. The fledgling was edgy and kept peeping and hopping from branch to branch until it finally flew off after its folks.

I timed the tide just right, and fetching a load of wood was quick and easy. The trip home presented no problem, even though a breeze blew up from the south, pushing a swell and some chop before it.

While building a fire in the evening, I thought about describing in the journal my sense of the day's easy rhythms. At that point, the fire was behaving well, and I planned to include that in the activities that had gone smoothly. Then when I added more wood, poof, the fire went out. I had to rebuild it almost from scratch, but even that went smoothly, and instead of fretting I made popcorn while I waited for the fire to take off. Something else to include as an example of the day's mellowness. But when I started to eat the popcorn, it tasted funny, and I realized I'd squirted ketchup all over it instead of hot sauce. I ate it anyway.

When I got home from cutting wood, I decided to take a vacation from pain and downed a Tylenol 3. I seem to have two distinct mind-sets about pain. When I'm focused inwardly, I can more openly experience and accept pain. That dissolves much of the tension. But when I'm trying to accomplish something in the external world, pain is in the way, and I just want it to disappear.

I've been reading Krishnamurti. He's a powerfully clear thinker and writer. "Suffering is the process of isolation." Bam. He also says obsession comes from imagining that our lives can be different from how they are, and so we don't accept the actual as it is right now. I've known that for thirty years, but still struggle against the simple truth that *things are what they are and not what I'd like them to be.* Apparently, my resistance to accepting things as they are is one of the things that are what they are. Jeez, that sentence gives me a headache.

JUNE 7, 2001

10:30 pm: 41°F today, a heat wave. I even saw a couple of blackflies. The rain barrel almost filled overnight. I had planned to go for wood today, but the sea started to move from the northwest in the morning, and there were white-caps by noon. I'm slowly getting a sense of the weather, and when the wind comes from the northwest it's apt to continue for days. I finally built the small outer porch today. I'm pretty much out of lumber, so I'll probably use rounds cut from a large log for steps.

Krishnamurti is stern and uncompromising, and very good at pointing out traps. I feel like a weekend spiritual dabbler when I read him. I've been here for four months, and my awareness of my inner processes is still dim and dull. I know that clutching after desired psychological/spiritual experiences is futile, yet I still grasp. I imagine I'll give it up when I finally get at gut level the painful futility of it.

JUNE 8, 2001

1 AM: 40°F and stormy. I've been sleeping on and off since 7 PM. Avoidance mode. Shoulder and back are tight and sore. I want to take a Tylenol 3 and drift off, but I'm not sure I will.

I finished the awning over the small front porch today. Sitting out there gives a whole new perspective on the world. Once I'd finished it, I felt relaxed for a little while, and then the deep discontent returned. Cycling between intense joy and intense anxiety or sorrow wears me out. Not sure what I can do, except stay with it until the cycles modulate.

In *Pedagogy of the Oppressed*, Freire writes that we can be fully human only in dialogue, in naming the world together. To do so requires humility, honesty, and openness. It's not my world or yours that's true, but *our* world that we discover/create together. This is the direction I need to move in my life. Away from pride and fierce self-sufficiency toward humility and communion. I started the book because I've had it on my list for so long. I didn't expect it to be particularly relevant to me here, but it's just what I need.

NO ENTRY FOR JUNE 9, 2001

JUNE 10, 2001

2:30 AM: 32°F. Gentle night. Clear, but softly so rather than crystalline. A wide ring circles the moon, and sea lions and seabirds are calling. In here, my heart is crying. It's been a hard two days of physical and psychoemotional pain.

Today was Sunday, my day of rest. Only I didn't. I cleared moisture from the propane regulator, cut the top off a tree too close to the rain gauge, cleaned windows, and buried garbage. Then, since the afternoon was sunny and calm,

I ran over to Staines. Halfway across, the motor started to miss, but the problem fixed itself. Three nice snapper.

Tonight, when I got out the mirror for my weekly shave, I looked into my face and eyes, and felt sorrow and compassion for the hurt I saw there. Anger and rebellion hid a boy longing for his father's approval, but receiving only harsh criticism. No wonder I'm a perfectionist — always hoping that if I do things well enough I'll finally feel loved and accepted. So much of my activity is driven by pain: if I can just do it right, I won't hurt anymore. The trap is that it works — temporarily. For a short time I do feel better, but then self-criticism sets in again and I need to accomplish something else — perfectly.

Sitting under the moon tonight, I briefly sensed that what I'm going through here is not to teach me how to get rid of pain, but to teach me to open my heart to myself in pain. Pain is part of life, and if I don't open myself to experience it, I can't be truly *alive*. Nor can I open myself to others because that would risk experiencing their pain. And God knows I've got enough of my own I'm trying to escape.

JUNE 11, 2001

MIDNIGHT: 41°F. A few stars show through the high thin overcast; the sea is from the south but calming now at low tide. This morning, there was no wind and only a light frost on the ground. It wasn't cold enough to freeze the sea, so I packed the survival kit for a trip to the bay where I'd originally planned to build my camp.

The pale winter sun hung low in the north as I left camp. Mountains loomed against the grey sky, and the sea was flat calm. I expected to make the fourteen-mile trip in just over an hour, but halfway there a breeze blew up from the south and started to chop the water. It wasn't bad, but I had to slow to ease the jarring. Soon, though, things turned foul as the wind picked up and shifted to the southeast. But I'd never seen really nasty weather come from that direction, so I kept going. Then the wind got mean, and I again considered turning back. But still didn't.

A dark line of wind-blown water, awash in whitecaps, streaked across the channel toward me. Oh shit. It looked much worse than what I was already in, and I was pretty sure I didn't want to be where I was. Just before the squall hit, I moved from my butt on the seat to my knees on the floor to lower my physical — and spiritual — center of gravity. The channel doglegged, and the wind now struck broadside. Steep and breaking waves caught the boat from the side and caused it to lift and tilt at a sharp angle. The wind whipped up streaks of foam, driving it into my face. I worried the boat might flip.

I decided I really should turn back, even though I was only two miles from the bay. Once I was moving with the wind and waves, the storm didn't seem so bad, and I knew I'd be unhappy if I gave up. So I turned toward the bay again. A ribbon of pale blue stretched low over the southern hills and I hoped the worst had passed, but the wind dug in to rage again. I was drenched with spray and thinking I should probably be wearing the life vest, but couldn't let go of the tiller to put it on. Finally, I ran into the protected bay.

I often find it hard to let go of what might have been and stay with what actually is. I'd hoped the bay would not seem as beautiful as the island where I'm settled, but that hope was forlorn. The bay lies in a bowl of hills, over which a condor soared. And while there isn't a view of wild mountain peaks, the smaller closer crests are lovely, too. Another lesson is that I must simply choose to be with what *is* rather than use a sort of inverted "grass is always greener" mind-set to rationalize that what I don't have isn't so good anyway.

I drifted in the still water for a while, then put on the life vest, said good-bye to the bay, and edged back into the raging storm. I was now crashing directly into the teeth of the wind and waves, but before I even made the channel, I hit a patch of drifting kelp and fouled the prop. Damn it! A nearby rock offered enough protection to clear the prop, and then out I went.

Holy mother, it was nasty out there — the kind of sea I've often watched from my island and thought, "I'm sure glad I'm not out in that" — but the boat and motor handled it well. Once in the channel with the sea on my rear quarter, the boat started to surf. I usually sit far forward to balance the outboard's weight, but now, to prevent the nose from digging in, I shifted to the rear.

In moving back, I accidentally jerked the kill-cord attached to my wrist and switched off the motor. (The cord's job, if I ever fall overboard, is to kill the motor so the boat won't keep going without me. It would still be nasty in the cold water and difficult to heave myself back into the boat, but at least I'd have a chance.) This wasn't good. I was close to shore with wind and waves driving me toward the jagged rocks. I reattached the cord and yanked the starter rope, but the motor had jammed in gear. Things were getting dicey. I reached over the side to jiggle the prop, and once free, the motor cranked up and I escaped.

Ten minutes later the sea was glassy calm again with just a gentle swell rolling the surface. Huh? Did I dream all that? No, I'm wearing the life vest, and in spite of being covered head to toe in rubber, I'm wet and cold. Behind me I see the sea still wind-whipped and churned with whitecaps. The ribbon of blue still stretches over the southern hills. I wish Cat could tell me if it stormed here at the island.

MIDNIGHT: Fried potatoes and bacon for dinner. I still have four days of fish in the larder, but decided to vary the menu. My usual meals continue to be beans and rice or fish and rice for lunch/dinner and oatmeal for breakfast, with instant soup and noodles thrown into the menu from time to time.

The solar panels won't see much sun for the next month and a half, so I've switched to propane to hoard electricity for the computer and satphone. The propane lamp is noisy, but not as noisy as the wind generator. There's been no rain to speak of in days. The mud in front of the porch where I pee and toss dish and fish-cleaning water is starting to smell rank. I'm finally tired of slogging through the mud holes and may take the boat to look for gravel soon.

It was a quiet afternoon. I spent time with sea, mountains, and myself. I'm seldom here when it's calm, and I relaxed and bathed in the beauty of it all. How joyful if I could see such beauty in myself and in other people. I asked Spirit to guide me, and the reply came back, "What do you think is happening, moron?" A softer voice reminded me to trust the process.

Later, the eastern face of Staines was shadowed, but rich yellow light shone on the highest domes from the setting sun beyond. The peaks and ice fields of the Andes glowed gold, and one leg of a rainbow, pointing nearly straight up, hung in the air. The northwest sky, translucent, almost glacial blue, was streaked an impossible orange, and below, just over the hills, were delicate whorls of cream-yellow cloud, the color of the ducks' breasts.

As night fell, I sat on the porch contemplating the world inside and out. Yes, beauty inside, too — of consciousness and visions and . . . I sat peacefully there with Cat until I came in to build a fire and take a nap.

I woke feeling grumpy and groggy, went to fetch some potatoes, and Cat got right underfoot. As usual, it made me furious. I often seem to feel "bad" after a spell of feeling "good." Almost like coming down off a drug high. I first noticed it in Vancouver last year, driving home from meditation. Instead of having patience, I'd get instantly angry at other drivers who were in my way.

In *Nature, Man and Woman*, Watts talks about feeling "blah" after sex, and points out that it's not the ecstasy of sex that creates this reaction, but grasping for that ecstasy. Perhaps it's the same here. I'm so hungry for joyful experiences that I cling to them and feel disgruntled when they pass. I also catch myself turning away from joy, believing it's not to be trusted since it won't last. It's useful to write about this since I hadn't seen it clearly before.

Pedagogy is displeasing me. Too black and white. Too Marxist dialectic. Freire also makes absolutist statements, comparing men to animals, and of course animals are just unconscious dumb brutes with automatic behavior. How can he *know* that with such certainty?

JUNE 13, 2001

MIDNIGHT: Starry and perfectly still, with just an occasional rustle of water against the rock. It's been a slow, steady day. Little by little, I'm relaxing (at least for the moment) into how things are. There is peace and inner light. I still long for the sense of wild aliveness I felt so strongly during my first long retreat, of being inside my life looking around rather than outside looking in, but it will come when it comes — or not...

I woke at first light and got up to exercise, make coffee, and watch the dawn. Then went to spend the day at the point. Four sea lions swam by, and an otter appeared below me in the kelp. I got out the binoculars and we peered at each other for a while. Actually, I think he snorted and sniffed more than looked. Maybe his eyes aren't so hot.

I also saw two new birds. An elegant hawk, colored café-con-leche brown with lighter flecks, landed on my beach. Tossing fish heads down there to attract raptors is a good idea. I spotted woodpeckers (Magellanic Woodpecker) for the first time, too. Either one male and two females, or one adult female with two young. All were black or gunmetal blue with topknots, and one had a brilliant red head. Their call was wonderful, but now I can't remember it.

I've often said with pride that I believe in God/Spirit sometimes. That is, I directly experience a Presence sometimes, and when I don't, I no longer know if there is or is not God. Since direct experience is transient, I've thought that people who expound their constant certainty that God exists don't actually *experience* the Presence, but base their claim on only a conceptual belief.

But I wonder... Jean Piaget showed that in a child, object permanence is a stage of cognitive development. Before it's established, a child thinks that a ball hidden out of sight no longer exists. Once object permanence is achieved, the child *knows* the ball continues to exist, even if she doesn't actually see it at the moment. Maybe this is so for spiritual development, too. Perhaps I'm just immature, and when I don't have a direct experience of Presence it no longer exists for me. Perhaps when I develop more, I'll have a sure sense that Spirit always exists, even if I don't sense it at the moment.

Yes, I remember now. Without the direct lived acceptance of death, I cannot feel truly *alive*. Death is part of life, but the ego/conceptual self creates an illusory sense of permanence and invulnerability. If I wish to dissolve the shell, I must accept what the ego tries to deny. Pain, too, is part of life. Period. No exceptions.

What a blessing today was. I can only offer praise and thanks.

NO ENTRY FOR JUNE 14, 2001

MIDNIGHT: I was just getting started on the day when I heard a motor. At first I tried to figure out what it really was, since I often hear sounds I think are a motor that turn out to be a hummingbird, bumblebee, boiling kettle, or waterfall. But this really was a motor. A boat appeared and stopped just past the point. I thought it was fishermen and went out to ask them to please go away. Two men walked down the beach toward my cabin, one carrying a box.

Ah, it's German from the National Parks Service; I bet they brought my barometer. Sure enough. As they approached, German held up the box, as though it were a talisman to ward off danger, and called out that he had brought the barometer. I think they suspected that after four months out here alone, I might have gone dangerously insane. While the Chilean mail service may be slow (Patti mailed the barometer to me in Punta Arenas a month before I left there), the door-to-door service is impeccable.

The men were curious to see my camp, and I invited them in for coffee and a look around. They liked the cabin and suggested I leave it standing when I depart, so there will be refuge here; but I'm not sure I will. It would be much easier not to tear it down and nice for others to benefit from my work, but I doubt it would last long. Soon the tarp would rot and scatter in the wind. As much as possible, I want to leave the island like it was when I arrived.

They showed me a kind of tree with red wood that burns easily even when green, and said that if I run short of driftwood, I can use some of it. I've been careful to cut as few living trees as possible, and was surprised that they suggested it. I showed them the wood that had worked so well for kindling before I ran out, and they confirmed that it's cypress, so I'll look for more soon. Useful information.

When I told them about the outboards being submerged, they asked if I would like them to take the flywheel off the 15 hp to check the electronics underneath. Since it's working ok, I decided to leave well enough alone. Hope that wasn't a mistake. They might pass twenty miles west of here again in six weeks, and if I need supplies, they'll bring them to me. I'm glad to have the barometer. It should help me predict stormy weather. German said it will be calm like this for the next two months, and I do feel a change in the air.

I enjoyed their company for a little while, and was glad they left when they did. Their visit reminded me of my first long wilderness retreat in Canada. I'd been alone for two months on a remote lake, when I was startled to hear an outboard. Skittish as a wild animal, I scurried to hide in the trees. I felt so shy and estranged from other humans that I couldn't face talking to them. I hoped they would pass by, but they saw my canoe and came in for a visit. They called "Hello," but I remained crouched behind a fallen log, thinking they would leave. They called and called until I finally came out of hiding. We visited for a few minutes, but I could barely talk, and soon they went away and left me alone again.

JUNE 16, 2001

11:30 PM: The grey sky sagged lower and lower all day, until the mist touched the water and my world shrank. Then I felt truly alone. Back, neck, and shoulders are stiff and sore, and my head is filled with noisy conversation. This morning I brought in half a dozen large flat rocks to lean around the stove. They should absorb heat and modulate the temperature. Later on, I moved the solar panels as far as I could from the tree line. I hope they'll collect at least enough juice to power the laptop for journaling.

NO ENTRY FOR JUNE 17, 2001

JUNE 18, 2001

NIGHT: I can't remember if I wrote yesterday or not; I'm losing track of time. It was misty in the early morning and then sunny all day. I spent most of the day just being at the point and letting myself flow with the world in acceptance and peace. I'm somehow reluctant to describe these experiences of release and freedom, but I've written a lot about the painful experiences of holding on and self-judgment. Such writing from pain is motivated by an urge to escape and by my desire to understand the source of the suffering. When there is joy, I feel less need to write about it.

Today warmed to a languorous 45°F. So far, June has been pretty mellow; not nearly as grim as I'd expected. If it doesn't rain soon, I'll take the boat to fetch water. I've had the generator hooked up all day, and there's just enough wind that it's humming without howling. Yesterday, the solar panels in their new location had direct sun for more than six hours, and I'm back to using electric light.

NO ENTRY FOR JUNE 19, 2001

MIDNIGHT: Rain and wind. This afternoon I crossed the channel. The sea was choppy and the fishing slow. When I tried to come home, the outboard wouldn't start. I checked the fuel filter and poured gas into the spark-plug holes; still nothing. As evening shadows from the towering Staines cliffs darkened the water around me, I gave up on the 15 hp and tried to start the backup motor, but it wouldn't kick over either. Anxiously, I kept tinkering, finally got it running, and headed back across the channel. It was a slow uncertain ride through the chop, but the small motor chugged along until just thirty feet shy of the island. Then it quit, too. Unbelievable. I tinkered some more in the gathering dark, and barely managed to limp into camp.

When I landed on the beach, Cat jumped into the boat to say hello. He wasn't near the fish so I didn't pay much attention to him. Then he cried out and I realized he had a fishhook in his mouth. I've been careful to always remove the bait from the hooks to avoid just this. But today, distracted by motor problems, I forgot. Happily, only the point pierced his lip. It would have been ugly if he'd swallowed the hook or buried the barb in his tongue.

I suspect both motors have electrical rather than fuel problems. If I'm lucky, the 15 hp might just need new plugs. I think the 4 hp is running on only one cylinder. Hard to believe that spark plugs and a carburetor kit are the only spare parts I brought for it. I'd hoped I wouldn't need to use it at all.

I probably have enough firewood if I'm careful, and it might be time to stay close to home for a while. Of course I'll probably feel differently if I can get the motors running again. Or I could email the parks service and ask German to bring spare parts and a socket wrench next time they pass near here. It would break my solitude, but if I can't coax the motors to run, it might be worth it.

What a relief to have made it back to camp. I could easily be stranded on the rocks across the channel or drifting downwind in the dark rain somewhere on the water. This alone makes it worth having and repairing the 4 hp. I'm lucky this happened not too far from camp on a semicalm day. The boat probably would have been thrown onto the rocks if the motors had failed in the windstorm last week.

Winter solstice. Tomorrow the sun starts back to me.

NO ENTRY FOR JUNE 22, 2001

JUNE 23, 2001

EVENING: As I suspected, the 4 hp is missing spark in one of the plugs. The 15 hp has spark in both plugs, and when I poured gas into the cylinders it fired up. So it looks like a problem with fuel, not spark. I hope it's just a clogged jet in the carburetor. I'm not in a hurry to fix either motor. I'm tired of dealing with machinery.

As I listened to the enchanting sounds of water flowing through me today, I realized how inviting they are as a path out of my static mechanistic consciousness. They are always subtly changing, and if I relax and follow them as the days and weeks go by, water sounds can guide me back to the living universe. I sense that emotions are part of the field of Life here. Like the physical movement of wind and water, the behavior of the animals, and my own activity, the emotions I experience are a manifestation of our common existence.

Yesterday morning the cove and basin were frozen. I sat for a long time listening to the ice groaning and creaking as the tide pushed it onto the rocks. In the afternoon I took the kayak fishing, but no bites. At first I anchored just west of here, but — since I was in the path of ice being carried by a powerful tidal current flooding through the basin — I quickly realized it wasn't such a good idea. So I hauled up the anchor rock, drifted out into the channel, and let the world flow through me.

I again like *Pedagogy of the Oppressed*, but in his writing Freire doesn't seem to practice what he preaches. He insists on the absolute need for leaders and educators to enter into dialogue "with the people" rather than "filling the people" with what the educators think is the truth — which would be brainwashing. But he doesn't approach his reader with the same open dialogical spirit. Instead, he lays out how education must proceed.

Ideologically he's a Marxist and asserts that dialogue with Elite Oppressors is impossible. He defines social reality as grounded in struggle rather than in mutual understanding. He points out the illusion of the myths Oppressors foist on the Oppressed — one being that Reality is given and unchanging — yet in defining social reality as a struggle between concrete classes, he does the same kind of mythologizing. I've never met anyone who is simply an oppressor or completely oppressed. We are all a complex mix of both.

The oppressor/oppressed schema is sometimes applied to inner life, where the ego tries to oppress the whole human being. Perhaps dialogue with the ego is impossible and instead it must be resisted or destroyed, but I tend to think this approach is mistaken. Rather than fighting the ego, my path lies toward balance and integration.

SUNDAY MIDNIGHT: The rain has poured steadily for thirty hours and has washed the stench from the mud out front. There was an inch in the gauge this morning and more today. The rain barrel is long since full. It warmed up 10 degrees and all the ice melted. Tonight the wind is roaring. First time it's blown like this in weeks, and I didn't expect it again until September. I hope the solar panels are ok. They're completely exposed where they are now. I anchored them securely, but I may walk down and check in a while. Depends what the tide is doing. It's hard to get there at high tide, especially in the dark.

I spent the day reading *Right Ho, Jeeves* and escaping into food and sleep. It's not that I'm unwilling to experience dark emotions and physical pain; I just get worn out with it. I'm feeling again the absence of clear insight and sense of *wild aliveness* I experienced during my first wilderness retreat. I keep trying to let the memory go, but it's difficult. Apparently, I've signed up for a crash course in humility, patience, faith, and compassion — for self and others. This evening, as is my habit on Sundays, I made bread, sponge-bathed, and shaved. My tooth is getting looser and I continue to rinse it with saltwater and peroxide. It's not especially painful, but I worry that problems lie ahead.

In a dream last night, a naked man was acting berserk. Several other men held long sticks with loops on their ends that were around the wild man's neck. He was screaming, struggling, and trying to attack the surrounding men, who were holding him away from each other. Another man, without a stick, kept darting in, attempting to do something to the wild man, who tried to punch and kick him. Finally he managed to remove some sort of insect or spider from the wild man's neck that was giving him an extremely painful bite and making him crazy. The wild man calmed down and started to cry.

This is what's happening to me here. Something painful is attached to me and is being removed, and I'm fighting against the process because of the pain and my ignorance of what's actually taking place.

MIDNIGHT: 41°F. Stormy day, with rain and wind almost as strong as the worst storms of summer. Last night the panels were fine, but today the wind has been much stronger so I went back to the point and lashed them even more securely. It was a challenge to work down there without getting blown into the sea.

Cat did something quite civilized yesterday. He gave his "I gotta shit" meow and went down to the low-tide water edge to do so. Very nice.

JUNE 26, 2001

12:30 AM: I taped the sound of rain today, and also taped myself singing. My voice sounds pretty good to me as I sing, but the recording sounded awful. I guess my vocal cords are rusty from long disuse.

I spent most of the day meditating and reading *Flow* by Mihaly Csik-szentmihalyi. He claims that *flow* arises from setting a goal and focusing full attention on achieving it. For me, that kind of engagement is ego-centered; the deeper experience of surrender, choiceless awareness, and nonaction in the moment is Life-centered.

I've been looking again at my ambivalence about whether I should work on "improving" myself or abandon the self to go into the beyond. In my mulling and indecision, I do neither. I doubt it must be either/or. It can be both: when in small mind, work there; when in Big Mind, flow there.

I've also been mulling over whether to ask Patti to send down replacement parts for the outboards. Do I want to break solitude and pay German to bring them to me from Puerto Natales? I could take a chance on the motors (assuming I get them running), but it would be a major drag to have them fail and leave me stranded away from camp. Just a few days ago I was settling down to stay put here on the island, then in *Flow* I read a quote from a mountain climber about meeting a challenge. Instantly my restless mind, which wants to feel competent and adventurous, was snorting and raring to go exploring.

Out came the marine charts, and I looked at the route to the glacier I want to visit. If I do go, it won't be for at least a couple of months; the days are too short and cold now. I need to be careful of how much attention and energy I spend on the trips I might make. Unless I have serious problems, I'll be gone from here for ten days at most. And I expect to be here for another two hundred days. If I let worry about ten days out of two hundred fill my thoughts, I'm a doofus for sure.

JUNE 27, 2001

MIDNIGHT: Cold rain and wind on and off all day, and a glorious double rainbow in the afternoon. I sanded and adjusted the points on the 4 hp, and got spark in both plugs. I'm not ecstatic about it since the motor *was* working perfectly — until it wasn't anymore. Still, if it continues to spark, it's a good thing. It's been a peaceful day. Feels like I'm slowly settling into solitude.

Flow seems to be a sort of peak experience, but it's apparently different from experiences reported by mystics. In *flow*, the self (Csikszentmihalyi uses the term self-concept) is still in charge, but you are not aware of it since you are so focused on the task at hand. The *flow* experience actually strengthens the self, while in Eastern spiritual practice you either abandon the illusory ego-self for the true Self, or discover there is no real self.

Flow is activity-based (including mental and aesthetic activity). When you have the appropriate skills, and you focus deeply on the goal you've set yourself, *flow* can develop. Many of my activities here *flow*, but such self-directed activity can also mask the deeper experience that sometimes emerges when my mind and body are still. In those times, I become aware of the universal flow to which I always already belong.

In meditation, peak experiences are not sought (of course I'm doing just that) but fully embraced and released as part of the flow of living. In *flow* they are an end unto themselves. Csikszentmihalyi uses reading and sports as examples of *flow*, but Krishnamurti states that reading is often an escape from facing the world as it is, and Buddhist meditation teacher Joseph Goldstein writes that losing yourself in an activity such as sports does not lead to spiritual growth. Csikszentmihalyi recognizes that the experience of *flow* can become addictive. I know. I've lived much of my life chasing the experience of *wild aliveness*.

> Sitting
> bundled up
> eyes closed,
> I feel Cat's weight
> pressing down
> through his paws.
> The rain has stopped for now.
>
> I hear
> water surge
> against rock,
> and wind slide
> through the trees.
> The far faint stutter
> of a woodpecker
> cuts me like a knife.
> The rain has stopped for now.

1:00 AM: Calm and almost balmy. It's been a strange day. Everything seemed to go wrong. I kept dropping things and stumbling, and then fell out of the chair while getting up. Not a hard fall, but just, "What the hell?" Dropping things and losing patience stems, at least in part, from pain, which sometimes overwhelms me.

I removed the carburetor from the 15 hp to clean it, and in doing so I carelessly broke the plastic cover. I didn't get as freaked as I would have expected, just as I didn't get too happy yesterday when the 4 hp sparked in both plugs. I sure hope I can fix it. I may also email Patti and ask her to send me some stuff.

Still reading *Flow*. I'm used to exploring and reading about a whole range of "nonordinary" experiences that, as an academic psychologist, Csikszentmihalyi seems to lump into a single category he calls *flow*. Most Western psychology has a rather limited view of consciousness: awake, asleep, dreaming, psychosis, *flow*.

Csikszentmihalyi claims *flow* is enjoyable because it orders consciousness, which is what religious activity used to do. But, he says, we no longer expect *flow* experiences to link us with the gods. Seems to me he's selling us pretty short. Spiritual experience may not link us with the gods, but it does meld us with the universe and with Spirit. Or rather, in these states we can become aware of the unity we have always been part of. It's extremely limiting to assume that *flow*-type experience is only about ordering the consciousness of the individual self to generate a dollop of enjoyment.

Is there a self or not? Tonight, it doesn't matter; presence or absence doesn't change the quality of the struggle to be free. And once I relax into the flow of Life, it also seems irrelevant, because the apparent self is at ease with all around it. The self may be illusory or not, but it's counterproductive to fret about it either way.

Tonight I sat listening to the sounds of water, and then focused on just one cluster of gurgles coming from a crack in the rock. With closed eyes I saw patterns of light and circles, somehow linked to the sounds. Little by little I feel the world and myself coming *alive* again. And once again I sense that the mechanistic laws of science have no direct link to the Life of the world, which is profoundly and mysteriously spontaneous. Yet those laws are also a manifestation of Life since they have been imagined by our minds.

I feel less fragmented now than I did twenty-five years ago during my first wilderness retreat. Then, human and nonhuman seemed radically at odds and I could find no place for myself. I was human, but felt I belonged to nature and not the human world.

As I sat on a rock by the sea, I wondered: Did consciousness arise via evolution with the development of the human brain and culture, or is it inherent in the universe? For me, the question cannot be answered logically, but only experientially — like the question, Does God exist? There is no right or wrong answer that can be proved or disproved. I either experience the world as conscious or I don't.

Is consciousness inherently language-based? That query certainly is, but when I step back to notice the space of consciousness, I have no idea of the answer — and can see no way to find out. As soon as I frame the question, I'm in language and carry the answer with me.

Such speculation seems trivial to me at the moment. What's important is whether my mind is swamped by and identified with the incessant chatter of rehearsing the past and planning the future, or I quiet my mind and float in the sounds, smells, feelings, and thoughts of the immediate present in all its shifting dimensionality. Because yes, that experience is beyond language.

NO ENTRY FOR JUNE 29, 2001

JUNE 30, 2001

11:00 PM: 36°F. Rain and wind. On the bluff on the other side of my cove, I've discovered a deep notch in a cypress, which, according to the tree's growth rings, was cut roughly thirty-three years ago. Perhaps it was a marker-blaze for something. It faces the sea and would have been visible from a long way out. Surprising to find it here after all these months. I wonder if people have been all through this country and no matter where I'd set up camp I would have found human sign. Someday someone may find my tracks here, too.

I repaired the plastic top of the carburetor. A couple of careless minutes required hours of repair work. I Krazy Glued the break, melted small holes on either side with a hot needle, and lashed the break with dental floss. Over that, I laminated a metal patch with Shoe Goo. I think it will hold, but plastic is strange stuff and difficult to repair.

Sitting outside last night, watching moonlight on the Staines rock face, I was quiet and still on the inside, too. Ah. The world truly is mysterious when I'm fully open to it. After just these few glimpses of flowing Life, I feel more relaxed and patient about letting solitude have its way with me at its own pace. I imagine this patience will also pass.

What is the relationship between conceptual theory and the flowing present? For me, the more aligned they seem, the more I'm living in a conceptual construct and experiencing the world as a collection of static objects, rather than as a living organism. But I seldom realize I'm not feeling truly *alive* in a *living* world — unless I pause to remember that experience and realize I've lost it.

I emailed Patti a couple of days ago and asked her to buy and send outboard parts and several other items, but I'm still not sure I want German to bring them to me. I might not need the parts, and it could be another way to hold myself on the surface of this experience. The two-hour visit wouldn't be a problem, but looking ahead to it could be a major distraction.

I'm still reading *Flow*. Csikszentmihalyi uses the concept of *flow* to explain the whole human experience. In some sense he's talking about escapism. He shows how to organize the mind so as to not experience the darker feelings of life, such as fear and doubt. He uses the example of Icelanders huddled in their shelters using storytelling to structure their consciousness so as not to dwell on the fierce winter wind outside. Here, I'm trying to allow myself to experience the wind and the fear. In that willing embrace, there is freedom.

Buddhist meditation is also a structured activity done for its own sake: it has the goal of sitting still and staying present to what is actually happening; there is feedback in noticing if you are actually present; it is about cultivating attention. But it is not about imposing an artificial structure on the mind or shutting out unpleasant experience. Sometimes single-pointed concentration is encouraged, but in the long run, the intention is to bring stability to the context of the mind — to awareness — rather than to the content.

Csikszentmihalyi seems to believe that consciousness is chaotic until we control it. He counsels imposing an artificially structured *flow* on the mind, instead of relaxing into the mind's living rhythm. He advocates excluding the dark side of life, but I think he's actually excluding the whole living world.

I need to be careful not to natter about abstract notions, but to stick with my actual experience. Deep peace and harmony seem to arise when I surrender to the flow of the world, not when I'm analyzing it or staying busy to shut it out.

INTERLUDE

A GLANCE AT OTHER SOLITARIES

*I would rather sit on a pumpkin and have it all to myself,
than be crowded on a velvet cushion.*

— HENRY DAVID THOREAU

My explorations benefit from a long tradition of writing about solitude, although most of what has been available until now is not about deep wilderness solitude. Here I would like to glance briefly at a few other solitaries to see what the differences and commonalities between our solitudes might be.

IMAGINARY SOLITARIES

Two imaginary solitaries, Robinson Crusoe and FedEx systems engineer Chuck Noland — played by Tom Hanks in the film *Cast Away* — are interesting examples. My circumstance was fundamentally different from theirs in that I went into solitude intentionally, knowing I could leave again at the end of a year; they were thrust into isolation and came to believe they would be stuck there for the rest of their lives. My reaction to each of their stories is distinct.

When I translate the Christian terminology of *Robinson Crusoe* into my own hybrid Buddhist/Christian/naturalistic idiom, I can recognize much of my own inner experience there. I find it intriguing that author Daniel Defoe had such profound insight into the spiritual transformations that occur in wilderness solitude — even though he, himself, apparently did not spend extended periods away from other people.

During his time alone, Crusoe settles more and more deeply into relationship with God, and in this sometimes painful transformation, he frees himself from the limiting perspective of his social identity. This is most clearly evident in his perception (from a hiding place) of the cannibals who occasionally come to the island to slaughter and feast on other humans they have brought along for the purpose. At first, Crusoe is disgusted with their pagan savagery and can think only of killing them in turn. Then, as he examines his own value system from the perspective gained in solitude, he recognizes that they are not evil but simply doing what is natural in their culture. He, on the other hand, by judging them and wishing to kill them, is committing an evil act — by his own Christian standards. It is this transformation of consciousness — the surrender of the culturally indoctrinated self as sole arbiter of right and wrong — that Defoe portrays so well in various ways. (I understand I've just opened a cultural relativism can of worms, but I won't dig into it here.)

In his book *In Search of Robinson Crusoe*, written in 2002, Tim Severin investigates some sources of information and inspiration that might have been available to Defoe when he wrote *Robinson Crusoe* in 1719. Severin also tracks down several living individuals who have experienced being shipwrecked. Strangely, Severin does not discuss the psychological or spiritual experiences of the marooned people he interviews. This strikes me as remarkable considering how important such aspects of experience were for Crusoe. What is going on? When Defoe wrote *Robinson Crusoe*, did the inner experiences of a castaway seem as strange and intriguing as the physical? Was there a more general interest in the spiritual/psychological aspects of life then than there is today?

I was disappointed with the film *Cast Away*. It seems to me that the filmmakers didn't really know what they were talking about. They simply portrayed our current cultural fantasy of what being alone must be like. The story begins, and ends, with a man alienated from, and struggling against, the nonhuman world.

Noland spent four years alone on a tiny tropical island, and during that time it never seemed to occur to him that he was embedded in a *living* world. His consciousness was cloistered from the world around him by the mind-set that intimate engagement is possible only with another human being. Instead of finding his way through this cultural conditioning to develop a relationship with the trees, sea, and sky, with his own inner depths and with Spirit, he created a surrogate human from a volleyball. Sigh.

He never surrendered himself to *living* fully in the actual present, but remained emotionally centered on his memories and imaginings. The film doesn't question this mind-set or hint at the possibility of meditation practice or nature mysticism, even given the recent flourishing of such practices in the West. Noland did lose the outward trappings of civilization, but he remained a man *against* nature — even though we in the audience were brought into relationship *with* nature via wonderful cinematography.

Although both these characters expanded their worldview, both also remained culturally bound to some extent: one by Christian dogma, the other by a belief in the all-encompassing value of human relationship. However, Crusoe's inner transformation seems more profound. Perhaps the authors of each story focused on breaking free from what they perceived to be the most limiting aspect of their culture: Crusoe from a self-centered life, Noland from a frantic obsession with time.

ACTUAL SOLITARIES

In the writings of actual people who have taken themselves voluntarily into solitude, I find a mix of various motives: spiritual quest; love of nature; preference for living alone; the challenge of achieving a goal. Generally, seeking absolute wilderness solitude involves some degree of meeting a challenge. At times, a whiff of heroism slips into the writings of such individuals as they overcome almost impossible odds to finally achieve some goal — which may then permanently transform their lives. During my first long retreat into wilderness solitude when I was twenty-eight, I felt certain my life had been healed once and for all, but I now doubt that such peak experiences ever endure. They seem, instead, to be part of the ongoing flow of our living.

Solitaries vary in their focus of attention: inward and/or outward. The Christian Desert Fathers exemplified solitaries who seek solitude primarily to surrender themselves and come into relationship with God. For secular seekers, the "Something Greater" may be physical Nature rather than nonmaterial Spirit, but it is still perceived as sacred. Solitaries Chris Czajkowski and Richard Proenneke, on the other hand, scarcely mention their inner life. Czajkowski built a log cabin in a remote area of British Columbia's Chilcotin wilderness and lived there alone for part of each of ten years. Proenneke built a log cabin and lived alone in the Alaskan wilderness for over thirty years. Yet the scope of their writing (in Czajkowski's *Nuk Tessli* and Proenneke's *One Man's Wilderness*, with Sam Keith) embraces only the external world — for which both have a profound appreciation — and, occasionally, emotional tone. It is unclear whether they are troubled by introspection.

An extreme example of a solitary refusing to explore his inner world is found in *Bold Man of the Sea: My Epic Journey* by Jim Shekhdar and Edward Griffiths. Shekhdar considers loneliness and depression to be his enemies and speaks of girding himself in his battle against them. He sees all inward looking as dangerous and probably pointless. He claims he was too busy during his nine-month solo ocean voyage to indulge in such frivolous activity, but in fact did everything he could to keep his mind on the surface of things. He played as many as fifty games of electronic solitaire a day, constantly listened to whatever commercial or shortwave radio programs he could tune in, called his family at least three times a week via satellite telephone, sent numerous emails, and worked out a business plan on his laptop. All of these activities were in addition to the basic survival tasks of maintaining himself and his boat as he rowed and drifted across the Pacific.

Shekhdar claims to have been disappointed to not directly experience the existence of God, but how could he? He kept his mind so full of trivial activity there was little possibility to notice God's presence. Yet still, from his description, changes took place during his trip — even if unbeknownst to him. His connection with nature deepened and softened somewhat. Necessarily, being in a small boat at sea, he surrendered his demand to be in control of everything. His perception of and relationship with a shark that followed him became less aggressive as he began to consider matters from *her* point of view.

Surprisingly, the solitaries I've read who did not go into solitude specifically in search of the sacred didn't seem to prepare themselves psychologically or spiritually. Even those on an inward, as well as an outward, journey devoted little time and attention to inner preparation. Perhaps this is why some had such difficulty dealing with the psychological and emotional stress they had to face. For instance, Kevin Patterson sailed solo from the South Pacific to Vancouver, and Alvah Simon sailed his boat to the far north of Canada just west of Greenland, froze himself in intentionally, and wintered there alone; both spent considerable time in introspection, but neither writes about meditation practice or other spiritual training.

This is, I believe, a reflection of how we fragment our lives — or at least our writing: we are either physical adventurers or spiritual seekers, but seldom integrate these different aspects of ourselves. Before my first long retreat into wilderness solitude I, too, did not prepare for the inner turmoil I would face, and I nearly went insane as a consequence. Until we acknowledge our interior life and the value of psychological and spiritual training, we will remain unprepared to journey inward with equanimity. For me, Shekhdar's account exemplifies how much we lose when we avoid looking within.

EXISTENTIAL TERROR

Existential terror, usually repressed or at least muted in the social milieu, can sometimes fill the solitary mind. Father Henri Nouwen (for quotes by Nouwen, see the Interlude "The Urge to Be Alone," page 203) uses Christian vernacular to exquisitely describe the terror of nothingness and the dissolution of the self. In solitude, I see more clearly how we use social relationships as mirrors to maintain personal identity; through our interactions we hold each other's persona in place. I have an idea of who I am — a conceptual identity — and in subtle ways invite and manipulate others to treat me as this persona needs to be treated to survive. In solitude, without this constant mirroring, the persona can begin to unravel. Believing we actually are our persona, we may feel like we are literally going to physically die. Hence the terror. This has been my experience, and I believe the process is common to many.

I see three possible responses to this unraveling: embrace it, avoid it, or go mad. If we have some understanding of what is happening and the desire to seek a deeper center of ourselves than the shifting sand of our persona, we might make the effort to stay with the terror, loneliness, doubt, and despair until our ego-self dissolves into Something Greater. Then there can be self-acceptance and peace. It is as if a carpet is being pulled from beneath our feet and we feel we are falling into the void. If we remain quiet and alert, we discover there is a solid floor (or rather, the *living* Earth) beneath the carpet. Even though there is no static solidity, doubt and insecurity disappear and we feel cradled and cared for. But this is possible only once we surrender the idea of who we think we are. Individuals on a spiritual quest may go into solitude exactly because it is an intense catalyst for such transformation.

Avoidance has many forms. Commonly, when terror and loneliness wash over us and we fear being swept away, we avert our attention by keeping ourselves busy with activity or some other escape, such as reading or television, food or narcotics, or other people. It's tempting to say that anyone who does not struggle with existential terror is in some sort of avoidance mode, but this may not be fair. I can know only that this is so for me. Solitaries Admiral Richard Byrd, Simon, and Patterson write about their psychological struggles, but Thoreau, Czajkowski, and Proenneke barely mention inner turmoil.

It's clear, though, that some solitaries, either because they don't experience the loneliness and terror or because they accept and transform it, feel at ease with themselves and express little desire to leave their life in solitude. Others come up to that dark place and do not allow themselves to embrace it — naked and alone. They escape their solitude one way or another. After a long eventful trip, Patterson called to be towed to shore rather than stay with his longing for other people for even one more day, and so sail in on his own. Simon and Byrd leaned heavily on their radios for companionship, and claim it was the endless winter dark of their low-latitude locations that was impossible to bear alone. Still, many spiritual seekers have walled themselves up alone in caves for years. Byrd was, apparently, seriously delusional and possibly close to death from carbon monoxide poisoning; it's intriguing to wonder how much of his suffering was due to poisoning and how much to natural psychological disorientation. Shekhdar, determined to reach his goal of being the first to row solo across the Pacific, hung on and waited for the wind and current to carry him to his destination — some three months after he had expected to arrive. Indeed, setting the record was apparently the only thing that made the journey worthwhile for him. He did not consider spending time alone to be a valuable experience in and of itself.

I've found commonalities among the experiences of solitaries as well. Patience seems to develop with the growing realization that we are not in charge of the world. Civilization is designed to buffer and to help us avoid facing the uncertainty of life. In wilderness solitude the illusion of control quickly drops away as we are confronted with our need to adapt to the world around us.

Solitaries have a tendency to anthropomorphize and describe the nonhuman world in metaphorical language. This is especially evident in some of Thoreau's writing. When I attribute thoughts, emotions, or intentionality to the world around me, I do it in a self-reflexive way, often with tongue in cheek. I'm not claiming I actually know what animals, or the wind, think or feel, but in solitude the visceral experience can be intense and magical — at times terrifying. And, if I can't logically claim to know the thoughts and feelings of animals, neither can I dismiss such intuitive identification. Perhaps in solitude I become more sensitive to connections usually invisible to our city-dulled senses. I simply don't know. In any case, personalizing animals and elemental forces seems to happen naturally in solitude.

A third, and for me vital, commonality all solitaries seem to share is the experience of feeling vibrantly, often ecstatically, *alive* in a *living* world. In *Walden*, Thoreau flatly states, "There is nothing inorganic."[1] Years later, in *Alone*, Byrd wrote, "There came over me, too powerfully to be denied, that exalted sense of identification — of oneness — with the outer world which is partly mystical but also certainty. . . . There were moments when I felt more *alive* [emphasis his] than at any other time in my life."[2] It is unclear from Shekhdar's writing whether he consciously experienced this sense of vibrant *aliveness*, but then he seemed intent on avoiding being psychologically alone with himself. Even so, I detect in his descriptions of sea, sky, and fish a deepening sense of feeling at home with the nonhuman world.

What beckons to my imagination are the solitaries we know nothing about; those who do not write or speak of their experience; those who fully shift their center of being from human culture to Something Else. What of Lao Tzu after he wrote the *Tao Te Ching* for the gatekeeper and then disappeared over the pass and into the mountains beyond? What of the silent ones who never wrote anything?

JULY 2001

Life is a mystery to be lived,
not a problem to be solved.

— ADRIAN VAN KAAM, REMINDER TAPED TO MY CABIN DOOR

NO ENTRY FOR JULY 1, 2001

JULY 2, 2001

MIDNIGHT: I've been using cypress for kindling the last few days. What a difference; makes the stove much easier to light. Soon I'll paddle the kayak around the island to cut some more. Yesterday was a busy Sunday. I mended clothes and rain gear, started a wash, organized monthly food, sent and received a check-in email, and reinstalled the carburetor on the 15 hp outboard. The repair job seems to be holding.

This morning I tried to fire it up. Nothing. I checked the plugs and there's no spark. I emailed Patti asking her to consult her local outboard mechanic for advice and to purchase the parts they recommend. I also asked her to buy a bunch of electrical items and some other things. I'm very fortunate to have her out there to do these things for me. She's perhaps the only person who I feel not only understands me, but deeply cares.

The 4 hp is running fine again — at least for now. If I can't get the 15 hp running, I won't be able to use the boat for the next seven months except for very short trips with the 4 hp. Technology is anchoring me to my social reality and identity. Mystics simplify their lives for good reason, and if I do another long wilderness retreat, so will I.

Just the other day I was berating myself for wanting to have so much firewood stockpiled. Now I'm glad to have as much as I do. I need to learn to

133

trust myself more, and also to think more clearly about perfectionism. It's not that I should do sloppy work, but only let go of harsh self-criticism. In believing that whatever I do isn't good enough, I destroy the joy of accomplishment and sap my creative energy.

Cat had another seizure today. Very strange. It must be even stranger for him. He's so spaced-out afterward. Tried to claw up my leg as if I were a tree. I freaked and knocked him down. Mostly, though, I was patient and comforting. He loses all sense of identity for a while, but seems to reorient himself in a couple of hours. It reminds me to be careful as I explore the depths of my mind beyond my own identity.

NO ENTRY FOR JULY 3, 2001

JULY 4, 2001

LATE NIGHT: I'm losing the urge to write again. Yesterday I emailed Alejandra, who works for the national parks. What a huge help she's been. She thinks there won't be a problem getting German to bring supplies, probably in August.

I've put the clock away to see if I can relax my grip on time. Losing that structure triggers anxiety. Yikes, what if I just drift away...? In counterpoint, I'm also going to be more formal in morning meditation: I'll sit for forty minutes with the intent to not move during that period. Then I'll send people, plants, and animals loving thoughts for a while. Including exercise, sweeping the cabin, and drinking coffee, the routine takes about three hours. I worry I'll lose this discipline when I leave solitude. It isn't easy in the social world to begin each day with that much personal work.

I continue to read *Flow* and continue to cycle between agreeing and disagreeing when he advocates controlling the content of the mind to exclude unwanted experience. In meditation I work with the space in which experience arises: learning to be with whatever happens without becoming overwhelmed. The chaos/psychic entropy Csikszentmihalyi believes is inherent to the mind is actually created by the separate self's desire to maintain its identity by excluding whatever it imagines as threatening or painful. It's like shining a flashlight in the forest at night and imagining monsters in the dark just beyond the reach of the beam. The only way to really deal with the fear is to turn off the light and realize the monsters are projections of our own imagination. If we always maintain control of our experience, there's no opportunity for the new and unexpected — for Life — to enter.

Here alone, I argue with Csikszentmihalyi about the need to stop the endless mental activity and allow the mind to settle and experience whatever comes into it. Then I realize I'm doing just what I'm telling him we should not do: filling my mind with activity. I'm really arguing with myself to understand what I think and feel.

I'm trying to let go and trust something greater than my small self to pull me to it. But what if that something is evil, not benign? It requires discipline and integrity to remain open to whatever arises, without being swept into darkness.

Today was slow and easy. Now I'm off to sit under the moon, and I imagine Cat will go with me. He usually sits on my lap for an hour or two a day. I get tired of him sometimes, but feel he needs the contact — as, perhaps, do I.

NO ENTRY FOR JULY 5, 2001

JULY 6, 2001

LATE NIGHT: A strong wind from the southeast is pounding the sea on the beach. The cabin trembles in the gusting blasts. I snuck away from Cat to sit alone on the rocks and feel the wind's energy more directly. With this wind, he wants to be on top of me, and I wanted some space for myself.

I found a loose wire in the 15 hp outboard yesterday, and once I tightened the connection, both plugs sparked. The motor started, but wouldn't keep running. Still seems like a fuel problem. The 4 hp was also hard to start today. Arghhh. Technology.

The sea was flat calm all day. No hint of stormy weather coming — at least not to my senses. I took the chain saw and paddled to the north side of the island. Felled a mostly dead cypress and brought back a dozen rounds. At one point the saw got stuck and I buggered my shoulder, yet again, by impatiently yanking it free. I wonder how long it will ache this time?

JULY 7, 2001

LATE NIGHT: 36°F. Just the remnant of a breeze; moon and stars are shining on snowy Staines, as a swell crumples softly on the low-tide beach. It's been a good technology day. I drained the laptop battery, which has been taking only a half charge lately. I thought the battery might be dying, but now it's charged right up again. I cleaned the chimney, and tonight it's dripping creosote like crazy, which stinks up the cabin.

I finally got the 15 hp running reasonably well. It's still a little rough and misses at high speed, but it is running. Not sure what the problem was. I opened the charts to check the route to the glacier, again. It looks to be about eighty miles each way. With good weather I might make it in a day, but more likely it would take two there and two back. If a storm slams in, who knows how long I might be stuck out there somewhere?

I was feeling good about getting the 15 hp to run, and then started to feel anxious again. *Flow* recommends staying occupied with goal-oriented activity in order to harmoniously structure consciousness. But that's exactly what I don't want to do. I want to go deeper and feel at peace in stillness.

In meditation I stay with the anxiety, and awareness itself is what establishes harmony. The price of psychological, as well as political, freedom truly is eternal vigilance. For some reason, I resent the constant attention that's required. But attention is also needed in the physical world to split wood, run the boat, or catch fish. So why do I believe internal harmony should happen automatically without conscious awareness? Perhaps because in our culture we're not taught to pay attention to our internal world in the same way we pay attention to the outer one.

Finished *Flow*, and, finally, I liked it. In the last two chapters Csikszent-mihalyi goes somewhat beyond the individual ego. The book is good in discussing interactions between individual and world, which is where meditation has less practical advice to offer.

JULY 8, 2001

I often sit beside an all-day fire on Sundays, and this is a good day for it. The wind raged up from the south during the night, and by morning it was driving spray and waves onto the beach. My tarp-walled cabin is shaking as if caught in a very long earthquake, or as if a train were passing right next door. This is by far the worst buffeting I've taken. Feeling too tightly bound inside, I step onto the porch to shake myself free from the tendrils of anxiety that reach for me from dark depths.

Condor! Sweeping low down the wind toward me. Entranced, I watch as he circles and climbs the updraft overhead. When he banks to turn, I see his back looks white but for a delicate black line on spine and splayed fingers of up-curved wing tips. Calligraphy painting a poem of grace across the sky.

I watch him float light as a feather in the roaring wind. What is this feeling that soars with him through the empty spaces of my heart? I watch and watch as he glides the wind stream, then — huge wings arcing into a hollow curve — flaps twice and is gone. I'm left staggered on earth, clutching a tree for support.

LATE NIGHT: Clear blue and sunny all day with a light breeze from the south. I went to lizard at the point. It's been a long while since I've had the chance to sit in direct sunlight, and I've missed it. I decided to go fishing, should the motors still be working. The 15 hp started rough, but smoothed out when it warmed up. The 4 hp wouldn't start at all. Grrrrr. I took off the cover, and the poorly designed choke linkage wasn't engaged. Once choked, it started fine.

I get angry dealing with the outboards. I don't know much about mechanics, am usually uncertain what the problem might be, and doubt my ability to fix it. Then, after I do everything I think I should do and it still doesn't run, I get furious and curse at the motor instead of calmly looking for the problem. My anxiety about the motors failing far from camp is probably out of proportion to the actual risk. Unless everything really screwed up at the same time, I don't think my survival would be threatened.

Tonight I caught myself thinking that I just can't stand any more demands on me. I felt totally exhausted from trying to fulfill expectations. Yet I'm alone here, and the demands are internal self-criticisms.

LATE NIGHT: Another cold beautiful day, but I didn't get to enjoy the sun much. Instead, I sat fishing in the shadow cast by the rock walls at Staines. I had to work for them but caught enough for four days. The motor cut out once, but otherwise ran fine. Hauling the boat up the beach is still hard on my shoulders.

I've started to read *Care of the Soul* by Thomas Moore and like it a lot. Moore was a Catholic monk for years before quitting to become a therapist. His approach is more spiritual than psychological: accept the mystery of life and explore and honor yourself just as you are. Very different from *Flow*, which — in its claim that *flow* is the best we can hope for — is seriously misleading.

Care of the Soul is catalyzing the sort of spacious self-acceptance I experienced twenty-five years ago on my first wilderness retreat. Moore clearly differentiates between cure and care. The goal of cure is to fix the self and be done with the problem. Care is a lifelong work. It's not about changing the self into an idealized socially normal person without hang-ups or problems, but about becoming more complex. The intent is not to get rid of or change anything, but to integrate all aspects of character — including the shadowy and painful. In this integration, all parts become acceptable and make sense:

then there is harmony. One of the joys and challenges of solitude is having the space to explore more and more of myself.

NO ENTRIES FOR JULY 11–12, 2001

JULY 13, 2001

LATE NIGHT: It snowed three inches overnight and this morning. Just enough to turn the world silent and white. Exquisite. Yesterday was clear with wind and waves coming straight onto the beach. I took the chair, warm clothes, thermos of coffee, and book, and paddled to the island just across the basin. I spent several hours on a flat, nonslippery rock that faces north, gets full sun, and is protected from the south wind. The water was rough in the basin, so I wore the life vest and was surprised at how safe I felt. Usually, I'm very aware that if I should go into the water with all my clothes and rain gear on, it would be very difficult to climb back into the kayak or swim to shore.

Last night I drifted into a sense of deep belonging and the awareness that I *am* the World. It's so easy to get lost in thinking about the experience, but when there is a moment of identity there's no mistaking it. More and more, I doubt whether there is any way to make such experience easily available to others. It just seems like a long, long journey, without set rules or regulations, into an unknown land. I can't imagine many people would want to follow such a pathless way. I've been at it for many years, and still have only rare moments of integration. Most of the time, I still experience the natural world as a mere backdrop to my individual activity.

I'm back where I was a month ago with the pain in my shoulders; using all my usual resources to try and ease the ache. Instead of firing up the chain saw to cut wood for the sweat today, I used the swede saw. The morning was too peaceful to disturb, and considering it's Friday the 13th, maybe it was a good thing. But I've apparently reinjured my shoulders.

A trip to the glacier has started to loom, bringing fear with it. Do I have to go? How will I feel if I don't go? Will the motor quit or the wind get ugly? Will I find places to camp along the way? Actually going or not going isn't the most important thing. Just watching my inner turmoil around the possibility is interesting and useful. I seem quite concerned about failure to face my fear.

I'm getting along better with Cat for the moment; trying to let him be who he is and not control him so much. If he wants to chase birds, so be it. I'm slowly waking up to the fact that he's part of the universe with his own existence, and I can learn a lot by listening to and watching him. An important step in learning to love him, the ducks, the trees and myself is to slow down and feel the world, rather than being so impatient to accomplish things.

I suspect the underlying dynamic for narcissism, perfectionism, and low self-esteem is the same. Different concepts to describe self-focus, isolation, and judgment. My intention with all this self-examination is to escape the narcissistic cycle and experience the world as vibrant and immediate. Jeez, what a twisted circular trap: focus on self because my experience is so self-focused. But in *Care of the Soul*, Moore claims I can love myself as a simple manifestation of the universe without being narcissistic. Such self-acceptance brings me back into direct contact with the universe as it manifests itself in me.

JULY 14, 2001

LATE NIGHT: 36°F. Two more inches of snow, clouds and wind from the northwest. I checked the email from Patti and sent her a reply. I'm still deciding on the supplies I'll ask German to bring.

I'm beginning to remember dreams for the first time since I arrived. Many are disturbing and I wonder what to do with them. For the moment I'm just letting them be without seriously trying to figure them out. I'm also starting to have sexual fantasies. I guess there's a bunch of stuff I've been keeping a lid on that's now coming up.

I saw a knockdown drag-out fight between the two pairs of nonflying butter-belly ducks today. They're very territorial, but until now their interactions have been vocalizations and ritualized posturing along the boundary line between their territories. Today the pair that lives around the island across the basin hammered one of the ones that live around this island. The lone one finally dove and disappeared. The other two patrolled a while and then swam off. A while later I saw a shape I didn't recognize. I put the glasses on it and it turned out to be the lone duck swimming very low in the water, head just above the surface, as though hiding. Earlier in the day the local pair came to drink the freshwater that seeps down the beach into the cove. Watching them, I realized I'm made from the same stuff and by the same processes they are. It brought tears to my eyes.

One reason meditation is so nice is that it's a simple spiritual practice: just pay attention. It does seem very impersonal at times, but perhaps there really is no need to deal with individual neurosis. Just leave it behind and move on.

NIGHT: Today I saw dolphins and an otter, and heard sea lions for the first time in weeks. I'd been thinking that maybe these critters had gone for the winter, but perhaps it is I who haven't been noticing.

Today is the third Sunday of the month and I sweat in the snow so I could join the circle at UBC. Halfway through the first round, I remembered that it's summer in Vancouver and they haven't been sweating since May. I had to laugh. Here I am, waking up early and dragging my sorry butt through the snow to honor my commitment to be with them when they sweat, and they're all lounging in bed. But some will be preparing for Sun Dance, and I can support them from here. What courage, especially those who tie themselves to the pole by piercing their chests and then tear their flesh to break free. I can barely imagine it. Even the thought of dancing for days without food or water frightens me.

Since February I've sent three spates of email: to request technical support for the electrical setup, for medical advice, and now for outboard parts and other supplies. In all three cases I think I've been seeking personal security by making things physically safe and controllable. If so, I've been confusing physical vulnerability with the need for spiritual surrender. I'm frightened of the powerful mysterious Presence I sense, even though I believe it's loving. The fear comes not from it, but from my ego freaking out over loss of control. Once the shift happens and I experience myself as part of something greater, there is wonder and peace, but beforehand it feels like impending death.

I complain about fear, but if it's true that we fear the unknown as a generic condition, then the path out of small self and into Life/Spirit must lead through fear. My feelings of anxiety seem to depend on how rigidly I build protective walls: the more open I am, the less threatening the Other seems.

I talk about the need to surrender, but the experience of feeling weak, vulnerable, and dependent brings up feelings of shame. The shame comes partly from our strong cultural ideal of autonomy and self-reliance, and partly from my own deep rebellion and pride. I don't want to be naked and ask for acceptance just as I am. Ah, but it's cold and lonely inside these walls.

NO ENTRIES FOR JULY 16–17, 2001

NIGHT: The temperature has been near freezing, and more snow has fallen. But last night was clear and I saw two shooting stars. Today I went to read in the sun and then worked on the 15 hp outboard, which is not running again. I worked for only a couple of hours, but I'm wiped out. In general, I'm doing much less daily work now than I did during the first six weeks here. I can force myself, but I don't have the energy to comfortably do much at all. Haven't felt like writing either.

These have been rough days psychospiritually. It's becoming clearer to me that I came here to transform my consciousness from this I/Bob Kull–centered experience to living in a collective decentered place where I'm part of the flow of the world. It's painful to feel I'm failing. When I leave here, I shouldn't say much to anyone about this year. Whatever I say will be a sort of lie since I'm only talking about the transformation, rather than actually *living* it.

This transformation has been my deepest goal for the past twenty-five years — since my first wilderness retreat, or even since I stopped doing LSD when I was twenty. I've given up so much for it: security, career, family. It's painful to feel that in some sense I've wasted my life. Of course, from another perspective, I've lived as I have because I've wanted adventure and not responsibility.

What makes it so hard is that after all these years and all this experience I still don't know how to break free of this small tight mind. It's ironic. The more I try, the less likely it is to happen — because it's the I/ego that's trying to break free, and that very trying actually reinforces the tightness. Yet the pain of being caught in the small I is what drives the urge to freedom. Once I slip out of the closed loop, I no longer feel the shame of failure; I'm content to just be. Of course from that open space, I haven't failed and I do have something to share.

At the point today, almost unnoticed, I drifted free. The same thing often seems to happen: I become exhausted, give up struggling, and relax. There must be an easier more sensible way to shift into that open space without so much trauma.

In terms of a method for bringing about this transformation, I'm as bewildered as I was twenty-five years ago. I read Ken Wilber and he makes the process of spiritual development seem straightforward. But in my journey, it seems like there are no clear signposts or procedures to move me in the direction I want to go. Everything I try keeps me stuck, and release comes only when I finally give it up. But when I try to consciously yield, that doesn't seem to work either, because there's always a small flicker of "looking over my own shoulder" to see if the capitulation is working. There's a sense of "doing it so that..." that is not true surrender, but negotiation.

When I'm more open, I realize that the success/failure dichotomy is a confusion of small mind. There is no absolute success or failure, just process and journeying. I won't leave here with any definite answers, but I will have something to share with others — even if only a warning against any set procedure that promises success!

Last night I sensed that the biological world that we lose by building a conceptual reality to buffer ourselves against uncertainty, suffering, and death is profound and meaningful. We've become trapped in our conceptualizations and cut off from the *living* world. Instead of trying to control Cat so much, I would do well to allow him to invite me into his world. I've been there before, and it can be frightening; but reentering that world is part of why I'm here.

This morning Cat jumped onto the food shelf where I insist he not go. I freaked and whacked him on the butt. He turned to stare at me and I smacked him on the side of the head. What instant anger when he thwarts *my* will! After a while I called and he reluctantly came and we sat together. He seems so forgiving, but who knows what damage I'm doing to our relationship? I would be ashamed for anyone to see me hit him that way.

I've noticed something recently. When I tell him to get down from my lap, I expect immediate action. When I don't get it, I assume he's willfully ignoring me. But if I get his attention first, then tell him to get down and wait a second or two, he usually does. It's as though it takes some time to process the information. I'm not sure if this is just the way cats are, or if his seizures have fried some circuits in his brain.

Enough. For not feeling like writing, I sure wrote a lot.

NO ENTRY FOR JULY 19, 2001

JULY 20, 2001

LATE NIGHT: Last night I got out the alarm clock and set it for 8 AM to be ready to go for firewood on the noon high tide. I've gotten so slow. I blink and an hour is gone. The outboard was cranky to start and ran badly until I fiddled with the low-speed fuel adjustment. After that it worked ok until I opened it up to full throttle on the way home; then it started to misfire. Amazingly, the repair manual describes exactly this symptom. It's probably the ignition module, which I can't do anything about until German brings the socket to remove the flywheel. It's nerve-racking to always wonder when I leave camp if the motor will crap out and leave me stranded somewhere.

I tried to be careful when hauling the boat up, but my shoulders are sore again. I should probably forget about wood for a long while, but can't afford to. I don't yet have a full supply, and once the constant winds return it will be much harder to bring in more rounds.

I saw two sea lions hauled out on the Staines rocks. They were big. Very, very big. Maybe that's why fishing has gone downhill. How many pounds of fish do they consume each day? I can understand why fishermen shoot them. Serious competition. Yesterday the redheaded woodpecker came by and landed on the wind generator's steel pipe tower. That threw him for a loop. I wondered if he would hammer it the way some Mexican woodpeckers hammer on metal billboards, but he just checked it out and flew away.

I'm reading *At Home in the Universe,* and it's a pleasant change from all the personal work. Stuart Kauffman seems to think he's made the profound discovery that life is at home in the universe. Well, of course we are; we're here. And if we're here, it's because, one way or another, the universe brought us forth and has sustained us.

He postulates that life arose spontaneously when enough different kinds of molecules gathered to build self-organizing, self-sustaining networks. This equates life with organisms. But if the whole universe is *alive,* he's missing the point. His notion seems analogous to the idea that given enough neurons in a network, consciousness arises spontaneously. This is still pure materialism and doesn't consider the possibility that consciousness is as fundamental to existence as matter.

The truly profound mystery is what any of this — including ourselves — is doing here. Why does the universe exist at all and why is it self-organizing? I think self-organization is a metaphysical rather than a scientific question. If you reject the idea of dualism and an external God, then the universe must be self-organizing. It's here and continues to exist. If you accept the notion of an external God, then God must be self-organizing.

I've also been reading Krishnamurti again. He's so extreme and absolute in his view. Everything is utterly this or utterly that. He talks about comparing what actually is to the myth of what we think should be, and says that this comparison is the source of most of our discontent, conflict, and confusion. The myth is pure illusion and has no reality at all. Wow. Social reformers like Paolo Freire would definitely disagree. They see the "should be" as most important, and the "what is" as grist for the mill of transformation.

Personal myth is a real risk. We tell stories about the past and forget that these stories are our own creations, built on selected aspects of experience.

The stories describe a self-identity we come to believe in: "I did this or I thought that." Once we believe the myth we've created to be literally true, we become — in our own mind — the character in the myth. Then the real problems begin. We must now live up to our expectations for this character based on what he or she has done in the past — what we have created him or her to have done. When who we actually are does not behave the way we've created the hero of our myth to behave, we feel like a failure.

I have expectations of what my current experience should be based on my first long wilderness retreat. But my memory of that retreat has been strongly colored by a story I later wrote about it. When writing the story I condensed and idealized the messy actuality into a more dramatic narrative. By now, I've come to take that idealization almost literally. This brings me grief since my current experience does not and cannot match that imaginary history. My task now is to be starkly honest and not mythologize this retreat.

JULY 21, 2001

LATE NIGHT: I notice different experiences when I step out of my small mind. Usually there is a sense of no-self, and I experience an open empty space within which there are sounds, feelings, and physical sensations (including this body). Things are simply happening. There is love for the world and for myself. Big mind. Peaceful and beautiful.

More rarely there is the sense of myself as other — as though seen from beyond — just a man in the world who belongs here as one being among many; all of us real and *alive* together. This experience is tenderly exquisite and what I long for.

NO ENTRY FOR JULY 22, 2001

JULY 23, 2001

NIGHT: 29°F. Two more glorious days. Since tomorrow is my birthday, I'll accept them as birthday gifts. Why not? I often take the wind as a personal affront, might as well claim the good days, too. Yesterday when I went for wood the chain saw misbehaved and finally quit completely. I finished cutting by hand with the swede saw. I'm glad to have more of the redwood German told me about when he was here. It burns hot and steady.

Back at camp Cat came running to meet me as usual. I don't know if all cats are as affectionate as this one, but he acts more like a dog than how I expect a cat to behave. Although I've named him Cat since he's the only one here, I usually call him Pup or Bud and think of him as the pup. He jumped onto the boat and I gave him some love before starting to unload. Then he went to check out the kayak that was tied alongside. He's not supposed to get onto the kayak since his claws could seriously damage the lightweight material of the inflation tubes. When I looked up he had his back paws still on the boat and his front ones on the kayak. I yelled, "No!" and he paused. Then the kayak drifted further from the boat and Cat was left hanging in midair… for just a moment before gravity helped him find his way down to the water. It was a classic spread eagle and funny, but I thought he might freeze and ran to scoop him out. No need. He instantly hoisted himself up and lit out for the cabin.

Poor Cat. He has thick fur and usually appears quite large, but soaking wet he was pretty scrawny. I zipped up after him to make sure he didn't go into his box and wet his bedding. I dried him off with my towel, which he didn't like much, but he acquiesced pretty calmly.

The rain barrel is so low that this morning I emptied three of the smaller food barrels and went to Staines to look for a stream. I followed the shore, stopping now and then to fish and listen for the sound of running water. It was so calm I didn't even need to anchor, but just drifted slowly along in the warm sun. A sea lion came by and hung around, swimming sleek and graceful in the clear water under the boat. Once she showed up, the fish quit biting, but I'd already caught six.

I finally found a small creek with an easy landing spot nearby. After I filled and loaded the barrels, I scootched upstream through some brush to where I heard water falling, and discovered a lovely grotto beneath the trees. Circling a rock that jutted up from the small pool, a collar of perfectly round half-inch spheres of ice had formed from the spray. They sparkled like a jewel necklace in the dim light. What a lovely gift.

Tomorrow I'll be 55. What does that mean? Headed toward 60, which sounds pretty scary. I look at my life and wonder what it's about. It seems to me that I am and have been living as if I have some goal in mind — but I don't know what it is. Perhaps it's an epigenetic journey whose destination I cannot know until I arrive. I wonder what I'll do when I leave here. I may keep wandering as I've done for so many years, but I'll need to make a living somehow. My physical adventures may be less extreme — or maybe not. Happy birthday to me!

JULY 24, 2001

LATE NIGHT: This has been one of the nicest birthdays I can remember. I woke to the trees and bushes covered with fresh sticky white. But the temperature has been above freezing, and all day I could hear the drip of melting snow. I've been doing just what I wanted: eating bread with honey, drinking coffee and some Scotch. I lit a fire in the early afternoon and have been inside and warm since then. Yum. Started to read *The Family Moskat* again — slowly — and it should last for many Sundays. I'll have fish for dinner and a bath after that.

This morning I sat on the porch and opened my gifts from Patti. She's such a sweetheart! Colored pencils and a small sketchbook. I drew a very rough sketch of the view from my porch. Too bad the pencil set doesn't have grey or silver — the most important colors here. She also gave me a yo-yo. What an apropos present. In Spanish, "Yo, Yo" means "I, I." If you focus excessively on the self, you will likely spend a lot of time going up and down....

Patti enclosed a note saying she hopes I'm finding my song here. As I read the note I started to cry and softly said, I hope so, too. It's been a long time that I haven't known my song. Painful to wander lost.

Nature also gave me a gift. I think it wonderful but I'm not sure everyone would agree. A hawk — perhaps a falcon — was perched in the dead tree on the far side of my cove. Suddenly, it lifted off, swooped over the sea, and just above the surface intercepted a small bird flying from the other direction; fwoop, snagged it midair in its talons and continued on its way. Fast, efficient, and very beautiful.

A while ago I cast an I Ching. I've intended to for some time, but haven't been sure what question to ask. In concrete situations the counsel I receive usually seems ambiguous, but for spiritual questions, my mind is often blown by the insight I find in the answers. Sometimes the hexagrams I cast seem mysteriously miraculous. Tonight was one of those times. Patti's birthday note catalyzed my question. I asked, "How can I find and live my heart song — deep meaning and fulfillment, peace, love, beauty, and *aliveness* — here on retreat and for the rest of my life?"

I cast the hexagram Holding Together. It's about community rather than individuality; waters flowing together in the sea. It's about being a leader, or, without that capacity, becoming a follower. It instructs the questioner to ask the Oracle whether or not he or she has the qualities needed to be a leader. I was tired by then, had lost concentration, and thought I would wait until tomorrow to ask whether I have those qualities. But something urged me to continue. This time I used coins instead of yarrow stalks because that method is quicker and less demanding.

I cast the same hexagram again, which, simply by chance, is extremely unlikely. The two results differed slightly because the second, instead of remaining stable, transformed from Holding Together to The Receptive, which is one of the two primary hexagrams: Creative/yang/male; Receptive/yin/female.

This hexagram is exactly to the point, since I'm struggling to shift from aggressive activity to acceptance and quietude. The commentary on the transformative line in Holding Together addresses the need for a leader to resist wooing or intimidation and to allow people to freely follow or to go their own way. If, someday, I do become a leader of some sort, I must stay true to myself and if others gather around, ok; if not, ok too.

One of the dangers with the I Ching is that it speaks in mythic terms, and I can easily start thinking of myself in those terms, too. Inflated ego. I can't deny that I have a strong character, but I also have self-doubt, fear, and a need for freedom. Perhaps I should swallow my pride and become a follower. The hexagram clearly states that going my own way as an independent is not a skillful path.

It's compelling to cast the same hexagram a second time. I have difficulty accepting that there is, or at least might be, a Something greater than me speaking through the hexagrams. Even with all that has happened here, I still tend to attribute such notions to projection. The I Ching is evidence — not proof — that there is something real beyond my own small self, and this is a good thing.

JULY 25, 2001

NIGHT: Washed clothes today. I don't much like doing it, but it feels good to have clean stuff to put on. I've switched to using homemade soap instead of detergent. Better for the environment and for my body, too. This way it doesn't matter if I've rinsed it all out.

JULY 26, 2001

NIGHT: 43°F. Calm and cloudy. The natives are restless tonight: dolphins splashing in the basin, and the bull sea lion bellowing across the channel. During morning meditation I heard the dolphins blowing and looked out to see them close by. One made a rare groaning noise, and I swear another blew bubbles. The snow is melting. I've enjoyed it, but I'm ready for it to be gone — until it snows again, if it does. So far, winter has been much nicer than the wind and bugs of summer.

I tried to start the chain saw today. Gas poured out the muffler. This, I presume, is not a good sign. I'm thankful it waited until I have most of the firewood I'll need. I also split wood this afternoon and that's all I did today, except my normal routine: meditate, exercise, sweep up, prepare food, and eat.

JULY 29, 2001

NIGHT: Every day it's getting harder to write; I just don't feel the urge. Today was Sunday, an empty day. I look forward to Sundays when I can read a novel and don't feel I must accomplish anything — not even meditate. But Sundays are probably the hardest day for me. Without structure or purpose, depression, doubt, and emptiness come rolling in. I feel like I've been wasting my life pursuing something, and I don't even know what it is. But I sense I will know when I find it. It's like fishing in rough water. There are lots of random tugs that might be bites, but when there actually is a bite, there's no mistaking it.

One premise in coming here was that our culture's pursuit of material possessions is not only destroying the environment but is also fundamentally futile. Material things cannot give us the satisfaction we seek, so we need to run ever faster, consume more and more, to stay ahead of the meaninglessness of our lives. I've claimed that when we shift out of the conceptual domain that we create and into the actual flow of Life, that experience — just in itself — is deeply meaningful and fulfilling. Yet in actuality, I seldom feel that way.

When physical and emotional pain rolls through, it feels somehow wrong. Buddhism teaches that suffering is inherent to living, but why should it be so? Even if, as the Buddha claimed, there is a way out, why should the journey be so difficult? The injustice enrages me; or rather, my own suffering does. I can be philosophical about someone else's suffering, but not my own. Self-centeredness is a dark aspect of my character, and I'm also seeing sadistic tendencies.

I don't think pain, loneliness, or emptiness, in themselves, are what really trouble me. What really troubles me is that they trouble me. If life is inherently worthwhile when we live it fully, then those experiences should also be valuable and welcome rather than rejected as unsatisfactory.

I've usually taken Krishnamurti's statement "Truth is a Pathless Land" to mean that conceptual theory cannot take us into the truth of our experience: each of us must find his or her own way home. But I'm slowly remembering that truth is not somewhere else that we must follow a path to reach. It is always right here in this moment, even though we're often blind to it. We don't have to go find truth; only open our ears, eyes, mind, and heart to what already surrounds and fills us.

Today it was 46°F, the warmest it's been in two months. A heat wave. The blackflies are out, the snow almost gone, and soon the winds will start again. I wonder if I'll go to the glacier before they become too strong, or if I'll go and get caught in a storm, or if I'll not go.

I built a fire and took a nap in the afternoon. I awoke feeling joyful. From a straitjacket of perfectionist self-judgment, I'd eased into the space of letting myself and everything else be just what we are. Often on Sundays I feel empty and lost most of the day, and then my experience opens into peace and harmony during the evening. I'm learning not to cling, but to let things be and then to pass away.

JULY 30, 2001

NIGHT: While eating breakfast, I heard a ruckus and looked out to see two male butter-belly ducks hammering each other. It looked like an aquatic cockfight. Flapping furiously, they rose to attack, first one on top and then the other. The females mostly just watched, but every now and then one would give her partner a rest and harass the other male, too. They never ganged up at the same time, though.

Until recently, the aggression and territorial defense has been symbolic. Maybe they're adjusting their boundaries. I'd like to be able to differentiate between the males and females, but I can't unless they're standing on shore together or two males are fighting. Neither partner seems to lead in swimming, landing, or diving. I think the one watching the fight made the honking sound I've associated with what I thought was the male.

Over at Staines today, fishing was excellent. I also cut rounds from a grove of redwood trees I found growing right on the beach. The outboard still misses if I crank it to full throttle. The left rear pontoon on the boat is losing air, but I don't want to patch it until the weather warms up. As I was adding air to it this morning, the foot pump broke. Then the other pump broke, too. Now I have two broken pumps to fix before I can use the boat again.

After I unloaded the wood, I decided to take Cat for a ride to see if he would be ok in the boat. He immediately climbed up onto the pontoon, and I immediately dragged him back down. It took a few times, but eventually he sat calmly on a life vest. If he's on the pontoon when I turn or the boat rocks, he might fall into the water. I can't say he really liked the trip, but he didn't freak out either. If I do go to the glacier I may take him with me. He'd probably rather be in the boat than here alone.

Last night I was considering the aphorism "Life is a Mystery to be lived,

not a problem to be solved." Do I really believe that? Do I want to surrender
and let Life live me? To be mysterious and free? If so, the problem to be solved
is how to shift from seeing my own life as a problem to experiencing it as a
mystery. But trying to solve the problem of learning to surrender at will is
another trap! The whole process of surrender is a mystery to be lived.

JULY 31, 2001

NIGHT: Winter is more than half over, and my time here is half over, too.
There are days when I think I might as well leave now, and other days when
I doubt I'll be ready to leave after the year. What a lot of energy I wasted
fearing winter. So far it's been much nicer than summer. More sun, less wind
and rain; only about 15 or 20 degrees colder.

A piece of the butter-belly puzzle fell in place today. A pair swam into the
basin, and something in their upright posture was different from what I'd seen
before. They glided casually along, looking around as though trying to appear like they belonged there. If they could have whistled, they would have.
Since all these ducks look the same to me, I didn't realize this wasn't the local
pair until I heard the locals sound a warning and saw them stalking the intruders. They, too, were swimming like I hadn't seen before. Low in the water
— crocodile eyes just showing — as though sneaking up. They dove and I
could see them swimming just beneath the surface. Up for air and down again,
then back up to attack. But the intruders spotted them coming and took off.
The locals chased them far out into the channel.

This all seemed pretty strange since the borderline interactions between
the ducks are usually visible and loud. Both pairs flap, call, and charge, but
break off while still about twenty meters apart — each pair in its own territory. Then I heard another warning call and saw the pair that holds the territory across the basin charge the pair that had just been chased by my local
guys. Huh? Three pairs? Ahhh, there is a new pair looking for a territory.

The territories of the two resident pairs are established, and their con-
frontations are largely symbolic to maintain the status quo. But this new pair
is being dealt with harshly to prevent them getting a foothold. That explains
the major fight yesterday and the sneak attack today. I wonder where the intruders came from. In my boat wanderings I don't recall seeing many of these
ducks. Is the whole area already covered with established territories, or is this
area of shallow kelp beds prime real estate? These ducks are fascinating. I
hope they mate and brood close by.

I'm more and more taken by light on water: soft shifting greys, whites, and pale greens. This afternoon, reflections from the sunset sky and shad-owed rock were exquisite. I watched as ripples from two directions created a crosshatch pattern that was broad and heavy close by, and became smaller and finer further away. The distance/texture relationship was beautiful. Like seeing boulders in a field diminish in size in the distance.

Tonight I decided to sit out on the rock at dusk, instead of later as I've been doing. I'm too drowsy later on. For a while, as dark set in and the moon lit sea and mountains, it all opened out into nameless color, shape, and move-ment. Softly, everything came *alive*. Yes, this is it. All of Existence together is *alive*. Experientially, a tree, a rock, a bird, is not *alive* because those things are conceptually created fragments, and concepts are not *alive*. The process of creating concepts is a *living* process, but the concepts themselves are nei-ther alive nor dead. Only the whole pulsating cosmos is *alive*.

INTERLUDE

DANCING IN THE HALLOWED HALLS

Existence is beyond the power of words
To define:
Terms may be used
But are none of them absolute.
In the beginning of heaven and earth there were no words,
Words came out of the womb of matter;
And whether a man dispassionately
Sees to the core of life
Or passionately
Sees the surface,
The core and the surface
Are essentially the same,
Words making them seem different
Only to express appearance.
If name be needed, wonder names them both:
From wonder into wonder
Existence opens.

—— LAO TZU

The world is not to be put in order, the world is order incarnate.
It is for us to put ourselves in unison with this order.

—— HENRY MILLER

One interesting, and at times disconcerting, aspect of this year in solitude is the strong academic component. During previous wilderness retreats I've been just a man exploring myself and my relationship with the world; this time, part of the context is earning a PhD. It's been a challenge to establish a personally meaningful relationship with the university and to present my research in a way that's academically acceptable. Here, I'll just touch on a few of the central ideas I've used to frame my work.

Previously, the only books I took into solitude were the I Ching and the spiritual teachings of Chuang Tsu. This time, many philosophical and psychological readings have influenced my thinking. At the beginning of my graduate studies, I approached academic reading as a requirement for earning a doctorate, but I slowly became fascinated by many of the ideas I encountered and began to realize that they are directly relevant to my life. Not only do they allow me to frame my explorations in academic terms, but they also help me make personal sense of my experience. They add a rich level of complexity and intellectual challenge to my solitary explorations.

At first, I believed I had to either accept or refute the ideas I was studying, as though they were true or false, right or wrong. Eventually I recognized that ideas are simply stories people tell to help them make sense of their world. Understanding this allows me to approach the work of other thinkers in a more relaxed and openhearted way: to take what makes sense and seems useful; to leave the rest or set it aside for later consideration.

My intellectual approach to philosophy is strictly pragmatic; I read and struggle with only those ideas that directly illuminate my experience of living. In my thinking and writing, as in my life, I don't feel obliged to be entirely consistent, and I sometimes embrace apparently contradictory perspectives. I see many such apparent contradictions as poles of false dichotomies. For example: mind/body; direct experience/conceptual thought; subjectivity/objectivity; religion/science; evolution/creationism. These are false dichotomies because they're not actually fractures in the world; they result from the conceptual categories we create to think about the world.

Intellectual activity can, though, distance me from the immediacy of the present moment. I have a lot of conceptual baggage to unpack when I step into the unknown. (Actually, whether we realize it or not, we all carry such baggage as a gift and a burden from our cultural heritage.) But the power of solitude sets these influences in perspective and allows me to again be just a man exploring myself and my relationship with the world.

SUCHNESS AND THE CONCEPTUAL MIND

In *The Experience of Insight: A Natural Unfolding*, meditation teacher Joseph Goldstein writes:

> The intellect is the thought-conceptual level of the mind. It can be trained, developed, and used; or it can be a hindrance. It depends how clearly we understand the thought process. If there's clear insight into its nature, it's not a hindrance at all. If we mistake the thoughts about things for the things themselves, it becomes an obstacle in that it

confuses concept with reality. But, in itself, the intellect is just another part of the entire mind-body process.[1]

This differentiation between conceptualization and the direct experience of the undefined Suchness of the world is found not only in Buddhist teaching, but in Western philosophy and psychology as well. Michael Polanyi writes:

> As observers or manipulators of experience we are guided by experience and pass through experience without experiencing it in itself. The conceptual framework by which we observe and manipulate things being present as a screen between ourselves and these things, their sights and sounds, and the smell and touch of them transpire but tenuously through the screen, which keeps us aloof from them. Contemplation dissolves the screen, stops our movement through experience and pours us straight into experience; we cease to handle things and become immersed in them. Contemplation has no ulterior intention or ulterior meaning; in it we cease to deal with things and become absorbed in the inherent quality of our experience, for its own sake.[2]

Abraham Maslow differentiates between abstract meaning and Suchness meaning, and sees them as complementary rather than mutually exclusive. Abstract, or conceptual, meaning is found in relating one experience to another; in creating a whole from the parts. Together, the whole and its parts have a meaning the individual parts did not have. Suchness meaning is immediate. The ultimate meaning of any experience is simply itself. There is no need to categorize or analyze. Maslow asks, "What is the meaning of a leaf, a fugue, a sunset, a flower, a person?" And he answers, "They 'mean' themselves, explain themselves, and prove themselves."[3]

A metaphor I sometimes use to describe the relationship between Suchness and concept is to imagine experiencing the world naively as a swirl of shifting form, color, and movement. In order to make sense of and add predictability to my experience, I begin to search for regularity and repeating patterns. Slowly I focus on the similarities and ignore the differences between the "things" I distinguish and wish to clump into groups that I might call cats or steamer ducks. I hold up a clear sheet of acetate in my mind and draw an outline around each of these things. This outline is the concept I (my culture) create to help organize my (our) experience. This is a useful process.

The problem develops when the acetate becomes opaque, and we can no longer see through it to the flowing Suchness beyond; when all we experience are the outlines that we, ourselves, have drawn. At this point, we're no longer experiencing the actuality of life, but only our own abstractions and ideas about those abstractions. We create such concepts of self, of other people, of everything. These constructs tend to be static and give a sense of solidity to the objects we've created. When — because everything in the physical world is always changing — the actuality no longer fits into these abstractions, there can be a painful sense of dislocation, and we more or less frequently, usually unconsciously, update our conceptualizations.

One of the intentions of meditation is to focus bare attention on our moment-by-moment experience of color, form, and movement, without trying to categorize, make sense of, or tell stories about it. Slowly, the conceptualizing mind, the intellect, begins to relax, and we can see both the impermanence of "reality" and our more permanent abstractions and thoughts about it.

But philosopher Ken Wilber, in *Sex, Ecology, Spirituality*, argues that making a sharp distinction between conceptual map and "real" territory is simplistic. He points out that what we experience beneath the layer of conceptual thinking is always already contextualized within a cultural matrix of meaning; it is not unconditioned "reality."

The conversation about concept and Reality is broad, evolving, and possibly endless. From my perspective, there's no need to complicate matters. I prefer to keep things simple and pragmatic. I actually experience a difference between thinking about something and experiencing it directly. As far as I can tell, all moments of experience include both of these activities. Conceptual reality is necessary if we are to function in the world, but if we get stuck there and no longer feel the world directly, life loses its joy.

WHAT DO I KNOW, AND HOW DO I USE MY KNOWLEDGE?

What we know has as much to do with how we study as what we study. A metaphor often used to describe education is that it's like building a tower one brick at a time. As each layer of knowledge is cemented into place, it forms the base for what comes next. But I feel more like an intellectual nomad, living in a ragged tent and wandering through a shifting intellectual landscape. The only facts and ideas I can remember are the ones I've most recently encountered — and those buried so deep in my mind they've become part of who I am.

Conceptual knowledge is often used to shield the mind from the unsettling experience of profound uncertainty; the uncertainty engendered by direct engagement with the world. But instead of building a self-enclosing fortress of knowledge, the intellect can be used to expand the space of awareness and enrich the experience of living. Conceptual knowledge isn't useless or bad, but it does tend to be self-referential, and we can easily mistake it for the world it describes.

In the university, clear rational thought is highly valued, and having a wealth of relevant "facts" at our fingertips is often vital to academic success. But modes of knowing other than intellectual are generally not cultivated. Emotion, body sensation, and spiritual insight tend to be overlooked or actively dismissed. Little official recognition is given to the appreciation of mystery and wonder.

THE MYTH OF SUBJECTIVITY AND OBJECTIVITY

During my academic studies, I embraced science and, for a time, believed what I was taught: science's mandate is to know the objectively "real" world as it exists apart from the mind of the scientist. Eventually, I was assured, science would develop a single universal all-encompassing theory of the universe.

Over time, I became less convinced of this, and it was a relief to find the writing of physicist-philosopher David Bohm, who argues that scientific theories are not objective descriptions or explanations of the world that should all somehow fit together. Instead, they each open a window and present a particular viewpoint. We don't imagine that some artist someday will paint the ultimate picture that completely captures the world. Each depiction is an interpretation that adds to the richness of our experience and understanding. Similarly, scientific theories do not directly describe the world; they are stories that describe what scientists experience when they engage with the world in precisely defined ways.

I also began to wrestle with the ideas of the Chilean biologists Humberto Maturana and Francisco Varela. Through their empirical studies in neuroscience, they came to realize that human beings do not have direct access to a supposed objective reality; each of us has a particular perspective dependent on physiology, culture, and personal history. We do not live in a universe, but in a multiverse.

There is no single god's-eye view that scientists, or anyone else, has access to. What we call objective reality is what we experience, or think we experience, in common. Because of this, Maturana and Varela argue that no one's reality is more valid than anyone else's, but some are preferable. We must each take personal responsibility for the world we prefer to live in and to behave in ways we believe will help create that world.

They do, though, clearly acknowledge that our realities arise through engagement with the external medium. While we cannot claim to know a strictly objective world, neither do we simply make up reality out of whole cloth. Varela writes:

> What we take to be objective is what can be turned from individual accounts into a body of regulated knowledge. This body of knowledge is

inescapably in part subjective, since it depends on individual observation and experience, and partly objective, since it is constrained and reg-
ulated by the empirical, natural phenomena.[4]

Instead of arguing about subjectivity and objectivity, a richer way of living is
to value as many aspects of the world as possible from multiple perspectives.
If we're willing to accept the world as deeply ambiguous, perhaps no single,
valid description is possible or desirable. This opens up a great deal of space
for exploration, without the need to negate any aspect of experience. The intent is not to prove that something is universally true, but to report an experience in a truthful way to see if it resonates with other observers.[5]

THE SPLIT BETWEEN SPIRIT AND SCIENCE

One difficult challenge for me has been learning how to integrate and justify
the integration of spiritual exploration with social science and academic study.
This challenge is most often resolved in our culture either by keeping these
two disciplines completely separate — as though they are incompatible and
might contaminate each other — or by equating spirituality with religion and
demanding that intellectual thought conform to religious dogma. Neither approach makes sense to me. If the mandate of science is to study the world,
and if the world includes spiritual experience, then we need to find a way for
science to study the inner as well as the outer world.

When I discovered Ken Wilber's integral model, I recognized it as a useful conceptual framework in which I could locate my own research.[6] While
the model is too rigidly structural to contain my actual life, it does help to organize my thinking — as long as I don't take it as a literal representation of
the world. Here I want to touch on two facets of Wilber's work that have been
particularly useful to me: his differentiation of kosmos and cosmos, and his
presentation of the evolution of consciousness.

One aspect of Wilber's model can be shorthanded as "Kosmos cannot be
reduced to cosmos." Kosmos refers to the full range of our physical, mental,
and spiritual experience. Cosmos is a subset of kosmos; it's the material aspect
of the world.

Natural science undertakes to explore, measure, and explain the physical
world, the cosmos. This is valid and vital, but science sometimes makes the
unwarranted claim that it can measure and grasp all that is real (the kosmos)
using the methodology of physical empiricism: that is, *everything really real can
be measured quantitatively*. But while all experience does have a physical component, purely physical explanations cannot account for all facets of experience (even though some scientists claim that eventually everything will be
reduced to and explained by physical laws).

This reductionist approach devalues or ignores those aspects of experience that cannot be observed with the physical senses. As a result, nonmaterial aspects of the world that cannot be measured — such as beauty, awe, and consciousness itself — lose substance and are neglected. Indeed, strict materialists deny the fundamental reality of nonmaterial consciousness; but this creates for them a nasty internal inconsistency because their own consciousness is making the claim that it, itself, is not real. This position seems seriously weird to me.

One of the subtle insights of solitude that's almost impossible to express in language is that spirit both transcends the physical and also dwells within the material world as the ground of all being. Spirit is neither separate from nor the same as physical form. In *Nature, Man and Woman*, spiritual philosopher Alan Watts uses a clear and simple image to describe this. He writes that spirit is the invisible inside of things and the material world is the outside. With the physical senses, you can never discover the inside. Pull apart an ecosystem and you find a collection of organisms. Dissect an organism and there are organs and cells. Spirit remains invisible inside the physical. Likewise, thought cannot grasp spirit. Spirit reveals itself to a quiet mind and heart.

Often, a hard line is drawn between spiritual intuition and scientific knowledge. Wilber argues that one way to heal this breach is for science to broaden the scope of its observations and recognize that there are different ways of knowing the different domains of experience: sensory observation for the physical realm; rational thought for the mental realm; meditation and contemplation for the spiritual realm.

He argues that all valid knowing (material, mental, and spiritual) can be grounded in some form of scientific inquiry. Such inquiry has three essential components: 1. An explicit practice or methodology: *If you want to learn about a particular aspect of the world, follow a specific procedure.* 2. Direct observation of data brought forth by the stated practice or method: *When I follow this procedure, I experience this.* 3. Communal confirmation or disconfirmation by other trained practitioners: *Is there commonality in our experiences, and if not, why not?*

Can such personal experiences as love, awe, and the felt presence of Spirit become public knowledge? Yes, but care is required. Since no collective observation is possible, my personal experience can become valid public knowledge only if I'm willing to openly discuss what I claim to observe in myself. Acceptance of my claim will be based on the community's assessment that I am truthfully reporting my inner experience, on the reasonableness of my claim, and on the consistency of my behavior with my report. And yet, even if the community does not accept my claim as generally true, this doesn't mean it's not valid and useful personal knowledge for me.

In asking science to expand its domain of inquiry to include the inner world, it's important to be clear that the exploration must be based on direct empirical evidence — not merely on belief that something is the case because someone else has said so. The actual phenomenon must be directly observed within oneself. Furthermore, the individual must be rigorously honest and precise in his or her observation and reporting so as to not conflate empirical evidence with preestablished dogma. This requires courage and clarity.

This aspect of Wilber's work was extremely useful to me in persuading my supervisory committee that studying myself in solitude would be a valid academic endeavor.

EVOLUTION OR CREATIONISM

We are frequently bombarded with fierce arguments from two extreme positions that each claims to explain how human beings came to be here: Neo-Darwinian evolutionary scientists are certain that our existence is essentially a fluke brought about by the purely physical process of natural selection working on random genetic mutation over vast stretches of time; strict creationists accept a literal interpretation of the Bible and insist that not so long ago, an eternal transcendent God created the whole universe, including us, from scratch in six days.

Both stances smack of hubris. Neo-Darwinian theory implies that, as far as affecting our existence, there is no intelligence in the universe greater than the (rational) human mind. Christian fundamentalism does not set the human mind as supreme, but it insists that we are created in God's image, and so we are certainly above all other beings in the universe. Neo-Darwinians refuse to acknowledge spiritual evidence; creationists deny physical evidence.

From my perspective, this argument is futile. There's a great deal of fertile ground to explore between these extreme positions. Clearly — unless we ignore the enormous volume of empirical evidence gathered in many related fields of science — the earth is old, and ongoing change is inherent to the universe. God simply did not create everything once and for all some six thousand years ago. But there's no scientific reason to deny that consciousness might be inherent in the universe and integral to the process of evolution. Keeping an open mind is a useful approach.

The evolution versus creationism argument reflects the philosophical assumptions of materialism and idealism. Materialism claims that matter is the fundamental stuff of the universe, and that mind emerged spontaneously when the nervous systems of organisms reached a necessary stage of complexity. Idealism, on the other hand, insists that Mind/Spirit/God is eternal, and matter somehow emerged from or was created by this nonmaterial force.

This debate is grounded in yet another false dichotomy: that mind and matter are fundamentally different and separate. But what if the fracture is due to how we conceptualize the world? Have we, in our thinking, split apart what is essentially the unified mindmatter "stuff" of the universe? What if matter is inherently always conscious? This panpsychist perspective is a useful description of my own direct experience in solitude.[7]

MEDITATION, SOLITUDE, AND EVOLVING CONSCIOUSNESS

Wilber argues that biology isn't the only aspect of Kosmos that evolves; consciousness and culture do, too. He points out that individual psychospiritual development takes place within an evolving cultural context. Consciousness and culture always interact and influence each other.

For Wilber, the rational ego is not the end of cognitive development. Humans have the potential to reach transrational stages of consciousness. At these stages, our self-centered identity is consciously recognized and simultaneously surrendered to Something Greater in which we are always already embedded. The vehicle for this journey of transcendence is not rational thought but meditation. For me, solitude also provides a context and a practice that catalyzes these shifts of consciousness.

When exploring and describing nonrational aspects of consciousness, it's important to not lump all such experiences together. "Higher" levels of consciousness should not be confused with prerational belief and magical thinking. These higher states are beyond rational thought; rather than deny rationality, they transcend and subsume it. Thinkers who value the rational mind above all else tend to see all nonrational experience as regressive — suspect at best and psychotic at worst. Differentiating pre- and transrational stages of development avoids the serious mistake of assuming that all nonrational experiences are roughly equivalent.

I began this retreat intending to use purely secular language — the language of academia, science, and the university — but that's proved insufficient. I've had to acknowledge and include the numinous Presence I sense in solitude. If I were in the wilderness only as a "civilian," I might be tempted to couch the experience solely in the mythical framework of the I Ching or the mystical writings of Chuang Tsu, but I can't. My mandate, as both a spiritual seeker and a doctoral student at a respected North American university, is to speak to and perhaps combine (if not resolve) both perspectives.

I could see this as a hindrance, but instead I've accepted it as a valuable challenge. Learning to integrate my personal spiritual search into the academic community and learning to use intellectual study as one modality of spiritual practice has provided an appreciated opportunity for development. From an intellectual perspective, my mind has sharpened and broadened, and from a spiritual perspective, it's all grist for the mill.

AUGUST 2001

Even if our efforts of attention
seem for years to be producing no result,
one day a light that is in exact proportion
to them will flood the soul.

—— SIMONE WEIL, REMINDER TAPED TO MY CABIN DOOR

LATE EVENING: 41°F. Calm and raining with the moon shining through. After sending the check-in email, I received a reply from Alejandra. She has the packages Patti sent and says German will be here on the 9th. I sent Patti a new shopping list. I'm not sure how she'll get the additional items to German.

Today was calm and sunny with prairie-cloud formations. It's rare to see such clouds floating in a clear sky. I went to Staines to fish and cut firewood. The outboard still acts weird when starting. It runs for a few minutes then dies. I wait for a while to restart it, and it's fine from then on. I fished deep and caught four, but reeling them up that far was hard on my shoulder.

The saw is still dumping gas out of the muffler when I fill the tank, but works ok when I fill it only halfway. For months, cutting and hauling wood seemed like a burden, but now, even though it hurts my shoulder, it's difficult to stop since it's the only task that gets me moving. I miss physical activity and feel restless.

I've started to read *Solitude* by Anthony Storr. Both books I've read on solitude justify spending time alone as healthy and valuable. I've never questioned that, but apparently many people — psychologists in particular — do. They define humans as exclusively social, and claim we are healthy only when engaged in intimate interpersonal relationships. Now that I think about it, I suppose some people do consider what I'm doing a crazy waste of time.

163

It's generally assumed that each of us is a fundamentally separate entity, and that we need to *come into* relationship with each other through social interaction. But we are more profoundly social than that — we are collective beings. My consciousness is always part of the human matrix whether I'm physically alone or with other people. I'm working to open myself to a deeper level of connectedness that doesn't depend solely on the form of surface engagement.

Am I being irresponsible when I disengage from social obligations to spend time alone? I've been supported financially, emotionally, and intellectually by other people and have a responsibility to contribute to their lives as well. I hope and intend to continue to do that. A key sign of maturity and emotional health is the ability to form intimate and mutually respectful relationships. It seems to me that when I've returned from past solitary retreats, my relationships with others have become more meaningful because my relationship with myself has deepened.

We are also Spiritual Beings. To be fully human we need to cultivate a relationship not only with other people but also with our deeper selves and with Spirit. Solitude can be a powerful context and catalyst for this process.

AUGUST 2, 2001

LATE NIGHT: Moonlight casts shadows from tree branches onto the translucent porch roof. Exquisite black on white calligraphy. I wonder why shifting from three-dimensional color to two-dimensional black and white affects me so powerfully. For the past few days, the barometric pressure has been low — about 29.6 — and the weather fairly calm and mostly sunny. Now the pressure has climbed to over 30 and it's raining and blowing. This is backwards. I had hoped the barometer would help me predict storms, but not so far.

There's been a shift in consciousness these past few days. An opening into spacious stillness and peace. I'm not always there, but when I notice I'm not and pause to relax, it flows back effortlessly. I can still sense doubt and self-judgment in the background, but they are faint. It feels like solitude is working on me. At times I look ahead to leaving here, and dread losing the sense of openness and belonging. I still have a lot to learn about equanimity, because I'm loath to lose this experience.

At these times, happiness is not the issue; there is peace, love, and joy, and I feel blessed — like we should be this way all the time. When I feel locked out of this space, then there is unhappiness. This is why I resist taking antidepressants to mask my depressive feelings. I really am missing something vital when I'm locked into my small personal self. Sensing the loss and trying to be good enough to get it back might be the source of my perfectionism. But trying to be perfect is not the way home. This feeling of absence is what drives so much of our culture's destructive materialism: looking for fulfillment in all the wrong places.

Mornings remain difficult. I feel grumpy and resistant to, well, everything. I don't want to get up and don't want to stay in bed. My shoulders hurt, and so does my heart.

AUGUST 3, 2001

NIGHT: Grey pus is oozing from around the tooth that's been bothering me for the past months, and it feels like another tooth it's attached to with a double crown has broken. I'm going to try to find the balls to pull the infected one. If I can't get it out, I'll have to catch a ride to the dentist with German when he comes. That would mean going to Puerto Natales for at least a week, and I really don't want to leave here. The worst will be if the tooth starts to seriously hurt, since the only way to visit a dentist quickly is to call the navy for emergency rescue. I'll start antibiotics tonight.

I guess I'll take a couple of Tylenol 3, smear Orajel on the gum, tie a string to the tooth, and try to yank it out. It's quite loose, but my teeth have roots that go down forever. So far it's not very painful, but I'm scared to pull it and have it hurt horribly or break off inside the gum. Assuming I can actually pull the tooth, I'm sort of glad I have to deal with it. The chronic infection may have something to do with my constant aches and lack of energy. I hope it doesn't explode with pain. I guess it will be what it will be.

AUGUST 4, 2001

NIGHT: Brilliantly clear and calm with a heavy frost over everything. The moon rose into a crystal sky and a mirror sea. It's so relaxing not to have wind. Today the returning sun touched the roof and front yard! Being relegated to the shade is almost over.

I've noticed myself thinking that I don't trust the weather. This isn't the same as being cautious because the sea can get rough in a hurry. That's a physical condition I must prepare for and adapt to. This feeling of distrust is emotional self-defensiveness; almost paranoia, as though Nature is out to get me. When I think of going to the glacier, I imagine a storm stranding me on a spray-battered rock, or having to call for help because the outboard packed it in. What I desire is to have calm clear weather, have the motor work perfectly, and find good campsites easily. Anxiety blossoms when I compare the two imagined situations: one I want and one I don't want, but expect.

Cat is so civilized. Today I confirmed that he goes to the low tide water's edge to shit. It's interesting to watch how I feel about Cat. I often go out to the porch quietly enough not to wake him, because I don't want him to stare at me and want affection. I feel imposed upon, like he's breaking into my private space. If he wants loving and I don't feel like it, I try to ignore him or give him just a quick scratch and a word to let him know he's not alone. Sometimes I let him pull me into affection, even when I don't feel like it.

The tooth is about the same. I can twist it almost 45 degrees and wiggle it up and down. Seems like it should pop out easily, but when I pull there's no give at all. I guess if I have the courage to pull hard enough in spite of the pain, it will come out. When I've had teeth pulled in the past, the dentist always carefully scraped the socket to be sure all the infection was cleaned out. I imagine that would hurt like hell without Novocain, so I may poke a piece of string into the socket to keep it open and draining for a week while the antibiotics do their work. I emailed Patti to ask if there's anything I should be especially careful of when I pull it and to admit that I'm pretty frightened of the pain.

AUGUST 5, 2001

NIGHT: I received a reply from Patti with answers and reassurance. She said that in the larger picture this is no big deal and won't be nearly as painful as my shoulders have been. She reminded me that people have been pulling their own teeth for centuries. She told me to stop being such a wuss; tie the tooth to the door, slam the door, get on with my life. Excellent advice! I feel inspired! Only problem is I don't have a door heavy enough to slam. Guess I'll have to tie the tooth to a heavy rock and drop the rock. Maybe it will come out without a huge hassle or excruciating pain. On the other hand, maybe not. I think I'll wait a couple of more days.

AUGUST 6, 2001

LATE AFTERNOON: Glum day. Well, I asked for rain to fill the barrel. It can be deafening on the porch when rain drums the tarp roof. Inside the cabin is quieter because there's a layer of fiberboard under the tarp. As usual, I sat on the porch most of day, but now I'm glad to be in this cozy nest. A few months ago I had to blow and fiddle, sometimes for an hour, to start the fire. Now I've learned to keep the chimney clean, use cypress for kindling, and split wood ahead to let it dry. When the fire is occasionally fussy, I'm not so freaked since I know that with patience it will burn and I won't die from the cold.

It's not going into solitude or the wilderness that brings a sense of peace. It's getting away from our normal life's concerns and engagements. Usually we stay only a brief time in the wilderness and our disquiet doesn't catch up with us. I've been here long enough that this has become my normal life, and all my usual concerns are in operation. But there are fewer distractions and escapes here, so I can see the process more clearly and must face my concerns more directly.

For a long time I believed that all art is grounded in coping with the pain of having an individual self. As a photographer, I could either depict my pain to glorify or rationalize it, or create escapist images to distract myself and others from our common pain. But both approaches reinforce the separate self and the suffering that arises from it. I decided to give up photography and work to dissolve the self and its inherent suffering. I no longer see the issue as so black and white. Art can simply be part of living and, perhaps, even a path toward self-abandonment; perhaps. Or maybe my dream of losing the self is just that, and I would do well to find a more realistic approach to existential pain. Meanwhile, the rain falls, and the tide and my breath ebb and flow.

AUGUST 7, 2001

NIGHT: This morning I knew I couldn't put it off any longer. I meditated, exercised, built a fire, and fetched a rock from the low-tide beach. Finding the perfect tooth-pulling rock took a while. It had to be the right shape and texture so the string wouldn't slip off, and heavy enough to pull the tooth with a single jerk. It would be nasty to drop the rock and have it yank on the tooth, but not hard enough to actually pull it out. Then I'd have to drop it again. . . .

I shaved in case my face might be sore and swollen for a few days, smeared Orajel on the gum, took two Tylenol 3, and held ice against my cheek while I meditated for a while longer to calm my mind. I took off my shirt so blood wouldn't splatter on it, and laid padding on the floor to muffle the thud of the rock.

I tied one end of a four-foot piece of strong nylon string to the abscessed tooth. It was a front upper and would, I hoped, get jerked straight down and out when the rock snapped the string tight. I started to tie the other end of the string to the rock, and as I did, a startlingly real sequence of images flashed through my mind.

In that prophetic vision I braced myself, leaned forward, and opened my mouth as wide as I could. I held the rock with both hands out in front of me at chest height and told myself to drop it. But my hands didn't open. I took a deep breath, adjusted my stance, and told myself again to drop the rock. And again nothing happened. "Drop the rock, Bob. Bob, drop the rock!" Simultaneously, another part of my mind was muttering, "I don't *think* so. . . ."

Just the thought of the rock crashing down and hitting the end of the string caused my butt-hole to pucker up.

I reconsidered my options and decided it might be more sensible to work the tooth out slowly by tying it to a leg of the table, pulling up with my neck muscles, and at the same time wiggle the tooth with my fingers. If I couldn't get it out that way, or couldn't stand the pain, I'd have to tie the tooth to the rock, drop that sucker, and be done with it.

I told myself it was ok to feel afraid. I thought about all the women who go through childbirth and about the old prospector in Canada who was trapped up the Nahanni River by an early freeze, got scurvy, and had to pull all his teeth with pliers. I thought about having my foot ripped off in the motorcycle crash and about the seemingly endless pain in my torn rotator cuffs. Pulling a tooth is really minor in comparison.

It wasn't just the pain I was nervous about, but doing it to myself. It reminded me of cutting a fishhook out of my thumb with a razor blade on a remote beach in the Dominican Republic. It wasn't the pain that bothered me, since it doesn't hurt that much to slice yourself with a razor blade, but the idea of intentionally cutting into myself. If I hadn't done it, I'd have had to leave solitude and go to a doctor. Same situation here.

I meditated some more, asked for courage, and began. I'd accidentally tugged the string while tying it to the tooth and had felt a small wave of pain just from that, so I figured actually pulling it out was going to be really unpleasant. I test pulled and wiggled the tooth. It hurt, but there was no give at all. I set myself to sink into the pain and started to seriously pull up with my neck, while at the same time twisting the tooth with my fingers. Just as I thought, "Ok, here we go," fwoop, the tooth popped out.

What a relief. The root was intact and my mouth hardly bled. As usual, what I imagined was much worse than what happened. I hung the tooth on my altar as a trophy, and to remind myself to not take my imagination's dire speculations too seriously. It felt great to have that mess out of my mouth, but as the Tylenol wore off, I noticed pain in the other bad tooth on the rear lower left. If it abscesses, it will be much harder to deal with. Hopefully I can nurse it along with saltwater rinse and antibiotics.

AUGUST 8, 2001

LATE NIGHT: 37°F. Calm and clear. I went fishing to Staines and brought home a dozen. Two of the fish were still twitching as I filleted them, even though I'd stabbed them in the brain when I caught them and they'd been out of the water for hours. I'm starting to feel all this killing. I also made a cooler by stuffing sawdust around a pail filled with ice inside a woven sack, and then wrapped the whole thing with the life jacket I don't use. Fish should last a week in there.

I emailed Alejandra to ask when German is coming (he's theoretically supposed to come tomorrow) and if she would send forty ampicillin capsules. I doubt I'll need them, but if I do, I'll sure be glad to have them. I feel bad to keep asking her for more favors.

I came here in part to slip into wildness and explore beyond our socially constructed reality, but I'm seeing more clearly that that reality is inside me. Each of us creates one and they're not identical, so we each live in a unique world. To some degree many of us share a common reality, but even so we supposedly can't enter each other's world. I wonder...

At times I sense I'm beyond my individually constructed reality and into a collective space we all share. If that's so, I should be able to meet others there, but so far I haven't. So perhaps that sense of common ground is only an experience I have in my personal world. We might each have the experience that there's a common space, but that doesn't necessarily mean there really is. No way to prove it one way or the other. You either experience a common space or you don't.

I've started to let Cat come right up and smell me, instead of keeping him away from my face because of allergies. He gets his nose just touching my lips, sniffs a while, and then settles into my lap. Today I sniffed him in return and it was captivating. A rich animal smell and strong sense of connection. No wonder animals smell each other like they do.

I suspect that Cat, like me, experiences a spectrum of emotional energy. Today, a glum rainy day, he sat at the door quietly moaning. That expressed just how I felt. On warm sunny days he's definitely languorous. Of course it's possible that he picks up my moods, but it makes cleaner sense to assume there's an "emotional aspect" to the world that animals as well as humans experience — each of us in our own way.

When the wind blows, I experience auditory, visual, olfactory, and tactile phenomena as physical manifestations of moving air. Perhaps there's also an emotional manifestation that can be experienced as excitement (when I'm confident in the situation) or anxiety (if I feel I might be overwhelmed). I have coevolved with the world and am woven into it, so why shouldn't a physical event have an emotional — and probably spiritual — component too?

AUGUST 9, 2001

NIGHT: The east channel, the basin, and my cove were frozen this morning. By late afternoon the sun and high tide had melted or moved the ice. Some new seabirds have arrived: black head, back, and chest; white belly; long red bill; high-pitched peep, peep cry (Magellanic Oystercatcher). A hint that winter is passing and migrating birds are on the move.

I was looking closely at Cat today. What an elegant creature. His face is beautiful. The exquisitely delicate swirl patterns of tawny hair around his ears remind me of a moth. His bent ear just adds distinction. He may have had a seizure while I was rock-sitting last night. I heard thumping, and when I came back to the cabin he wandered in. That's a pretty sure sign of disorientation. I picked him up, gave him some loving, and he went to sleep. Seems ok today.

Trying to characterize solitude is like trying to describe relationship. Impossible since there's so much variance. In solitude you can focus on the external world, become entranced by trying to create conceptual order, immerse yourself in artistic work, study inner emotional experience, or explore spiritual dimensions of universal wholeness and love. Solitude is liberating because the only limiting factor is your own capacity, but difficult because there are no other people to help catalyze growth. In solitude you pretty much must do it on your own.

Twenty-five years ago, during my first long wilderness retreat, I decided that the only thing worth dying for is *living* fully. In a sense I've remained committed to that, even in the face of disapproval from others for being selfish and irresponsible. I need to remember that if I'm true to my own nature, I'll be making the contribution I'm meant to make, even if everyone else disapproves. Over and over I see that my fundamental task here is to live this experience to the fullest.

I finished Storr's *Solitude*, and it reminded me of Jung's belief that all psychological growth is essentially religious. I must trust my own natural process of growth. It's not particularly relevant *which level* of spiritual development I'm on. *Orientation* is much more pragmatically important. If I hold onto my self as the center, I stagnate and suffer. If I'm open to change and being part of something greater, I experience joy and peace.

AUGUST 10, 2001

LATE NIGHT: 36°F. I awoke today to a fogbound morning. The only sounds were the distant rumble of falls on Staines Peninsula and sea ice rustling against the beach: a momentous mystic moment that stretched into timelessness. The eastern mountains, vague and ephemeral in the melting mist, reflected from a sea as glassy as I've ever seen.

I took out the camera for a single shot, and used up half a roll of film instead. Where does the photographic urge come from? Is it the light or my soul calling? It was relaxing to focus on framing, images, and quality of feeling evoked. I'm still working with blacks, whites, and grays that are just faintly touched with color. My shots are becoming less studied and more simply what I see though the lens.

Curious language: catch fish, shoot photos. It doesn't actually feel that way. I do catch fish, but when my heart is open it feels like the fish are given to me. I don't take a photo, shoot a scene, or capture something on film. It's more like my eye and heart are attracted to a moment of form and color, and I feel called to honor and frame it to share with others.

These past three weeks would have been good weather to go to the glacier — if the outboard was running properly. I spend hours thinking about going and about the risk and possible discomfort involved. If I don't go, I believe I'll feel deep sorrow for a long time, as though an important part of my task here was not completed.

And there's a twist to this. I've been thinking about perfectionism on a large abstract scale — e.g., this retreat won't be perfect if I don't go to the glacier — but today I realized that perfectionism affects me here and now, moment by moment. Well duh, when and where else could it affect me? My psychological explorations often start this way in the abstract, and then I slowly become aware of habits manifesting the actual present.

I also read books this way. At first I'm just distantly engaged with the ideas, then little by little I begin to consider how they relate to my own journey. Often, I imagine that books are supposed to be perfect. But they are written by people just trying to make sense of their lives.

AUGUST 11, 2001

NIGHT: 30°F. Calm, partly clear. Just another day. Back to the daily routine of meditation and exercise. Little by little I'm giving up the struggle to change myself as a no-win endeavor. I'm weary and want to let myself be who I already am.

I tinkered with the chain saw to see if I could figure out why it's leaking gas from the muffler. Nope. Just as well, since I didn't really want to shatter the evening quiet. One good thing about being alone is I don't hear anyone else's noise and don't need to worry about anyone hearing mine. I wonder sometimes if the animals mind the racket.

AUGUST 12, 2001

LATE NIGHT: Another day, *no más*. Got up, meditated, exercised, and started building steps. I've been planning to do them for months, but hadn't gotten around to it. Today, almost without thinking, I began to build. Letting things happen in their own time.

This evening I was sitting out on the rock and Cat was wandering around whining. I kept saying shhhh, shhhh, and finally screamed "SHUT UP!" That did it, but I had to smile. Peaceful evening, dark settling in, and then the bellowed "Shut up!" rolling across the channel and bouncing off the rock face of Staines Peninsula. One reason I get so upset when he whines is that he's interrupting me while I'm talking to myself (thinking). It might be good for me, though, since I could do with a lot less thinking.

When I daydream about talking with other people, I'm talking to myself in every sense. Not just because I'm talking internally, but also because all the thoughts are different points of view that I, myself, hold. In one daydream I ask an imagined critic, "Who gives you the right to decide what a human being is or should be?" An interesting question. I spend an enormous amount of time and energy trying to fix myself, but who am I to know how I should be? All this self-improvement work is just a way of trying to escape from my life as it is.

Care of the Soul talks about the need to marry soul with spirit. I don't usually think in terms of soul, but once I adjust to his language, I find that Moore is saying things that describe my experience more closely than anything else I've read. He points out that one aspect of the *puer* personality is sadism/cruelty. It's hard to admit, but I recognize myself there. I do have a mean streak that I cover up with charm and supposed spiritual awareness. Moore describes *puer aeternus* as the aspect of the soul that's eternally youthful. Because the puer attitude is so unattached to worldly things, it's often prevalent in religious movements. Feeling the confinement and humdrum of everyday life, we try to transcend it through spiritual practice. Hmm, yes, that sounds vaguely familiar.

It's been blowing all day from the northwest and feels like the summer winds may have started again. Down at the point, I felt sudden gratitude toward brother wind for helping me explore my soul. It felt good to give thanks for a change instead of screaming, "Fuck off!"

NO ENTRY FOR AUGUST 13, 2001

AUGUST 14, 2001

NIGHT: *Care of the Soul* argues that soul work is right where things are hardest and where we don't want to be. That's where the ego wall is weakest and where we can most easily open up and let something from beyond come in.

Does this mean I should celebrate my *flaws?* That's certainly where I'm apt to be more humble about my life. The trick is not to try to fix the weak spots, but to acknowledge them and be with myself as I am.

In the last section of the book, Moore talks about reanimating the world. There is a collective world soul that every being and object is part of. It's rare to read about this feeling of existing in a *living* world. I paused and it washed softly over me. The cabin and everything else came *alive*. Such tenderness and love. Tears blurred my eyes. This is what I've been seeking for so long, and as usual I've had it backward. I've been focused on *my* experience of sensing the world as *alive* rather than focusing on the world itself. Now, my attention naturally and softly touched the world around me — including myself as part of that world. It felt cozy and comfortable, like I was cradled and held. At the same time, I was aware of the fierce aspects of existence: fear, pain, death.

In some sense this is what I've been looking for since I left home at eighteen to chase phantom feelings and grasp for experiences. Without this sense of being *alive* in a *living* world, no place, job, or relationship feels right. But Life can't be grasped. I can only open myself and allow it to wash in. With this sense of *aliveness*, it doesn't matter where I go. Anywhere is fine since no place is more *alive* than any other place. It's like being in love, but in a soft quiet way rather than a passionate love affair. I was surprised by the unexpected shift today. It just happened and brought a sense of deep relaxation, like I can rest now. I've been searching for so long and have finally come home. But restless mind is an unruly beast and habits take time to change.

During the past twenty-five years I've had the sense that I've wandered down many dead ends and detours along the spiritual path. *Care of the Soul* says that in seeking Spirit there may be a direct path, but in cultivating the soul it's a labyrinth of wandering and wondering. Somehow in following my heart these past years I have been caring for my soul. I'm grateful for *Care of the Soul* and hope I might touch someone else this way through writing or storytelling.

AUGUST 15, 2001

LATE NIGHT: 39°F. Started to rain at dark and has been coming down ever since. It's also been blowing hard all day. I'm glad I'm not out on the sea somewhere, but I sure would like to go to the glacier.

I've felt for a while that my altar is incomplete. There are rocks, feathers, a piece of firewood, sage and sweetgrass, a bird's breast bone, a few things from Patti, some photos, a bit of Mom's ashes, Dad's ring, my tooth, and my amulet. Today I added a small dead windswept branch to remind me I'm not in charge and in gratitude to the wind for helping me learn/remember that. It's also an offering to propitiate the wind in the hope I'll not be caught on the water in a storm.

Good news. I was wrong again. I didn't think the fluorescent bulbs were causing the electric light to dim, but I tried the spare bulbs, and bright light again! I'd forgotten how much nicer it is not to have the noise of the propane lamp. And I've been thinking again (always a dangerous thing to do). In the future, I need to remember that I can never take enough plastic twine when I go camping. It's so useful. I just happened to grab a roll to bring with me at the last minute and I'm glad I did. I'm using and reusing it over and over.

I finished the steps and I'm glad to have them done. Only took six months. All my outdoor projects are complete except to spread gravel in the mud holes. Of course the boat, outboard, and chain saw continue to need attention, and I want to move the solar panels back to the more protected location now that the sun is returning. I hope the cabin doesn't start to have problems.

AUGUST 16, 2001

NIGHT: 44°F. Windy and overcast, sea on the move. Things are falling apart. Just yesterday I wrote that I've finally gotten almost everything done — unless something falls apart. This morning I discovered the stovepipe has rotted through in spots. Unbelievable. I had the pipe made in Punta Arenas, and even their best-quality metal was not very good. I've rotated the pipe, patched the holes, and emailed Alejandra to ask German to bring new pipe when he comes. Ironic if I can't use all the firewood I've brought in. So much for dreams of life being trouble-free until I leave. I suppose equipment problems on this kind of adventure are to be expected. I just hope the satphone and laptop continue to work because I haven't a clue how to fix them.

I've been pissed off all day about having to fuck with the stovepipe. It felt like the world was actively thwarting my efforts. I'm often angry when I work with the physical world. Rather than engage my materials in dialogue, I want them to obey my will without resistance. I seem ok with routine tasks like splitting wood, cooking, or fishing, but as soon as repairing something mechanical is involved, I become too tightly focused, start to rush, and get impatient. When I relax my grip on my goals and plans, the process again becomes an engagement instead of the world confronting and limiting me. Ah God, I should have learned this is stuff when I was a kid.

I was watching the butter-belly ducks today and admiring how self-contained they are. No matter what the weather, they seem comfortable in it. No equipment to worry about. All they need do is preen. But they patrol and defend their territory many times each day. Cat also seems to constantly test boundaries (or perhaps he's playing and teasing me). Maybe that's just how the biological world works. Each organism expands until stopped by others around it. Yet I'm trying to solve my problems once and for all so I can live from now on without any challenges. But in that case, I wouldn't really be alive.

AUGUST 17, 2001

NIGHT: I dragged the boat up further and moved some of the firewood, too. This was as high as I've seen the tide, and tomorrow will be higher yet. The water swirled around the chopping blocks and into the sweat lodge. No damage as far as I can tell.

Another mishap with Cat. When I go to the outhouse, he follows me and cuddles right up. He'd climb onto my lap if I'd let him. As I stood to pull up pants and rain gear, he — still on the seat — stood on his hind paws with his front paws on my lower back. I reached back to brush him off, and whoops, down the hole he went. It's only eighteen inches deep and full of water, so he climbed out in a hurry, but he didn't come out smelling like a rose. No, in fact he smelled like shit and looked like a sewer rat. I had to laugh. What a creature. Figured I better dry him or he might get seriously chilled, but the only thing I have to dry him with is my towel. So then my towel was full of shit and I had to wash it. Ah lord, the tribulations of an impatient man.

I've started to read *The Eye of Spirit* by Ken Wilber. It's very different in tone from *Care of the Soul*. I'm reading it to reorient myself before I dive into Wilber's major work, *Sex, Ecology, Spirituality*, again, which is much more difficult. I appreciate Wilber's intellectual depth and scope, but he often seems to take his model of the Kosmos literally. I get hung up on his apparent certainty and heavy focus on structure. It speaks to my mind but not to my heart. It's good to be reminded that in contrast to modernity's scientific materialism, variations of the so-called Perennial Philosophy (physical matter, animal nature, rational mind, soul, Spirit) have formed the basis for many cultures' worldview.

The dual aspects of Spirit as transcendent and immanent are useful in conceptualizing my experience: transcendence is the peace, clarity, and inner light I often call Big Mind; immanence is what I call *aliveness*. I've been trying to sense the physical world around me as alive, but it still often seems mechanistic. Actually, that makes sense. If I focus only on sense perception of the material outer surface, the world will appear dead and mechanical. *Aliveness* is inward — the awareness that arises in a still mind.

EARLY NIGHT: While fishing today, I was more mindful to pause and give thanks for the fish as I caught them, and to be sure I stabbed the knifepoint into their brain so they wouldn't suffer. Even so, several were still twitching as I filleted them later, and it again brought home that I'm taking lives. If I didn't like to fish and to eat fish so much, I might stop killing them.

At the very low tide tonight, I walked down from the cabin to see more of the sky over the trees. Cat's eyes glowed wild and eerie in the flashlight. I felt chills run up my spine and feel them again now as I write these words. I trembled as though some repressed energy was struggling to break free. I've felt this before and it's led to release and opening, so I stood in the dark and stayed with it. My rational mind was frightened of the unknown, but I reassured myself that it was ok.

Then something dark and savage surged up. I felt my face twist into a snarl, and a dark *presence* growled, "You are mine!" I hung on and worked with it as best I could — asking the inner light for help and the ominous presence what it wanted. It said that if I allowed it to come in, it would give me power. No, thank you. Courage and strength, yes, but power, no. I stayed steady and allowed it to be, but didn't let it control me. I gave myself love.

I'm frightened of this darkness. It seems to come from outside me, but that's the nature of the shadow. It told me that it is who I am, whether or not I want to recognize it: the rage that roars when my will is thwarted; the brutality that smacks Cat for doing something I don't like; the subtle cruelty to women. My anxiety and anger toward the wind are somehow linked with this darkness, too. I sense that in denying and projecting this shadow aspect of myself, I'm left with fear. The rage may come from denying my manhood in fundamental ways. I hope I have the courage to face and acknowledge this darkness as part of who I am.

I finally came inside to light a fire and warm up. Later, when I went out to pee, the *presence* hissed from the dark, "I'm waiting." While slicing bacon for dinner, I almost cut my finger and the voice mocked, "I'm gonna get you."

I usually believe that I do acknowledge my shadow, but in truth I seldom viscerally own this side of myself. Tonight I had to admit in my gut the darkness of some of my behavior. What's truly frightening is to be unaware of my own dark side, because then it emerges covertly in my actions.

Meditation teachers say that terror and other dark energy will likely surface from time to time. As always, the skillful response is to observe without judging: neither reject nor get sucked in. And there's Patti's courage and support. If I really need to, I can email or even call her. I know I can't face this on my own, and ask the inner light for courage, strength, patience, and humility. Five more months alone might be pretty tough. Well, I expected there would be difficult issues to face out here. It will be interesting to see what happens in the coming days and weeks.

How to explain the existence of evil in the world? Mystics claim that Spirit, the ultimate ground of existence, is Love. If so, and if the entire manifest world is Spirit Incarnate, how can there be evil? It seems to me that *without resorting to dualism*, there are only three basic options: 1. There is no God. The cosmos is blind chance at worst and impersonal process at best. In that case there's no reason why there shouldn't be evil in the world. 2. God, like everything else, has a shadow side. Pain, disease, and death — as well as human cruelty — are inherent to Life. If God is Love, then Love cannot be what we normally think it is. 3. There is no actual evil in the world. It's created through perspective and attribution. In this case, evil is defined in relation to ego. I label as evil anything that seriously threatens me, my people, my way of life, or my ideals. But if I'm able to see the world without my extended self as its center, then yes, there is suffering, but not evil as such.

If I truly give myself to the swirl of life and death, then I cannot judge the acts of another as evil — even though that person may be doing wrong from his or her subjective perspective. However, their self-judgment would be based on the notion of free will. I wonder... do we actually have free will, or is it an illusion that allows us the comfort of supposed control in the face of our mysterious existence?

AUGUST 19, 2001

LATE NIGHT: Empty Sunday. All day I've felt like a stone rattling down an empty well. Over and over I've decided to stay with the feeling, and over and over have eaten something instead. Tomorrow I intend to fast and drink only tea. Perhaps I'll fast on each new moon from now on.

This morning the wind was blowing and the sea on the move, so I prepared for a super high tide. I tied the boat more securely, moved the chopping blocks, and lashed rope around the woodpile. I've been expecting this high tide for months. The water didn't come very high at all. Heigh-ho.

I wonder if I need psychotherapy. Little question but that I have some serious neuroses going on. No surprise, since most of us do. But I wonder if the personal work I've been doing over the years — alone and with friends — is accomplishing what therapy would accomplish, or am I going in circles? A futile question for now, but I'll consider it when back among people.

What am I learning here that's worth sharing? Anything I say will be meaningful only if, in my own life, I walk the walk I talk about. New-age gurus often flash a big smile to show that they have found the Answer/ System and it WORKS. I find this style distasteful and don't trust it. We need to come clean with each other about our doubts and flaws. I've always liked Insight Meditation teachers who don't claim to be gurus but see themselves as simply fellow travelers who can guide those who have not walked as far along the path. This, of course, assumes there is a path to follow and that we aren't simply wandering a pathless land.

One thing does seem clear, though. Joy comes from living fully in the here and now, no matter what the circumstance. To live like that I must give up wanting things to be different. The hardest is to give up wanting to give up wanting things to be different.

AUGUST 20, 2001

NIGHT: Last night, after writing in the journal, I went out to the rock, and sensed the world as Holy. I tried to see what usually keeps me from that vision. It seems like desire prevents me from experiencing all of Life — the good, the bad, the painful — as Holy. Peeling away layers of desire allows the sense of sacredness to flow in. Desire often includes the rejection of what is and the wish to have something different.

The high tide I expected yesterday came today. Whew. The water surged eighteen inches higher than I've seen before: to the foundation posts of the cabin and halfway up the woodpiles, onto the rock where often I sit, and into the trees where I was pretty sure it never goes. The boat, pulled as far as possible into the bushes, was still floating. The lowest porch step washed away. Good thing I lashed the woodpile in place. Even where I lived in the tent when I first arrived was under water.

Watching the waves wash into the trees, I remembered that the intertidal zone was one of the first places I realized that beauty and harmony can arise from the conflict of opposing forces. But today I found myself identifying with the plants being *attacked* by the sea, and didn't feel the peace and equanimity that arise when I stand back to let the process go its way.

I wondered how I could stop feeling attacked by the elements, and then remembered that I came here to be *shaped* by the experience of solitude in nature. In that moment, I relaxed my grip on who I think I should be and how the world should treat me, and opened myself to the process of change and growth.

This hasn't been the easiest day for a fast perhaps, but symbolic. Physical, emotional, intellectual, and spiritual fat is being trimmed off.

AUGUST 21, 2001

NIGHT: Another stormy day, but not as intense as yesterday. I walked to the point this morning, and along the way picked up some plastic washed in from who knows where. Mounds of uprooted sea grass and kelp lie high in the bushes. The beach has a new face. No major structural changes, but it looks scraped and polished, like it's been born again or gone through a major spring cleaning.

Cat continues to intrigue me. I've been looking deep into his eyes lately. I've also been sleeping with the door unlatched; in part I was latching it against him. Yesterday was roaring with wind and rain when I went to check the solar panels, so I told Cat to stay at the cabin. Instead he came with me. By the time we got back he was soaked, and even though it was a warm day, I dried him off. I'm not sure if he's neurotic to be so attached or just a loving friend.

AUGUST 22, 2001

NIGHT: Last night the wind generator started to howl so I went down to short the wires. The wind at the point was savage. Cat, as usual, came with me. This morning I moved the solar panels back to the more protected spot where they were before they lost the sun in early winter. Again Cat came along. I couldn't believe it. Pissing down rain, but he stayed with me and got drenched.

Last night in the outhouse Cat, as usual, got in the way. I've scootched him over a bunch of times, but he keeps getting right where I need to sit. I lost my temper, grabbed him by the scruff of the neck, and tossed him away. Instead of coming right back when I called, he just looked at me. He finally came back and I gave him some loving. Even though I hate to admit it, I actually enjoyed blowing up at him. It gave me pleasure to dominate and maybe even hurt him a bit. This feels really shitty.

I noticed that afterward I felt affectionate, even though previously I'd been distant and cold toward him. I project my internal distress onto him, and once I dump it, I feel softer — and remorseful. I do the same thing with women, though nonphysically, which is classically abusive.

Cat often seems to demand that I attend to him, and I feel guilty when I don't. The guilt triggers anger. Or maybe I didn't get my needs met when I was a boy, and Cat's demands touch off my own rage. I often feel that women I'm in relationship with want something I either can't or don't want to give, and then I feel guilty and become angry and mean or withdraw emotionally or physically. Patti is aware of this, and over and over tells me I don't owe her anything.

Wilber points out that narcissistic rage is a characteristic of early development. If so, I'm not unique but just haven't outgrown it yet. In any case, I need to remain open to the feelings that come up so I can let them go and stop taking them out on Cat. I also need to remember that Cat is a separate being with his own life and distresses.

I sat out in the pouring rain for a long time today and slowly realized that I only sense the world in front of me rather than on all sides. I'm outside looking in, not inside looking around. This is the basic phenomenological experience of dualism, and I think it's linked to fear of death. If I remove myself from the sweep of life, nothing can sneak up on me from behind!

In doing this, I'm no longer truly part of life. Life is always out there somewhere else and I'm always trying to get to where it is. But this, too, is a subtle kind of dualism. Even feeling lifeless at times is part of being an actual animate person. Why is this so hard to get?

NO ENTRY FOR AUGUST 23, 2001

AUGUST 24, 2001

NIGHT: Cloudy this morning, but clear in the afternoon. First time I've seen the sun in almost two weeks. I hope it freezes tonight so I can collect ice for the cooler. A plane flew by out of sight on the other side of Staines Peninsula. I'd forgotten how peaceful it is here. I spent most of the day in the kayak and stopped here and there to pick up plastic the storm tide washed in. Apparently, one of my jobs in life is to be God's garbage collector.

Still no word about when German is coming. Except for the outboard parts, I could almost say don't bother. If the motor was working well, this might be a good time to go to the glacier. But to create a special challenge like going to the glacier won't lead to a balanced way of being, day to day.

Sitting on the porch, watching the day darkening to night, I looked out to see the orange-bill butter-belly ducks swim into the basin. Silhouetted in the steely grey light, they looked like gunboats or battleships cruising in to patrol their territory. I suddenly sensed myself to be one among many — just part of existence. Lovely to feel profoundly *part of the world*. . . .

NIGHT: After being here for seven months, I finally left the beach and went into the middle of the island. I decided to not wear rain pants — eek, my security blanket! I rarely go anywhere without my rain pants. I knew I'd get wet, but it would be much easier to climb through the trees and brush without them. I managed to sneak away without Cat. He probably wouldn't have liked the trip, and I certainly wouldn't have liked him crying the whole way.

I've never been in anything so tough. Dense vegetation and very rough ground. A tangle of fallen trees and steep jumbled rock formations. Several times I barely saved myself from a bad fall when, thinking I was on solid ground, I started to take a step and found nothing but air under my foot. When I peered through the underbrush, I saw I was standing on a fallen log seven or eight feet in the air!

Once I lost sight and sound of the sea, I'd absolutely have lost my way without sun and compass. I might have wandered in circles for a long time among the ridges, gullies, and fallen trees. It took over an hour to cross the island and it's not more than 150 yards. On the far shore I somehow felt like an explorer to a new land, even though I've been there before by water.

I found a cypress log that must have washed in on the storm tide. Someone somewhere sometime chopped some notches in it. I wonder who and where and when. I also picked up some plastic. It hurts to think of the mindlessness of people who toss such stuff overboard.

On the trip back I stopped to rest on the highest point of the island, where it was semi-open and I could see the water and mountains in several directions. The dark *presence* came again, and again I felt I was being attacked from outside. I must appear demonic to Cat when I rage at him for crying. More projection.

Wilber describes the defense mechanisms that operate on different levels of psychological development: neurotic and immature people use repression and projection; healthy mature people, suppression and sublimation. When I read that, it didn't make sense, but on the hilltop I got it. A lot of dark stuff that is usually buried and unconsciously held in check by cultural mores is free to emerge here. If I want to experience these aspects of myself, I need to assume personal responsibility to not become swamped by them. This seems like the move from repression and projection to suppression and sublimation. Repression is an unconscious process; suppression is consciously acknowledging the shadow material and choosing not to act it out. There are many ways to sublimate the shadow's energy, but I think the most direct is to channel it into being aware of the energy itself.

NO ENTRY FOR AUGUST 26, 2001

AUGUST 27, 2001

36°F. Tender night, calm and quiet. A half-moon showing through broken cloud. Strange how much easier it is to write about daily doings than inner experiences. Yesterday, Sunday, was, as usual, a melancholy day. Feeling empty like I've failed in my life. I've been working on inner stuff for so long and have made so little progress. Sometimes I feel that all I really want is a job I can enjoy and a relationship that's joyful.

This morning I woke at first light to the sound of wavelets crumpling on the beach. As day came on I could see the small cypress through the window shivering in the breeze. Not a day to be out in the boat, so I went back to sleep. Later I meditated, exercised, and got busy with domestic tasks: washed windows, buried garbage, reorganized the food on the porch, stacked wood, and cleaned up the debris the storm tide left near the cabin. Small jobs, but it feels good to have them done.

I've been reading *Gaia: A Way of Knowing*, a collection of work by various thinkers. The introduction by William Irwin Thompson expresses clear thoughts with lovely words. On the other hand, biologist philosopher Humberto Maturana (whose work I've studied before) has got to be one of the worst writers I've ever read. I think what he says is probably interesting and valuable, but I'm never sure, since the way he says it is barely comprehensible to me at the best of times.

He claims that as humans "we live in language," but I don't think he could make that statement if he was fully embedded in language. He can perceive our relationship to language only because he has a perspective from beyond language. A fish cannot say, "We live in water." If water is all you know, then it's the context of experience, not content.

Wilber points out that the process of psychospiritual growth is disidentifying with one level of consciousness and transcending it to the next, more inclusive, level; context at one level becomes content at the next. He also claims that Spirit is the same as awareness, and defines enlightenment as waking up to notice that we are always already aware and so always already enlightened. The task is not to become aware, but to notice that we already are.

One good thing about reading Wilber is that I'm finally coming to accept the importance of daily meditation. Anyone working to become more aware has to go through the same process one way or another.

NO ENTRY FOR AUGUST 28, 2001

38°F. Clear night with light clouds. A medium breeze and the sea on the move. I'm regularly staying up almost all night. Without so many daily tasks, I've just sort of drifted into this schedule. Yesterday was calm and clear. I went fishing and exploring. I wanted to see if Cat would go with me, and put him in the boat; he jumped out. I put him back in and held on, but when I thought I'd pushed far enough away from the beach and let him go to start the motor, he made a mighty leap back to land. Since it was a test to see whether I'll take him with me if I go away for more than a day, I decided to try one last time. I rowed back to shore, called him, and, lo, he jumped into the boat.

He was sooo good all day. I had to tell him to get down off the pontoon only once. I liked having him along, and he was completely calm and seemed to enjoy the trip. I caught a dozen snapper, then continued northwest to investigate a deep inlet on Isla Owen, about six miles from here. Delightful in there. As usual, I was nervous about the outboard, but it worked fine. According to the GPS, I covered 20 miles. If I go to the glacier, it will be four times as far just to get there.

Today I went to the other side of the island to pick up the cypress log I found the other day. I took Cat with me and he seemed to like the ride, even though it was choppy. He stood with his front paws up on the pontoon so he could see out, and looked like a dog in the back of a pickup truck. I cut and loaded the cypress, and when it was time to go, called Cat and put him in the boat. He immediately jumped back out. Grrr. By this time the wind was up and pushing the boat onto the sharp rocks. It took quite a while to coax him back to where I could reach him and lift him into the boat. I gripped him tightly until I'd pushed the boat out, but when I let go to start the motor, he leapt to shore again. Fuck it! If he made it home the other day, he could today, too.

My behavior continues to trouble me. I get so angry at the little guy and then act violently. He's starting to shy away from me at times. He still comes when I call, jumps onto my lap, and likes to play, but the harsh treatment — even though rare compared with the gentle strokes I give him — is having an effect. I must try harder to be aware of this stuff and not act it out.

I picked up two loads of gravel from the island north of here and spread it in the mud holes around the cabin. Then I split the cypress into slabs. What great kindling: well seasoned and hardly any knots. When I'd finished I paused for a look around.

The peeping cries of the newly arrived red-billed seabirds call to me from where they share the musseled rock with the pair of white-and-black geese. The Orange Bill Butter-Belly Diving Ducks work the kelp beds in the falling tide. Across the channel to the west, the rock walls of Staines Peninsula drift into and out of sight behind swirls of mist and slanting streaks of rain. But here, just here on this rock and the small island beyond, sun pours down and the trees shed their drab shadowed green and shimmer, almost iridescent. Rapt in wonder, I watch a rainbow magically appear and then fade again to wherever it came from.

Into this mystic stillness an eagle flies; majestic or ponderous, depending on your eye. The male goose honks a warning but doesn't move. Tending to its own affairs, the eagle flaps steadily past. But what's this? One of the red-billed peepers lifts off, climbs in a steep curve, and attacks from behind. And now, as the light fades to grey again, the ducks join the others on the rock. Community.

I drop the notebook and feel myself sink more deeply into the world. All desire to write disappears. What has happened to my flow of language? I fall mute before such wonder and beauty. I try to describe the delicate shades and patterns of shifting color as wind swirls water around immovable rock, but my images feel dull and trite. There is no dance between word and world. What I see and feel begs a sensuous tango, but my words march static and stiff in lines across the page.

AUGUST 30, 2001

NIGHT: 36°F. The weather continues to mystify me. Today the barometric pressure went up, the temperature dropped, and it started to rain. I'd begun to believe that rain comes with falling pressure and the temperature hovering around 41°F. Oh well, another theory shot to hell.

I read for most of today and also filled the five 5-gallon gas containers from the 55-gallon drum. I usually hate to siphon gas because I always get some in my mouth and it tastes nasty, but I think I've finally found the trick. I used to use a short opaque hose and couldn't see where the gas was, but I brought a ten-foot piece of clear hose with me here, so I can see when I've sucked the gas out of the drum and it's running downhill toward me.

And I got my first good laugh in months today — from a thought. I was reading Maturana and struggling to understand an impossibly convoluted sentence when I felt my mind tighten down. I looked up from the book to the sea and sky, took some deep breaths to relax, and tried the sentence again. And again felt my mind cramp up. Back to simply breathing in the beauty around me until I felt my mind soften, and back to the torturous sentence. Then a supremely sensible thought drifted into my mind, "I'd rather suck gas through a hose than read any more of this crap." Cracked me up and I closed the book.

For the past few days I've been leaning toward making an overnight trip to an inlet twenty-five miles north of here. The days are getting longer and the temperature warmer. I'm tired of waiting for German to bring outboard parts, and the motor does work pretty well as long as I don't rev it up too high. Tonight I was looking for the description of the inlet a naval officer gave me, and found a note saying the best months to explore are April to August; the winds start to blow hard again in September. Ah hell. I easily could have made the trip to the glacier during the past two months. Of course I didn't know that in advance, and the temperature was cold and the days short.

This feels like a rationalization for not facing my fear. If I was going with another person, I'd have gone long ago. My imagination has held me back. I think the actual danger is slight. I could run into serious problems, but the worst that's likely to happen is to get stuck for days on some exposed rock waiting for a storm to pass, or if the motor quits, I might need to call for help. If I don't at least try to make it to the glacier, I suspect I'll carry the failure for a long time.

AUGUST 31, 2001

NIGHT: 38°F. The second half of August has been generally foul. Today it blew, rained, hailed, and snowed. I'm feeling restless and discontent. So is Cat. He's been whining and whining.

I often project my fear onto the world so I can avoid the external situation I imagine to be the source of the fear. Today I noticed that this same dynamic operates in *facing* fear. I project fear out so I can confront the situation I've convinced myself is the source. Once I confront the fear, I've dominated it and don't need to experience it any longer. Projecting fear into an imagined future, instead of actually experiencing it in the present moment, is another kind of cognitive dislocation. To truly face fear I must simply be with the experience and do nothing to avoid or attack it.

SEPTEMBER 2001

Traveler, the path is your footprints
and nothing more;
traveler, there is no path
but what you make by walking.
Your footsteps create the path,
and looking back
you see the track
where you won't pass again.
Traveler, there is no path,
but only wakes on the sea.

— "CANTARES" BY ANTONIO MACHADO, 1929

NO ENTRIES FOR SEPTEMBER 1–2, 2001

SEPTEMBER 3, 2001

NIGHT: 41°F. These past days have been cloudy and raining on and off. The wind not fierce, but strong enough to raise whitecaps. My shoulders seem to be slowly improving. Tonight I took ibuprofen for the first time in days. I haven't gone to Staines for a while, but if the weather is decent tomorrow, I might head over to fish in the lee of the cliffs. I still have one meal of fish, and the ice in the cooler should last another week.

I'm considering where I might plant a garden in the sun and out of the wind. The solar panels are keeping up with my electricity use, and I hope I won't need the wind generator again. If I'd known how noisy it would be, I'd have bought two more solar panels instead.

I've rigged a plastic shelter to stretch over the boat in case I go exploring for more than a day and can't find a place to camp on land. I've also built a spray shield on the boat that I hope will keep me dry in rough water. A few days ago I annotated the marine chart with the longitude and latitude of various prominent points along the route to the lake with the glacier so I'll be able to track my position on the map using GPS. I've been watching the barometer more closely, too, but can still make no sense of the relationship between it and the weather.

Still no word from Alejandra, and I'm considering not checking email anymore. German will get here when he does. I'm actually sort of glad he hasn't shown up yet. It's allowed me to realize I can make do with what I have and don't really need all the stuff I've asked Patti to buy and send.

I've been spending more time sitting in the rain and wind at the point. Cat usually comes with me. Today I snuck away and went to sit alone in the woods. I found a lovely nook down near the point. Delicate ferns, mosses, and lichen. It's much quieter in there, very wet, and very green. Not a square inch of bare earth.

Yesterday was full moon and I sweat. Sweating is important to me, but it's so much work that I'm glad I don't need to do it again for a month. I gave thanks for my life and again asked for the courage and steadiness to keep trying to accomplish whatever it is I came here to do. I can't do it on my own, or even figure out why I came.

Perhaps the darkness I fear so much is not evil, but loss of control. Ego hanging on for dear life, even though its need for control is killing me. Moments of surrender come and go, and perhaps one of the lessons I'm learning is that I can't depend on peak experiences to change my way of being. It's a long process, a lot of work, and it may come to naught.

It's getting easier to tell the butter-belly ducks apart. I don't know if my eyes have become sharper or if the male's color is changing with the coming of mating season. They came to drink on the beach today, and after they went back to the water the immature eagle landed to score one of the fish heads I've been tossing down there. The butter-bellies didn't like that at all. They came charging back up the beach and chased the eagle away. Poor eagles, no one wants them around. They must scavenge eggs or hunt the chicks.

A new pair of beautiful birds (Ashy-headed Goose) arrived recently: rusty brown breast, filigreed black-and-white belly and sides, light grey head and neck, some white on the wings.

The butter-bellies do their territorial defense routine several times a day. Both pairs know where the boundary is, so why not stop wasting time and energy defending it? Because that's not the way the world works. I don't believe science will ever really explain how the world is because the rational mind is incapable of doing so. Yet in my personal life I become furious when the world doesn't behave in a rational way — which, of course, isn't very rational.

SEPTEMBER 4, 2001

NIGHT: I just heard a commotion of flailing wings outside. The butter-bellies do this now and again, especially at night. Maybe the otter is out there. How do they ever sleep when they must always be on the lookout? I just noticed how odd it is to be typing on the laptop and pause to add wood to the fire. What a mix of technologies.

I went to Staines today and the spray/wind shield worked perfectly. I can just see over it and only my face gets wet. Fishing was poor. I guess it can't be good every day, but why not? Coming back, I got hit by a wave of restlessness. I wanted to go somewhere or do something, but I couldn't think of anyplace I want to go or anything I want to do. Not even make love. Just feeling restless. I might not actually *want* to go to the glacier, but I do feel called to go as part of the process of being here. My shoulders and back are very sore from pulling the anchor rock up two hundred feet and dragging the boat up the beach. No wonder I like to catch a bunch of fish when I go.

Late last night after writing, I went out to the rock. I didn't really want to, but something urged me on. Soft mystic moonlight fell on a calm sea and snowy Staines cliffs. I sat for a while — thoughts drifting in and out — calling my mind back over and over to my breath and to the sounds around me. Then one of those wandering thoughts snagged my attention.

I've been trying to feel part of the community of Life, but in that moment I remembered that I, myself, am already a community comprised of bacteria, viruses, fungi, mites, and who knows what else. And according to the biologist Lynn Margulis, even each eukaryote cell in my body is a symbiotic community, made up of organelles that at one time were independent prokaryote cells.

In the past, the thought of having all these critters living on, in, and with me — who are me — has been kind of creepy, but last night I was carried softly and gently into the flow of the world. Sacred indeed is everything. And me, sacred, too. Slowly I'm relaxing and healing. Not the earthshaking transformation I'd expected, but the ebb and flow of solitude carrying me along.

I remembered sitting in the Peruvian desert years ago beside a mummy dug up by grave robbers. I'd read about the Buddhist practice of going to the charnel house to meditate on impermanence, and through my Christian goggles had interpreted that practice as a penance to face the hard fact of death. But with the mummy I felt a quiet sense of brotherhood and spaciousness; I, too, would go where he had gone, and my immediate concerns were not as all-consuming as I usually experience them to be.

There was the same unexpected freedom last night when I realized that this me is not really just me. A sense of being woven into the world. In the past I've sensed the world as a unified field of sorts. Last night I sensed Life as myriad individual organisms, each maintaining its own inner coherence and all of us organized into a hierarchical web. I sensed myself as belonging to a world of individual beings, but there was no feeling of fragmentation; we were all still one flowing whole, too.

Lately I'm less concerned with trying to figure out how other people can easily find their way to a shift of consciousness. No theory or system can make it happen faster or easier. Like a child growing up, our spiritual lives need to be lived one day at a time.

In spite of these openings to Spirit, my behavior toward Cat is not improving. He got in the middle of my work today and I put him aside. He came back and I forcibly tossed him to the ground. No patience or compassion; just "Get the fuck out of my way while I'm trying to work." I don't know how to change this behavior. I'm aware of what I'm doing, and I do it anyway.

SEPTEMBER 5, 2001

NIGHT: First blue sky in a week, and I woke to morning sun slanting in through the window. Joy. I didn't expect it back at the cabin this soon. I hung the wash out to finish drying, and then Cat and I sat lizardlike on the rock. Ah me, what a spring day: slight breeze, 50 degrees, no bugs. I wanted to stay in the sun, but worked on the boat instead, so tomorrow I'll be ready to go away for a few days if the weather holds. At the moment it doesn't look too good: barometer falling and sky clouding over.

In one of the Gaia essays, Francisco Varela writes that through their behavior, animals allow us to see the world they have created for themselves. The butter-belly diving ducks are a good example. Their behavior both creates and points to the boundary line that stretches across the shifting sea between their territories. Without them to show me, I couldn't perceive it.

It's interesting that when a question arises in my mind I often see the answer soon after. Today I saw the female butter-belly sleep. She settled into a patch of kelp to keep from drifting, tucked her head under her wing, and dozed off. The male was feeding close by and seemed to keep watch.

SEPTEMBER 6, 2001

LATE NIGHT: My intuition last night about the weather was correct. I set the alarm for 7 AM. By 8 it was cloudy, a light breeze had sprung up, and small wavelets were washing the shore. I figured the channel might get rough, but my fish and wood supply need replenishing, so I headed to Staines anyway.

The wind was blowing way too hard over there to fish, and the waves breaking on the beach were big enough that loading wood would have been a hassle. I bagged it. Whoa! I actually let it go and started home without even trying to fish or cut wood. Just gave up.

Instead of coming straight home, I stayed out in the channel for a couple of hours to practice handling the boat in rough water. The motor started to miss so badly I thought I might not make it back. I need to run the motor in calm water to see if it misses even when water is not splashing up around it. I don't think I'll go far until German gets here with the parts whenever that might be. I'm definitely not going anywhere unless the day is flat calm.

According to the marine chart, the inlet I want to explore is about twenty miles northeast of here where a river runs from a small lake into the sea. A second lake, into which a glacier seems to slide, lies a short distance up a second river. On the topographic map, each river appears to be less than a quarter of a mile long and to gain very little altitude, so depending on how rough the country is I might be able to hike to the upper lake carrying the deflated kayak. If I can't reach the glacier eighty miles north of here, perhaps I can make it to this smaller closer one.

Even if I intend to go for only one night, it will take hours to prepare the gear, since I might have to wait out a storm before I can make it back. I'll leave Cat here with plenty of food. I imagine he'll hate being alone, but I worry that when I land somewhere he might not come back into the boat when it's time to move on.

SEPTEMBER 7, 2001

LATE NIGHT: 40°F. Cloudy with scattered stars. Only a light breeze and the sea is fairly calm. Last night was luxurious. I built a fire early and took a nap; got up, ate, read for a while, and took another nap; got up, read, and took a third nap; got up, ate, read, and watched dawn come through the window into the warm cabin. Each time I woke from a nap the fire had burnt to coals but started easily again. I spent a while at the point, and then came back to bed. I covered the sleeping pad with sheets, and for the first time since I've been here, took off my long underwear and slept naked.

Tonight is less peaceful. I've started reading *Thoughts without a Thinker* by Mark Epstein, a Freudian psychiatrist and Buddhist meditator. The book relates the two practices to each other, which is interesting and useful, but triggers all my psychological stuff again. I'm sick of rehashing the same old crap. Maybe that's the point. When I get sick enough of it, I may finally give it up.

In two weeks it will be spring equinox. How did that happen? Just yesterday it was winter solstice! I received an email from the national parks office that said, "Only a little time remains now," as though the main point is to be able to stay the full year. I've been here seven months and have five to go, so I'm just over halfway. But in one sense they're dead on. Time will begin to fly, and there really is only a little left.

A famous Zen koan asks: "If the many return to the One, to what does the One return?" If I think that returning to the One refers to the atoms and energy of the individual returning to the common flux of the universe, I'm mistaken; atoms and energy are matter. The challenge is to sense not only matter, but also nonmaterial Emptiness.

Deep, still, pool in my mind.

Is this why
    the quiet sea
        beckons so?

I sit on solid rock
    as wind and sea move me,

plying the clouded sky
    as gull, as condor.

Late I sit
    on solid rock
        sunk in this deep still pool.

And the sea mirrors my reflections.

SEPTEMBER 8, 2001

LATE NIGHT: Ha! I saw the butter-bellies screw today. The one I've thought was the male was on top. They had sex in the water and then head-bobbed and preened for a while; he worked mostly on his wings, while she concentrated on rearranging her ruffled tail feathers. Tufts of down stuck to her bill and dangled down on both sides like a Fu Manchu mustache. What cool birds. I'm glad to have them for neighbors and hope they nest where I can watch what they do.

The close pair had several strong interactions with the far pair and chased away a single intruder. When performing the ritual territorial defense, both pairs make noise and try to look as large as possible: the females stretch their necks up and point their bills toward the sky; the males push their breasts out, rear back, and beat their wings to hold themselves high out of the water; both sexes have their tails spread. The males sometimes charge each other, but always turn away to show their white tails before actual contact. Both pairs then swim parallel to the boundary — males between their female and the other pair. When intent on mayhem with an intruder, they attack silently and sink low in the water or even dive as they go after the outsider.

I think this female will begin laying eggs soon. I suppose she'll deposit one a day and start to brood once the whole clutch is laid. Will both of them brood the eggs in turn, or only the female? Will they guard the nest before they start to brood? If not, and if I can find the nest, I might rob an egg or two for dinner. Yum. They *probably* won't mind. . . .

Thoughts without a Thinker is clean, straightforward, and subtle. Epstein discusses the two false selves we all create: one is inflated and the other de-flated — in Buddhist terms, solid existence and solid nonexistence. I can certainly feel myself flip back and forth between these states. When I'm successful in something I feel grand, and when I fail I feel like shit. This is the exact dynamic Epstein describes. Happy day, I'm normal! Whew, it's pouring down rain.

NO ENTRY FOR SEPTEMBER 9, 2001

SEPTEMBER 10, 2001

NIGHT: 40°F. Yesterday, Sunday, was a long empty day. I awoke with that old feeling of not getting anywhere. I hear about people making progress in therapy and spiritual practice, but I've been at this shit for thirty-five years with little to show for it. I feel like Sisyphus, and question why I've wasted my life doing this when it's clearly not going anywhere. I try to maintain emotional and cognitive space so I can see what I find hard to deal with. At one point I sank deeply into the feeling of emptiness and it opened out and transformed into love and peace. Anxiety, I think, transformed into joy. This seemed important at the time, but less so now.

Emotions — like wind and rough sea — lose their apparent ferocity when I go into them, but gain power if I hold them at bay. When I hide in the cabin, the Wind threatens; if I go out, it's just wind. Instead of going out to transform Wind into wind yesterday, I remained inside with the anxiety. Clarity is important, too: emotions, like the sea, can swamp me if I don't take care to remain steady and alert.

Last night I got out the charts and marked the longitude and latitude for eighteen points along the route to the far glacier — just in case. As I was working on it, the wind shifted to the southwest and smashed straight into the cabin. I took it as a sign . . . but I'm not sure of what. Was it that the wind will fuck me up if I go, or, since in spite of my anxiety the cabin and I survived with no damage, that I shouldn't let my fear prevent me from going?

As far as I can tell, there is no way to predict the wind. Yesterday was cloudy with a moderate breeze from the northwest, as it has been for the past two weeks. Then — barometer holding steady and not especially low — the wind just slammed in. I still feel frustrated, threatened, and vulnerable, especially when considering a long boat trip.

This afternoon I was washed with a wave of grief for Mom. I cried as I acknowledged to myself how much I caused her to suffer by my inability to open up and be soft with her these past years. I tried so hard, but each time I went to visit I'd feel threatened, guard myself, and hold her away. Where did such hurt and rage come from? I have a dozen narratives to explain the family dynamic, but so what?

In my grief today, I also discovered shame. I've never really acknowledged how deeply ashamed of myself I am. Shame for who I am and who I am not. Especially my fear, weakness, and self-centeredness. I also must admit that I was ashamed of Mom, and I'm ashamed of myself for this, too. Feeling ashamed of someone who loves you must be one of the most hideous and damaging things you can do. I've done this to all the women who have loved me. Perhaps when I can't face my own shame, I dump it on others.

Running from these feelings has led me to be suicidal in subtle ways. To stay ahead of the shame or to disprove my cowardliness, I've done things that have almost killed me. But even as I write that, I must admit that I love to be out on the ragged edge where things are risky.

SEPTEMBER 11, 2001

NIGHT: 44°F. Calm and raining, and another day of difficult emotions. Some psychologists claim that fear is the fundamental emotion underlying anger. I don't think so. It seems to me that anger and shame are as basic as fear, and all are inherent in having an individual self. If I step back and visualize the universe as a whole, it's fluid and centerless. But when I experience it with my own ego-self as the center, this angle of view creates a distortion that manifests in different ways depending on circumstance: fear, anger, shame, etc.

I took the kayak to look for the diving ducks' nest but couldn't find it. When I got back, Cat wasn't around, which is unusual. I called, waited, and called some more as evening came on and it started to rain. I was beginning to worry that something had happened to him when he finally came strolling in from the direction of the point. He'd circled the island. I was very glad to see him. When he's around I often feel irritated and crowded, as if I'm not free to be myself, but when I think he might be gone, I feel the loss and miss him.

In *Thoughts without a Thinker* Epstein talks about being able to experience anxiety and excitement at the same time. I've often sensed that these two emotions share the same physiological arousal: when we believe we can handle an intense situation, we feel excitement; when we believe we can't cope, anxiety.

What's the difference between fear and anxiety? If fear is a biological response to something happening now, and anxiety a psychological response to an imagined future threat, then anxiety sucks. After all, the *future* exists only as certain kinds of thoughts we think in the present.

Epstein also writes that low self-esteem is endemic in our culture. This is useful to read because it sets my own experience in a broader context. We all suffer such pain, and in realizing our commonality, individual suffering is eased.

In some sense the suffering of starving, tortured, and diseased people seems unreal to me. But what does seem real is the pain of the countless people who experience themselves as failures and their lives as disappointing. I grieve for those who suffer so. This pain may be inherent to the existence of a self: in the end, we all fail because we all die.

SEPTEMBER 12, 2001

LATE NIGHT: 42°F. Grey windy day, sea on the move. After a night of dreams, I woke this morning feeling lost and confused. Then I just let it go and asked for help. Surrender brought peace, but also the disappointment that I'll never *understand the world*. It felt like another kind of failure.

I attempted to reglue a loose patch on the boat without removing the floor, but it didn't work. Maybe the pontoon material is damp and salty. I might try to rinse the area and use a heated rock to dry and warm it. Other than that, I meditated, read, and continued to struggle with fear. I'd considered not reading anymore, but instead I've started Wilber's eight-hundred-page book, *Sex, Ecology, Spirituality*, and will try to read fifty pages a day. I'm reluctant to give up reading and simply be with my own life 24/7.

Cat seems to have found playmates in the butter-belly diving ducks. He stalked them today and got very close before the male noticed him and flinched away into the water. Cat then turned his attentions to the female. She just lowered her head and hissed. He reconsidered his options and wandered away. I was sort of hoping he would jump on one of them. I doubt he could hurt them, unless he was very lucky, and the image of him clinging to a duck's back as it ran flapping across the water struck me as pretty funny. Of course I would have had to launch the kayak to go rescue him if he hung on for very long.

This afternoon I heard a warning call and saw them swim out into the eastern channel. I couldn't see anything until I used the binoculars to finally spot an intruder. They have amazing eyesight to recognize one of their own species so far away.

Can the formation of strong pair-bonds and territorial defense behavior be explained within some theoretical framework? Does neo-Darwinian Theory, which presupposes individual competing organisms, actually make sense? As I continue to watch them, such questions fade and I'm left with blank amazement and wonder at their bare existence.

SEPTEMBER 13, 2001

Fierce night. Rain and northwest wind roaring in the trees. I feel like a wild animal out there is trying to get to me, but as the months pass I'm becoming more confident that the cabin will hold. I'm also realizing more clearly that what I fear will come for me is already part of my mind.

I woke early to go for firewood at high tide. A light wind was already blowing, but I decided to go anyway. As I got out of bed, feeling groggy from not enough sleep, an inner voice said, "Don't go." How to listen to inner voices without going crazy and how to know which to believe? What is sound intuition and what only fear? When actual danger is involved — like taking a small boat into rough water — questioning whether an intuition can be trusted has more heft.

I loaded survival gear and chain saw into the boat. It started to piss down rain. I decided it was a sign to not go, but then changed my mind again. The water was very rough in the channel, and waves were breaking on the beach where I cut wood. It's the second time I've come home empty-handed.

Today pretty much convinced me to give up going to the distant glacier. The motor is running rougher than it was and knocking louder. I still plan to explore the inlet twenty miles north of here and see if I can hike and paddle to the glacier there. If I don't go to the far glacier, I imagine I'll have the opportunity to face my fear sooner or later anyway.

For a long time I've been relating to myself and my parents as if my character was the result only of upbringing with no input from my own inherent nature. How strange. Given the family dynamic, I could have responded differently. If I want to attribute all my stuff to nurture, I need to do the same for them. We've each done the best we could. Mom gave all she could in the face of her own fear and despair. Dad's severe criticisms came from his own sense of inadequacy; he must have judged himself cruelly — even if not consciously.

I read fifty pages of Wilber today. One whole section seems hopelessly muddled to me, but at the end he gives a summary that makes perfect sense. So he continues to be an interesting challenge.

I wonder about new knowledge. Perspectives might be refined, and the language used to express ideas evolves, but really new ideas are rare. Thinkers have seen the world in various ways for a long time, and the scope of potential worldviews probably doesn't change much.

SEPTEMBER 14, 2001

A lovely day, only the second in over a month. Mostly sunny, 45°F, light breeze from the southwest. I went fishing to Staines, but no bites at all. I did pick up a load of redwood, though.

After I unloaded I took the boat back out for a slow easy circuit around all four of the islands in this cluster where I live. It was relaxing to be close to home and not so worried about the motor, even though it sounded pretty unhealthy.

During the extreme low tide I walked out on the mudflat and watched buried clams squirt sparkling spouts of water, backlit by the late afternoon sun. I found a tiny sea urchin and a couple of small spiral snail shells—none of which I'd seen before. My eyes must be getting clearer.

I came in to put on warmer clothes, happened to look out the window and saw the kayak sitting untied right at the water's edge, with night falling and the tide coming in. If I hadn't noticed, I might have woken up tomorrow with the kayak gone — drifted away in some unknown direction. Can't believe I did that.

It's been a long day and I'm tired and sore. *Thoughts Without a Thinker* suggests focusing bare attention on pain. So I haven't taken any ibuprofen yet. I want to see if I can relax into the pain and sink beneath the conceptual label to experience it directly as a flickering complex of strong sensation. I hope to stay with it until it dissolves on its own.

SEPTEMBER 15, 2001

NIGHT: 49°F. Cloudy, calm. I was up early to go exploring, but a breeze from the northwest already whispered in the trees. Sunrise was astonishing. Maybe I miss a lot of beautiful sunrises by sleeping late. I didn't meditate, which changed the tone of the morning: a sweet lonely why-are-we-alive feeling.

This afternoon the close pair of diving ducks swam into their neighbor's territory. At the boundary the male hung back, but the female swam right in and started to feed. She kept calling, and finally, apparently against his better judgment, the male followed her. They continued to feed and even climbed onto the other pair's home-base rock. Suddenly a warning cry as the other pair rounded the corner into the basin and charged. Whoops! These guys were off the rock and underwater in a heartbeat. Once back in their own territory they resumed their normal boundary defense display. (Ah, the female . . . always leading the male astray.)

This behavior was new to me. Are all animals as individual as these? If I watched them for five years, would they continue to act creatively the whole time? Maybe the belief that instinct drives most animal activity is overstated. Studies often focus on commonalities and ignore differences. But doing so can create a distorted picture and give the impression that we understand the world better than we actually do.

At the extreme low tide I took the shovel out onto the mudflat and waited until I saw a squirt. I dug but didn't find whatever squirted. As the afternoon light softened, my mood shifted to a sort of sweet sadness. Looking around at the mountains and sea, I imagined being already gone from here and missing it terribly. Al Green singing *For the Good Times* has been going through my head all day.

I like Wilber's claim that differentiation and integration are both necessary aspects of development: too much autonomy, the individual loses vital connection with the environment; too openly receptive, the individual is overwhelmed. I suspect I'm much too differentiated. The only time I feel fully integrated is alone in the wilderness. This sense of excessive independence is common in our culture, especially for men.

According to Wilber, we're evolving on all levels: physical, cultural, and cognitive. Humans haven't left behind some ideal state of being and run off the rails by developing a strong differentiated ego. The emergence of the ego is a vital stage of development, but not the end of the process. The individual still needs to integrate the ego into the soul and into the embracing swirl of the universe. We haven't gone astray, but neither have we arrived to where we're going.

On my way to the point yesterday I noticed a path has formed where I walk through the grass. It gave me a sense of comfort and security. Maybe what I'm doing here is laying down a path between different states of consciousness. Not coming up with an abstract theory of how to control the shift, but simply covering the ground again and again until I know the territory and have laid down a path in walking.

LATE NIGHT: It's been a tranquil day. I woke to light rain and a flat sea. Ah, quiet. On the high tide I went fishing to Staines and caught a bunch of snapper. Since my ice is gone, I sealed the fillets in a plastic container and floated it in a pool of groundwater beneath the trees. The water is 40°F and the fish should keep for at least four days. It was wonderful to slide over glassy water without being jarred by wind and chop; like leaving a rutted dirt road to roll along smooth pavement.

It drizzled most of the day and I enjoyed being out in the gentle rain. Wisps and streamers of mist wrapped themselves around the hills and drifted into the hollows. The rock walls and waterfalls were perfect and perfectly beautiful. How blessed I am to be here.

Out on the water I felt my heart softly open, and remembered that this is the feeling I have when I leave the safety of home for the unknown. I still fear the trip to the glacier, but being far from the cabin might carry me more deeply into this openness. Something in me is calling, or I wouldn't be so concerned about whether I go or not.

While fishing, I heard the sea lions and went to visit. There are ten of them now. A dominant bull, eight smaller adults, and the calf. They were a delight to watch. I drifted to within thirty yards of them, but was leery of going closer since I don't know how far the bull will defend his territory. They all swam back and forth along the rock in a tight pack, sometimes sort of leapfrogging over each other. They would pause, lift up to gaze at me, and then resume their swimming. It looked like play to me — like they were swimming together just for the fun of it.

Mom and calf stayed on a ledge, leaning this way and that, as if the movement gave them a better look at me. They were always touching: mostly the calf had a flipper over mom's back. Finally, she, too, dove into the water and left the calf alone. Their ledge was four or five feet above the sea, and if the calf had gone in, I couldn't see how it would get back up again, so I kept my distance. How nice to have them for neighbors.

NO ENTRIES FOR SEPTEMBER 17–21, 2001

Spring Equinox.

Time is:
a worm
a caterpillar
a grub.

Minutes creep into days
days trudge toward the end of the week.

Then lost in the long grey sleep of our absence
a sudden startling shift.

A transformation.

Years have flown and carried us toward
the implacable moment of death.

Are you remembering to remember.
to pause and notice Life *living* in you?

to feel
the tender autumn light
flicker across your waters?

to drift
with the clouds and mist
into the mountains and canyons
of your soul?

to float
in the ebb and flow
of joy and sorrow, love and grief
through the wide empty basin of your heart?

What a glorious first day of spring. The past five days were raw: frequent rain, no sun, and nearly constant wind. But yesterday afternoon the weather shifted to calm and clear, with only a light breeze from the southeast.

I had hoped to finish *Sex, Ecology, Spirituality* by now, but I'm only on page three hundred. I mostly like what Wilber writes, even though he makes the spiritual journey seem very straightforward — almost like solving an engineering problem or learning to play tennis. For me, opening my heart and mind to what is, rather than trying to control everything, remains a mysterious art.

Although I've been staying up until nearly dawn most nights, I decided to go to bed with the chickens last night and get an early start today. But before I knew it, it was 5 AM. I woke three hours later to a clear calm sunrise. The breeze didn't build, and by noon I was on my way to the inlet southeast of here where I've wanted to go for six months.

At first I trudged along at only 8 or 9 mph since the motor started to miss when I cranked it up enough to plane. I'd like to get that fixed, but there's still no word from Alejandra about when German might come with the parts. Other than that the motor ran ok. Then I remembered that if I slow to a crawl and accelerate rapidly, the boat lifts up much easier. After that I was flying along at almost 14 mph in the calm areas and 11 or so in the light chop.

It feels like movement is a deep part of who I am, but once on the water today and less tightly bound, I remembered that such exploring is not the main reason I came here. On the contrary, I came to practice being still and receptive, rather than constantly active and seeking. Still, it felt great to be on the move.

Along the way I stopped at what looked like a good place to fish, where the rock wall had crumbled into the sea. Wham. Even before the bait reached bottom I had a nice snapper on. The next three times down I pulled up six fish — all of them as big as the biggest I've caught at Staines. Dinner secured, I motored on.

The inlet is beautiful. At the far end I fished the mouth of the small river that drains a lake I'd considered trying to reach in the kayak. No bites, but it was a treat to listen to the babble and watch the sun sparkle on moving water. I miss that here on the island. The river was much too fast and rocky to paddle up or walk with kayak in tow. The land was flat and sparsely treed, and I could, perhaps, have deflated the kayak and carried it cross-country, but I didn't try.

Along the way I looked for possible campsites, but there were always signs that the tide floods into the heavy brush. I followed a narrow side inlet reaching south into the foothills. It was alluring in there, but at the far end — as far from anywhere as you can go — I found a bunch of plastic crap that had drifted in with the wind and tide. I cleaned it up and brought the trash home with me.

Back here, I went to visit the sea lions. Woooeee! The colony is growing fast. It started with one last fall, and I counted eighteen today. Where do they come from and how do they know there's a colony forming here? Do they leave and return each year? No wonder fishing is now slow over there.

A beautiful bird (Rufous-chested Dotterel) has recently arrived. Maybe eight inches tall, neutral grey back, creamy white belly with strips of white running up in front of the wings. The breast is a rich rusty brown and separated from the belly by a heavy black line. The eyes are ringed in white, and a white band circles the head just above the eyes. I saw two of the males fighting yesterday and it was just as exciting as a cockfight.

My psychological struggles have continued these past days and I'm getting pretty damned tired of them, too. I guess I'll give it up eventually. In the meantime I'll cook fish and rice for dinner and then go to sleep. I may sit under stars for just a little while first, though. . . .

NO ENTRIES FOR SEPTEMBER 23–30, 2001

INTERLUDE

THE URGE TO BE ALONE

He who does not enjoy solitude will not love freedom.
— ARTHUR SCHOPENHAUER

Solitude is a torment which is not threatened in hell itself.
— JOHN DONNE

Our language has wisely sensed the two sides of being alone.
It has created the word loneliness to express the pain of being alone.
And it has created the word solitude to express the glory of being alone.

— PAUL TILLICH

Solitude has long been recognized in many cultures as an opportunity to look inward, but in our current cultural climate seeking solitude is often considered unhealthy. Many psychologists and other therapists say we are social beings and claim that meaning is found only through relationship with other people. For me, this is only partially true. We are also spiritual beings, and to be fully human we need relationship not only with other people but with the nonhuman world, our own inner depths, and with Something Greater. In solitude there is the opportunity to deeply explore all these domains of relationship.

What is it that calls or drives some people into solitude? Abraham Maslow, in his study of the human hierarchy of needs, found a greater detachment and desire for privacy in self-actualizing individuals, but Anthony Storr writes:

> Most psychiatrists and psychologists agree that human beings differ in temperament, and that such differences are largely inborn, however much they may be fostered or suppressed by the circumstances of childhood and by subsequent events in a person's life. This is especially true when considering the individual's reaction to solitude. At the very least, we all need the solitude of sleep; but, in waking life, people vary widely in how much they value experiences involving human relationships and how much they value what happens when they are alone.[1]

Storr also describes how our feelings may urge us to leave our habitual social setting to spend time alone:

> In the ordinary way, our sense of identity depends upon interaction both with the physical world and with other people. . . . My relationships with my family, with colleagues, friends, and less intimate acquaintances, define me as a person who holds certain views and who may be expected to behave in ways which are predictable.
>
> But I may come to feel that such habitually defining factors are also limiting. Suppose that I become dissatisfied with my habitual self, or feel that there are areas of experience or self-understanding which I cannot reach. One way of exploring these is to remove myself from present surroundings and see what emerges. This is not without its dangers. Any form of new organization or integration within the mind has to be preceded by some degree of disorganization. No one can tell, until he has experienced it, whether or not this necessary disruption of former patterns will be succeeded by something better.[2]

In our culture, specialization has been carried to such an extreme in the service of efficient productivity that daily life can become narrow and boringly repetitious. Activities we used to enjoy in childhood and youth are lost to the demands of adulthood. In wilderness solitude there is the need and the opportunity to do everything for oneself. For me, the satisfaction of self-reliance is one of the joys of living alone in the wilderness.

Solitude can provide a respite from the demands of social life, in which personal healing might take place. In the words of Father Henri Nouwen:

> Although the desire to be useful can be a sign of mental and spiritual health, in our goal-oriented society it can also become the source of a paralyzing lack of self-esteem. More often than not we not only desire to do meaningful things, but we often make the results of our work the criteria of our self-esteem. . . .
>
> When we start being too impressed by the results of our work, we slowly come to the erroneous conviction that life is one large scoreboard where someone is listing the points to measure our worth. And before we are fully aware of it, we have sold our souls to the many grade-givers. . . . A life without a lonely place, that is, a life without a quiet center, easily becomes destructive. When we cling to the results of our actions as our only source of self-identification, then we become possessive and defensive and tend to look at our fellow human beings more as enemies to be kept at a distance than as friends, with whom we share the gifts of life. . . . In solitude we become aware that our worth is not the same as our usefulness.[3]

Solitude provides an opportunity to investigate the sense of alienation many of us experience in our culture and to realize that being alone is not identical with feeling isolated and lonely. The core of my loneliness, when I feel lonely, is not separation from other people, but feeling disconnected from myself and from Spirit. In the absence of external judgments, I can see more clearly how often I demean myself, and I can begin to develop a sense of intrinsic self-worth. Paradoxically, choosing to spend time alone can help heal our sense of alienation from others.

Possibly the most often cited reason for going into solitude is to seek spiritual communion. This involves surrender of individual autonomy to something greater: God, Spirit, Nature, or our human family. Charles Alexander Eastman writes about the attitude of American Indians toward the Eternal, the "Great Mystery" — before contact with Europeans:

> The worship of the "Great Mystery" was silent, solitary, free from all self-seeking. It was silent, because all speech is of necessity feeble and imperfect; therefore the souls of my ancestors ascended to God in wordless adoration. It was solitary, because they believed that He is nearer to us in solitude, and there were no priests authorized to come between a man and his Maker.[4]

According to David Abram, the shaman in many aboriginal societies spends time in solitude so he can mediate between the human and suprahuman realms. Although such surrender and communion are commonly acknowledged in religious writings, many secular authors do not seriously discuss them.

DEFINING SOLITUDE

In *Solitude: A Philosophical Encounter*, Philip Koch identifies three features that define solitude — physical isolation, social disengagement, and self-reflectiveness — but argues that the essence is disengagement from other subjects:

> What, then, is solitude? It is a time in which experience is disengaged from other people. All of the other features of solitude that come intuitively to mind, the physical isolation, the reflective cast of mind, the freedom, the silence, the distinctive feel of space and time — all of these flow from that core feature, the absence of others in one's experiential world.[5]

I agree with this definition, but would add a caveat. Solitude may not depend on the physical absence of others or even the absence of others in our consciousness, but rather on how we react to their presence. If we engage with others, in either a positive or negative way, we are not alone. However, if we do not reach out to beckon them closer or push them away, but simply notice their presence, we remain free in our solitude. Finally, though, trying to define solitude is, like trying to define relationship, an impossible task, since there is no one thing called solitude. The experience varies among individuals and within one individual across time and circumstance.

By almost any definition, living alone in the wilderness is solitude; even so, I have always been keenly aware of how my felt relationship with other people and with the world around me changes. Even while I remain physically apart from and generally out of communication with others, the quality of my solitude varies widely. At times, I'm fully engaged with the present moment, with the flow of the nonhuman world, with the mysterious presence of Spirit. At other times, I'm lost in memories of being with people or in imagining future social interactions.

When building the cabin, I often wondered how what I was creating would seem to Patti. Was I in solitude at those times? When writing an email to request information about my electric system from a tech support person, was I in solitude? When I'm writing in my journal and sly thoughts of an imagined future reader creep into my mind, am I in solitude? In some sense it may be impossible to ever completely leave the cultural matrix, since the consciousness with which I experience solitude is itself a collective cultural phenomenon.

Koch also identifies five virtues — valued states or activities — most easily realized in solitude: Freedom, Attunement to Self, Attunement to Nature, Reflective Perspective, Creativity. I would add a sense of vibrant *aliveness*. My journal contains many scattered references to these virtues, and I have considered using them as a framework to organize and describe my experience, but to what end? If I were to do so, I and the reader would gain little and we would lose much of the spontaneous immediacy of the journal.

OBJECTIONS TO SOLITUDE

There are also objections to spending time in solitude. Until recently, I'd never questioned whether spending time alone is psychologically healthy or socially acceptable; it has simply been an important part of my life since I was a young boy. I've discovered, though, that there has been a rich and sometimes acrimonious argument about the matter, at least since biblical days.

Ecclesiastes (4:9–12) warns:

Two are better than one; because they have a good reward for their
    labor.

For if they fall, the one will lift up his fellow: but woe to him that is
    alone when he falleth; for he hath not another to help him up.
Again, if two lie together, then they have heat: but how can one be warm
    alone?
And if one prevails against him, two shall withstand him; and a threefold
    cord is not quickly broken.

But the great biblical mystics Moses, John the Baptist, and Jesus all went into
solitude to face their demons and commune with God alone.

Since then there have been many others who have condemned the pointless selfishness of spending time alone. David Hume snarls that:

> Celibacy, fasting, penance, mortification, self-denial, humility, silence,
> solitude, and the whole train of monkish virtues; for what reason are
> they everywhere rejected by men of sense, but because they serve to no
> manner of purpose; neither advance a man's fortune in the world, nor
> render him a more valuable member of society, neither qualify him for
> the entertainment of company, nor increase his power of self-enjoyment?
> We observe, on the contrary, that they cross all these desirable ends;
> stupefy the understanding and harden the heart, obscure the fancy and
> sour the temper.[6]

Storr credits object-relations theorists with fostering the current widespread
belief that the only value and meaning in life are found through social relationships:

> If we were to listen only to the psycho-analytic "object-relations" the-
> orists, we should be driven to conclude that none of us have validity as
> isolated individuals. From their standpoint, it appears that we possess
> value only in so far as we fulfill some useful function vis-à-vis other
> people, in our roles, for example, as spouse, parent, or neighbor. It fol-
> lows that the justification for the individual's existence is the existence
> of others.[7]

Apart from the dangerousness and apparent uselessness of spending time
alone, perhaps the most common objection to solitude is that withdrawing
from social engagement is self-indulgent and irresponsible. Thoreau answers
this at length in the conclusion to *Walden*, and Nouwen writes:

> Many arguments for the value of solitude do not defend solitude in and
> of itself, but only the beneficial effect it can have on one's relations with
> other people and one's contribution to society.
>
>   Solitude is essential to community life because in solitude we grow
> closer to each other. . . . We take the other with us into solitude and there
> the relationship grows and deepens. In solitude we discover each other

in a way which physical presence makes difficult, if not impossible. There we recognize a bond with each other that does not depend on words, gestures or actions and that is deeper and stronger than our own efforts can create. . . . There we grow closer to each other because there we can encounter the source of our unity.[8]

And also:

In solitude we realize that nothing human is alien to us, that the roots of all conflict, war, injustice, cruelty, hatred, jealousy, and envy are deeply anchored in our own heart.[9]

Social responsibility is a balance of give and take. My own sense of responsibility and belonging to a social network seems to deepen in solitude. After my first long wilderness retreat, I volunteered to teach organic vegetable gardening for two years in the rural mountains of the Dominican Republic. After this retreat, I trust I will also find ways to contribute to the lives of others.

At times, when I'm unhappy and confused, I wonder if spending time alone is selfish, but when I'm clear I realize I cannot know what contribution I'm making to the world. I'm part of the world, and to the extent I heal myself — assuming wilderness solitude promotes healing — I heal the world. To say a solitary is shirking responsibility is to claim to understand the full workings of reality. All we can do is be true to our deepest calling and trust that we are doing what we are meant to do.

To the objection that solitude is escapist and that the choice for solitude is a choice for a world of unreality, Koch replies: "Direct encounters with Nature, Self, and the Mysterious in solitude are in fact generally acclaimed to feel more self-authenticating, more luminous with Being, than most social encounters."[10] Many of the claims that solitude produces deleterious effects are couched in terms with loaded meanings that are often carelessly conflated. Thus solitude, aloneness, isolation, alienation, loneliness, and longing are sometimes used interchangeably, even though they have quite different meanings. Aloneness, for example, refers to a physical state, while loneliness and alienation are emotional experiences.

Perhaps we should use the term solitude to refer to the experience of spaciousness in being alone, and isolation to the experience of being cut off. The feeling of isolation does not depend on external circumstance. Alone in the wilderness, I often feel isolated not only from others (in my mind and heart) but also from the nonhuman world around me; from Spirit; from myself. At other times, with no change in physical circumstance, I feel fully integrated into the flow of the universe, which includes not only the world immediately around me but also my web of human relationships. Nor are loneliness and longing identical. I often feel lonely in solitude without actually longing to be with anyone. Perhaps my longing for another person, when it arises, is actually longing for my lost connection with myself and with Spirit.

CONTAINMENTS AND COMPLETIONS OF SOLITUDE

Can we ever be completely alone or completely engaged with others? In *Labyrinth of Solitude*, Octavio Paz writes: "Solitude is the profoundest fact of the human condition. Man is the only being who knows he is alone."[11] Marcel Proust puts an even sharper edge to it:

> Not withstanding the illusion by which we would fain be cheated and with which, out of friendship, politeness, deference and duty, we cheat other people, we exist alone. Man is the creature who cannot escape himself, who knows other people only in himself, and when he asserts the contrary he is lying.[12]

Ken Wilber and Christian de Quincey, on the other side, argue that intersubjectivity is fundamental. Our sense of isolation arises from a particular perceptual angle. Buddhism sometimes claims that all sense of separateness is an illusion. One reason for going into solitude is to explore the unity that lies beneath our apparent aloneness; beneath the need to connect through social engagement, mediated by language. For me, the only way to satisfactorily answer the question, "Are we truly alone, locked into separate minds and bodies?" is experientially through a transformation of consciousness.

M. C. Escher's drawing *Bond of Union* beautifully depicts our situation. Each of us has a distinct perception of the world, and we can never know the actual experience of another. We are profoundly alone. Yet we can intertwine and to some extent share our experiences. More, if we are willing to quiet our minds and peer beyond the allure of language, we might discover that we are fundamentally united. But the drawing is not inclusive enough, because I sometimes experience all people and all nonhuman organisms as manifestations of our common flowing Life. And finally, the planets among which we float are us. Our sense of separateness, while not exactly an illusion, is not the whole truth.

In discussing how solitude and relationship fit together, Koch develops the notion of containment. Social relations act as a container for our time in solitude, just as our solitariness is always present in our relationships. In interweaving these two aspects of our being, he heals the false dichotomy between social and solitary.

He depicts the lives of St. Anthony and other Desert Fathers as an example of containment. Even though each lived a solitary life out of sight and hearing of the others, they met for prayer once a week, assisted each other in times of need, and always welcomed guests with hospitality. Their solitary lives were pursued within a web of social and spiritual relations. I believe, though, that this containment can be (and in the lives of true solitaries is) reversed. Relationship with God, Spirit, or nonhuman nature becomes the containment for social relationships.

Some of the layers of containment for my retreat are: the Buddha, the Dharma, and my Sangha; the one-year timeframe and subsequent return to the social milieu; journal writing; and the memory of my first long retreat into wilderness solitude. I work to expand, dissolve, or at least soften the boundaries of my conceptual containment, to relax my grip on social identity and settle into the mystery of living in the present moment.

Koch also speaks of the completions of solitude: the experience is completed in sharing it with others. I find this need in myself and question it. If I claim that solitude is valuable and meaningful in and of itself, but I need to share, even validate, the experience through journaling, am I living a lie? Is trying to share our solitude a futile endeavor, in any case? Perhaps some experiences are so sacred they should be honored in silence and not be diffused or profaned by trying to talk about them.

Koch presents points of view from both sides of the argument concerning fundamental human nature — solitary or social — and concludes:

> Collecting all these observations in a summary: the ways in which communicative encounters with other people are incomplete have either been falsely exaggerated by the lonely philosophers, or, when true, do not prove that aloneness is any more ultimate a state than encounter.

And

> What is the place of aloneness in human existence? Given the failure of arguments to the contrary, I am inclined to accord to it an equal status with encounter. Both are states of Being and Knowledge, both are full of illusions and lies.[13]

IS SOLITUDE FOR EVERYONE?

Petrarch, defending solitude in the fourteenth century, wrote: "I am not so much proposing a rule for others as exposing the principles of my own mind. If it commends itself to anyone, let him follow its suggestion."[14] Thomas Merton, with his tendency toward global prescription, promoted a stronger view:

> Not all men are called to be hermits, but all men need enough silence and solitude in their lives to enable the deep inner voice of their own true self to be heard at least occasionally. . . . If man is constantly exiled from his

own home, locked out of his own spiritual solitude, he ceases to be a true person. He no longer lives as a man.[15]

Nouwen, using Christian language I must translate into my own idiom, reminds me that the dark times I experience in solitude do not arise simply from my own neuroses, but are a manifestation of the difficulties faced by anyone who turns inward. In his words:

> In solitude I get rid of my scaffolding: no friends to talk with, no telephone calls to make, no meetings to attend, no music to entertain, no books to distract, just me — naked, vulnerable, weak, sinful, deprived. Broken — nothing. It is this nothingness that I have to face in my solitude, a nothingness so dreadful that everything in me wants to run to my friends, my work, and my distractions so I can forget my nothingness and make myself believe that I am worth something. But that is not all. As soon as I decide to stay in my solitude, confusing ideas, disturbing images, wild fantasies, and weird associations jump about in my mind like monkeys in a banana tree. Anger and greed begin to show their ugly faces. I give long, hostile speeches to my enemies and dream lustful dreams in which I am wealthy, influential, and very attractive — or poor, ugly, and in need of immediate consolation. Thus I try again and again to run from the dark abyss of my nothingness and restore my false self in all its vainglory. . . .
>
> The task is to persevere in my solitude, to stay in my cell until all my seductive visitors get tired of pounding on my door and leave me alone. . . . That is the struggle. It is the struggle to die to the false self. But this struggle is far, far beyond our own strength. Anyone who wants to fight his demons with his own weapons is a fool. The wisdom of the desert is that the confrontation with our own frightening nothingness forces us to surrender ourselves totally and unconditionally to the Lord Jesus Christ.[16]

We each have a social identity, a persona held in place by our interactions with other people. In solitude, without others to mirror this persona, it begins to lose solidity and dissolve. The process can be terrifying, and one powerful aspect of solitude is that there are few easy escapes from such difficult experiences. There is opportunity and necessity to face inner darkness. Emotional cycles — both highs and lows — usually modulated by social engagement, can become extreme. In solitude I experience a full range of emotions, from feeling painfully isolated to feeling joyfully woven into my physical surroundings and into my fabric of personal relationships. I discover that I'm not identical to the conception I often have of myself as an isolated individual. I'm more fluid and profoundly part of the flowing whole.

Koch recognizes that he cannot objectively defend the value of solitude; that it is an inner debate between our various selves about how we wish to live our lives: "My purpose, rather, has been to enable us to better understand the origins of certain inner questions which nag at our solitude."[17] I find his writing valuable in that it makes more visible the interweaving of solitude and engagement in my own life.

The claim that we can find real value and meaning in our lives only through intimate interpersonal relationships has not been widespread in our culture for very long, but its power is difficult to resist. Even after the wonder, peace, and joy I've experienced in solitude, I still feel at times that something vital is missing from my life when I'm not involved in an intimate physical relationship with a mate. No matter how rich my engagements with nonhuman nature and Spirit (as well as with friends and family), I sometimes lose my balance and slip into despondency when I live in a solitary state.

This feeling of lack is more difficult to accept in the city than it is in the wilderness. When I'm feeling the pain of loneliness and longing in solitude, I can justify it by telling myself, "Well, of course I hurt. Look where I am and what I'm doing." In the city, it's easy to feel that no one wants to be with me and to forget that I actively choose to be alone because I find peace, joy, and fulfillment in solitude. The boundary between solitude and engagement does not always seem permeable to me, but a wall I must climb — in both directions. I often feel isolated rather than simply alone, and I continue to work to make the boundary more porous.

The value of spending time in the wilderness has been studied empirically by Robert Greenway, who has been leading groups of students on two- to four-week retreats for many years. Spending three days alone is an option for those who wish. He has documented the following effects of the experience on some of his students:

90 percent of respondents described an increased sense of aliveness, well-being and energy;

90 percent stated that the experience allowed them to break an addiction (defined very broadly — from chocolate to nicotine and other foods);

80 percent found the return [to "civilization"] initially very positive;

53 percent of those found that within two days the positive feelings had turned to depression;

77 percent described a major life change upon return (in personal relationships, employment, housing, or lifestyle);

38 percent of those changes "held true" after five years;

60 percent of the men and 20 percent of the women stated that a major goal of the trip was to conquer fear, challenge themselves, and expand limits;

57 percent of the women and 27 percent of the men stated that a major goal of the trip was to "come home" to nature;

60 percent of all respondents stated that they had adopted at least one ritual or contemplative practice learned on the trip; 18 percent of those studied longitudinally (nine out of fifty) stated that they were still doing the practice after five years;

92 percent cited "alone time" as the single most important experience of the trip; getting up before dawn and climbing a ridge or peak in order to greet the sun was cited by 73 percent as the second most important experience. "Community" or fellowship of the group was cited by 80 percent as the third most important experience.[18]

But Greenway makes no universal claims about the supposed beneficial effects of spending time in the wilderness:

I do not believe the therapeutic effects of wilderness can be proven by scientifically objective measures and with statistical confidence. Nor am I fully confident that, within the dynamics of my own culture, these effects are in fact therapeutic, whether proven or not. I have observed many (mostly futile) attempts to prove beneficial outcomes of various psychotherapeutic approaches and realize wilderness therapy deals with even more variables.

He goes on to say:

While studying the wilderness experience, I honor it as an experience of exquisite beauty, of obvious impact on individuals, and so profound and complex that using the word *spiritual* seems appropriate. Whatever the wilderness experience is, and whatever its benefits, it is worthy of respect and a flexible research approach.

As with much participatory anthropological research, my approach has been rooted within the process and confirmed by experience. Objectivity is an interesting and useful mode of knowing, but should not be mistaken for the reality of experience. I have tried to avoid grabbing hold of symbols and findings to create theories.[19]

Even though Greenway's focus is more on the effects of wilderness than of solitude per se, and the retreats he leads are shorter, I find parallels between the effects he has documented and what I experience in wilderness solitude. I, too, although my intention at the beginning of this retreat was to explore solitude through a purely secular lens, have had to admit that I cannot fully live nor write about what is happening without using spiritual terminology.

SURVIVING WILDERNESS SOLITUDE

Living alone in the wilderness demands the ability to survive physically, emotionally, psychologically, and spiritually with minimal external support. Such independence is sometimes frightening, but trusting and relying on oneself is also deeply rewarding.

Survival in the wilderness and survival in solitude require two distinct sets of skills. Both are needed to survive in wilderness solitude. This doesn't mean there is one standard set that is the same for all people in all circumstances: it depends on topography, climate, and psychospiritual orientation. But a broad range of skills, developed over time, will be called into play.

The ability to build a shelter, stay warm and dry, obtain and prepare food, repair clothing and damaged equipment, maintain personal health, and use a map to navigate on land or water are all necessary physical skills. It is also vital to have the psychospiritual tools and experience to deal with the mental effects of long solitude. There are various ways to do this, but most fundamental is the capacity to experience with equanimity (or to ignore) whatever arises in the mind.

OCTOBER 2001

If you understand,
Things are just as they are.
If you do not understand,
Things are just as they are.

—— ZEN PROVERB TAPED TO MY CABIN DOOR

NO ENTRIES FOR OCTOBER 1—9, 2001

OCTOBER 10, 2001

I'd thought I would stop daily journaling around the equinox, but I'm surprised how suddenly it happened. Bam, I just quit writing. It's been an intense seventeen days since my last entry. The weather has been mostly glorious. Only two days of wind and heavy rain; the rest of the time was calm and clear or calm and cloudy. During the day, temperatures ranged from the low 50s to low 60s, and at night, high 30s to low 50s. Now it's storming again.

On September 23, I packed the boat, sent a code yellow email with my proposed route and destination, and at noon headed up the east channel to try hiking with the kayak to the lake with the glacier. The sea turned choppy for a while, but the wind came from behind and was not troublesome. I used the GPS to track my location and compared its readings with the chart on which I'd noted the longitude and latitude of prominent landmarks along the route.

Traveling by small open boat through an uninhabited wilderness of mountains, islands, and unknown waterways is like nothing else I've ever done. At times I feel an ethereal expansion of who I am, and at other times sense myself and the boat as a tiny moving speck in the immensity. Narrow passageways, a larger boat couldn't enter, lure me to investigate. Then, at the far end, they fling me out again into a seemingly endless shining sea.

Running with a small outboard in calm water is not like paddling a kayak or driving a powerful speedboat. It's more exciting and free than paddling, more relaxing and intimate with the water than speed boating. Small variations in velocity can make a big difference. Trudging along at nine miles per hour is slow; lifting to a plane at thirteen is fast. Although excitement builds at the higher speed, it still allows enough psychic space to appreciate the quiet around and within. Sometimes, when conditions are right, a harmony grows between boat, motor, body, and mind. Standing motionless in the bow, just shifting my weight for balance and tweaking the steering pole now and then, I zoom at mellow speed through an endlessly expanding universe.

The trip that day was beautiful. I followed the channel north for fifteen miles, turned east for another five, back south along a narrower passage, and finally east again deeper into the foothills. During this final stretch, the banks closed in and lofted overhead into sheer cliffs. At the end of the inlet, where I expected to see a shallow river rush into the sea and where I'd hoped to camp, I found magic instead. A narrow notch split the rock and allowed the boat to ease into a hidden tidal lake.

In a trance, I motored through and saw seven condors — the most mythic of birds — wheeling overhead. An eagle, curious about this strange apparition, circled low to inspect me, and then soared back up as though wishing to be a condor, too. All around, the steep rock walls rose to form a secret amphitheater and frame the clear blue sky. For the first time in a while, I felt protected and safe.

I beached the boat near the river that poured crystal water from the upper lake into this one. Trees I hadn't seen before showed pale spring leaves. I made my way across a soggy brush-choked flat and climbed a bluff, trying unsuccessfully to reach the upper lake. The terrain was too rugged and the rocks too slick to risk a serious fall. I did, though, reach a vantage point from where I should have seen the glacier I was seeking. But it wasn't there. It was either still hidden from where I stood, or the map is wrong.

It was the first time I'd hiked on this wild coast, and it felt good to be high above the sea. The view back to where I'd left the boat was stunning: Plunging through a gorge in a long series of rapids and falls, the river sparkled in the late sun. Here and there, the slanting rays filtered through moss-draped trees to touch and warm the forest floor. I couldn't leave the play of light on land without tracing its memory on film.

Unable to find a dry level place to camp, I tied the boat between one anchor in the water and another dug into the beach, then arranged my gear to make room to sit, cook, and sleep. The night was cold and clear, and at dawn I woke to sunshine in a sleeping bag damp with frost. I decided to stay, fast, and ask for a vision that would transform my life — taking the lake and

surrounding cliffs as my quest circle. I spent a quiet day on the beach and in
the boat. The condors shared the sky with me, and the golden red rock walls,
sculpted by sliding shadows, morphed into geometric shapes and dragonlike
beings.

I received no startling vision. Instead, from deep within, a profound
recognition: All that I experience — joy and pain, light and dark, courage
and fear, kindness and cruelty — are part of me and filled with Spirit. I need
to accept and honor everything just as it is, just as I am. And reaching out, I
realized there is no real separation between me and the world. All is Sacred
and seamless.

That night I dreamed I was hitchhiking and picked up by an evil man
with a knife. Later, I came to, lying wounded in the hospital, and asked if I'd
managed to kill the man. I was told no, but that the police had. The dream
seemed a warning that in accepting all of myself, including the shadow, I must
be careful to not lose my sense of balance and responsibility. If I act out my
own dark impulses, literal, rather than symbolic, death might result.

I rigged a tarp over the boat that second night to keep off the frost, and
woke at first light to eat, pack, and leave. Back in the inlet, I headed south for
a few miles and was entranced by fantastic ice fields, carved by morning light
and shadow. I finally turned back and followed the inlet to its distant northern end to look for an old military refuge the navy captain had told me was
there. I went ashore and searched without success among the trees and around
a meadow rough with hummocks of tall grass. It seemed an odd place for a
military refuge, but it was built, I was told, in the late seventies during the
difficulties between Chile and Argentina. It's not far from the border, and
perhaps there's a pass through the mountains nearby that allows passage between the two countries.

I spent all day in the boat, and the sky and sea remained clear and calm
except for an hour of breeze and light chop. A different route home took me
west along the broad reach north of Owen Island, then south down the channel between Owen and Evans islands. Wide stretches of open water allowed
new and expansive views of the Andes to the east and scattered islands far
to the west. I soaked in the beauty of ice fields and jagged peaks, waterfalls,
radical rock formations, and a multitude of tiny islets topped with gnarled
bonsai-looking trees. For most of the journey, I stood at the front of the boat,
and as it skimmed over glassy water, I felt myself flying through the wild
unknown. To be completely alone in such spacious unspoiled beauty was
glorious, and I sometimes sang with joy.

As I approached my island, I didn't feel ready for home, so camped on
the Staines beach where I often go for firewood. I built a small fire, and for the

first time since I've been here slept under the stars. The next morning, inspired by one of the most amazing sunrises I've ever seen, another deep realization dawned: Not only is everything I experience part of who I am, Spirit-filled, and not to be rejected, but there is no need to go searching for something special anywhere else. Everything life has to offer is always right here wherever I am right now. There is no place more *alive* and sacred than this place. No time more *alive* and sacred than this time.

I spent the morning on the beach and came home. Cat was glad to see me. I was gone three days and had traveled eighty-seven miles. I sent a code green email to say I was back safely, and spent the next two days bringing in loads of firewood.

I felt content that I'd gone to the lake and reconciled to not taking the longer journey to the far glacier. But soon, the inner conflict I'd been struggling with all winter resurfaced: desire to see the glacier, face my fear, and bolster my self-image as an adventurer in the (imagined) eyes of others — versus fear that the motor would quit or a storm rage in and leave me stranded in that immensity of broken islands and endless tangled waterways.

The following day, September 29, I woke at first light to a mirror sea. Not a breath of wind. I hesitated briefly, communing with the water and sky — trying to divine whether a storm, still hidden from my senses, was approaching — then decided I'd go to the glacier. I lashed a temporary plywood deck over the bow of the boat and loaded it with extra fuel, the deflated kayak, rope, and an anchor. I packed more fuel, camping, fishing, and rain gear, warm clothes, first-aid kit, stove, 4 hp outboard, tools, spare parts, tarps, camera, binoculars, satphone, etc., into the boat. I took food for two weeks — just in case I got caught in a storm — and left Cat plenty, too. When everything was loaded, there was barely room for me. Finally, at noon, I sent a code yellow email and took off. Within five minutes the wind blew up. Arrrgh!

My continuing inability to predict the weather triggered raw feelings of frustration and vulnerability. I couldn't believe it. It had been calm for a week, and now, just when I finally started for the glacier, the northwest wind was back. Since it sometimes blows lightly for just a couple of hours at midday and then calms again, I decided to push ahead against the wind, chop, and mounting swell. After six miles, I ducked into the protected inlet on Owen Island to hide and wait.

I tied up and dozed off, soothed by the soft gurgle of a brook sliding into the sea. At 5 PM I went out to check the channel, and the wind and water seemed to be settling, so I continued north. I decided that if the sky remained clear and the sea continued to calm, I'd keep going under the full moon. I again tracked my position by comparing GPS readings to the marine chart, and eventually crossed the intersecting east/west channel that separates Evans Island from the mainland to the north. In the lee of the hills I headed west with gathering hope for a gentle night and peaceful journey.

It was almost 9 PM and nearly dark, since clouds had covered the moon, when I rounded a point into the main north/south channel thirty miles from my camp. Instantly, the water was turbulent: swell, chop, and tide, all driving in different directions. I could neither continue nor turn back, and spent a dangerous half hour creeping along the rocky shore, searching in the dim light for a semiprotected nook where I could hide for the night.

By then, it was too windy to rig the plastic shelter over the boat, and I thought it would probably rain, so I didn't roll out the sleeping bag or Therm-a-Rest pad. Bundled in sweaters, heavy coat, snow pants, rain gear and rubber boots, I wrapped up in a tarp and passed an uncomfortable night. The boat jerked on its tether and it was cold, but at least it didn't rain.

The wind howled through the trees all night, and in the morning I crept out to check the channel — my route to the glacier. It runs for many miles on the same bearing as the prevailing northwest wind, and a heavy swell, as well as frothing surface chop and driving spray, made the channel impassable. I turned tail to begin the slow rough ride home. Most of the way the wind and sea came from behind, and I had to stay intently focused to keep the boat on course, as it wanted to surf the swells and broach to. Exhausted and discouraged, I made it back to camp and sent a code green email.

Two days later, the sea was mirror calm again. Tense with anxiety and frustrated that the weather is so fucking unpredictable here, I again packed the boat, sent a code yellow email, and took off. Again the wind came up almost immediately, and again I hid in the same inlet on Owen Island. At 2 PM the sea seemed to be settling, so I kept going. My remaining supply of gas wouldn't permit another aborted attempt; this was my last chance to reach the glacier. If a storm raged in, I'd have to wait it out and then press on.

But the sea continued to calm, and by the time I reached the main channel where I'd had to turn back on my previous attempt, the water was almost glassy again. Because the boat was too heavily loaded to plane, it lumbered along at only 8 or 9 mph. I stopped in a small cove to cache one empty and one full five-gallon gas can to drop some weight and give myself more room.

But the boat still wouldn't lift into a plane, even though, after burning five gallons of gas and caching another five, I'd lightened the load by seventy pounds. This wasn't good since it both limited my speed and was hard on the motor. I tried slowing and accelerating, going with, against, and across the light wind riffle, swerving back and forth, but nothing worked. The motor was clearly losing power, even though it didn't sound worse than usual. I'd reconciled myself to plowing through the water instead of skimming lightly over it, when the boat unexpectedly lifted and its speed jumped from 9 to 13 mph. What a relief.

After that, I kept going without pause since there were still four hours of light, and if I lost the plane, I might not get it back. The further I went, the more I thought I could make it to the glacier that day. It was eighty miles, but I decided to go for it since I wasn't sure how long the calm would last. A return trip in stormy weather would be with the wind, sea, and spray, and if not pleasant, at least easier than fighting against the storm.

As the hours stretched and the motor throbbed, sound and movement carried me more and more deeply into the present. Shifting currents constantly changed the texture and color of the sea as I rounded jagged headlands from narrow straits to open water. Fifteen miles from the glacier, I left the main channel and turned east toward the mountains. Strange and beautiful shapes of sculpted ice floated in this narrower passage. They didn't slow me, but did focus my attention. Crashing into one would have been disastrous. At one point, my small boat began to lurch for no apparent reason. I felt I was in the grip of some hidden power, and then realized that several large dolphins were playing directly underneath. Their slipstream was messing with my trajectory.

Finally, I had to pause and siphon gas from a reserve container into the outboard's tank. Once under way again, the boat easily lifted back up, and I continued to check the marine chart against the GPS readings. Things started to not make sense. For the first time, I was uncertain of my location and began to feel lost in the complex maze of waterways and islands. In the flat evening light my perception of distance was confused, and the land looked more or less the same in all directions.

I turned south into what I thought must be the inlet leading to the glacier — even though it didn't seem like I should have reached the opening yet, and the rolling hills on shore didn't quite match the contour lines on the chart. It also seemed strange that the floating ice had disappeared as I approached the mother lode. Five miles later I finally realized I was headed north instead of south.

An overcast sky hiding the sun offered no hint of direction, and I was so focused on the GPS, I hadn't paid attention to the compass. When I'd stopped to siphon gas the boat must have drifted 180 degrees. I was tired, semidazed from long hours of travel, and in a hurry to reach the glacier before dark; once the tank was full, I just fired up the motor and kept going in the direction the boat was pointed. From the middle of the channel, both shores looked similar and I didn't notice I was going back the way I'd come.

By the time I'd returned to the east/west passage, it was too late to reach the glacier by nightfall. On the chart, I saw what looked like a good place to camp only a few miles ahead. A narrow entrance led into a circular lagoon and I tied up in a tiny cove, protected from the wind by trees and rock walls. The floor was wet from spray, so I laid a tarp to keep my bedding dry and rigged the plastic shelter overhead. Snug and cozy, I felt safe; glad to be there far from my cabin and from Cat. I heated and ate some rice and beans and went to sleep.

The wind blew up in the night, and I didn't hurry to pack the next morning since I assumed I'd be in the protected lagoon all day and that night, too. It was almost noon when I took down the plastic and went looking for drinking water and a place to shit on the beach. I decided to at least nip out and look at the channel to see how rough it was. Surprisingly, it was calm enough to go on to the glacier. I was jarred by light chop for part of the way, but mostly the trip was fairly smooth, even though at times the motor ran rough and the boat refused to plane. Finally I could see the faint fractured line of the glacier far off to the southeast.

I wove my way for half a mile through ten thousand smallish chunks of floating ice that filled the inlet where the glacier met the sea; looking for and following interconnected gaps to edge as close as possible to the glacier's still distant wall. When — among many other tourists — I visited the Perito Moreno Glacier in Argentina years ago, enormous slabs of ice calved off its towering wall and crashed into the lake. This wall was lower and seemed more rutted and streaked with silt. At first I felt disappointed. It was not as overwhelmingly impressive as I had expected. But then, as I have with so many other expectations, I let it go and brought myself back to what was actually happening around and within me.

I was completely alone in an immense field of shattered ice as the glacier slowly slid into the sea. Through binoculars, I followed its sloping surface until it disappeared in the distance, and I sensed the massive weight of the Southern Patagonian Ice Field, stretching for two hundred miles down the length of the Andes. This glacier, like the one high in the mountains near my camp, and the Perito Moreno over in Argentina, was part of that larger body.

I felt I was beyond even "the middle of nowhere"; a landscape of drifting ice; otherworldly, yet also intensely real. I turned off the outboard and listened to the silence. Only the occasional faint call of a seagull punctuated and expanded the vast stillness. I floated for a time in the quiet, but the glacier called me to come closer. I started the motor again and crept forward. Movement among floes caught my eye, but when I focused, there was nothing but the endless mosaic of shining ice and indigo water.

Then five dolphins surfaced to swim around the boat. Rising and diving, they created circles of slowly spreading ripples that caused the ice to undulate. I was pleased to have their company in this seemingly lifeless domain, and shut off the outboard again to share the silence with them. Once the vibration ended, they abandoned me and swam away. But it didn't matter because now something else was calling.

Even with all the incredible beauty, something still lacked, and I felt a hollow ache, but for what I didn't know. A black rock spire, lifting from the sea, seduced my eye but didn't ease my heart. I lingered until I became formless, out of time, and simply there.

The sky shifted and a hazy sun showed through the clouds to fall full on the floating ice. And there it was: intense blue glowed deep within the world around me. It didn't shine from far away, but from intimate pockets in the surrounding floes. I remembered then what I'd forgotten.

During these past months, beneath all the mental chatter about needing to face my fear, the mystic light of glacial ice had been calling to my heart. That luminous blue, created by massive weight through time, reflected an ancient quality within me so numinous I couldn't describe it even to myself.

In that wordless moment, I realized that the mysterious call of blue ice was also a call from my soul, and I felt a shift as the fragmented parts of my being found peace in profound integration. Even worry-mind was welcomed and honored for bringing me there safely — and hopefully taking me home again.

Oddly, perhaps, images of scuba diving deep and alone drifted into my thoughts. When far beneath the surface, no matter how entranced by the underwater world, a dispassionate part of my mind always remains focused on survival. It monitors depth, time, and air supply. I often argue and plead for just a little longer in that shadowed otherworld, but finally I always give in and head back to the surface.

The thought that the motor might fail and leave me stranded in that frigid seascape, or that the temperature might drop and freeze the boat and floating ice into a solid mass, was troubling, so I put the thought away and continued to soak in the beauty. But the thought kept creeping back. I could also hear the faint hiss of air escaping from the pontoon that had started to leak more rapidly. It was time to go.

I headed back to where I'd camped the night before, to have an early start the next day. Out in the east/west passage, I again saw the sculpted icebergs, which I now realized came from some other glacier further to the east. I wanted to follow their trail, but my fuel supply was limited. Their source would remain unknown to me.

Dolphins leaping nearby woke me at first light the next day, and I packed to leave. Again the boat didn't want to plane but finally got up, and I kept going without stop all the way back to where I'd cached the gas. The return was as smooth as the trip out had been. Beautiful rock formations and secret inlets beckoned to be explored, but the unpredictability of the weather kept me moving. In the main channel, I saw two boats far away across the water.

I found the gas cache without problem, having marked the location as a waypoint on the GPS. What a handy gizmo. It would be extremely easy to get lost among all the islands and waterways here. As long as I keep close track of where I am on the chart and in relation to camp, I'm ok, but if I were to lose track of my location, it would be very difficult to figure it out without the GPS. The wild seascape seems endless, and many of the rolling hills are similar in appearance. It blows my mind to think of the original explorers who came here with no maps or aerial photos. Did they sail and row down every channel to see where it might or might not lead? How did they not become totally confused?

The sea and sky were holding steady, so I stayed in the shipping route along the west side of Evans Island rather than cut east into more protected water. By the time I came level with Vancouver Island across the channel to the west, a breeze had sprung up and was ruffling the sea into a light chop, but I decided to risk it and complete all the trips I've wanted to make while here. I originally considered Vancouver Island as a possible place to live for the year, since much of the island's total area comprises a large enclosed circular lagoon with many islets and passageways. But when German told me fishermen regularly go there to harvest urchins, I shied away.

I crossed the four-mile-wide channel and passed through the narrow opening into the lagoon. It was protected and very peaceful, but I doubt I would have been content there. There is no mountain view and the fishing is probably poor due to the shallow water. Powerful tidal currents swirl and streak through the narrow passageways, which would make kayaking exciting on extreme tides. The landscape here continues to fascinate me; so many nooks and crannies to putter in. I wandered for a while, then crossed the channel toward home. Cat, as he usually does, rushed to the water's edge to welcome me back.

The trip to the glacier was one of the hardest things I've ever done. Not the actual trip, which — because wind and sea remained calm — was smooth and easy, but facing the fear and uncertainty beforehand. One of the challenges of solitude is that potential or imagined danger can loom to fill the mind. Without other people to help maintain perspective, fear that would normally be manageable can overwhelm. I would challenge the fear, prepare everything for the trip, and at the last minute the wind would come raging in. Or it would look like it was going to blow so I wouldn't leave, and the sea would remain flat calm all day.

Over and over, I imagined myself caught in a ferocious storm huddled for days on a wind-whipped, spray-soaked rock or as a small vulnerable speck lost and alone — drifting helplessly with a dead motor among an endless labyrinth of mountains, islands, and waterways. I'd see myself trying to limp home with the 4 hp outboard that I don't trust or, worse, needing to call for rescue.

Besides facing my fear and uncertainty, perhaps what made the trip so intense was the complex and prolonged preparation. Then, the long hypnotic hours in the boat concentrated my mind as the droning outboard carried me further and further from the security of camp and from the frequent aggravations of Cat. The unreliability of the motor triggered hypervigilance as I constantly listened for increased knocking or other problems.

I can see the trip to the glacier as a metaphor for my year here. Something called me to come, and I've had glimpses of that numinous *Something*. I've sensed it, but cannot put it into words. My time at the glacier was magical and profound; then the experience, like all experiences, becomes part of the on-going rhythm of living. I sense, though, that it has left an indelible trace in me. I wonder what mark this year will leave.

I suspect those first two weeks of spring were my last window of opportunity for travel, and I'm very glad I made all the trips I'd planned. Their total distance was more than 350 miles. I feel a sense of completion, as though I've accomplished something important and can now relax and allow myself to simply experience whatever arises with no further destinations in mind. I can focus on simply being here without the distraction of feeling bummed that the wind is blowing every day and that I didn't make the trips when I had the chance. I have enough firewood to last until I leave, almost no gas for the outboard, and I'm pretty sure I don't want German to bring spare parts for the motor. Unless I have a serious problem, I don't plan to send or receive any emails — except the monthly check-ins — for the next four months.

OCTOBER 11, 2001

The Orange Bill Butter-Belly Diving Ducks continue to fascinate and mystify me. I now think the close pair purposefully instigated the fight I saw three weeks ago. Although this male lost on that occasion, perhaps there was another fight while I was away; the territorial line has shifted to increase the close pair's territory. I think the territorial squabble is about nesting site rather than feeding area. The old boundary cut across the islet where the close pair is nesting, and now it's completely within the pair's territory.

I have an intuitive sense that it's not necessarily the stronger male who wins, but rather the male of the pair that wants the territory most. In any case, there is much less territorial defense activity now than in past weeks. I wonder what the males will do about the boundary line once the females are brooding. Maybe they'll say, "Ah screw it, let's just relax and try to get along."

When the close pair went ashore on the islet today, the male stayed on the rocks near the water while she waddled up toward the brush, stopping a couple of times to preen — as though checking to be certain she wouldn't give away her nest location to a lurking predator. Then she disappeared into the brush and didn't reappear until three and a half hours later. I like how the male keeps watch when she goes to build a nest or lay an egg. Once they'd left the area I went to search for their nest in the dense brush, but couldn't find it. It must be incredibly well hidden. I didn't want to tromp around too much for fear of scaring her away from the area.

Generally, territorial defense is interpreted as competition between individuals, pairs, or groups. But if instead of focusing on each individual pair, I look at the system of organization as a whole and consider the fact that they seldom actually fight, I can see their territoriality as a cooperative strategy to organize resource use most efficiently. If there were no defined territories, a pair might waste time feeding in an area another pair had recently harvested.

OCTOBER 12, 2001

I used fingernail polish to number thirty limpets today to find out if they move over time. In a couple of days, assuming the polish sticks, I'll check their positions again. If they haven't moved, I'll check each week for a month. If they have moved, I may start to track their positions daily.

I spent most of day watching the ducks. She's feeding much more than he — either to balance the energy drain of laying eggs, or to build up reserves for when she'll brood them. While they were sitting on a rock near the point, I went to see how close they'd let me approach. When I was twenty-five feet away, they acted nervous, so I stopped and sat. A little later she waddled to within ten feet to drink from a pool. Then he came over, hunkered down beside her, and tucked his feet into his belly feathers — to keep them warm, I suppose. They'd close their eyes for a second or two, open them briefly, and then close them again. Their eyes close from the bottom up, which is pretty cool.

It was nice to share the sun, wind, rock, and water sounds with them. I felt a sense of unity: all of us manifestations of Life together; life studying life. From that perspective there was no observer and no observed — just observation. I wonder how much of that basic experience we were actually sharing. Do the ducks and I have identical awareness? Not the content of awareness, but the simple space of being aware of the world?

Philosophers of science argue that all facts are theory-bound. Without theory for context, we cannot actually see facts. Facts are not just lying around waiting to be discovered; in some sense, theory creates them. I try at times to give up my theories and the search for facts, and just keep company with the ducks — a sort of Zen biology.

After sitting with me for a while, they swam into the basin and disappeared behind the islet — and never came back out, even though I watched closely in all directions. Then I happened to glance toward the point, and there they were! How do they do that? It's magic how they disappear and then reappear somewhere else.

NO ENTRY FOR OCTOBER 13, 2001

OCTOBER 14, 2001

I didn't see the ducks until afternoon when I finally spotted the close male alone. It feels as though he's just a visitor in the female's territory now. The white goose of the black-and-white pair has been standing sentinel on the far island. Did I have their sexes mixed up? Is the black-and-white one the female — now brooding — and this, the male, guarding the nest? I like to witness these creatures reproducing and keeping the cycle going, but I feel sort of left out.

I checked the positions of the limpets this afternoon. Whoa! Did they ever move, and some have completely disappeared. Starting tomorrow I'll check them daily. I've come up with an efficient method to locate their positions on the rock. I made a dial from a plastic bucket lid by painting numbers from 1 to 12 around the rim and dividing these segments into ten smaller units, each 3 angular degrees wide. I weighted the dial with a stone, attached a fifteen-foot string to the center, and marked the string at three-, six- and twelve-inch intervals. To measure the positions of the limpets, I set the dial on the rock each day in the exact same spot with the same north-south orientation, stretch the string to the top point of a shell, and note its distance from the center of the dial and the angle at which the string crosses the dial's rim. This yields a vector I can later transform to an XY coordinate system using the dial as the origin.

It's rainy and cold; a day of painful emotion. In the past I might have attributed this feeling to loneliness, but now I wonder if it's spiritual long-ing. Missing other people feels similar to the experience of being cut off from Spirit — from my own deep being. Several times I determined to simply stay with the feeling, but over and over I ate something, drank coffee, or engaged in some other escape activity.

Then tonight at dusk, I slipped into a joyful inner space of light and vi-sions. I think it was a sentence in *Sex, Ecology, Spirituality* that triggered the shift. Wilber was talking about exploring this huge mysterious world of con-sciousness, and bam — of course. This journey is an exploration, not some-thing I must do just right so I'll be ok or so I can teach others.

In that openness I heard the waterfalls from Staines and experienced them as inside my body. With another shift of perspective and consciousness I was no longer enclosed in my body, but expanded freely into space all around. Both body and waterfalls were aspects of consciousness.

Then Cat started to cry and the sound hammered me. As I crashed into that tight painful space I thought, "Not again! Why can't I stay where it's light and joyful?" But when I'm physically traveling and exploring I don't expect everything to be easy and pleasant. I expect it to be tough, dirty, painful, and frightening at times. That's what traveling, as opposed to tour-ism, is. So why do I expect these inner explorations to be different?

Cat doesn't live in a world that's very attractive to me. Or rather, when I'm caught in what I imagine his experience to be, I'm not happy to be there. The biosphere is, in some basic way (I think), oriented toward flight or fight. Cat's yowling plunges me into that dark space and tightens me up. The ten-sion may (quite likely) have nothing to do with Cat at all, but may be my own resistance to feeling certain things, like vulnerability and fear of death.

It's as though I have an inner switch. Either I'm flowing easily in the de-centered space of Big Mind, or, wham, locked down into small tight mind. When I slip from small mind — where I cling to my isolated ego-self and the security of the known — and radically shift into a larger more relaxed space, I recognize that this is where I've always wanted to be. I don't understand why, after all these years of work, I still resist the shift so fiercely.

Sometimes I'm still caught in magical thinking when I want something. Talking aloud, I ask the wind to stop blowing or tell the rain to wait a while, or I thank them for behaving in a way that pleases me. On one level I know I'm playing and that this is simply a way to express my feelings, and yet . . . not en-tirely. I really am trying to persuade the elements to consider my desires. Ra-tionally, I know this is silly, but emotionally I still sort of believe it might work. In some sense that magical space feels dark and threatening, as though the wind is a willful entity with the power to attack, and so must be propitiated.

OCTOBER 15, 2001

This morning there were sensuous van Gogh clouds over the mountains that looked more like a painting than real sky. I received an email from Patti saying she has purchased a ticket to visit Chile in February. I'll be glad to see her. I sent a message to Alejandra saying I don't want German to bring me outboard parts and other supplies.

There wasn't much soot today when I cleaned the chimney; hopefully, it will hold up until next March. I put some of the soil I dug up when building the outhouse into containers to start lettuce and radish seeds. Planting a garden will be a lot of work. I'll need to mix sand with the soil to allow for drainage, and I may use clear plastic to keep off the heavy rain. Just taking care of survival pragmatics today.

I suspect the female duck is brooding her eggs. I didn't see her at all yesterday or today. There are, though, lots of other birds. It's a sort of avian gestalt on the rocks when I open myself to the collective swirl of all the birds, instead of focusing so tightly on the butter-bellies.

From one perspective, the birds can be seen as a simple movement of energy — like wind or rain. I was thinking that way before reading Wilber again. Now I wonder if that conception reduces them to the physical movement of matter, and attributes no efficacy to biological motivation. The birds can also be seen as internally motivated in the normal, *every bird for herself* way, but if I shift perspective, they are all expressions of Life. Then there is no real separation between them, and the terms competition and cooperation lose meaning.

OCTOBER 16, 2001

I woke early this morning to the sun coming over the mountains into a clear sky. I went out to the rock to have tea, watch the day come on, and meditate. New moon, my day for fasting, and I'm hungry. I want to at least put honey in my herbal tea, but so far I've resisted.

In a couple of weeks, I may review the limpet data. I'm curious about three things: Do the same two limpets stay close together over time? Is there much variance in the amount of movement between individuals (are some wanderers and some couch potatoes)? Is there a pattern in their collective movements? Of course there is some sort of pattern, the question is: what kind? Will it be something my eye and mind can detect as repeating behavior, or will it be the kind of free-form irregular pattern found in jade?

Personality always has an impact on scientific findings. What the researcher is looking for largely determines how he or she designs a study and, consequently, what can be discovered. If I were looking for average limpet movement, I might ignore the few individuals that move long distances, or average them in — and so ignore their significance. But personally, I'm interested in the oddballs — the wanderers.

As part of the study, I might lift some limpets off the rock and re-place them as a cluster in a flat area I'll clear of mussels. I question the ethics of uprooting and likely killing hundreds of mussels to satisfy my curiosity. If there wasn't red tide I'd have little reluctance to kill that many to eat, even though I don't need them to survive. What's the difference between killing to satisfy intellectual desire and killing to satisfy physical desire?

Today I watched myself making measurements under the slanting afternoon sun — a lone man far from others of his kind, kneeling on low tide rocks trying to discover something about the lives of limpets. In some sense, it's not so much about the limpets as about exploring ideas; playing with the notion of integrating science and aesthetics by looking at limpet movement as a dance rather than a feeding activity.

There are times when I feel a deep love for Cat and am very glad for his company. But often, too, I would prefer not to have him here, especially when he's crying. And he cries a lot, or at least it seems to me that he does. A wonderfully peaceful morning or evening is just shattered by his moaning cry. I've tried everything to get him to stop: reasoning with him, yelling at him, swatting him, and squirting him with water. But nothing really works.

He is truly creative in his vocalizations; what variety! But most of the sounds he makes are unpleasant to my ear: there is a sort of mindless complaining sound like the whining of a five-year-old child; a demanding yowl; or his hunting cry. The other day he made a sound so truly disgusting that it stopped me in my tracks. It was so nasty I had to laugh. I mean, if you can imagine the sound rotting meat might make analogous to its stench, this sound would be it.

I gave him some limpets today from a part of the study I've discontinued because it wasn't working out. Now they won't clutter up the rock. Science at its finest: Don't like the way an experiment is going? Test subjects not behaving as you want them to? No problem. Cancel the study and feed the subjects to the cat!

OCTOBER 17, 2001

I wonder if I'll ever come back here. Of all the places I've seen, where would I build next time? It would be nice to be somewhere more protected, but then there might not be good fishing or such a spectacular view of the mountains. All things considered, this is an incredible spot.

I just imagined being back with people and feeling not as good as others. Then I remembered that we're all embodiments of Life and immediately felt calm again. This decentering from such strong narcissistic self-focus seems to prevent judging myself and others so harshly. The shift requires discipline; it's not enough to depend on flashes of insight, but I also sense it's called up by something higher or deeper and not controlled by my ego.

OCTOBER 18, 2001

Well, that woke me up. I just tended the stove, and after adding wood I noticed a small piece of orange tinfoil on the floor. It seemed strange and I wondered where it could have come from. I picked it up. Yeow! It turned out to be a live ember that must have popped out the draft hole. I now have a juicy blister.

Since I've only occasionally gone to sit outside in really foul weather, doing science is taking me into the elements, where I'd expected to spend more time than I have. I caught another far glimpse of myself today measuring the movement of snails on a slippery rock in a rainstorm in the middle of nowhere. Human beings are truly an odd species.

NO ENTRY FOR OCTOBER 19, 2001

OCTOBER 20, 2001

The pair of rusty-breast geese is very skittish. I hope to get a photo, but will be lucky if I do. Another new bird has arrived. It's lean and angular, and flies the same way — like it will fall out of the sky if it pauses for an instant. It looks like a seagull wired on speed, except it's graceful and lovely, which hasn't been my experience with the meth heads I've met.

Things are falling apart. The folding chair broke today and I repaired it with wood, wire, and duct tape. I've been repairing the chimney inside the cabin since midwinter by wiring sheet metal over the rust holes, but the outside pipe was almost completely rotten. Yesterday, as I sat mulling this and that — one thing about being alone out here, there's plenty of time to think — it occurred to me that the seven cans of powdered milk I brought might be about the same diameter as the chimney pipe. I measured them and they were exactly the same. After the milk went into plastic bags, I cut out the tops and bottoms of the cans and replaced the rotten sections of chimney, using duct tape to hold it all together. I even made a 90 degree elbow from two of the cans. I feel quite clever. What would I do without duct tape? I suspect that if Napoleon had had duct tape, we'd all be speaking French now.

I found myself disagreeing with Wilber again today. He claims it's an egotistic activity to find Spirit in nature through the feelings that arise when in the wilderness. He argues that we cannot bring Spirit in from nature, but that Spirit moves through us out into nature. Sounds like horseshit to me. Spirit is everywhere, and being in nature can help us perceive it. And we can perceive it in nature only if we experience an inner transformation.

Wilber also criticizes the strong *no-self* doctrine of Theravada Buddhism and claims that most schools of Buddhist thought don't hold that view. They teach, instead, that there is a self, but that it's relative rather than absolute. I've wondered about the no-self doctrine for a while. At times, I've had the experience that there really is no one at home in here, but I've also sensed that the self may actually come into existence through mental or physical activity, and dissolve only in the stillness of meditation.

I've been meditating much more these past days and want to keep it up. The winds continue to blow, which is good because it keeps me off the water and focuses my attention inward. There are moments of joy, peace, and love, and also moments of longing, lack, and hollowness. I still avoid the difficult moments, although I repeatedly make resolutions to stay with them. I might settle into a basic sustenance diet for a while and give up using food treats as pleasure and escape.

OCTOBER 21, 2001

Grey rainy morning. I stayed in the cabin most of the day hunkered down by a fire, and the Sunday blanket of depression and torpor settled over me. I still have no understanding of its source or place in my psyche. Is it a valuable balance for something, or a useless distraction to get rid of with antidepressant drugs?

How can I accept myself just as I am, when part of me is judgmental? It seems like a vicious circle: another catch-22. I can't accept the flaw of my perfectionism because it causes me to reject myself for not being perfect! But the circle is broken when I do accept myself just as I am — imperfect in my perfectionism.

When I leave here, I must be sure to remember all these ups and downs — rather than create an idealized myth of this journey, to which I compare the rest of my life.

Today is Sunday, my day of rest.
All week, now and then, I look forward to Sunday.

I exercise just enough to ease my shoulder ache, do not meditate,
reread a novel rather than philosophy or spiritual teaching, build a
fire, and feel no obligation to sit outside in the rain and wind.

Sunday is, perhaps, my hardest day.
Unstructured and undisciplined, deep aches and longings wash over
me and lie as heavy as gloom on my heart.

On Sundays, even more than on other days,
I escape into coffee, popcorn, and chocolate.
I long to be elsewhere, but nowhere I can think of.

On Sundays, I see how far and for how long these feelings have
driven me: to wander; to drugs; to each new woman's body; to here.
No, not the feelings but avoidance of them.

On Sundays, I look at these feelings and question, unsuccessfully,
their source and niche in this fabric I call myself.

On Sundays — after all these months —
I feel no closer to peace, freedom, or understanding.

On Sundays, I look out my window and the Orange Bill Butter-Belly
Diving Duck is just a bird: eating, shitting, breeding, dying,
over and over again.

On Sundays, I look down the remaining years of my life
and see fleeting joys but no lasting peace.

On Sundays, I look forward to Monday and wish I didn't.

NO ENTRY FOR OCTOBER 22, 2001

OCTOBER 23, 2001

Another windy, sometimes rainy day. Measuring the limpets was a nasty
proposition; I was almost blown off the rock and into the sea. Most of the
limpets are pretty sedentary, but a few have taken off for parts unknown. I
wonder how far they go and why. Hunger? Sex drive? Wanderlust?

Scientific studies begin in various ways for various reasons. Sometimes
the impetus is intellectual curiosity, sometimes emotional drive, sometimes
desire for status or monetary gain, often simple happenstance. My original

plan for this year was to go into the wilderness alone, do animal behavior research, and include in the study reflections on my own cognitive, emotional, and spiritual behavior as the researcher. But along the way, my orientation shifted from a biological study of some other organism to direct observation of myself in solitude. I became not only the researcher, but also the subject of the research — a fairly circular state of affairs.

Once here, I saw the limpets, started to wonder how much they move, and eventually decided to track their movements quantitatively over time as a sort of hobby. All this was just a mind tickle for several months, until one sunny afternoon I felt motivated to mark a number of limpets and actually begin a study.

The qualitative Orange Bill Butter-Belly Diving Duck study I seem to be doing began differently; I just drifted into it. Day after day, there they were in my watery front yard, and as I casually watched, I became intrigued by what I saw. Little by little I started to pay closer attention.

In addition to measuring the limpets and watching the ducks, I started to build a sling chair today. But the wretched materials wouldn't cooperate and I immediately got angry. My current practice is to focus on the anger and on letting it go, instead of acting it out. No matter what I'm doing, when I become aware of getting angry and frustrated, I stop, relax, and let it go, before I continue. This is the most important behavioral thing I can do here, and since I have no need to accomplish anything more, I certainly have the time. I'm seeing more clearly how anger and self-centeredness feed each other and are grounded in frustrated desire and thwarted will.

I finally finished *Sex, Ecology, Spirituality*. It seems to me I've been reading that book forever, and by now I'm thoroughly tired of Wilber's style. I don't know if he's just so brilliant that he's right all the time, outrageously arrogant, or both. He's the deepest and broadest thinker I've seriously studied. His four quadrant model is a complex and extremely inclusive cognitive map; a useful tool in helping me organize my own thinking — as long as I approach it metaphorically, rather than reify the quadrants and levels as actually existing in the world. Reading Wilber has been very valuable to me and I owe him a great deal.

OCTOBER 24, 2001

There was definitely weather today. Strong wind from the northwest and then from the southwest; rain, hail, and even some snow. Tonight it's calm for the first

— or maybe second — time since my return from the glacier. It probably won't last until morning, but if it does I might go fishing. The dolphins came to play in the basin for a while this evening.

I started to dig a garden plot near the point; or rather, I tried to turn over a shovel of soil. But there's an impossibly dense tangle of roots under the grass. No way am I doing a garden down there. It would be far too much work for one season. I may build a couple of wooden boxes and fill them with dirt from the outhouse hole. They won't produce much, but at least something to supplement the lentil sprouts I'm eating.

This afternoon, one of the small grey land birds came to rob food from Cat's dish. She's very aware of Cat. If I'm sitting on the porch alone, she goes straight to the dish. If Cat is with me, she turns and leaves. Cat often stalks these birds, and I've given up yelling at him to quit. As far as I can tell, he hasn't caught one yet.

NO ENTRY FOR OCTOBER 25–28, 2001

OCTOBER 29, 2001

I don't feel much like writing. But it's nearing the end of the month and I expect to stop journaling for a while, so I want to put down some thoughts I've jotted in the notebook these past days.

I intend to give up reading for the next three months to open more space for inner exploration. I want to stay with my own moment-by-moment experience. I've been heading toward this year alone for a long time, and if I don't live it fully I'll regret it. Perhaps I'll read a page of *A Path with a Heart*, Chuang Tsu, or the I Ching now and then to catalyze inward shifts.

I'm also going to give up coffee, cocoa, chocolate, sugar, and bread for at least a month. I've become more and more aware of how I use food and caffeine to escape physical and emotional pain and to change from feeling a sort of hollow depression to feeling pretty good. Then a short time later I slump or doze off, and head for some stimulus again. Round and round. At some point I'd like to fast and stay outside for three or four days and nights. Sleeping in the rain seems extreme to me, even though I'd wear rain gear and try to stay as dry as possible. I guess I've become soft with this cushy lifestyle.

I'm still questioning the place of language in my experience. Is the space of consciousness the result of language? Clearly, all thought is language-based.

Pure sensation (e.g., seeing moving water) does not seem to be; but is the awareness of myself seeing moving water?

According to Wilber, some mystic philosophers claim that Spirit "hid from itself in its eternal play" by becoming matter, and in doing so lost awareness of itself. From this perspective, physical and cultural evolution is the process of Spirit growing back toward itself. The middle stages of the process are language-based; to reach the higher stages we must pass through these middle levels. But the direct experience of awareness seems to be beyond language. I'll continue to chew on this stuff.

I wonder if pure Spirit is not self-aware, and in attempting to know itself manifested as the material universe and began its journey of self-discovery. Perhaps pure Spirit can know itself only through being mirrored by itself incarnate. If so, then Spirit calls to us in order to know itself; not just from compassion. That would make us more than mere epiphenomena. At times I sense a Presence here that I can experience but not put into words or understand rationally.

I feel commonality with the male butter-belly in my body, and definitely sense that he's more than a feather-draped stimulus/response machine. I can't know for sure, but why would I want to reduce this wonderful being to an unconscious automaton? Why would I want to do that to the universe I live in? Why would I want to do that to myself?

As I've gotten more serious about possibly writing up my study of the butter-belly ducks, I've switched from simply being with them in curiosity, love, and wonder to wanting to take something from them: information, public approval, etc. This shift from sharing to taking is a form of greed. I believe much of science is grounded in taking, but truly creative scientists give themselves to the world instead of taking something from it to fulfill their own desires and expectations.

What can I give to the world? I'm receiving so much. Is bringing my awareness to this place a gift? Does the loving-kindness meditation I send daily have an effect? Is it necessary to give if there is no boundary between us?

Nature is going nowhere. Evolution is a conceptual notion to give us a sense of progress, purpose, and meaning. Things do change via evolution, but very, very slowly compared to the endless repetition of the daily/yearly same old, same old. Life is drudgery when looked at from the outside. That's why we've invented so many ways to escape. Even personal growth (I think at this moment) goes round and round, up and down. The only way life — as it is in nature — becomes meaningful is to step out of conceptual abstractions and into the flow of living.

This cloudy night
the wind has finally died
and the sea whispers softly.

Her sensuous murmur
drifts and echoes
through the infinite empty space
of our mutual existence.

I can no longer speak
of solitude without admitting
the presence of Something
here with me.

Something nonmaterial and nonpersonal.

Often
I'm deaf and blind,
and my heart is closed.
But again and again
an inner softening
yields love, peace, beauty,
and deep, deep gratitude.

Then
all there is to get
I've already got . . .
if I simply open my mind and heart
to what is.

There is no place to go
other than here.
No time to be
other than now.
No way out
and no way further in
to Life.

OCTOBER 30, 2001

Just a day.

OCTOBER 31, 2001

Last day in October, and if things go according to plan — no reason why
they should, they rarely have before — this will be the last entry for a while.

It's been a busy day. I woke fairly early to quiet. No wind in the trees or waves against rock. I looked out to the first completely calm day in three weeks. Excellent conditions to measure elevations on the limpet rock.

Two days ago on a very low tide, I stretched a level line from the highest point on the rock out over the study area. Then using a fishing weight tied to a string as a plumb bob, I went along the line, measuring down and marking the sloping rock with nail polish every four vertical inches. Today, as the tide came in and the water level reached each mark, I worked quickly around the dial — set in its usual position — and recorded the distance from dial to water at each 30 degrees of angular displacement. From the measurements, I'll be able to re-create the contour lines of the rock on paper, one line for each four vertical inches. I feel quite clever for having thought of using the sea as a level. Even a laser beam would not have been as accurate or efficient.

I went fishing to Staines in the afternoon. I paused to honor the gift of each fish and to acknowledge the life I was taking. As I killed them, I looked into their eyes to watch the life fade. Tonight will be the first time in a month I've eaten fish.

The sea lions are still on their rock. I wonder how much fish eighteen sea lions eat. They have no sense of sustainability. First a single one moves in, and before you know it a whole herd has invaded. They use up our common resources, stay up all night making a racket, property values go all to hell. Perhaps this calls for yet another letter of complaint.

It rained on and off all day, which is good because the rain barrel was low from washing clothes a few days ago. Wash day was semiclear with a good wind, and it occurred to me to string a line at the point and hang everything there. Even the heavy shirts and pants dried within three hours. Not bad; it took me only eight months to figure out.

Yesterday, I read an essay in *Ecopsychology* by Steven Harper, a wilderness guide who leads people on trips to reconnect with nature and with their own inner being. He claims they do *no impact* camping; but it's impossible to do any physical activity with no impact. It's like the famous oxymoron sustainable development, which is also impossible. But *sustainable impact* — not damaging the world faster than it can replenish itself — is possible and is context dependent.

My current impact is, I believe, sustainable — even though I'm fishing, cutting firewood, using a gas-powered chain saw and outboard, and allowing a small amount of detergent to enter the sea. But I'm the only person here or likely to be here for a long time to come, so the damage will have an opportunity to heal. If I behaved this way in a heavily used area, it would be unsustainable and irresponsible.

Harper writes that *crossing over* into the wilderness is like culture shock. It puts us into a stranger context than we are used to, and shows us a broader reality. His job as leader is to "trust and support the process, get out of the way, and let the actual wilderness teach the lessons." This mirrors my thoughts and feelings about letting solitude have its way with me.

I also read an essay by Robert Greenway, who has led groups into the wilderness for thirty years. He claims it is common when returning to society to feel depression and lose the wonderful sense of vibrancy. He suggests that to prevent losing the positive effect, people can meditate and get together with the others who were in their wilderness group. I think, though, that trying to hold onto the wilderness experience once we return to the city is actually part of the problem.

Clinging to past experiences, instead of letting our lives unfold naturally moment by moment, is just what we usually do — and tend to stop doing in the wilderness. To maintain the sense of *aliveness*, we need to be deeply open to our actual lives in the present, wherever we are — not cling to our memory of the wilderness experience.

When I finish writing this entry, I'll turn all my books around so the titles face the wall as a symbolic way of putting them out of reach; I have nowhere to hide them out of sight. I intend to not use the computer for some time. If I really want to record something, I'll jot short notes longhand.

There isn't much physical work to do now, which is good because I want to create space for new discoveries — to open myself more fully to what the wilderness has to teach me. It's going to be hard losing all these avoidance mechanisms at once, but it's time. It feels like I'm stepping into the unknown, and I'm frightened by the thought of the long days and nights ahead without activity to fill the hours.

INTERLUDE

TECHNOLOGY AND DESIRE

*Any sufficiently advanced technology
is indistinguishable from magic.*

— ARTHUR C. CLARKE'S THIRD LAW

*All technology should be assumed
guilty until proven innocent.*

— DAVID BROWER

*Men have become the tools of their tools. . . .
Most of the luxuries, and many of
the so-called comforts of life, are not
only not indispensable, but positive
hindrances to the elevation of mankind.*

— HENRY DAVID THOREAU

Like many people, I have an ambivalent relationship with technology. Sometimes the relationship is pleasant, even joyful. At other times the relationship becomes more adversarial. In solitude, I have only my own ability to keep the machines I depend on functioning. I often feel at their mercy and question my wisdom in creating such a high-tech environment for myself. On previous wilderness retreats, I took nothing more complicated than a fishing reel, and it was a relief to not have to deal with mechanical devices. The downside was that if I'd been seriously injured, I would have had small chance of survival, since no one knew where I was and I had no way to tell them. This time, for my own peace of mind and to comply with requests from friends, family, and the university, I brought a satellite telephone.

Then, one thing led to another. Since I would need electricity to charge the satphone, I brought a wind generator, solar panels, and storage batteries. Since I would have electric power, I decided to bring 12-volt lights and use a laptop for journaling. In such a fierce climate, a chain saw would be useful,

and, of course, a boat with outboard motor would be more pragmatic than a
kayak for exploring the rugged seascape. Having only one outboard is risky,
so I brought a backup. As long as I was bringing gasoline for the outboards
and chain saw, why not add propane and a propane stove for cooking? I wonder: Could I have survived in any sort of comfort without these technologi-
cal aids?

It's become clear to me during the past months that using one machine
fosters dependence on another. When in the boat and far from camp, I'm glad
to have the satellite telephone in case the motor fails and leaves me stranded.
I feel at the mercy of the outboard because it can break in a way I don't have
the replacement parts, tools, or skill to repair. I've never felt this vulnerable
when relying on a canoe or kayak. I've always felt that unless I broke an arm,
I could make it back to camp or out to civilization. The feeling of vulnerability
due to my dependence on faulty machinery is unpleasant. The frustration and
anger I experience while trying to repair the outboards and chain saw when
they *refuse* to run is even more painful. Thus, having technology for my own
peace of mind is often counterproductive.

The existence of technology in our lives has become so ubiquitous that
what was once a rare luxury has become not only a necessity, but a seemingly
eternal reality. Electric lights, refrigerators, stoves, running water, and toi-
lets are as fundamental to many people as air, gravity, or their own bodies:
simply there and rarely noticed — until there is a breakdown. We often avoid
this shadow side of our dependence on technology by relying on others to
maintain the machines we believe we need to survive.

Ah, but when our machines are working well, what an amplification and
extension of power and perception. On days when the sea is calm, I sometimes stand in the bow of the boat as the motor sends me flying across the
water and out into the universe. What freedom, what joy! In those moments,
I'm a cyborg with human mind/spirit and mechanized body. To me, as a male,
machines often seem like phallic amplifications; I wonder how females feel.
Does the focus change from amplification to extension? Do the drive of the
wind generator and thrust of the outboard give way to the solar panel's quiet
concentration of energy and the satellite telephone's broad embrace?

Satellite technology is truly amazing. Sitting on a far-flung rock, I can
reach out and connect with people far, far away. I can point a small GPS
gadget toward the sky and locate myself exactly on the Earth. Does this wonder cast a shadow? Is there loss as well as gain?

At the beginning of each month I send a check-in email and wait
for replies. As my attention focuses on connecting with people who are

somewhere else, I tend to feel tight and withdrawn from my immediate environment. My involvement with technology distracts me from settling into solitude. And not only do I become perceptually cut off from my surroundings, but I also often feel less spiritually and emotionally connected with the people I'm contacting. It's as though I lose awareness of our underlying unity when I focus my attention on linking electronically via technology and language.

Relying on the Global Positioning System to locate myself also tends to take me out of the immediate environment. Instead of paying close attention to and identifying landmarks along my route of travel, I can simply read a number from the display screen and find my position on the map. During my first months here, I relied on thermometer, barometer, and clock, instead of my direct perception of the world around me. Such instruments are clearly useful, but in depending on them we lose some of the immediacy of our relationship with the environment, with other people, and with ourselves.

The absence of internal combustion engine noise is profoundly relaxing. We have become so inundated by noise in our culture we no longer know what it is to live without the racket of machinery. It's glorious. Machine noise is often physically painful to me. However, this seems to be so only when I'm not running the machine! In solitude I find the noise of the chain saw intense but not unpleasant. However, if someone else were running the saw within my hearing, I would experience it as very disturbing.

Although I sometimes feel wild joy standing in the boat, flying across the sea, driven by the throbbing motor behind me, I'm also aware that the noise disturbs my tranquillity. The dolphins, on the other hand, seem attracted to the sound or vibration. They never approach when I'm paddling the kayak, but often have come to play around the motor-driven boat.

The banshee howl of the wind generator is seriously intrusive, and I've mostly shut it down and minimized my use of electricity. I feel more comfortable with the solar panels that passively gather and convert sunlight than I do with the generator and its often wild activity.

IN AND OUT OF TOUCH

Cell phones and email can narrow and impoverish our experience of the world. As the shadow side of allowing us to remain in contact with our social group, cell phones and email tend to buffer our engagement with the people physically near us. To the extent we are actively linked to those we already know, we are less available to interact with strangers we might encounter along the way. This is particularly evident when traveling in foreign cultures.

During the last forty years, I've often traveled and lived in Latin America. In the past, when I set off with my backpack into remote areas, I knew I'd be out of contact with the people back home for weeks or even months at a time. I only rarely received mail along the way via general delivery, and pausing to write letters or postcards was an infrequent and significant event. Traveling alone, my only social interactions were with local people or with other travelers. I always felt I had stepped over the edge and into the unknown.

But on this trip to Chile, before going into solitude, I felt I hadn't stepped cleanly out of my familiar social group. Daily, I visited internet cafes to engage in electronic conversation. As I became aware of myself doing this, I noticed many other "travelers" doing the same. We were all maintaining active relationships with friends, lovers, and family back home. This made it more difficult and less imperative for us to engage fully with the people around us.

I'm not suggesting that electronic connectivity is entirely negative in our lives. I've met many interesting strangers via email, and my relationships with Patti and others live via email and telephone. But I am aware that these relationships tend to distract me from engaging as fully as I otherwise might in person with those in the community where I live.

If this is the personal price we pay when we use technology, there are also deleterious impacts on the people who manufacture these machines (but who sometimes don't have access to this same technology), on our common environment (particularly air and water), and on our nonhuman neighbors. Technology enriches our individual lives, and we are loath to give it up, but we pay an enormous collective price for it.

SHOPPING FOR ILLUSIONS

Technology has the capacity to amplify and extend our desires. Consider the shopping list that bloomed in my mind during the months of July and August. What I experienced seems iconic of our culture's relationship with material goods.

It began with a small hole in the chimney. I noticed it when I'd been here for only about five months. It seemed evident that the chimney wouldn't last the full year, and I'd then be left without the means to heat the cabin. I considered alternatives, such as removing the damaged sections and running the shortened pipe straight up through the roof, but none of the alternatives seemed acceptable. The rusting chimney, in and of itself, would probably not have pushed me to consider breaking solitude by asking the CONAF officials to bring me a new one, but the outboard was running poorly, and I was also worried I might run out of ibuprofen and antibiotics. Once I decided to ask German to bring in a few items, I discovered more and more things it would be nice to have.

Slowly the list grew, and, via email, I sent Patti on various wild-goose chases in Texas as she faithfully fulfilled my requests and talked to outboard repairmen and other technicians, trying to determine exactly what it was I thought I so desperately needed. For quite a while I couldn't see what was happening, and my shopping list lengthened to include electric supplies, cheese, onions, and many other goodies.

The bubble of desire grew in my mind, and what had been things it would be nice to have *just in case* became necessities I felt I needed for my survival. Fortunately the CONAF boat didn't arrive when promised, and this gave me the opportunity to see how subtly and easily my desires became identified with my physical survival. Then, poof, the bubble burst as I realized I didn't really need anything I didn't already have.

We have seriously confounded luxury with necessity in our culture, and can no longer differentiate between what we want in order to maintain a particular lifestyle (with its social relationships and sensual pleasures) and what we actually need for physical survival. We have confounded social identity with biological and spiritual being to the point of believing we will die if we lose our social standing, which is often based on the material wealth we have accumulated. This accelerating spiral of desires becoming necessities is driving our suicidal rush to destroy the Earth we depend on for our actual physical survival.

Our rush is not only self-destructive, it is unnecessary. Recent studies suggest that wealth and happiness do not necessarily go hand in hand. Once the basic necessities of life — food, water, shelter, clothing, and health care — are provided, additional material goods often do little to enhance our sense of well-being.

NOVEMBER 2001

People say that what we are all seeking is a meaning for life.
I don't think that's what we're really seeking.
I think what we're seeking is an experience of being alive.

— JOSEPH CAMPBELL

Here I am writing.... Yet another plan shot to hell. But I'm again writing longhand, as I did for the first few months.

I've been thinking about Cat again and how "willful" cats are in general. A pure manifestation of self-centered *wanting mind*. I've also been looking at the shadow aspects of myself Cat might be triggering. Then it dawned on me: the traits I don't like about Cat are part of me, too. I can't believe it took me nine months to see this.

NO ENTRIES FOR NOVEMBER 2–3, 2001

The notion that animals in their *natural state*, unspoiled by human contact, are unafraid of people is myth. It seems likely that none of the resident birds have had previous contact with people, yet most have become less afraid of me over time. At first, they tended to be shy of this large unknown animal. Only after I didn't bother them did they become desensitized to my presence. It probably is true that they didn't actively fear me as a *human*, and so their nervousness has relaxed more easily.

My expectation based on cultural mores led me astray; my earlier attribution of sex to the black-and-white geese, based on the apparently dominant behavior of the one I thought was the male, was wrong. The female emerged with six chicks today: grey fluffy little balls. She led them from their hidden nest down the steep rock to feed, and I paddled over for a closer look. The white male was close the whole time, peeping like one of the chicks. The little guys had a hard time climbing back up to the nest. I wonder if she chose such a tough nest site because of otters.

NOVEMBER 5, 2001

Solid walls of hail and even some snow interspersed with sun and blue sky.

The black-and-white geese brought their chicks to this side of the basin. They were very alert to the eagle, who also seemed interested in them. The chicks didn't seem bothered by the hail, but at one point mom crouched, wings slung low to make a shelter, and tucked them under her. It was very beautiful.

Do they feel love or concern for their chicks? If I saw a human couple behave this way, I'd say, Yes! I can't attribute human emotions to the geese, but it seems just as unwarranted to claim they feel nothing — that it's all instinct. If Life brought forth human emotions, why not equivalent goose emotions, whatever they might be?

Why would we want to insist that animals have no feelings? Perhaps because it's hard to live with ambiguity. It's easier to believe that animals feel as we do or to turn them into automatons with no sense of self or feelings at all. It's much more difficult to live with the mystery that they have their own lives we will never know — except to some degree through empathy, intuition, and quiet observation of their behavior. But the world is so much richer this way. Although I sometimes playfully attribute human qualities to the non-human world, this acceptance of mystery is what I actually think and feel about anthropomorphic projection.

It seems to me that the most parsimonious theory about anything is: none. Everything just is as it is. Of course that's not very intellectually satisfying. There's a huge difference between being openly aware of mystery — the bare attention of *don't know mind* — and prescientific magical explanation.

NOVEMBER 6, 2001

I was sitting on my porch peacefully watching the red-billed peepers happily murdering mussels on the low-tide rocks, when a malevolent visage suddenly loomed into the lens of the binoculars. Like a crocodile intent on mayhem, two beady eyes glared from just above the waterline. Then the male butter-belly roared in to attack. Whee! Nearly knocked me from my chair. The red-bills seemed startled, too, and scattered in flight. The butter-belly strutted a step, then returned to the water, and the red-bills settled back to their meal.

The attack was unusual since they frequently all hang out together, and it seemed strange given that they're allies in chasing the eagles. It reminded me how rarely I actually see conflict. In general, the interactions between plants and animals are neutral or mutually beneficial. It just needs a more inclusive point of view to see things that way. It's like a basketball game. On the surface the two teams compete fiercely, but from a broader perspective they cooperate much more. Both teams agree to meet at the same time on the same court, play the same game, and abide by the same rules.

NOVEMBER 7, 2001

Anxiety.

NOVEMBER 8, 2001

At low tide I went to see what the limpets had been up to. It was nasty out there. Driving rain and thirty-mile-an-hour wind, gusting to fifty. I doubt I'll ever publish the data, so why collect it? Perhaps doing for the doing rather than for the result is a good thing. Why should we study nature only to share the information with others? Why not primarily for our own interest?

When it started to hail, I was briefly blown out of *data collecting mind* and saw myself as other: a lone man in the middle of nowhere on the southern coast of Chile. What was I doing? Then my mood shifted — and hunched on the slick rock, encased from head to toe in rubber, buffeted by wind, rain, and hail, I started to laugh. What else could I do? No one — except perhaps half a dozen other lunatics somewhere — could give a damn what the limpets on the tip of South America are doing. Hell, until a few months ago I didn't care either.

So why was I doing it when I could have been inside my warm dry cabin? Well, in some sense this kind of scientific fieldwork is fun — like any outdoor sport. Skiers try to go fast, climbers try to scale mountains, field biologists try to make accurate measurements under sometimes-adverse conditions. Weird, but there it is.

From a nondual evolutionary perspective, I'm not outside the universe but have emerged from within and am part of it — this includes my knowing mind. So this study is not the separate mind of a scientist learning about the world, but the world learning about itself through a scientific study. Probably, even the limpets don't know where they've been, so through my activity the world is becoming more consciously aware of itself.

NOVEMBER 9, 2001

I saw the female butter-belly for the first time in days. I was meditating when I heard them call and opened my eyes to see her and the male run across the water to greet each other. She bathed in the sea and was gone again — back I presume to her nest.

NO ENTRY FOR NOVEMBER 10, 2001

NOVEMBER 11, 2001

All six goose chicks — grey puffballs with black legs — are still alive. Their parents led them from place to place, feeding on the rocks and swimming in between. It was almost like an obstacle course to strengthen them. At one point they had to leap off a ledge into the water. One chick after another launched into space, almost like parachutists, plop, plop, plop.

NOVEMBER 12, 2001

I often sit on the point and let myself be battered by wind and rain. Part of my grief and sorrow is that I'll never be good enough to get rid of this feeling of not being good enough. The death of ideals. Could this death lead to freedom from the straitjacket of perfectionism? I know I've been through this before, but then I forget, and each time, I need to rediscover the need for acceptance.

I watched as a rainstorm veiled the face of Staines Peninsula with a lovely swirling grey pattern. For months I've listened to rain on the tarp porch roof. It comes in waves of intensity. Changes in drop size and quantity, and the force of the wind, create a complex rhythm of shifting sound. Looking at the swirling pattern today, I suddenly realized I was *seeing* the sound of rain.

NO ENTRY FOR NOVEMBER 13, 2001

NOVEMBER 14, 2001

Today might be only the third time I've seen sun and blue sky since the beginning of October.

The female butter-belly emerged with her chicks: brown-grey on back and top of head; white belly, rump, and sides of head; black legs, feet, and bills. They're much smaller than the goose chicks, even though the butter-belly adults are larger. When I first saw her, the male was across the basin, and I thought maybe these males don't help with rearing. How quickly theories leap into my mind. But when he saw them, he came over and stayed nearby.

Sometime later, the chicks butted their way under her, even though she wasn't very welcoming. Her wings are atrophied and there's not much to drape over the chicks. I found myself judging her; disapproving that she didn't welcome them more readily. Good thing new life is emerging. I feel tired, sore, and used up today.

NOVEMBER 15, 2001

The butter-belly chicks can already run across the water and dive. They all went into the waves beyond the point. The chicks were washed around like fuzzy corks, even up onto the rocks, but it didn't seem to faze them. On land, the female keeps up a low steady single cluck. If the eagle appears, she clucks more loudly and rapidly, and the chicks rush to her.

Today it seems I'm doing the limpet study just because that's what I do. A form of meditation. The results or lack of results don't matter; what does matter is to develop a sense of grace while making the measurements.

NOVEMBER 16, 2001

Rain outside and glum within. Two expressions of one underlying... what? Yesterday was intense: new moon and my day for fasting, so perhaps the mood today is a sort of hangover.

It's getting harder to not think Cat is playing games with me. At times it seems like he cries just to get my reaction. He'll yowl from about ten feet away and then turn to look at me, knowing he's out of water-throwing range. Sometimes when I throw a cup of water at him and he dodges it, he seems to take more pleasure in that than in not getting wet. Sometimes when he dodges the cupful, I try, unsuccessfully, to nail him with a bucketful. Hmm, I might be getting a bit crazy about Cat. In his cry I hear all the hurt and want of the universe.

NOVEMBER 17, 2001

When I'm honest with myself, I admit that my intended destination for this journey — and my life — is enlightenment, whatever that is. I long to feel part of not only my family and society, but the universe. A high-flown notion, but when I hold it loosely, this destination creates a huge space for living. I notice, though, that I become uptight and unhappy when I focus too tightly on the destination and neglect the present moment.

In land travel I've learned that what I most enjoy is not to seek special tourist sights/sites, but to relax on roadsides and park benches and notice whatever Life brings into my field of view. On this inward journey I haven't fully learned that yet, and still grasp for exciting and meaningful experiences.

Nature is red in beak and talon today. As I sat meditating, a drama was unfolding in the basin. Something told me to look out and check the butter-bellies. I spotted both pairs on their disputed boundary line. The far pair had nine or ten chicks with them, but the close pair was chickless. All four adults were calling loudly and engaged in their stylized territorial defense dance, which became more and more intense until the two males started to fight.

Meanwhile, the eagle had apparently been busy. I first noticed him when he swooped on the far pair's chicks. That female lunged to ward him off, and then a red-bill attacked from the air. The eagle gave way, but circled to land on a rock fifty feet from the fighting males.

At that point the close female swam rapidly away, calling, and two of her chicks rushed out from shore toward her. Although I didn't see the attack, I assume the eagle took advantage of her inattention and nailed the other chicks while they were undefended. As I watched, the eagle swooped on the two remaining chicks, but they dove beneath the surface and the red-bill drove him off again. Whew, what an intense encounter!

For those who see the living world — rather than a disembodied creator God — as our source, we sometimes look to nature for possible lessons or metaphors. What does this episode teach? 1. A romantic vision of idyllic harmony and cooperation in nature is as misguided as an exclusive focus on competition. 2. Aggression/competition can be so extreme as to seem self-defeating. The close butter-belly pair expended considerable time and energy breeding and brooding their chicks. Then, caught up in aggression against the other pair, they left the chicks unprotected against an eagle attack. 3. Patience pays off. The eagles have been patrolling this area regularly since the chicks hatched, apparently watching for just such an opportunity. 4. The enemy of an enemy is not always a friend. The red-bills, which are strong allies against predation by the eagles, have been attacked on occasion by the male butter-belly.

Nature can also mirror internal process. I've become attached to the close pair and their chicks, and saw the eagle's attack as vicious, but he was just feeding chicks of his own. I disapprove of the female butter-belly for leaving her chicks unprotected, and I mentally scold the male when I see him away from the female and the chicks. The feeding chicks seem cute and innocent, even though they are killing, too. This, more than any other event here, has reminded me how risky and impermanent individual life is. I'll also be gone soon — dead with all the others.

The female butter-belly is very vigilant and protective, especially on land, but today she let me come within four feet to photograph her and the two remaining chicks. At one point one of the chicks snuggled under her wing, and the other tried to butt its way under the male. He leapt like he'd been goosed.

During morning meditation, I wish the butter-bellies and the eagles freedom from suffering. But how can they all be free from suffering when it's a zero-sum game? Life for the eagles means death for the ducks. I'll stay with that *truth* and see what opens up for me.

I had a lovely dream sequence last night, inspired, I think, by Maturana's ideas about language and consciousness (or perhaps by my Sunday dinner of bacon and greasy fried potatoes). According to Maturana we enact the world we live in through the distinctions we make in language. In the dream I was copulating with an empty pant leg (I wonder how much of the fierce activity of amputees is an attempt to re-create the lost limb) and bringing a world of *things* into being. It was apparent that: 1. The cognitive act of distinguishing *things* from a background and naming them is inherently procreative and so has an erotic aspect to it. 2. Since the *things* we create this way are insubstantial, transient, and exist only in relation to the background, they don't truly exist and this creative act is never completely fulfilling.

In the dream I kept copulating on and on — unsuccessfully seeking completion and fulfillment. The process of creating a world of individual things in language is inherently frustrating and unsatisfying. Perhaps this is partially what spiritual masters mean when they talk about the fundamental dissatisfaction of living.

I've noticed over and over these past days that it's words — some kinds of words — spoken to myself or read that shift me from small to Big Mind. So words themselves are not a prison, but only certain uses of them. A lot of densely packed analytic words tend to tighten my mind. A few lyrical words often open an inner space. I need to remember this in my writing and speaking — both with others and with myself.

In the long slow evening twilight I shifted from small to Big Mind, and for the first time ever (or so it seemed) I got the koan of "Listen for the sound of one hand clapping." How magical and beautiful the phrase. This is all the sound of one hand clapping: wind, water, and rain, trees, rocks, and far foggy hills.

It's been a day of conflict and insight. This morning I saw some of the beautiful brown-breasted geese near the point. I've been trying for a good photo of them since they arrived, but they're very skittish. Cat was with me and he likes to harass them because — unlike the butter-bellies — they're afraid of him. He headed for them but I called, "No!" several times and he finally stopped. I praised, petted, and carried him back to the cabin. Told him to stay and took the camera back to the point.

Halfway there I heard him coming after me. I told him to get back, and he ducked into the trees. I talked soothingly to the geese (which really does work), and they let me sidle to within thirty feet. I was moving still closer when Cat stalked by me and the geese scattered.

I was furious and decided that when I caught him I'd hammer him. I was aware of my decision and asked myself whether I really wanted to do it. I took the camera to the cabin and went out to measure limpets. There he was, casually sniffing around. I grabbed him hard by the skin on his back, yelled, and slapped him. He bared his claws and snarled — rage in his eyes. I slapped him again and yelled that he'd better not fucking snarl at me. Then I dunked him in a pool of water and threw him from me. He ran off into the trees.

In the afternoon he asked to come on my lap, and I petted him and thought the confrontation had passed, but later he blatantly strolled into the cabin. I grabbed him and threw him out into the mud. I remain ambivalent about my behavior. I think most people would upbraid me for cruelty, and some might even slap me in turn. Still, it seems to me that cats in general, and this one in particular, are very willful and expect to do as they please. Most people let them, but I'm not willing to. I'm not comfortable either letting Cat do as he pleases or smacking him. Throwing water at him doesn't work, so perhaps dunking him again will be my next recourse.

Toward evening, I heard the close pair of butter-bellies call and saw them swimming across the basin fast and alone. She was searching for her last two chicks: head high, looking around, and she even went up to her old nest site. I could feel her agitation in my own body: loss? pain? grief? I imagine the eagle got the chicks, but how? Since losing the other five, she's been extremely protective of the remaining two. I'm sad both for her and for me. I was looking forward to watching them grow up. I've tried to simply be with the experience and level no judgments or rationalizations.

Examining the listening process is an excellent way to see how the mind creates categories and uses them to identify and organize sensory experience. From a unified field of sound, I choose the ones I want to group together as rain on the roof, water falling from gutter, waves on the beach, waterfalls, wind in the trees, etc. It's my mind that distinguishes distinct "sound entities," and attributes a source to each of them. When I hear a sound I can't identify, my mind becomes alert and uneasy until it places the sound into a category.

All this is useful for survival, but it has a downside. In conceptualizing, organizing, and thinking about these sensory impressions, the immediacy of experience can easily be lost. It requires patience and practice to soften this habitual activity by over and over letting go of thoughts and analysis to simply stay with the swirl of sound just as it is without trying to *do anything with it.*

Today I watched my thoughts trying to create the sense of a solid self. The dream is to establish that self and then not have to hustle anymore; not have to fake it; actually be really real. But the hoped for solidity is an illusory dream. The only way to be free from the hustle is to give up trying to create a solid self or solid social presence. This doesn't mean we disappear or stop being active, only that we can relax and let ourselves do whatever comes naturally without worrying about results. For the ego, this can be a truly scary idea.

There seems to be a thinking aspect to any *Aha!* insight. Thought may trigger that gestalt of apprehension, as well as solidify it. It's a kind of dance to move in and think in a directed way, and then, when my mind begins to tighten, move back and simply notice the thinking from afar. Then once there is some space and stillness, move back in again. I'm learning that thinking is an art form. Too bad they don't teach us how to think in school.

We train/condition members of society (especially kids) to be a certain way. But this is backward. It's like seeing natural selection as selecting *for* some ideal form or behavior. But that isn't how natural selection operates. Rather, some biological forms and behaviors that don't work are selected *against* and die or become extinct. This allows enormous freedom of variety for things that do work well enough to survive and reproduce. It's the same with socialization. We should train citizens to refrain only from behaviors that are unacceptable to the collective (murder, stealing, etc.) and allow full freedom for individuals to develop as they will within those constraints.

Jeez, for planning to not write anymore I sure am writing a lot.

NOVEMBER 21, 2001

I woke to a calm sea and hard steady rain; then snow began to fall. I thought it would be just a flurry, but it snowed all afternoon and evening — big wet flakes drifting straight down until ground and trees were glorious white. The sound of snowfall is so much softer than that of rain.

I fished for a long time from the kayak. Mist cloaked the solid rock of Staines Peninsula; the only sign of its existence was the sound of waterfalls and sea lions. The hills and mountains to the east had vanished, too. My world became this small cluster of hidden islands. From far above, I could see myself drifting in an opaque fog on a shining sea.

NOVEMBER 22, 2001

Is this Thanksgiving Day? I think I'll treat it as such since it's a beautiful calm morning, *alive* with silver light.

I'm neither stuck in language nor able to leave it behind. Language is like my body: I live in my body, and it's an aspect of who I am. I'm not stuck exclusively in my body, but I'm never separate from it either. In one sense I began as body and then developed thinking mind. It's the same with language and culture. I have the potential to grow through them and beyond. Language and culture are always an aspect of who I am, but I'm not stuck exclusively there. What a thanksgiving gift this simple realization is. I've been struggling for a long time with Maturana's claim that we live in language.

Attachment to wilderness is still attachment and an attempt to prevent change. Global warming is — one way or another — part of the cyclic drift; populations grow dense and crash; life goes on. But we may be able to influence the process to prevent disaster to ourselves and to the ecosystems that sustain us.

NOVEMBER 23, 2001

The far pair of butter-bellies reclaimed the rock that had been their home base but that they'd lost to the close pair. All the chicks from both pairs are now dead. While my first long wilderness retreat showed me unity and harmony in all things, this time there seems to be conflict on all sides: wind, sea, and rock; all creatures eating and being eaten; birds fighting for territory; me struggling against myself. Nature, though, expects nothing from me but to be just what I am.

NOVEMBER 24, 2001

This afternoon I went to the point to brace against the roaring wind like a football player on the line of scrimmage. Something in me finally let go and I started to dance and holler for joy in the fierce power of it. Dolphins were playing in the basin, and I took the kayak out to play with them, but they left as soon as I arrived. It hurts my feelings when they do that. Perhaps the shape of the kayak reminds them of a killer whale.

NOVEMBER 25, 2001

SUNDAY MORNING: I keep slipping out of the present moment by imagining future conversations. How strange to make such an effort to leave the social matrix and then spend so much time there anyway. A lot of my inner small mind dialogue is me telling others about this experience . . . swell. The only thing I'll have to tell others about is being lost in fantasies of telling them about solitude.

I'm not sure if I've been imagining such future events the whole time I've been here, or just since I stopped staying busy with daily activity. These imagined future conversations may have replaced thinking about cutting firewood, going to the glacier, etc. It all seems to be activity of the ego trying to maintain a solid sense of self and self-worth.

I seldom have sexual fantasies, and when I do they have little seductive power. But over and over I get lost in fantasies of telling other people about this year in solitude. From a positive perspective, I could say the fantasies are about wanting to share with others. But if I'm lost in an imagined future rather than being fully *alive* and present in this moment, I'll do the same when back with people. And that's just the problem: spending life lost in the past and future. When I'm settled into the present moment, these fantasies don't seem to suck me in. What a relief to relax into how things actually are.

NO ENTRIES FOR NOVEMBER 26–30, 2001

DECEMBER 2001

Gaining enlightenment is an accident.
Spiritual practice simply makes us accident-prone.

— ZEN SAYING

Two of the missing limpets showed up. One has probably been in plain sight all along, but in a very unexpected place. It crossed five feet of sand and broken shell to attach itself to a separate rock. I wonder why it went there. Slowly, I'm starting to feel close to them as brother organisms.

Last night, for just a little while, the world pulsed with signs and portent — *alive* and enchanted under a moonlit sky. The trees on the bluff stood sentinel; awe and wonder everywhere. Today, Cat is moaning and I am dark and grim. Even though the sun has broken through the clouds, it falls on a world that's just the world again: beautiful island, mountains, and sea.

Each day I spend time at the point with the wind, and ask it to teach me what I need to know. Death is everywhere: in the diving ducks and swooping eagle, the leaping dolphins and waiting kingfisher — all are hunting and killing. On the tidal flat, each step I take crushes life.

At the point, the plants are always there; they can't retreat from the wind. I hide behind them and warm myself by burning their bodies. I eat their flesh and breathe their exhalations. I'm beginning to love and care for the plants.

How would logging have to change if we accepted Native Americans' statements about "brother tree" as a literal rather than a metaphorical or sentimental expression? How would we live if we actually experienced the

257

world and ourselves as fully *alive* and sacred? We would still need to take life
to live, but I think we would try much harder to avoid wasting lives unnecessarily.

I continue to bully Cat at times and continue to feel lousy about it. I'm seeing more clearly how cowardice and bullying are linked. Afraid to face my
own fear and rage, I take it out on him. I'm not afraid of death, but of un-
ending pain. Last night I struggled with a bout of phantom limb pain. It's
eased off today, and I have no idea what triggered it.

I often look forward to measuring the limpets. It structures my day, links
me with the tide, and pushes me into the wind and rain. The experience can
be exciting, almost like riding a motorcycle.

Rock-sitting in the evening rain — and then a shift. Light, that seems to come
from beyond, floods my soul and brings love, peace, beauty, and the gift of
Life. Perhaps I, myself, am the source of that light, but for now one step at a
time. When I try to force the identification, I seem to lose my way.

Perhaps describing the shift as a move into *wild aliveness* isn't so skillful.
The term seems too self-important and macho. These changes are softer than
those I remember from my first long wilderness retreat. They arrive as a gift
and bring a sense of gentle transformation. As with a mathematical transformation, there's a relationship between small and Big Mind, but here the relationship is mysterious rather than numerical.

Low day, grey and rainy, inside and out. When I'm down, I have no stable
worldview or life goal to hold me steady, so I'm at the mercy of the ebb and
flow of immediate experience. I long for meaning and purpose that's not ego-
based but comes through me from a deeper place. If all my work here only
makes it more tolerable to pass through life, then it doesn't seem worthwhile.
There needs to be joy.

That's the last thought — with its negative tone — I remember having
before I noticed the rain rippling in the puddles. Then the soft shift to peace,
love, and beauty. Why? What triggered it? It's as though my conscious mind
has little influence. Big Mind/tender heart just comes and goes. For stability,
I need to live in a context that includes both wonder and gloom. Else, I'm always on a roller coaster.

Often now, I feel love for the rain. The drumming on the roof I used to find oppressive has become comforting; it concentrates my attention and carries me inward. Today, fierce wind is hammering the cabin, and even that, with twinges of anxiety, feels ok.

I spend so much time worrying about whether people will like and respect me in the years ahead, but there is nothing I can do to make that happen. I can only work on liking and respecting myself and others, look for Spirit in each of us, and learn to accept inevitable frustration, fear, and anger without blaming myself or the external world. My task is to stay centered, not manipulate others to make me feel ok.

In the long lovely twilight, the butter-bellies swam into the Big Mind space of the basin. But as I focused on them, I flipped into small mind. So I loosened my gaze and turned my eye, with a less attached interest, to a cormorant floating not far away. Flip. And again, with more care this time, back to the butter-bellies. I felt something in my body, some intentionality — perhaps from their posture or the speed of their movement — and wondered where they were going. Then I realized they were heading for the cormorant. Surprising, since they usually coexist peacefully. But the cormorant sensed it too and flew away. As soon as it lifted, the ducks changed direction.

From the perspective of Big Mind, everything is *perfect* just the way it is —*just because it is*. Things are not perfect in an *ideal* sense, but they are *what they are*. We all exist as natural manifestations of Life, no matter what I might feel and think about it.

Some psychologists argue that we become depressed when we're unwilling to consciously feel anger toward the world, and instead direct it toward ourselves. I wonder. I've felt openly angry for a long time, and I still get depressed! Perhaps, instead, depression is just the sense of lifelessness that comes when I'm unwilling to feel painful emotions of any kind and so hold all experience at bay. Leaning in, to experience the depression directly, breaks the cycle because then I am feeling and letting the world touch me. By leaning in and accepting it, I can shift my perspective to Big Mind, and then the depression loses its power to dominate; it becomes a natural part of the universe. Sometimes when I sink lightly into the depression, it opens out into joy.

Ah, that this clarity would last, but it, too, is transient. Just this afternoon, I was thinking that for twenty-five years I've tried everything, and I still get caught in fighting against depression. Now, of course, that all seems behind me... until next time.

DECEMBER 9, 2001

Lovely warm mostly sunny Sunday. It's windy on the point, but there's only a breeze here. I had a surprise today I'm hesitant to write about — my first real lust attack in the ten months I've been here. I've had occasional mind bubbles before this, but they didn't really move into my body. This one did. I found myself fantasizing about making love with a Latin woman, and then I realized that on a subconscious level I've always wanted to have sex with my mother. I've thought I kept my physical and emotional distance from her because I resented the demands she put on me and because I sensed rejection, but sexual desire is one of the feelings I've been avoiding. I suppose I shouldn't take it too personally, since Freud claims this is a universal aspect of the mother/son relationship. Still, it's not easy to actually face.

I let myself feel the sensations and found myself masturbating. The wave of lust passed before I climaxed, and I was glad. Sitting in the Sunday sun, I felt more relaxed than in a long time. But the body lust returned and I went with it. Afterward, I remained aware of my feelings, but not much guilt or anything else came up. I realized that sexual love wasn't what I'd really wanted with my mother. I wonder if this has opened a dark corner in me that will take a lot of time and work to accept — like acknowledging (if not liking) my sometimes physical attraction to men. I sort of hope not, because I've enjoyed the peace of nonlust out here.

DECEMBER 11, 2001

I sit and watch what aversion and desire do to my mind. I practice the balance of leaning lightly into pain and lightly away from pleasure; practice letting go of the past and trusting the unknowable future. And I explore the shift that transforms the path to somewhere else into an endless opening in the here and now.

A strange male butter-belly swam into the basin today and made himself at home. He acted so much like the resident that I couldn't be sure he wasn't, until the local pair showed up and drove him off. It was, perhaps, a glimpse of how a male acquires territory: move in *as if* it's already yours, and then defend it *because* you experience it as yours.

Often, the limpets still seem like objects to me. But I do feel them as animate beings when, for the study, I pry them from the rock and see the animal beneath the shell. I've accidentally nicked a couple of them with the putty knife, and felt the cut myself. I filed the sharp corners of the blade, and have been more careful, since.

Low-tide rock-sitting, listening for the Voice of God. Then the soft subtle shift: my whole being relaxed and I was listening (am now, and always have been) to the Voice of God in every sound.

Such a small difference — from *for* to *to* — yet massive. In one I strain for what isn't; in the other I find peace in the wonder of what is. Listening *for* the Voice of God implies duality, as though whatever I'm experiencing is somehow not the Voice of God.

I spend so much time and energy listening for the Voice of God with my mind, but I listen to the Voice of God with my heart. My mind has definite ideas about what it wants God's Voice to say; it wants answers, certainty, conceptual understanding. My heart hears God's Voice saying, "I Am," and it is peaceful and content.

NO ENTRIES FOR DECEMBER 16–23, 2001

This is the most peaceful, if not the most painless, Christmas I've spent in a long time. I'll share it with the sea and sky, the mountains, the trees and the wind.

Since early October, only a few days have been calm enough to fish from the kayak, so mostly I'm land-bound on this small patch of earth. When I do go fishing, I recognize the life I take in killing a fish. I feel deep connection and gratitude for the gift of sustenance from the sea, and also sorrow in ending the life of my fellow creature.

Yet out here alone (except, of course, for the whole world around and within me), I see death daily and know that all beings survive by ending the lives of others. There are underlying harmony and oneness in our common existence, we are all alive together, but there is also surface conflict — competition for food and space.

Long ago I put away my watch and calendar, and now spend much of my time quietly listening to the rain on the roof and the sound of waves against the rocks, watching the tide and my breath flow in and out; bringing myself back to my own direct experience of the here and now, to my body and heart and sometimes spacious mind. To the question: *Who am I?* Daily I go to the exposed point to sit or stand and be hammered by the wind — slowly being shaped in ways I cannot tell.

This morning I completed four days of fasting and intensive meditation. Sitting for long hours in the wind and rain, encased in rubber from head to toe. The process is often difficult. There is darkness and anger and grief. There is pain. But there are also times of radiant joy when my heart and mind and body are filled with the light of peace and love and beauty. Times when wonder fills the world. Times when I want to never leave here.

During the days of fasting and meditation, I was centered enough to let Cat's cries arise and fall without reacting to them, and he cried very little — perhaps because I slept on the porch. Over and over, I've vowed to not react to his cries, and over and over, I've failed. This morning I nailed him full in the face with a pan of water, and again I vowed that until January I would take no physical or verbal action against him from a state of anger and aversion.

When such feelings flood me, they poison my relationship with the whole world. My heart hardens and I become implacable; everything, including myself, is unpleasant. What triggers these feelings is often insignificant, but seems huge and like it will last forever. Even when the event is short in duration, the painful state can persist because I remain on guard, waiting for the event to recur. In this state, I focus only on the negative.

During the fast, my nose ran from the cold and wind. At one point I felt a drip form and slowly dribble down my lips and chin, but I managed to stay with it instead of wiping it away. My whole being focused on the intense tickle and the aversion it aroused. After that, the dripping became just a normal sensation. Without aversion, perhaps Cat's yowling will be just a sound.

Ha! I just went out to the porch and caught him watching alertly, ready to dodge flying water. It's as though he enjoys this conflict; as though it pumps adrenaline into him. So my actions may actually be reinforcing his crying. Maybe all these maybes are just babble and Cat is just as he is. I notice again how much intentionality I attribute to him — as though he, and everything else, is intentionally thwarting my will. But the world is simply doing what it does; each being living its own life. Why is this so difficult to see and accept, when insisting on being the center of everything causes such pain?

Dang. In a moment of mindlessness I fried the Mac laptop by plugging it into the PC charger. After fasting I was very dehydrated. All the symptoms were there — droopy skin, dry mouth, disorientation — but it took a while to recognize what was going on. Yet another catch-22: how to recognize your own dehydration when one of the symptoms is confusion. While I was foggy, I plugged in the Mac and pffttt. I really liked that small machine and used it for journaling until I switched back to pen and paper a couple of months ago.

Now for a well-deserved cup of coffee — the first since the beginning of November.

NO ENTRIES FOR DECEMBER 25–28, 2001

DECEMBER 29, 2001

I still seem to feel less urge to write about the non-ego-centered experiences of love, respect, awe, and peace than about inner darkness. I think I use writing as both an escape from the intensity of painful feelings and as a means to discover and describe how and why I trap myself in suffering. But during these last few months I'm making an effort to more frequently describe the light as well as the dark.

I've also come to realize that these entries aren't simply a record of my life in solitude. They are also a teaching tool for the future, a way for me to remember what I'm learning and will likely forget once I return to the social world. Like Hansel and Gretel, I'm leaving a trail of crumbs to lead me home again.

DECEMBER 30, 2001

Rock-sitting in a warm moonlight breeze
through the night and toward the dawn.

Drifting into and out of the Now.

Keeping company with Spirit and with myself.
Nowhere to go, nowhere to not go either.

INTERLUDE

SPIRITUAL PRACTICE

Never think that I believe I should set out
a "system of teaching" to help people
understand the way. Never cherish such a thought.
What I proclaim is the truth as I have discovered it
and "a system of teaching" has no meaning
because the truth can't be cut up into pieces
and arranged in a system.

— BUDDHA

Spirituality has been integral to my life for as long as I can remember, although I didn't always call it that. I was raised in a conflicted Baptist family: my father had been recently born again, and my mother had no use for organized religion. She was, though, unwilling to argue about it, so we kids went to church or Sunday school every week. Nature was my mother's church, and by inclination, mine, too.

The first time I swore was at a fish. I was twelve years old and working a stream in California's Sierra Nevada. A trout kept stealing my bait, and in frustration I finally muttered, "Damn you!" That was the beginning of the end for me and fundamentalist Christianity. I became a backslider: troubled by fears of hell, but eager to live a free and adventurous life here on earth.

By the time I was fifteen, Baptist dogma no longer made sense. My deepest question (then and now) was: "How can both predestination (determinism) and free will be true?" The church had no satisfactory answer, and this gap in logic nudged me further from the fold. At seventeen I announced that I didn't want to attend Sunday school any longer. My mother cheerfully agreed and said that I could, instead, stay home and help clean the house. Although I didn't realize it at the time, her response was a fine example of the Sunday school teacher's explanation of predestination and free will: I could, of course, do what I wanted, but my mother knew beforehand what I would choose. There was, however, a difference between my mother and God. My mother didn't *really* know, not for certain.

When I left home a year later, my faith was gone, and I'd begun to deny the existence of God. For a time, while experimenting with LSD, I again considered the spiritual aspects of the world, but it wasn't until my first long solitary retreat in the wilderness that I directly experienced a Presence I could not explain away. This was both joyful and troubling.

During the next year, I struggled to make sense of what had happened to me in solitude. Along with consulting the I Ching, I read the Bible and Carl Jung, searching for a way to acknowledge the mysterious Presence I still sensed at times — without sliding back into fundamentalism's rejection of all spiritual experience that doesn't conform to a literal interpretation of the Bible. For a while I visited various churches, seeking a community where I could feel at home. I often recognized the presence of Spirit, especially in evangelical meetings, but they wouldn't accept the validity of any path but their own.

BUDDHISM

One day my sister told me she had recently attended a Buddhist meditation retreat and had hated it, but thought I might like it. She was partially correct: I didn't actually like it, but I did find it enormously valuable and reassuring. Soon after, I attended a three-month silent retreat, and then lived for a time in a small hybrid Buddhist/Christian/Tai Chi community in New Hampshire.

Over the years, Buddhist meditation and thought have been very useful as I attempt to explore, accept, and, perhaps, understand myself. Although I've devoted considerable effort to inner work, I still consider myself a beginner on the way as I work to develop moment-by-moment, nonjudgmental awareness and acceptance of living in all its ambiguous wonder.

My thinking about Buddhism tends to be pragmatic and straightforward. For instance, most Buddhists believe in the birth/death cycles of reincarnation. I spend little time wondering about what might or might not happen after death, focusing instead on life in the here and now. I do recognize, however, that I must die to each moment in order to be fully *alive* and present in the next. This seems to be how the Buddha taught as well. Instead of answering questions about abstract metaphysics, he dedicated his words to the practical alleviation of suffering.

The Buddha taught Four Noble Truths:

1. Suffering exists in our lives.
2. Attachment, aversion, and delusion are the cause of suffering.
3. There exists a way to alleviate suffering.

4. Freedom from suffering is found through the Middle Way practice of the Eightfold Path.

Life involves physical, emotional, and psychological pain. This is self-evident once we stop pretending otherwise. One of our most ubiquitous forms of denial is to hope for a future in which pain will no longer exist in our lives — to imagine that our current pain is a temporary anomaly. Our cultural drive for progress is based, to some extent, on the utopian social ideal of an end to pain. Belief in a pain-free eternal life after death is another manifestation of this longing. There is also suffering in our lives, but pain and suffering are not the same. Pain is inherent to living, suffering is optional.

Buddhism teaches that the root causes of suffering are attachment, aversion, and delusion. We are attached to sense pleasure; to our opinions and theories about how the world is and how it should be; to various social, political, religious, and scientific rites and rituals; to the belief in a permanent separate self — I, me, mine. This teaching can be loosely summarized as: the desire for and attachment to pleasure and security cause suffering because nothing in the world is permanent; everything changes.

The other side of desire and attachment is aversion to and avoidance of pain. The strong sensations we generally label as pain are inherent to living, but we can work with the quality of our experience in relation to these sensations. If we resist them, our resistance actually intensifies the sensations and thus creates additional pain. Another common way we intensify pain is by taking it personally and having a "why me?" attitude. If we can relax into pain as a natural part of living that everyone experiences, and let go of the self-judgment that something is wrong with *me* because *I'm* experiencing pain, we can alleviate our suffering to a large degree. Much of our suffering is caused by attachment to our sense of a separate autonomous "I" that can somehow achieve a permanent state of affairs with only pleasure and no pain. Attachment to pleasurable spiritual experiences and aversion to other darker experiences also causes suffering.

The Buddha taught that the journey from suffering to freedom is along the Noble Eightfold Path: right understanding; right thought, right speech, right action; right livelihood; right effort (in meditation); right mindfulness; right concentration. Still rebelling somewhat against my fundamentalist Christian upbringing, I tend to resist prescribed ethical rules. But Buddhism doesn't use language of condemnation; instead it speaks in terms of unskillful and skillful means — actions that do or do not lead to more suffering.

One Buddhist teaching, based on insight that may arise during meditation, is that to a great extent our normal experience consists of conceptual categories, and that beyond/beneath/within these categories the world flows without fixed boundaries. When we clearly see that nothing is solid or permanent, see into the process of how we construct and name objects by distinguishing them from the surrounding matrix, see that without the background matrix an object cannot exist, and see that each object is part of the background for each other object, our lives are transformed and we can relax — until we forget again and slip back into conditioned habits of perception.

The terms Emptiness, Groundlessness, and Suchness slip and slide and cannot be pinned down. They remind us that the world of discrete objects — including the self — is conditional and empty of permanence or self-sufficiency. And they direct our attention to the flowing physical reality beneath the level of conceptualization. But they also point to something more. Wilber writes:

> This is why, in nondual Suchness [Emptiness], it is absolutely *not* that each being is a *part* of the One, or participates in the One, or is an aspect of the One. In other words, it is not, as in pantheism, that each is merely a *piece* of the "One," a slice of the pie, or a strand in the Big Web.... As Zen would have it, Emptiness is not the sum total of Form, it is the essence of Form.

And:

> Pure Emptiness and pure Consciousness are synonymous. Consciousness is not a thing or a process.... It is ultimately Emptiness, the opening or clearing in which the form of beings manifest themselves, and not any particular manifestation itself.
>
> [All italics and quotation marks are Wilber's.][1]

And then the *Heart Sutra* from the Buddha further boggles the mind: "Form is emptiness, emptiness itself is form; emptiness is no other than form, form is no other than emptiness." Here it might be useful to give up trying to "understand" with the rational mind and simply return to following the breath.

From a Buddhist perspective, spiritual practice is not primarily intended to structure the content of experience and prevent unpleasant thoughts and feelings from entering, but rather to stabilize consciousness itself — the context within which all thoughts and feelings arise — to honor and care for all aspects of ourselves and our experience. We do not fear the dark and chaotic, but allow everything to arise and dissolve — as all experiences arise and dissolve — without rejecting or clinging to anything. It is this equanimity, the confidence to be with life in all its manifestations, that brings peace and joy.

CONTROL OR SURRENDER

The extremist dichotomy — control or surrender — between West and East is an artificial generalization I don't want to defend as literally true, but I would like to look at it as a possible metaphor with broader implications for how we live our lives. Posit a spectrum. At one end is the efficient modernist technician: fully focused on getting the job done, improving his personal life by seeking more status and a higher salary that will fulfill his desire for more material goods. He is intent on developing ever-more-powerful technology to control and improve the world and his own body. At the other end is the caricature of the Eastern mystic: scrawny, long matted hair and beard, dirty, covered with flies, making no effort to better his lot or improve the world in any way.

The technician accepts his inner self as given (indeed, it is often invisible to him), sees pleasure as good and pain as bad, and works to change the external world — including his own body — to improve his quality of life. The goal of the mystic is to embrace pain as well as pleasure and to experience all as sacred. He works with his own mind to accept and value the world — including himself — just as it is and so improve his quality of life. Both seek to be happy, but go about it in different ways. Which approach is correct and which mistaken?

Both are right. If we attempt to avoid all pain by controlling the world, our emotions, and our bodies, we run in an ever-more-frantic circle, trying to deny who/what we actually are, as though we can somehow escape from the universe. On the other hand, we (or someone who cares for us) do need to act to survive, and we do have the capacity to alleviate some of the pain of life through adjustment of external circumstance. It is not activity *or* acceptance, but rather acceptance *and* activity — based on wisdom rather than avoidance and greed. This is the middle way of Buddhism.

TRADITIONAL TEACHINGS AND PERSONAL EXPERIENCE

I sometimes question the relationship of my own direct experience to traditional spiritual teachings. Buddhism is an empirical practice: students are encouraged to accept only what they directly experience for themselves. Yet great value is placed on the ancient teachings of the Buddha, who was, it is claimed, a fully enlightened being and saw the truth of existence. When my own experience does not accord with traditional teachings, there could be several possible reasons: my understanding of the teachings is partial or confused; the original teachings have been idealized or corrupted over time; my perceptions are distorted; the cultural context of my experience is different from that of the Buddha; our current collective understanding has evolved beyond that of the Buddha.

Ken Wilber criticizes philosophers who see current culture as degenerate and want to return to some supposed Golden Age. He argues that the knowledge and sophistication of spiritual explorers as well as that of natural and social scientists continue to evolve.

I value both my own explorations and traditional teachings. I also continue to question whether our understanding of ourselves and the world is progressing in a fundamental way, or if we are simply developing explanations that reflect our current language and cultural context.

POTENTIAL TRAPS

Tension often arises between adherents of different organized religions. There may also be edginess between those committed to a traditional spiritual practice and those who follow a more personal idiosyncratic path. Both approaches carry risks. In adopting an established tradition it can be tempting to literalize the teachings and idealize the teacher. This creates the illusion that there is someone or something outside ourselves that can "save" us. How often I've imagined that someone somewhere must have the *Answer* and a system he can teach me that will end my suffering. Buddhism is frequently presented as a system of practice and thought that will lead to enlightenment, but as the epigram above suggests, the Buddha himself, at least in some contexts, denied he could provide such a system. Finally, we must each find our own way home.

In recognizing this, it is easy to become a spiritual dabbler. Instead of deepening our own contemplative practice, we take the easy way out and spend our time reading and thinking about what others have written. This can be extremely useful, but such teachings are only conceptual descriptions of someone else's insights and understandings; they are not a direct examination of the light and shadow of our own inner world. There is also an opposite risk. In following a personal meandering path, it's easy to become lost in thickets of doubt and confusion. At such times, a trusted teacher can be invaluable.

Always skulking in the shadows is the ego's need to perceive itself as special. This need is often present but unrecognized in spiritual communities. A sort of "us and them" superiority can develop among groups of spiritual seekers. It's easy, when surrounded by a group of like-minded people, to believe that you have found the Truth others are still seeking. Teachers, too, when held aloft by ardent followers, can be seduced into seeing themselves as special beings. This limits everyone involved. The teacher is no longer a fellow being in the flow of life, but set apart and above.

In following your own path, on the other hand, there is the risk of spiritual arrogance and excessive independence: an "I don't need any help; I can do it all on my own" attitude. Surrendering the ego to Something Greater is at the heart of spiritual practice, and the process is endlessly subtle and challenging. The temptations of self-deception and hypocrisy are always present.

Some years ago, feeling myself to have veered too far into independence, I began to participate in a Native American sweat circle. It's an interesting and powerful practice. Some of my brothers and sisters take the traditional teaching quite literally; others less so. I work to relax my habit of doing things my own way and to join respectfully in the ceremonies, without attempting to be other than I am.

LEARNING AND CREATING A SPIRITUAL PRACTICE

I approach spirituality as integral to ordinary life, not something special and apart from it, and I see the spiritual journey as simply becoming a mature human being. Some spiritual systems categorize stages of development in great detail. I'm too pragmatic to be attracted to abstract discussions of theology. What fascinates and beckons me is direct experience and understanding of the mind/body process as lived here and now. One of my own — and my culture's — immediate tasks is to acknowledge and integrate our inner shadow and heal the rifts between mind and body, self and other.

It can be seductive to project an abstract idea of spirit out into the ether and seek salvation in our own imagination, but this is as misguided and deadening as is denying the existence of spirit altogether. In *Religion in an Age of Science*, Ian Barbour points out that spiritual traditions tend to either understand spirit as transcending the physical, which leads to disembodied dualism, or they equate spirit to the physical world as in nature worship. Western religions lean strongly toward the transcendent, and there is now hunger to redress this imbalance. We are beginning to rediscover spirit in the immediate, in our flesh — even perhaps as our flesh. Of particular and intense interest for me is the experiential shift from feeling alienated from an essentially static and lifeless existence to a sense of belonging in a world that is vibrantly *Alive*.

My basic spiritual practice is daily meditation and retreat into solitude. Alone in the wilderness, my awareness deepens. I slow down and frequently pause to come back to myself in the here and now. In loving-kindness meditation each morning I ask for peace, happiness, and freedom from suffering for all people, plants, and animals in the world. Before each meal I pause to give thanks and offer a small portion of my food to the earth. In solitude, daily rituals spontaneously develop that enrich my life and express my sense of gratitude. These regular practices create a sense of stability that helps maintain equilibrium.

JANUARY 2002

Everything is Sacred.

— REMINDER TO MYSELF TAPED TO MY CABIN DOOR

NO ENTRIES FOR JANUARY 1—3, 2002

JANUARY 4, 2002

Amazing. A flock of parrots (Austral parakeet) has landed in the trees behind the cabin and set up a raucous screeching. What are parrots doing here? They're not very large, have a yellow-green body, shiny blue-green wings and tail, some red on the belly. Many other birds that I didn't notice last summer have also moved in.

One tiny one (Magellanic tapaculo) that appears to be black flits among the dense brush. I've only caught a glimpse of it once, and I wasn't wearing my glasses, but I hear it frequently. Its call is two sharp notes: "Wake up!" or "Come back!" or "Look out!" I've named it Dharma bird because of its frequent reminders to stay in the present.

A few days ago I saw two swallows (Chilean Swallow) flying nearby. One had a feather in her beak. She dropped it, and as it fluttered down, she swooped round to pluck it from the air. I think she did it twice. It looked like play to me.

A jellyfish bloom floated in yesterday and Cat seems to enjoy eating them.

JANUARY 5, 2002

What a hoot! My neighbors surprised and delighted me again. Three dolphins were here as they frequently have been during the past month. They

273

were roaring around whapping the surface with their tails, and one was swimming on his back, white belly in the air. I'm pretty sure I saw a pink erection pointing toward the sky.

From the corner of my eye I saw the butter-bellies swim casually into the basin. I thought it was the close pair, but they swam across the boundary into the neighboring territory and climbed up onto the other pair's home rock. Odd. Then a single intruder appeared and the pair ferociously charged. I watched through binoculars as they came running/flapping in a froth of spray across the water toward me.

It's hard to imagine — without having seen something similar — such an intense adrenaline-pumped rush of movement. I suppose the frenzied flutter of a flock of chickens when Farmer Brown's wife appears in the hen yard, meat cleaver in her hand and Sunday dinner in her heart might come close. Usually, the ducks thrashing over the water seem sort of comical because they're frantically trying to escape the imagined danger I pose in the boat or kayak. But to see them charge straight in through binoculars toward me was a different matter entirely and very threatening.

All of a sudden, like a scene from the Keystone Cops, all three switched direction and the intruder now pursued the resident pair! Huh? Then all three hustled up onto the rock together! This was absolutely unprecedented since they're intensely territorial.

An interesting side effect of looking through binoculars is that they tunnel vision and focus consciousness. The rest of the world disappears and the only thing that exists is what I'm seeing through the lenses. So I was quite startled when the three dolphins swept into view right behind the ducks. I suspect they were excited by the commotion and playing rather than hunting, but the butter-bellies didn't seem to think so.

The dolphins like to frolic in the tidal bore that runs through that part of the basin, and they swam leaping and splashing past the rock to disappear behind the small island. Once the dolphins were gone, the butter-bellies seemed to remember what they'd been doing. The intruder scooted back into the water and ran flapping off in the direction the dolphins had gone — the pair, still intent on mayhem, in hot pursuit. Within seconds, all three came flailing back from behind the island — the pair in the lead, then the intruder, and the dolphins close behind. The pair leapt onto the rock again, but the intruder just circled it, and once the dolphins had passed, fled back in the direction he had come. Then all was quiet once again. Meanwhile, the black-and-white geese with their chicks were peacefully feeding not far away.

NO ENTRIES FOR JANUARY 6–7, 2002

When my heart opens, the world seems small and intimate, and I feel tender love for all that exists. Everything feels more real and *alive* somehow, even the table and stove. I find myself listening not only to sounds, but also to the silence within which sounds arise. It's this gestalt of form/emptiness that seems full and *alive*.

Back in the human realm, I have still received no word from the navy about bringing Patti here, even though in the January 1 check-in email I asked them if they would. Trust the Process.

I've started to build a meditation box for Patti. She's been a huge loving presence in my life and has contributed so much to my journey here. Months ago I found a rock I often hold when meditating. A while back I found a long slab of cypress washed up on a beach, and the notion of making a box for the rock came to me. I'll nestle the rock in a chiton shell set into the bottom of the box. I saw a chiton for the first time last week. The inside of a chiton's shell is exquisite turquoise blue, so I immediately thought of using it in the box. But I didn't want to kill the only one here. Today I found another one. I'll make the lidded box just large enough to hold the sun-bleached breastbone of a seabird, which will cover the rock.

I don't have many tools, and a major job is to saw, chisel, and smooth a thin board from the driftwood slab before I can start to actually build the box. It will take a while, but I have time. The sandpaper I brought was ruined early on, so the most efficient way to smooth the wood is to scrape it with the machete. Cypress is exquisite: beautiful grain, golden color, intoxicating smell.

The past few days have been calm and I've been leaning toward fishing, but I've also been questioning killing. It didn't feel right to go until today. After I'd caught seven, I came back to protected water and floated quietly in the kayak. I felt a strong sense of the Sacred, and honored what is beyond/within me. Taking the life of the fish and acknowledging that we must kill to live catalyzed my awareness of the Sacred. Somehow death is a central aspect of all this.

It doesn't affect me so much to kill fish; the pain hits when I'm filleting them with a calmer mind and heart. While fishing, I feel joy, excitement, and gratitude for the capture/gift. In filleting, I'm deeply aware that I've killed this creature — especially since some of them still twitch as I slice through their flesh.

It's impossible to truly follow the Buddhist precept to refrain from killing. I'm a biological animal as well as a spiritual being, and to live I must take the life of others. Today I finally accepted that there is no way to avoid the pain and responsibility of taking life. Truly, we cannot live without killing. Some choose to kill only plants, some refrain from even that. Yet if our immune system stops destroying viruses and bacteria, we will not survive. When we walk in the forest, each step crushes life.

I'm weary of killing, but not yet ready to give up fishing. It's an important part of my sense of who I am; my wilderness competence. If I'm unwilling to kill here and wish to avoid hypocrisy, I'll need to give up eating meat back in town.

In some sense, environmentalism, with its focus on physical sustainability, is not asking the deeper questions. How can we live — and respectfully take other lives — in a way that allows us to honor the sacredness of all Life? How can we live so our activities don't rend us from the experience of belonging to the Earth and being part of the flow of Life? How can we sustain not only our own lives, but also the Life of the land and reestablish our sense of belonging and longing for the Sacred? I must have the courage to publicly ask these questions and to admit that I have no clear answers — even for myself. Each of us must search within for our own answers, and they won't be conceptual, but how we actually live our lives. If we don't make this search, we may not survive.

There is a familiar loneliness and heartache awakening within me again; a profound emptiness and longing that somehow seems connected to embracing the sacredness of Life. I will miss this place when I leave, especially my small cabin. From the kayak yesterday I looked at the cabin and was flooded with a deep sense of care and tenderness. Yet soon I will tear it down. All things are impermanent.

JANUARY 11, 2002

I must admit I don't have what it takes to be an intellectual macho. I admire and sometimes envy thinkers who can maintain and defend a coherent and comprehensive worldview, but each time I try I end up with internal contradictions and the realization that *this* construct doesn't really work either. Then I'm thrown back to immediate experience and the pragmatic heuristics that let me muddle through. Of course I always find internal contradictions in other people's worldviews, too....

JANUARY 12, 2002

I continue to question, "How can I know what's the right thing for me to do in any situation?" But perhaps there isn't any *right* thing, and what's important is the intent of what I do and how I do it. If grasping, aversion, doubt, and fear motivate me, then whatever I do won't work. Perhaps in times of indecision, I need to focus on my state of mind and heart and let my actions follow from that.

Since no one can *know* the right course of action, all decisions involve uncertainty. But I still somehow believe there must be a way of being in which this profound sense of uncertainty is not present. Some inner space in which there is wisdom and confidence that what I'm doing is right.

This brings up the old question of free will. Do I have freedom or is it an illusion? It seems clear that I can often do what I want, but much less obvious that I can actually choose what it is that I want. I think it was Isaac Singer, the same Isaac Singer who wrote *The Family Moskat*, who responded to a question about whether he believed in free will: "Of course I believe in free will; what choice do I have?"

For a long time it's seemed to me that since my body is totally enmeshed in the physical world with each molecule following the law of equal and opposite reaction, there is no possibility of free will — unless science's ideas about matter are seriously incomplete. The notion of personal freedom has seemed like a useful illusion to soften the stark awareness of our vulnerability and impermanence. But, paradoxically, I've also felt I'm completely responsible for my actions.

I think Wilber has persuaded me that matter behaves differently in different contexts, and to treat biological matter the same as a rock is crazy. Apparently, consciousness affects matter in some mysterious way. Still, if there is no separate self, who/what is free? I sense that I often ask this question in the wrong way. Conceptual thinking cannot answer it. It requires a deep transformation in my view of reality. The notion of spontaneous freedom begins to make sense only when I experience myself as universal Life.

I have only three more weeks here, and they will be gone in a heart beat. For twenty-five years I've assumed that during a year in solitude I would find the *Answer* that would make everything ok and my life coherent. If I don't get *it* now, I feel I'll never again have such an opportunity for quiet reflection. I've learned, though, that the *aliveness*, peace, beauty, and love I seek are never out there, but always right here right now.

JANUARY 13, 2002

It feels like I've prepared as much as I'm able. Now, all I can do is wait with an open heart for the Voice of God, for transformation and insight. To quietly return over and over to the present moment and work with spiritual hindrances.

JANUARY 14, 2002

I've stopped wearing glasses most of the time and my nose is coming alive. Without glasses everything is more immediate. Floating in the kayak this evening, the world seemed freshly created in each moment. I haven't often felt the Earth as my mother here, but finally floating in the kayak, yes.

The frog calls and I hear: life calling to life. Telling me that I, too, belong. In these moments, it doesn't matter if others are interested in my experience or whether I have anything to teach. More and more I must admit I know less and less. It may be hard to turn such awareness into a PhD dissertation, but that's ok, too. This is worth so much more.

But this is evening. Mornings are different and dark with doubt, restlessness, and depression. It's as though something happens in my sleep and I must begin the journey again each day.

JANUARY 15, 2002

Nothing fits here . . . no system at all. Nature just is. To feel *alive*, I must see the world as for the first time in each moment. As soon as I begin to record, classify, and compare, I move from *living* nature to conceptual mind — no wonder I feel I don't know anything.

It isn't that in order to feel *alive* I must accept death; life/death is a single process. Deny death and life goes with it.

JANUARY 16, 2002

I've been building a kite on and off for over a month: whittling a frame from cypress, attaching a clear plastic cover, trying to remember from forty-five years ago the correct angles and curves. Getting it into the air seemed hugely important because building a kite is one of the few happy memories I have of Dad teaching me how to do something when I was a boy. He, himself, learned the art in the early nineteen hundreds, when flying kites was still something boys did as an integral part of their lives.

Last week I took the kite and my fishing rod to the point in a stiff wind and tried different lengths of tail and different ways of hooking the kite to the line, but nothing worked. It kept spinning out of control and I was getting frustrated and angry. Finally, the kite crashed so hard onto the rock the crosspiece broke, and then it flew — sort of. Aha! I need more curve in the crosspiece.

I repaired the kite, tied on a huge long tail for stability, hooked it to my rod, and released it into the sky. What fun! I let out different amounts of line and watched as the kite soared and swooped in the turbulent gusts, like a fish fighting for its freedom. I could actually see the complex patterns of the gusting wind. Sometimes the kite would dive so radically that I barely managed to stop it from plunging into the sea. Sometimes it did crash and I had to slowly drag it back to shore. Since then I've gone often to play with the wind.

Flying the kite reminds me how my relationship with the wind has changed these past months. When I first arrived, I often felt the wind as a malevolent force intent on my destruction. As I've worked to surrender to the world, the wind has become a powerful teacher. Rain has taught me about tenderness and love; the wind about acceptance and about how I project my own denied demons onto the world. Watching the seagulls and condors playing high in the fierce wind a couple of months ago, I realized I wanted to play there, too, and the idea of building a kite flickered into my mind.

JANUARY 17, 2002

Again and again I get caught in greed — not for things, but for experiences. At those times it's not enough to just be here with things as they are; I want something special I can hold onto and take back with me. Better character, wisdom, and especially the completely fulfilling experience that will make me whole. The problem is that in order to know if I've actually *got it*, I must step out of the ongoing flow of the present to compare what's happening with the expectations I have from my own experience or from what I've read. In doing this I cut myself off from the experience I long for.

Again the catch-22: as long as I want to be in the flow of Life, that very desire prevents me from seeing that I'm always already here. But if I don't want it, I won't make the effort to look for what is usually hidden.

JANUARY 18, 2002

Coming into Wilderness Solitude is like studying where everyone speaks a language you have forgotten so long ago it now seems completely foreign. You know you have something important to learn, but you don't understand. It takes patience to keep listening and listening. I hear the voices of nature and try to translate what I hear into conceptual thought language so I will know I understand in my mind. But the language of nature cannot be translated into human concepts. It is deeper and different. I realize I have heard and understood when my heart softens and opens to love and peace and beauty around and within me.

JANUARY 19, 2002

Empty morning and I'm feeling sorrowful that finally I won't get what I came here for — the ultimate fulfilling experience. When I allow that feeling to be part of the flow of my immediate actual experience, it feels rich and complete. It's when I get caught in that feeling to the exclusion of all else that I feel the loss of Life.

I was up until dawn sitting under the stars, feeling my way toward Spirit as transcendent and immanent. Transcendent can't mean somewhere else — like heaven — because there's nowhere else to be. Perhaps the aspect of Spirit I usually think of as immanent, because it's right here everywhere, is really transcendent because it seems to be *within* everything — and not the *actual material* itself. Perhaps true immanence is when Spirit becomes the material world.

NO ENTRY FOR JANUARY 20, 2002

JANUARY 21, 2002

Two days ago I was feeling lonely and missing Mom; upset that I never fully opened my heart to her when she was alive and haven't really grieved since she died. Something in me broke and I went naked into the wind and rain. Waving my arms and bellowing my frustration and pain, I strode the rocks at the point. Eventually, cleansed and drained, I returned to the cabin, where I shivered for a long time. I might have looked insane to an observer, but it felt natural to me; a sort of do-it-yourself primal scream therapy.

And what does it matter what other people think of me — or I of them? We are what we are no matter what we think about it. What does it matter what I think of a tree or a rock and whether I approve or not? It matters nothing, nothing at all.

Later that day I felt called to sleep in the woods, so at dusk I dressed warmly, tiptoed away from Cat, and made my way into the dense forest. In the dark, I crawled up and perched ten feet above the forest floor in the root mass of a fallen tree. I'd expected blackflies and rain, but neither happened, so I arranged myself semicomfortably and dozed. I awoke to joyful visions in the night and journeyed far in mind and heart. I sensed that perhaps the physical world and consciousness arise together from some beyond-perception Something that is not a thing at all. When it splits into two it comes into existence as matter and consciousness. At dawn I came home to sleep.

Late last night as I sat on the ground and leaned against a tree, I felt it come into me and I sink into it — part of and belonging to the Earth. Again I felt deep gratitude and fulfillment. This is in part why I came here. I've been so focused inwardly that I've sometimes lost sight of the Earth as my home.

In some way I feel I've accomplished my work here, and yet I've just begun. All these experiences can be seen as grasping for the pleasures of spiritual materialism. The real work, the deep steady practice, is to relax and be with whatever arises in body, mind, and spirit.

JANUARY 22, 2002

I took the kite to the point, attached it to my rod, and let out nearly three hundred yards of line. Translucent and small in the sky, it sometimes disappeared into the clouds; then I was sky-fishing for the wind, an imagined kite my lure. The ultimate in catch and release.

NO ENTRY FOR JANUARY 23, 2002

JANUARY 24, 2002

I returned at dawn from the island to the north of here. I went at dusk the day before yesterday and slept under a clear sky and half moon. Last night it clouded over and started to blow. I had no sleeping bag or pad, but did the best I could with a piece of plastic in a rocky nook.

Although I usually spend most of my days outside or on the porch, I feel I've become too attached to the security and comfort of the cabin. So for now I'm staying outside as much as possible. I didn't come here to live in a cabin in the wilderness, but to join the ebb and flow of nature. The climate, though, is so intense that I've spent more time than planned behind closed door — shutting out cold and Cat alike.

It sometimes seems I've always been homeless, but this isn't quite so. What I've done is cycle between homelessness and close attachments. When wandering free and easy, I love it and dread being closed in and tied down. Then I reach a point where physical, psychological, and emotional comfort and security — no matter how disagreeable they sometimes are — seem very attractive, and I jump into a new relationship, a new job, a new life. I lose all balance and tether myself so tightly that I eventually become restless and break free again.

It's as though these are separate worldviews and personalities. One loves security, my own nest, friends and lovers, peer respect, etc. When in that mode, the thought of wandering homeless and alone, with all the fears and discomforts, frightens me. Yet once I set off, I love being *out there*, and the comforts and relationships I've left behind lose importance. Then, in some vital way there isn't any out there. It's all right wherever I am.

I experience this same apparent dichotomy between the security of a contained familiar self — no matter how uncomfortable at times — and the longing, fear, and joy of letting go into the mysterious unknown of the flowing now. What I forget over and over is that in surrendering to homelessness there is the possibility of being at home everywhere.

Self or no-self? The seeming dichotomy comes from all-or-nothing thinking. It's actually a sliding scale, a cline. Little by little I open to the universal ebb and flow, then it gets too hard and I shut back down. Then that gets too tight and I open up again. Cycles of closing and opening: like relationships, like the tides and the seasons; morning head and afternoon head, small mind and Big Mind.

During this year I've repeatedly resisted giving myself to the freedom of the unknown, and over and over I've let go and stepped off the edge: physically (opening to the wind, going to the glacier, giving up food treats and the cabin's comforts); emotionally (giving up email, self-analysis, and thinking about the future); intellectually (giving up reading); spiritually (giving up the security of Buddhism to just be here alone in the wilderness).

My craving for answers is really a longing for security. When I let go of that need, and step into unknowing and trust, I'm much more relaxed and peaceful.

Defenselessness is a question I've been struggling with for days. If I stop defending myself, will nature roll over me? I think the problem is seeing myself as a separate thing instead of as a process that's an integral part of nature. Just because I let go of the conceptual idea of who I am doesn't mean I stop caring for myself physically. The actual processes of life continue. My immune system continues to function, I wear protective clothing, I'm cautious while walking on slippery rocks and while paddling the kayak. Rather than defending myself against a world I imagine as my enemy, I buffer myself as much or little as I feel necessary for survival.

JANUARY 25, 2002

First light, first birdcall. I'm just back from the lovely nook in the forest by the point. It rained hard before I snuck away from Cat at dusk yesterday and now again after I've returned, but only light showers fell during the night. At one point Cat came searching for me, sounding his hunting growl in the dark forest. I wanted to be alone and kept very still, hoping he wouldn't find me. Right. As he prowled closer and closer, the hair on my neck stood up and I had a small taste of what it's like to be prey. Perhaps my aversion to his crying has genetic roots.

He's become a skillful hunter. Yesterday I accidentally flushed a bird from the grass and he leapt to snag it midair almost three feet above the ground. He let it go when I hollered "No!" and it flew away. Some time ago I saw him gnawing on a foot-long fish he'd apparently scooped from a tide pool. He also caught another rodent recently. I didn't know there were any on this island until one morning a few months ago I found a mouse/rat nose on the porch.

Last night I explored the source of the images and visions that appear in my mind. Nothing happened except cold restlessness and broken sleep until almost dawn. Then, beyond doubt and fear, I moved into a place of . . . nothing. No visuals, no feelings. I felt myself drifting and asked for strength to stay focused. There was a shift: from searching for to waiting with an open heart. Then love and life came pouring in.

An inner voice said I'll never really understand, and I still resist accepting that, but if I want the joy of living in mystery, that's how it is, I guess. The voice said I don't need to understand and explain the world but be a source of life for others the way solitude is for me. And in my relationships keep an open heart so we can be together in peace, love, and beauty.

Today is another day in paradise. I'm trying to savor each one, and I'm slowly getting it that each moment really is unique and then is gone. Nothing stays the same, but most things return. The sensations of sight, sound, taste, touch, and smell, as well as thoughts and feelings, are all in endless flux. Death is always with me. Frequently now — with eyes closed in meditation — I experience myself as patterns of light, vibration, and energy. What am I really?

There is quiet joy in feeling Cat resting on me. I sit here a man with a cat on his lap. But when I open up, I become a cat/man on the porch, and then cat/man/porch in the wilderness. Finally I am — if only briefly — the flowing All.

JANUARY 26, 2002

I spent last night in the woods again. This time I took the small Therm-a-Rest, made a plastic hood to keep the rain off my head, and wore rain gear over the down parka. It rained lightly most of the night, and I slept on and off.

Ontologically, there's no proof that Spirit actually exists; it might be projection. But I do experience Something that I sometimes call Spirit. If I deny its actuality, I can equally deny the actuality of the physical world. Accepting the ontological existence of Spirit, like believing in matter, is a question of taste and balance.

JANUARY 27, 2002

For months I've wanted to make something to express how I feel toward the condors that soar in the fierce wind. When I finally got a kite to fly, I decided to make a more elegant one as a gift for Susan — not knowing whether I'll ever give it to her or even see her again. I've made it from white tarp, and painted on a stylized black condor, using a bird feather for a brush.

JANUARY 28, 2002

Stormy morning. I sit and feel myself sink into the now; into the experience of being the world; into being *alive*. So often I rush to get something or to somewhere, but what I'm seeking I have always had. I am Life. I am the world.

Where are we trying to get to with our incessant activity? To the stars? But we're already as among the stars as we will ever be. Better quality of life? The quality we seek is lost in the seeking. Truly we have it backward with our continual striving for what we don't have and avoidance of what we do. What we crave most deeply we have always had.

What's the meaning and reason for our living? Only this. Life is its own meaning. Nothing to get out of it, and nowhere to take anything to. Like a tornado, we spin in the tip of the funnel, restlessly seeking. Let the fierce winds subside, and settle back into the flowing now of the universe.

NO ENTRIES FOR JANUARY 29–31, 2002

INTERLUDE

SMALL MIND/BIG MIND

A human being is a part of the whole called by us "the universe,"
a part limited in time and space. He experiences himself, his thoughts
and feelings, as something separate from the rest — a kind of optical
delusion of consciousness. This delusion is a kind of prison for us,
restricting us to our personal desires and affection of a few persons
nearest to us. Our task must be to free ourselves from this prison by
widening our circle of understanding and compassion to embrace
all living creatures and the whole of nature in its beauty.

— ALBERT EINSTEIN

It is important to see that the main point of any spiritual practice
is to step out of the bureaucracy of ego. This means stepping out of
ego's constant desire for a higher, more spiritual, more transcendental
version of knowledge, religion, virtue, judgment, comfort or
whatever it is that the particular ego is seeking.

— CHÖGYAM TRUNGPA RINPOCHE

In the journal, I use, but don't define, the terms "small mind" and "Big Mind." Like Emptiness, Suchness, Spirit, God — all of which, for me, are different terms for *Numinous Mystery* — Big Mind is not a thing I can pin down. Small mind is a bit easier, but any definition is still suspect. I use the term to refer to: my habitual egocentric way of perceiving and defending myself as a separate entity isolated from an external world out there; the painful experience of holding tightly to my opinions and to my insistence that the world be as I want (construct) it to be; repetitive thinking about things, rather than being in the present moment.

PURSUING BIG MIND AND ENLIGHTENMENT

Experientially, the shift from small mind to Big Mind is not a shift from one state to another, but from a static and tightly structured awareness into an open flowing awareness whose essence is mystery and freedom. This experience of openness is sometimes called "Beginner's Mind" or "Don't Know Mind," because it's not bound by the conceptual distinctions of small mind. The following quote from Mel Weitsman evokes the relative tightness of small mind and the spacious freedom of Big Mind:

> Big Mind is the mind which goes beyond discrimination and includes everything. Suzuki Roshi would admonish us to always live in Big Mind, but that small mind is an expression of Big Mind. It's not bad. Small mind is necessary; otherwise we would not have it. But small mind should be guided by Big Mind, and as a channel for expressing Big Mind. So our everyday life should be based on Big Mind so that Big Mind is expressing itself through our speech, actions, and thoughts.
>
> [Small mind] is the world of comparative values: this one is good, this one is not so good, the realm of like and dislike, value judgments based on personal preference. But Big Mind is the realm beyond comparative values, where we can accept everything the way it is without being judgmental and partial. It opens our mind to seeing things as they really are.[1]

I call different experiences Big Mind. Sometimes consciousness opens wide and I sense the whole world as within me, instead of "out there," and I'm one with Spirit. At other times I feel small and tender; one of innumerable beings living together on the Earth. In the words of Trungpa, I become tiny like a grain of sand — an infinitesimal part of the infinite universe. It's not all happening within me, but I am part of everything and deeply identified with the rest of existence. Both experiences are filled with mystery and sacred wonder, but the latter carries the rich sense of deep *aliveness* and gentle humility.

One reason I spend time in solitude is to explore the process of shifting from small to Big Mind — which, at the moment, I equate with enlightenment — and to learn to control and teach that shift. When I write in the journal about not finding the *Answer*, I'm referring to my failure to learn how to catalyze the shift at will and how to explain it in words.

The difficulty is that once I find the answer, or rather slip into it, it disappears. Only from the perspective of small mind is enlightenment a specific state to be achieved. From the perspective of Big Mind, the concept of enlightenment — as something to be gained — is no longer meaningful. In other words: Only when caught in a web of conceptual definitions do I think it's possible to attain enlightenment. In Big Mind, when I'm free from the *this* and *that* of conceptual structuring, enlightenment no longer exists as something distinct from nonenlightenment.

Experientially, small mind seems to be a subset of Big Mind. It's the domain of natural laws (or descriptions of regularities, depending on point of view). In the flowing present of Big Mind, all is spontaneously arising in the moment. It is the domain of direct unmediated experience in which no conceptual explanation is possible or desired.

In stating that small mind is a subset of Big Mind, I imply that Big Mind is primary and small mind derivative. But perhaps we're simply more familiar with seeing ourselves as separate individuals and have largely lost the experience of being one with the flowing universe, so the shift in perception carries a sense of profound portent.

If small mind is a subset of Big Mind, then we must always be in Big Mind even when we experience ourselves to be in small mind. This logical conclusion coincides with the Weitsman quote above and my own experience that enlightenment is not something we can attain. We are always already enlightened but usually fail to notice. Thus enlightenment — the shift to Big Mind — is simply waking up to what always already is.

Using the metaphor of spiritual journey may be misleading because it can point away from immediate experience — as though there is somewhere else to go. But while the journey from small mind to Big Mind may be long and arduous, the journey from Big Mind to small mind does not exist. From the broader perspective, there is no separation. There is, however, definitely an experiential difference between small and Big Mind, and while the difference can be conceptually deconstructed, it is nevertheless something I live.

It's easy to become confused when moving from Big Mind to small mind. One confusion is to conceptualize the Big Mind realization that there is nothing to seek or to gain, and then understand this idea to mean that there is nothing to experience beyond small mind. This is misleading and seduces the ego into defending its own rational status quo as all there is. A second confusion is to carry the memory of the experience of Big Mind into small mind, and then assume that the experiential difference between the two means that there is something called enlightenment that can be sought and grasped.

It's precisely the act of seeking and grasping that reinforces the sense of a separate self. Such seeking and grasping devalue the actual experience of the here and now, and the mysterious slip from small to Big Mind happens only in the here and now. This circularity can make spiritual practice challenging and frustrating. If we accept the (small mind) here and now and stop seeking, we stagnate in the status quo. But if we reach for liberation, and in the process devalue the here and now, that very act cuts us off from what we seek. The small mind ego cannot unlatch this catch-22 by itself. The peace of Big Mind comes as a gift and brings a deep sense of gratitude.

Liberation, enlightenment, the shift to Big Mind: These are spoken of differently by different Buddhist teachers. Some focus on a single sudden transformative flash of *realization* that permanently alters consciousness. Others present a more gradualist perspective and see consciousness as a series of extremely short-duration mind-moments that constantly arise and dissolve. Each moment we are free from greed, aversion, and delusion is a moment of enlightenment. As we practice, we come to experience more and more moments of liberation. Here are how three Buddhist teachers and masters have characterized it:[2]

> As far as Buddha Nature is concerned, there is no difference between sinner and sage. . . . One enlightened thought and one is a Buddha, one foolish thought and one is again an ordinary person.
>
> — HUI NENG, SIXTH ZEN PATRIARCH

> Strictly speaking, there is no such thing as an enlightened person. There is only enlightened activity.
>
> — SHUNRYU SUZUKI-ROSHI

> The true path to liberation is to *let go of everything* even the states and fruits of practice themselves, and to open to that which is beyond all identity.
>
> — JACK KORNFIELD

In spite of such counsel, I still sometimes long for the pleasure of an imagined permanent state of enlightenment. One of my favorite Sufi teaching stories succinctly depicts the foolish stubbornness of such an attitude: The Mullah Nasrudin was sitting in his yard eating hot chili peppers from a bowl on the ground beside him. His mouth was on fire and tears were streaming down his face. One of his students asked why he was eating the fiery peppers. "I keep hoping for a sweet one," said the Mullah.

Equanimity is a difficult lesson to learn, and giving up grasping for pleasure isn't easy. There seems to be no good reason why the joy, love, peace, and wonder of Big Mind shouldn't be the permanent conditions of my life — except that they are not. Yet the willingness to be with whatever experiences arise is also deeply satisfying, and at times equanimity, itself, opens into joy, love, peace, and wonder.

ACCEPTING THE DARK AND THE LIGHT

It's easy enough to say that dark and light condition — even create — each other, that only in contrast to the dark can we know the light. It's much harder to live such abstract knowledge. Easy enough to philosophically recognize pain as the necessary counterpoint to pleasure — until the pain becomes personal. On an inwardly sunny day, I can nonchalantly embrace the idea that dark clouds and rain are needed for life to flourish, but when depression wraps its wrenching arms around my heart so tightly I cannot see beyond despair, nothing at all is okay.

My experience of light seems less trustworthy than my experience of dark. Light is a rare and transient gift, dark is always waiting. But when I look more closely at this belief, I realize it includes the implicit judgment that light is better than dark. I accept darkness only because I must and with the hope that acceptance will transform it into light. I see darkness as the absence of light, but seldom recognize that light is also the absence of dark. Yet I love the comfort of the night and feel softly at home in her accepting embrace.

When I imagine that the conditions of my life are different from how they are, or that I'm different from the way I am, I dislocate myself from my actual experience, with all its swirls of light and dark. In either case I tie myself into a knot that I tighten with each effort to escape. When I'm able to relax into what actually is, there's a remarkable transformation as my self-imposed inner and outer boundaries soften and sometimes dissolve. Once I stop holding unwanted aspects of myself and the world at bay, I become the world; or rather, I am free to notice that I have always been the world. I've repeated this lesson over and over because it's so difficult to remember.

Two aspects of darkness are easy to conflate. The first is the actual experience, such as rage, fear, pain, loneliness. The second is the rejection of that experience. This also holds for the two meanings of *light*: one is a sense of clarity, happiness, excitement, and so on; the other is an openness of heart that accepts the impermanence of all pleasures, including intellectual and spirituality clarity.

The first aspect in both cases refers to the content of experience; the second to context — to the rejection or acceptance of the content; to telling what-and-why stories or simply noticing what actually is; to small mind or Big Mind. There is, of course, no clear difference between the two meanings. The context of this moment's experience becomes the content of the next. The empty clarity of Big Mind becomes a pleasure to cling to in small mind.

One alluring trap on the spiritual journey is to confuse the pleasure of peak experiences with the quiet joy of equanimity. It's spiritual pleasure, not pain, that most seductively calls me to abandon equanimity. Wonder and clarity feel so right, as though they should be permanent in my life. Thus, I abandon the quiet depths of equanimity to sail the shining surface of pleasure. But inevitably, another storm rolls through, and I'm caught in waves of emotion once again.

Only when I allow my inner waters to ebb and flow in accordance with their own natural rhythms do I experience peace. Such equanimity modulates both deep pain and deep pleasure. There's nothing wrong with experiencing extreme emotional cycles (unless such cycles create needless suffering), but when the storms threaten to overwhelm, it's useful to remember there's an alternative in the peace and steadiness of equanimity.

Is it possible to live permanently in Big Mind? I don't know, and such queries are in any case beside the point. They seek a conceptual answer to a question that can be resolved only experientially. Thinking about it will not get the job done, and experientially there's no confusion at all. The practice is to experience each moment as it is: to let be and let go; neither reject nor cling. If there is dark, there is dark; if light, light.

FEBRUARY 2002

Truth is a Pathless Land.

—— KRISHNAMURTI, REMINDER TAPED TO MY CABIN DOOR

I'm just back from four days camping near the point. It rained half the time and was clear the other half. Wearing rain gear instead of using the sleeping bag, I slept for two nights in the nook in the woods and two beside the sea. I built a tiny fire for cooking, and spent most of the time simply being rather than doing anything. Continually outside, I felt more closely linked to sea, sky, and forest than I often do here at the cabin.

On the morning of the third day, my heart urged me to give Dad's ring and the remainder of Mom's ashes to the sea. I also hung the amulet I've worn for the past five years on a dead branch, where it will stay in the wind until and after I leave here. The ring is a beautiful lion's head with a diamond in its teeth and rubies for eyes. Dad wore it for almost fifty years until he died. The amulet and ring were two of my most valued possessions, and it still hurts to have parted with them. But I've received so much here that I wanted to give back something important. I feel I've finally invited both Mom and Dad into my heart.

The rock walls of Staines Peninsula are full of faces. Three of them have become very real to me these past months. Even though I realize they're projections of my mind, viscerally I experience them as beings who live in the stone. One is a sensual full-lipped woman: desire, rapture, and ecstasy with the wonder of life. Another is a bitter old man: my dark side of aversion and judgment. The third, an ancient wise man: steady, patient, and tranquil. Exposed to endless wind and rain, the face manifests profound equanimity. Each day at the point I bow to all three and to the wind.

I can't really see the earth anymore when I look that way, but only the faces I've created from the shapes and textures of rock, trees, and waterfalls. Nonhuman stimuli have become eyes, nose, and mouth in my consciousness, and it's difficult to let them go. Now that my time alone is coming to an end, I'm working to bring those faces back to my mind and give the rock walls back to themselves.

This anthropomorphizing has allowed me a clear look at how — by abstracting from the flow of experience certain features that I focus on and make concrete (and by ignoring whatever doesn't fit) — I create an image of myself that I then believe is me. When we do this to each other, we largely create our collective social realities. Even more difficult than seeing the mind create such images is breaking the habit and returning to the flowing, ambiguous *living* world.

It's not that creating a conceptual entity — a mountain, for example — is problematic as such, but when I stop really seeing the endlessly changing shape and color, and instead see the mountain as static, I then lose the experience and joy of being alive. It's especially damaging when I do this with other people and with myself. I have a semifixed idea of who we are and so stop experiencing the ever-changing rhythms of our living together. Perhaps the best way to see through this layer of conceptualization is — as meditation teaches — to pay attention to the details: to the changing colors, smells, shapes, movements, feelings, thoughts.

NO ENTRIES FOR FEBRUARY 2–5, 2002

FEBRUARY 6, 2002

Yesterday the year was completed, and what an amazing year. At times I still feel an inner disquiet that I never fully let go to wander wherever the winds of Life would carry me physically, psychologically, and spiritually. As I sit here feeling this doubt and regret, I recognize that it's this very niggling that keeps me from letting go in this moment. And I do let go. . . . With surrender, the inner clenching dissolves into the flowing now. I sense this cycle will be with me for some time yet, and I'm learning to open my heart to the doubt and sorrow, too.

I went boat-camping to the Owen Island inlet for the last three days of the year. I wanted to give the process all I had. It was a wonderful time. The first two days and nights were stormy, but my plastic boat shelter kept me dry. It wasn't elegant in appearance, and it rattled in the wind, but I was cozy inside and delighted to be away from the cabin and Cat.

On the second day, a pod of dolphins came into the cove where I was anchored. They'd followed me in when I arrived, and now returned to coax me (actually the boat and motor) to play. They kept leaping completely out of the water — straight up or in an arc to twist and land on their backs. What a lovely treat. When I didn't start the motor they gave up and left.

After the storm passed, it was cloudy and calm; perfect weather for black-flies. I used spray, shooed many away, killed some, and let a few bite to share a meal with them. Unless I'm inwardly very still and focused, it's hard to wish them well as brother creatures.

I took the kayak for a paddle down the inlet. How peaceful and beautiful it is in there. Sheer rock walls drop to clear water, and gnarly trees cling to the tiny islets that dot the winding waterways. I was glad I'd come, even though I'd again been anxious about leaving the security of the cabin. I hope to take Patti there, and if she wants, I'll anchor the boat near the inlet's mouth and let her paddle in for some time alone.

That night was still and I awoke to a silent dawn. I sat and soaked in the silence and in the faint murmur of a tiny stream a ways away. In that moment I felt my time here come to completion. I know that the cycles of ups and downs, joy, peace, doubt, fear, aversion will continue; but they — for me at least — are part of the flow of the universe, the fabric of my life.

I'm not sure what enlightenment is, but I believe there have been moments. If so, enlightenment is not something I can get. It's the process of abandoning myself to the world. There have been times when, like a clear bell, I could hear the sound of one hand clapping and feel the sacredness of everything. It's the sound of the world, once I remember in my heart that there is truly nothing to get. What I'm looking for, I already have.

On the way home I crossed the channel to visit the sea lions, but they have gone. Along the way I came upon a pair of butter-bellies with four chicks. As I approached, the adults fled running/flapping across the water — dad that way, mom straight ahead — and the chicks dove; every duck for herself. I looked and looked along the shoreline and in the kelp beds, but never saw the chicks again. How do they disappear like that? Perhaps, like electrons, they have a discontinuous existence and pop into and out of this physical world. That seems the most parsimonious explanation, but I don't really know; I just don't know.

Back here, I set up the lodge and sweat beneath the stars, then checked my email. Patti sounds great. She's hooked up with the navy and will arrive here on the fifteenth. I'm glad to have another nine days alone.

Today, a new year begins, and I wonder where my life will take me. It's a grey, rainy, windy day, and I'm feeling restless.

REENTRY

How am I to find the naturalness, artlessness,
utter self-abandonment of nature in the utmost
artificiality of human works? This is the great
problem set before us these days.

— D. T. SUZUKI

I heard a siren a while ago and it surprised me. I'd forgotten sirens. Here in town, I'm surrounded by sound: horns honking, motors roaring, dogs barking, and the hum of human voices — laughing and talking — grounding and punctuating all else. Human-generated noise is so different from the wind and water music of the island. Only the creative meowing of Cat is absent. I miss the pup. He's in Texas with Patti and her family — lounging like a prince inside their house.

It's cold and grey outside. Winter is closing in and I'm sitting in the cozy kitchen of this small pension because my $4 a day room has no heat. I'm the only guest now that tourist season is over, and it's peaceful here. I don't know how long I'll stay, but I'm in no hurry to leave this quiet corner of the world to head up to the hurly-burly of Santiago. Still, it's cold and grey outside and the warmth of the North is calling.

I'm fasting for the first time since leaving the island more than two weeks ago and my head aches. I've neglected exercising and my shoulders are tight and sore. But little by little I'm reestablishing the daily practice of meditation, thanksgiving, and exercise. I've also been reading the frivolous stuff I found in the lobby, left I suppose by previous guests; *GQ* magazine, of all things. I was deep into an analysis of the social significance of Britney Spears's religious orientation when the church bells started to ring. I walked over to hear Easter Mass.

Today is the resurrection, the heart of Christianity and a truly joyful day, yet I feel awash in loneliness and sorrow. Strange that in solitude I was often lost in imagined social belonging, and now among people I sit alone and long for solitude again. Even though I've made warm acquaintances here in town, I often still feel cut off and disconnected. I miss Patti. I also miss Susan. She's decided to not continue our relationship, and I feel hurt and angry even though we made no promises. Ah shit, life does go on.

It's been weeks since my last journal entry, and a lot has happened since then. In the days before Patti arrived on the island, I was both eager to see her and sorry that my time in solitude was ending. I kept counting the days, and time flew. I worried — with good reason — that once no longer alone I would slip off center, become entangled in distractions, and forget to open and re-open my heart to Spirit. Wham! Now I must learn to integrate solitude with social life.

LAST MONTH ON THE ISLAND

On the day arranged via satellite phone, the Chilean Navy arrived with Patti in a semiwild sea, and I ran out in the inflatable to pick her up. The navy left and we toured some to give Patti a quick sense of the place. Then we went ashore where Cat was waiting. "Whoa, what's this? Another human being? I thought there was only one." It took him a few days to get used to her, but then they became good friends. Hearing voices in the cabin, he stopped yowling on the porch. What a relief.

On the second day of Patti's visit we took the boat for an afternoon cruise along Staines Peninsula and watched a gorgeous sunset. Next day we crossed the eastern channel and up an inlet to the foot of the Andes. Far from camp, the motor started to seriously misfire. I didn't dare shut it down to tinker, so we limped along and hoped to make it home. Luckily, the weather held and we managed to crawl to our beach before the motor died completely. It never ran again, even though I worked on it quite a bit during the following days.

I was disappointed that Patti wouldn't have a chance to see more of the area, but what a blessing that the motor hadn't died during the previous months when I was far from camp. I took it to a mechanic here in Puerto Natales and it turned out to have a blown head gasket. Amazing that it lasted the year.

Patti brought a video camera with her to the island. In Punta Arenas she'd met a crew of documentary filmmakers, and when she told them about my project, they encouraged her to buy a camera, and also showed her how to use it. I'd never thought about videoing during the year, but now it seemed the perfect thing to do. It was another way to depict life on the island, and would also serve as a mirror in which I could see myself from a different perspective.

We began to shoot . . . or rather Patti began to shoot and I began to talk. In fact, I seldom shut up — whether the camera was recording or not. This startled Patti since she was prepared to find me a semimute recluse and had expected little conversation for the first week or so. Instead, she found a raving jabber box. Patti was a natural behind the camera: good eye for framing and angle; delicate perception; smooth transitions and zooming. I pretty much directed the project, even though I tried to not be too demanding. Happily, we agreed on what needed to be recorded. Cat turned into a ham. He wanted to be in every shot, or perhaps, to be wherever I was. As he had all along, he continued to assert his presence.

For the first days Patti was there, the weather was amazingly warm and sunny. This would never do. For a year I'd been journaling about how tough the climate is, and now the video footage would show only warm sunny days. The lull lasted less than a week, and then the wind and rain raged in again.

Being in front of the camera was interesting. At first it felt perfectly natural. I was simply telling my story without concern for effect or appearance. But as the days went by, a subtle shift took place. I started to feel like an actor concerned with my image — my external appearance. In conjunction with this change, I started to lose my sense of steady centeredness, began to feel a bit hollow and less real. And this was after just a few hours of playing an actor portraying my own life.

Two questions: The first, of course, is the obvious one about how professional actors and actresses manage — or perhaps don't manage — to maintain a sense of their own inner reality when they're constantly in the limelight both on and off the set. The second may be just as obvious, but we're so constantly "on stage" in our lives — always projecting an image for those around us, often at the cost of our own sense of self — that it seldom gets asked. How can we live in the social whirl and not become so caught in the dance that we lose track of our own inner rhythms?

One answer is to make do with less in almost all aspects of our lives: less money, less excitement, less peer respect, less. . . . This creates space to explore who or what craves more of everything and why. It is, in part, this exploration that keeps the home fire burning.

We finished most of the shooting by March 1 and received word that the navy would pick us up on the fifteenth. Ouch. That day life would change in a big way. We relaxed for a few days and then started to pack.

But first I harvested my lettuce crop. It was pretty meager, even though I had tried everything I could think of to encourage the plants to grow. I'd mixed kelp into the soil and peed onto it; put the plants into direct sunlight and brought them inside on chilly nights. Nothing worked. The largest leaf on the dozen scraggly plants that still survived was about the size of my smallest fingernail. But I harvested it with a flourish and ate it with tweezers, glad I hadn't spent a lot of time and energy planting a garden.

I was tempted to leave the cabin in place; much easier physically and emotionally to just pack the gear and go. German had suggested I leave it as a refuge for others since it was the only shelter in the whole region. It was painful to destroy the home I'd worked so hard to build, but I didn't want to make it easy for someone else to come there. It had been difficult for me and I felt it should remain that way. Mostly, though, I didn't want to extend our human hegemony. I'd come as a visitor and stayed as a guest. I wanted to leave the island as much as possible as it had been when I arrived. I wanted to give the sea and sky and mountains back to themselves and to the beings who live there. I wanted the island to remain unnamed.

One day at the point, I asked Patti if she could see faces in the rock walls of Staines Peninsula. She could, and they were the same faces I'd been bowing to for the past months. I told her how viscerally real those beings seemed to me, even though I *knew* they were projections of my mind. She smiled and asked, "How do you know that?" Her question stopped me in my tracks. How indeed did I know that? In many animistic cultures those faces would simply be accepted as real beings. It's the scientific rational mind that denies such possibilities.

Preparing to leave the island was a lot of work. We waterproofed everything we didn't need, moved onto the porch, evicting Cat in the process, and tore down the cabin. Then we set up the tent on a temporary platform, covered the whole area with a tarp, and demolished the porch. The weather was foul the whole time and it rarely stopped raining. I worried that the lumber would be too wet to burn and we wouldn't be ready to leave when the navy arrived, but we were lucky and had two almost rain-free days just when we needed them.

Patti kept the fire stoked while I carried the cabin and outhouse floors, roofs, and framing. She stripped to sports bra and shorts, and, drenched in sweat and semicooked by the heat of the roaring flames, looked like a stolid peasant woman or a minion of hell. Only coals remained when the tide came in and washed the beach clean.

Once everything burnable was burned, we scoured the site for screws and nails. We were left with ten large nylon bags of trash that was mostly plastic I'd picked up from beaches during the year and tarp that had covered the shelter. What a muddy grueling job it all was. I pushed both of us pretty hard to get it done, but Patti never complained. There were a few prickly moments between us, but considering the circumstance and the fact that I'd had the island to myself for a year, we did well together. Patti always cares for me, and I tried hard to be kind to her in turn.

As a going-away present, the wind shifted and day after day howled in from the south to pound our exposed shelter. It wiped us out, but we had to keep working to be ready for the navy.

LAST DAY ON THE ISLAND

CONAF emailed that the navy would arrive at noon. We would be ready. All we had left to do that morning was take down the tarp, unhook the propane tank, pack up the tent, and dismantle the temporary platform. We got started about 8 AM and thought we had plenty of time. But at 9 the navy ship hove into view. Another storm was brewing and they wanted to reach Puerto Natales before it hit. The officer in charge of the landing party told me that we had only an hour and twenty minutes to leave the island. He said their orders were to take Patti, me, and our important gear, and to leave the rest behind. I told him I wouldn't leave until we had cleared everything from the beach, and if we hurried, we could make it.

The enlisted men were fantastic. We were all rushing to tear down the tarp and temporary platform, and haul everything out to the ship a quarter mile off shore. Meanwhile the officer kept saying that we'd have to leave the trash and that they would come back another time to pick it up. I kept saying no. The discussion grew more intense and confrontational until I flat out told him that unless we took everything, I wasn't going either. He repeated that he had to obey his orders to take Patti, me, and our important gear.

Patti was great. She told me to do what I needed to do, and if they left me there, she would find a way to come back and pick me up. I knew that if they did leave me, I'd be in serious trouble because all the food and camping gear was already on the ship. The officer said his commander had told him via radio to bring me to the ship so he could talk with me in person and that they would finish bringing the stuff from the beach. He gave me his word that they would bring absolutely everything, but at the last minute I decided that leaving before the beach was completely clean would be a major mistake.

That's when things got nasty. I finally held out my hands and said that with respect for him and his point of view, I had to honor my commitment to God, to nature, to myself, and to CONAF to clean up before I left. Otherwise my whole project would be meaningless. The only way I'd go before the beach was clean was in handcuffs. He backed down. It was time for me to compromise, too, so we could all feel ok about the situation. I agreed to leave the 2×4s from the tent platform since they're raw wood. I hid them under the trees where they'll quickly rot.

Once on board the commander greeted us politely, and I apologized for the corner I'd put him in. Everyone cooled down and we got underway. Patti smiled and said, "Welcome back to the world." I'd built a traveling box for Cat, and the crew said I should put him in the hold with our gear. I didn't argue even though it was dark and noisy down there, and I think he was sort of freaked by what was happening. At least it was warmer and drier there than on the deck.

The confrontation on the beach was, I think, mostly a misunderstanding and a minor part of all my interactions with the Chilean Navy. It would have been much more difficult and expensive to travel to and from the island without their support. Shortly before we reached Puerto Natales the crew apologized and said it was a national law that they had to charge us $16 USD per person per day on the ship: a total of $64 for taking me and my gear, bringing Patti, and picking both of us and all our gear up again. Imagine that. The storm never materialized and the trip back to Puerto Natales was flat calm. We arrived after dark and the crew unloaded the gear onto the dock and covered it in case of rain. We were exhausted.

DEATH OF A MENTOR AND 9/11

When Patti arrived at the island in February, she brought the first news of the outside world I'd had in over a year. Deneal Amos, the leader of the spiritual community where we'd met, had died the previous spring. He'd been a strong presence in our lives as a mentor and source of strength and comfort. We'd both felt close to him for a long time, and we'd known that if things ever got really rough, we could always go to Deneal. Now he was gone, and it seemed like there was a hole in the world where he'd been.

It felt strange not knowing about his death for so long, especially since I'd sent him loving-kindness meditation each day during the year. It also felt like the torch had been passed. As long as Deneal was alive we could lay the main responsibility for maintaining spiritual practice in the world on him and on others like him. Now it was time for us to assume that responsibility ourselves; time for each of us to do our part in keeping awareness of Spirit alive in our lives. If I've learned anything of importance in solitude, it's how empty and futile life is without spiritual grounding — however Spirit manifests itself to each of us.

Patti also brought news of September 11, 2001. Hearing about it didn't affect me very deeply, because by then all the activities of humanity seemed no more than a vague smudge on the far horizon. From the city, and even from this small town where I now sit writing, the island — and other remote corners of the Earth where we humans have not yet left our mark — seems distant and somehow unreal; a fading remnant of what once was. But on the island, especially during the last months, that far-off region of nature was the ancient center of my world. All the frantic activity of human society — cities, highways, pollution, and endless frothing news reports — were an ethereal dream.

So hearing that two of those phantom buildings, among so many, had been destroyed didn't mean much in the huge endless pulse of the universe.

Since my return to the electronically interconnected social world, I've been asked if being one of the few literate people on Earth unaware of the events of 9/11 until five months later, and being spared the incessant media barrage, gives me a unique perspective. I don't know. But much of the U.S. political commentary I've read online these past two weeks feels alien to me. Spending a year in solitude seems to have changed my perception of many things, including politics. I now have a more spacious view than I did. This doesn't mean my view is the only right one, but some things do seem clearer than before. This apparent clarity is a bit odd since the universe is also deeply mysterious to me.

We sometimes lose sight of the basic facts of our existence: Life will continue — maybe not just the way we would like it to, but continue nonetheless. Everyone dies. There always has been and apparently always will be pain and darkness in our lives. Killing other people, except in immediate self-defense, is rarely, possibly never, justified.

Many more than three thousand people die in the world each day from unnecessary starvation and preventable disease. Probably more people die in the United States each month from gunshots, smoking, drug and alcohol abuse, and the lack of affordable medical care. These deaths usually go unremarked and often seem as unreal to most people as 9/11 does to me. The news media are largely responsible for unnecessarily and overdramatically whipping up public alarm after 9/11.

In learning about the attack five months later, I couldn't understand why so many people had felt such panic until I realized that at the time no one knew what was happening or where events might lead: perhaps to nuclear holocaust! But the actual physical threat of nuclear war was negligible.

I think it more likely that the level of public anxiety rose so sharply because people began to doubt one of their fundamental assumptions: Modern social structures are more real than, and can control, the inevitable and endlessly changing cycles of life ... and death. Suddenly, everything felt much riskier than before. I felt that same anxiety as I struggled to accept my vulnerability alone in the wilderness.

From across the political spectrum here in southern Chile, the opinion I've most often heard expressed is that while all acts of terrorism are abhorrent, the United States is not blameless. People from all social classes point out that for many years the U.S. has interfered with the internal politics of sovereign nations throughout the Third World in the service of its own economic interests — sometimes benevolently, but often by supporting murderous dictators. This doesn't mean U.S. foreign policy is worse than that of many other countries, but in spite of rhetoric to the contrary, it's frequently no better. The major difference, one that makes the U.S. unique in our time, is its unprecedented power to impose its will.

Craving physical, emotional, and psychological security can lead us to project our fear, hatred, and cruelty onto those we label Evil. In the often violent relations between adversarial cultures, each may honestly believe it is peace-loving and innocent — even holy — and is defending itself against others intent on its destruction.

In the collective projections of the cultural groups involved in 9/11, I believe I recognize the process by which I projected my own dark shadow onto the wind, and so experienced it as malevolent. I began to see through this unconscious process only when I relaxed my psychological defenses and allowed myself to become vulnerable. Doing so was terrifying, precisely because I believed the wind was intent on my destruction.

There is, though, a difference between my personal shift in perception of the wind and the collective shifts required if different cultures are to live together in peace. Even when I viscerally felt the wind was out to get me, I knew cognitively that it was unlikely to be so. This is not necessarily the case among humans. We are at times viciously aggressive, and we do sometimes seek revenge for past wrongs.

It is difficult and also useful to take a large step back and attempt to disidentify with our "own side" in the current conflict and try to imagine how we would view the situation if positions were reversed and we were the Saudi or Afghan (or Iraqi) people and they were us. We might remember that in spite of everything, we are all in the soup of Life together, and that each of us is a manifestation of underlying Spirit. But sadly, and perhaps suicidally, we appear to be choosing a different path.

Did the world radically change with the events of 9/11? Psychologically, it probably did for a lot of people. Like it or not — though many are still in denial — it's now clear that the United States can no longer dominate the

globe with impunity. The question is whether we will join the dance of the in-
ternational community gracefully as a willing partner, or be dragged onto the
floor kicking and screaming. My perspective may seem hopelessly naive to
those who believe there will always be some nations above and others below.
Better that we should stay on top. Perhaps, but the price of dominion is high.
Blinded by projected fear and assumptions of their own righteousness, and
certain that their personal beliefs are True, secular and religious fanatics on
all sides insist that global cooperation is impossible, but I think it worth a try.

There are so many ways to think about and describe our encounter with
the Sacred. What enormous suffering and destruction we have wrought by
mistaking our descriptions for what they describe and by becoming slaves to
the dogma we ourselves have created. Instead of seeking common ground, we
often demand compliance and condemn apparent difference.

As far as I can tell, life in southern Chile seems much the same as it did
when I went into solitude. If I hadn't been told about 9/11, I doubt I would
notice any difference between the world as it is now and as it was before. And,
of course, the world has not changed for the sea, the sky, and the wind, or for
the Orange Bill Butter-Belly Diving Ducks.

BACK IN PUERTO NATALES

From the dock where the navy left us, Patti, Cat, and I caught a ride to the
pension where she had stayed before coming to the island. We settled in and
stayed for the next ten days. Cat had no experience with town or traffic, and
I thought he might get either lost or killed, so we kept him confined indoors.
He was very good considering that he'd previously had total freedom to roam
the island hunting and fishing. But jeez, switching him to canned catfood sure
caused him to shit a lot. Truly amazing amounts for an animal his size. The
smell was also pretty amazing.

I went round and round about whether to give Cat to the national parks
people, who wanted to take him to a field station in a remote location with no
roads, or to ask Patti to take him to Texas. Since he didn't understand Spanish or the local customs, I finally decided to send him north and hoped he
would be ok in the change to a new environment. I purchased an official traveling cage and arranged for shots and the necessary permits.

Town wasn't difficult only for Cat; it was for me, too. I had a lot of work
to do, and even though Puerto Natales is a small place, I felt battered by the
noise and the swirl of people and traffic. But there were also the delicious
pleasures of hot showers and ice cream.

Last Tuesday, we caught the bus to Punta Arenas and checked into a fairly nice hotel. They would accept Cat only if we promised to keep him shut up in the bathroom. As soon he was alone, he started to cry. To comfort him, I laid my coat on the floor so he would have something to lie on and to smell. I'm not sure if he had a seizure in the night, or if he was expressing his general displeasure with the arrangement, but as a going-away gift he peed on my coat. On Thursday morning I said goodbye to Patti and Cat at the airport, and spent the day talking to the owner of a transport company about shipping my gear to Santiago, visiting acquaintances from last year, and wandering the city streets.

Patti calls the island Soledad since it has no *written on the map* name. It lies just south of Owen Island, so I sometimes think of it as Son of Owen. Mostly, though, I like to remember it through its own language rather than through mine. It is its own place and better left without a human name.

MAY 11, 2002, LA ÚLTIMA ESPERANZA

I'm a silent loner here on board, without much urge to mingle. In the midst of all these people, just being who I am feels not good enough. On the Puerto Natales beach, sitting alone with the sea, the mountains, and the sky, peace and self-acceptance flowed back so easily. But Puerto Natales is gone now, a day and a half to the south. I'm on the NAVIMAG ferry heading north through the channels of La Última Esperanza toward the town of Puerto Montt, still two days away. An hour ago we passed the passage that leads to the island where I spent a year of my life, but I was sleeping and missed it. Still, it's wonderful to be among the wild islands and waterways again.

It was easy to be in Natales, hard to leave. During the last two weeks there I met several people I really liked and became closer to Ruben and Jovina, the owners of the pension where I stayed after taking Patti to the airport. My lessons — over and over — are to accept and forgive my own flaws and those of other people. Will I ever learn?

During the last days in Puerto Natales I finally built and packed two crates with all my gear. I gave my leftover food supplies to the Red Cross, and didn't have much luck selling the stuff I didn't want to ship. One of the batteries went for $30 and I traded the other for this ferry passage. I gave the pick and shovel to Ruben in trade for eggs and phone calls, and also left him the fishing float I found last year, so I'll have something to come back for. The transport company is charging very little to ship the crates to Santiago, and it should cost only $500–600 USD from there to Vancouver.

I went fishing twice with the Puerto Natales Fishing Club. The first time we waded out over slippery rocks to cast for salmon in the ocean. Everyone caught fish but me. I didn't have even a strike and suspected I was ruining

Canada's sporting reputation. The next time we fished for trout from the shore of a lake with a cold wind blowing straight in at us. Eighteen of us were closely scattered along the water's edge casting out and reeling in. The guy to my left caught a nice one; the guy to my right caught a nice one, too. Me, not even a strike.

Semiwet and chilled from half falling in, I was muttering to myself how much I dislike this kind of communal fishing when, wham, a fish on the line. My very lightweight rod and reel ensured a fierce fight. An hour later another strike and another nice fish. Something called me to let this one go, which I did — to the amusement of the other guys for whom fishing is a competitive social activity. They always keep and weigh everything they catch to see who has caught the most and the biggest fish. But nothing goes to waste. They either eat the fish themselves, or give it to their neighbors.

They quit fishing before sunset, but I stayed on with the lake and sky to myself. As the sun fell behind the hills, I told myself, "Just one more cast, then I'll quit, too." Wham! This one fought much harder than the other two, and each time I had it nearly to the beach, it stripped out line again. I finally landed and kept it, too. Each fish weighed more than six pounds and was bigger than any trout I'd caught before. There was still light when I made it to camp, so I picked up a bunch of trash left strewn by previous campers. What a joyful day.

I became a mini-celebrity in the South — interviewed for newspapers and on radio and television. The first interview was with a reporter from the Punta Arenas daily newspaper who was waiting for me when I returned to Natales. He'd heard about my retreat the previous spring, and during the year had checked with CONAF from time to time to see if I was still out there and still alive. His article captured the spirit and some sense of what the year had been about. The local television and radio stations invited me on for long interviews, and a reporter from the national newspaper, *El Mercurio*, wrote a front-page story.

That same day I received an email from the magazine *Revista Caras* in Santiago asking for an exclusive. Friends say that if I want to be known in Chile, *Caras* is the way to go; everyone reads it. But the article will likely be shallow and trite. The journalist wants to title it "Tale of a Shipwrecked Man," which is dumb since being forced to survive in solitude after a shipwreck has little to do with choosing it freely.

I had a brain wave, though. Rather than trust them to write an accurate story, I could write it myself in Spanish and give it to them. Last night I started to write and soon realized I didn't know what I could say that would give a glimpse of what I've been doing for the past year. With the recent attention,

I've sort of lost sight of the fact that I really don't have any polished gems of wisdom to offer. I'm still just ambling along myself. Up and down.

I can't tell if the public recognition is swelling my ego or not. It's nice, but under the surface glitter my life is still just what it is. I can feel myself building a shell around my heart, and even with people I still feel lonely and alone. I tell myself it's because I'm not involved sexually with anyone, but in the past this hollow longing has arisen even in relationship.

I think Cat is dead. He disappeared from Patti's house over a week ago. I miss him. Given my lifestyle, I wasn't sure if I'd ever take him back from Patti, but I miss him nonetheless. I wonder if he was hit by a car, killed by a seizure or a coyote, or got tired of waiting and set out to search for me. North America seems to have gobbled him up. I wonder if it will devour me, too.

I also wonder what the year would have been like without him. He was such an integral part of my life in solitude, and I learned so much in my interactions with him. In some ways, our relationship was as intense as any I've shared with another human.

My heart hurts when I think of Cat; I can feel myself shutting down with the unwillingness to go through the pain again. Over and over I invest so much emotional energy in relationships just to lose my partner. Still, I'm glad for what I shared with the pup.

MAY 13, 2002, PUERTO MONTT

The ferry docked last night, but we were allowed to sleep on board. I could have gone on to Santiago with the truck carrying my crates, but decided not to. Yesterday I cast an I Ching asking if I should go straight to Santiago, and received hexagram 12: Stand Still. (Ascent of dark, inferior people. Withdraw into inner calm and accept no remuneration.) Important advice. I can see that I'm becoming caught in my desire for recognition. If I do, I'll lose the peace and joy of simply living in the moment.

For now, I'm anonymous again; just another tourist sitting on a bench writing in a notebook. No more glum than I often felt on the island, but here it's harder to accept as part of life's ebb and flow. This morning I went to Calvary Hill in a nearby town and followed the Stations of the Cross. I felt stronger empathy, respect, and gratitude for Christ than ever before. He had such courage to follow his spiritual path to the end/beginning. Do I? Is my path also etched in suffering and loss? Is everyone's?

I also visited a small cathedral built by the Germans who settled here a hundred years ago. It replicates one in the Black Forest near where my mom grew up. The cathedral was closed, and an old woman passing by said it opens only for morning mass. No matter. Just looking into her kind black eyes gave me the peace I was seeking. We can so easily, and often unknowingly, give such gifts to each other.

MAY 15, 2002, PUERTO MONTT

Puerto Montt is a friendly old seaport of maybe a hundred thousand or so. I'd thought to stay only one night, but another cold is trying to get a grip on me, the weather is rainy, and I haven't felt the urge to move on. Maybe tomorrow.

Yesterday on the way to check for buses to the town of Pucón (where there are hot springs!) I passed a construction site during siesta break. All the guys were playing soccer. Lots of laughter, but they were running hard and playing skillfully, even though many wore rubber boots. One guy had on bib-style rain pants, and another removed his baseball cap with a flourish each time he headed the ball.

Last night I ate shellfish chowder at the fish market by the docks. It cost $3 for a big bowl of clams, mussels, abalone, and barnacles. I was the only customer there and chatted with the lovely fourteen-year-old girl who was cooking and serving. She works eight hours a day every day for $150 a month and goes to school full time, too. She said she gives it all to her family since her dad can't find work.

MAY 21, 2002, SANTIAGO DE CHILE

How strange to be here again. I'm staying in the same pension and the same room I stayed in nearly a year and a half ago. The cycle has completed itself, and it's almost as though nothing has changed. That, of course, is frightening. The dread of backsliding, of things never really changing. Already the insights and transformations on the island seem far away.

I caught the bus from Puerto Montt to Pucón, and spent several days soaking for hours in the glorious hot springs not far from town. It was a delight to float in the steaming water under a clear sky and feel warm and relaxed for the first time in many months. I remembered looking forward to such bliss when chilled and hurting on the island.

The bus ride from Pucón to Santiago was a long twelve hours, and during the trip I finally felt I was leaving the wonder of the South behind. The last three hundred miles were especially dull, the highway often lined with billboards and industry. The bus broke down along the route, and while I was waiting beside the road for another one, a man started a conversation and quickly recognized me from the newspaper article. I must admit it's kind of fun to be *famous* for a little while.

The Santiago bus station and streets were packed with people. I felt nervous and crowded; watchful for thieves. I'm intimidated here in the city, yet it isn't much different from needing to be cautious on slippery rocks or in a rough sea. It's about survival skills and staying alert to the world around me.

JULY 18, 2002, MIAMI, USA

By now I'm used to the new airport security procedures and have learned to not wear socks with holes in them.

My month and a half in Santiago was often socially busy and sometimes quietly lonely. I met and made friends with several people at the Canadian embassy. The woman in charge of public relations arranged a television interview on a program called *La Belleza de Pensar* (*The Beauty of Thinking*). The host, Cristián Warnken, is a well-known intellectual, and famous philosophers, authors, scientists, and artists are guests on the show. I felt honored and somewhat out of place to be invited. During the interview I suggested that from my perspective a better name might be *The Beauty of Not Thinking*. At one point Cristián asked what I'd learned from my study of the limpets. I said, "Not much. Limpets, like humans, just sort of do what they do." That got a laugh. The interview was fun and interesting, and afterward both Cristián and studio crew said they'd really enjoyed it. I hope so because I sure did. I'm glad I'm fluent in Spanish. It's a beautiful language.

I gave talks at the CONAF headquarters, the Canadian embassy, and a university. I also described my year in solitude to many people over meals in their homes. But I spent much of the time alone in my room watching English movies on cable TV, wandering the streets, or sending and receiving emails in an internet café.

The *Caras* magazine story came out, and it was reflective, comprehensive, and accurate. In part because I reached an agreement with the journalist that she would write the article and show it to me before publication. I requested some fairly extensive changes, and since I still had the photos they wanted to use, it all worked out.

I also met a wonderful lunatic who is making a full-length animated movie about unemployment in Chile — while he and all the people working on the film are themselves unemployed. He invited me to use his editing equipment, and I put together a twenty-five-minute video from the six hours of tape Patti sent back down from Texas after extracting it from the thirty hours we shot on the island.

During my last two weeks in Santiago I moved out of the pension and stayed with a beautiful woman I met. She was kind and thoughtful, and sharing intimacy gave us both pleasure. I enjoyed not being alone so much of the time and hope we'll see each other again in Canada. Although painful to leave, it was time, and I flew north to Miami. On the way I stopped for two weeks in the Dominican Republic to scuba dive and visit friends I hadn't seen in ten years. Ah, to finally feel warm again!

Tomorrow I fly to Texas to spend time with Patti and meet her kids. Then it's on to Vancouver and whatever awaits me there. I'll need to find a place to live, see if I can get my car running, and begin to pick up the threads of my life. There's also the small matter of a dissertation to write.

EPILOGUE

*The wonderful thing about Zen practice is
that you get to do it whether you like it or not.*

—— ZEN SAYING

*Penetrating so many secrets, we cease to believe in the unknowable.
But there it sits nevertheless, calmly licking its chops.*

—— H. L. MENCKEN

When I first returned to Vancouver, it felt like a foreign city where I had no place to live and no idea where I would find an apartment I could afford. Then by chance I met a man who lived in a quiet neighborhood and had a small trailer parked in his backyard garden. In exchange for some rent and ten hours work a month, he let me live there, use the bathroom in his basement, and store my gear in the garage. It was perfect for my needs.

Before leaving for Chile, I'd added fuel stabilizer to the gas tank of my old Datsun station wagon and covered her with a tarp, but by now she'd been sitting for almost two years in a wet climate. Moss was growing on the outside and mold covered much of the inside. The carburetor was so gummed up it had to be rebuilt.

Although I thought I was returning to an empty bank account, I discovered a forgotten $3,500 term deposit. Still, that wouldn't go far. Then I won a fellowship that would see me through the next year and a half if I was frugal. I hoped to complete my PhD by then.

I had, though, no idea how to turn my year in solitude into a dissertation. Some of the nearly nine hundred pages of the original journal was already typed, but almost a third was scribbled longhand in spiral notebooks. When I'd stopped to visit Patti in Texas, she had heroically offered to transcribe the written portion, which she did with virtually no errors — even though I had trouble reading my own writing. I felt overwhelmed by this huge amount of raw data.

I sat facing my computer for more than a year waiting for a vision of how and where to begin. The traditional social science approach would be to use conceptual theory to structure the work, and then add short excerpts from the journal to support and give life to the abstract ideas. But what I'd learned in solitude was as much in my heart and body as in my mind, and I couldn't even put it into words, never mind theory. All I knew was that somehow the daily journal, itself, would be central to the work.

During that year I told myself over and over that I simply had to begin to write, but resistance and inertia bound my imagination and energy. On some level I wasn't yet ready to write; I was still processing what had happened to me alone in the wilderness. I again became a semi-recluse, spending long hours hidden in my office.

I even asked my supervisory committee to delineate the minimum requirements for a dissertation that would be academically acceptable. They declined the bait and said that I'd fought long and hard for the freedom to follow my inner call, and now I needed to trust myself. They encouraged me to stop worrying about some supposedly acceptable dissertation and instead to write from the heart. They reassured me I could write absolutely whatever I wanted, and then my job would be to convince them that it deserved a PhD. I appreciated the gift, but still didn't know how to begin.

THE SLOW DANCE OF THE CHILEAN LIMPETS

In the meantime, I returned to the limpet study. That data — numbers in tidy columns — I did know how to work with. I defined a simple computer procedure that would plot on a graph the limpets' daily low-tide positions. Vaguely at first, and then with growing interest and excitement, I noticed that the sequential positions of some of the limpets showed strong geometric patterns. It was as if they might have been using the earth's magnetic field to orient their movements. My mind was captivated by the patterns that were emerging from the limpets' apparently random positions on the rock. I wondered if I had discovered something that no one had noticed before.

Then, sitting alone late at night, hunched over the eerie glow of the computer, things got a bit weird. I began to imagine setting myself up as a sort of soothsayer — using the patterns of limpet movement as my tea leaves to predict the future. I might even develop a cult following as the limpet guru. Such are the bizarre imaginings of a, or at least this, solitary scientist.

But in a flash of understanding, the prosaic and disappointing source of the pattern suddenly became obvious: my own methodology. While measuring the positions of the limpets on the stormy southern rocks, I rounded my measurements up or down to the closest division mark on the radius of the dial

I'd made from the bucket lid. I also rounded up or down to the closest mark on the string attached to the center of the dial. This twofold rounding up or down created the artifact of apparent geometric pattern in the data. Alas! Once I reintroduced a random element into the measurements to compensate for the rounding off, the geometric — almost mystical — pattern disappeared.

It's fascinating how readily the mind creates and projects regular patterns onto the world, and how exciting it is to then "discover" those apparent patterns. Scientists consciously examine their methodology and data for just such artifacts, but on a deeper level, the mind constantly and unconsciously creates and projects patterns. This process is pragmatically useful because it allows for some degree of predictability, but it can lead to a false sense of power and security, and to the extent we become caught in our own projections, it can dampen our experience of the mysterious wonder in the world.

Often when we clump things together into categories (such as species of limpet) we lose the grounded actuality of the individual. I was intrigued by the uniqueness of each limpet's daily behavior. Each just seemed to do what it did rather than follow a regularly repeating pattern or a pattern common to all individuals.

I still imagined the limpets to be doing a kind of very slow free-form underwater dance, and persuaded Axel Anderson, a fellow grad student, to write a computer program that simulated their movements. I could watch it for hours. I presented the results of my statistical analysis and the computer simulation at a conference, but no one else seemed particularly thrilled. I guess without having spent time in the wind and rain with the actual limpets, the graphs and moving dots on the screen didn't mean much.

POST-SOLITUDE BLUES

I was often asked if coming back was difficult, and I usually replied that since I was familiar with the process it was not as hard this time as it had been after previous retreats. Nevertheless, although not aware of it at first, I slowly settled into depression. I felt confused about what I had and had not learned in solitude. This was a continuation of the doubt, frustration, and anxiety I'd often felt on the island about not finding the answers I was seeking, and the belief that I should have *Answers* to share with others.

Many spiritual teachers claim to have found ultimate peace and joy and that they can show others how to find it, too. I would love to be able to say the same, but that would be dishonest. In any case, I tend to mistrust people who profess to have evolved beyond uncertainty, doubt, and pain, and appreciate those who openly share the ups and downs of their journey and the partial wisdom they have found.

Eventually, troubled by my lack of a sexual relationship and my lack of productivity in writing the dissertation, I began to see a psychiatrist. Perhaps someone formally trained in the workings of the mind would be able to help me see what I could not see and accept on my own. From my office in Vancouver, southern Chile seemed far away both physically and psychologically.

At the UBC mental health center, a nice therapist talked with me for a while and then said she felt I should seek professional help. I'd thought that's what I was doing there, but apparently not. She referred me to a psychiatrist, who after talking with me for fifty minutes told me, with no apparent doubt, that I needed long-term therapy and strong medication if I wanted to be free of my obsessive-compulsive perfectionism.

I declined his invitation and found another doctor who was not as eager to prescribe pills. I worked with her once a week for about three years, and the process was very healing. I didn't learn much I hadn't figured out on my own, and I was disappointed that I couldn't deal with my distress alone, but her steady mirroring of positive regard gently began to soften my self-deprecation.

Although I hadn't found any ultimate *Answers* in solitude and sometimes still felt grief at that failure, more often I remembered to not take my questions so seriously. Slowly the gloom of depression lifted, and there was a gentler sense of quiet spaciousness in the movements of my heart and mind.

TELLING MY STORY, AND FIFTEEN MINUTES OF FAME

I spent a lot of time working with the images I'd brought back from Chile. I'd taken photographs for a year without seeing any results, and I was very happy that many of the images were beautiful. As a way to share my research and evoke for others the experience of solitude, I started giving slide-show presentations at the university and in other venues around Vancouver, using storytelling and journal readings in conjunction with the images to create a sort of guided meditation.

My work was definitely nontraditional, and it triggered interesting responses — most of them positive. One of the people who came to a slide show said that what she appreciated most in my talk was that I didn't try to provide some universal *Answer*, but rather, by openly sharing my journey, created the space for her to follow her own path of exploration. Via the website my nephews helped me create, I received frequent email from people I didn't know thanking me for sharing my experience with them.

One day in the spring of 2003, as I was sitting quietly in my office, the phone rang. It was the UBC Public Affairs Office. They said they had heard about my year in solitude and asked if I would do an interview for an article in the university newspaper.

Two weeks later the story appeared and within hours I received a call from the *Canada National Post* also asking for an interview. That story made the front page and was picked up by the *Vancouver Sun* and the *Ottawa Citizen*. Local and national radio and television stations invited me onto their programs. I often go days, even weeks, without having phone messages, but for those few days I was sometimes on the phone talking with one reporter or producer and would hang up to find messages waiting from other programs.

I knew it was a transient bubble that would soon pass, and I didn't take any of it too seriously. People kept saying, "Hey, I've been seeing you everywhere in the paper and on radio and TV. You're famous now." I'd laugh and say, "It's just my fifteen minutes and will soon be over." But it lasted longer than I expected. The media attention didn't change my private life or my relationships, though. It's odd that our culture values public recognition so highly when it seems to make so little difference to lived experience — except during the (usually brief) times of public performance.

A PhD IN SOLITUDE

One day during this period I ran into my friend Anne who had recently finished her PhD in nursing. In celebration, she'd flown back to Ottawa to visit her family. Her mom met her at the airport, and the first thing she said was, "Well, your PhD from UBC isn't worth a damn!" This startled Anne and she asked why. Her mom showed her the Ottawa newspaper and said that some guy out there was earning a doctorate for sitting on an island and telling a story about it. Anne laughed and told her mom that I was a friend.

But when she told me, I wasn't amused. One of the painful aspects of doing unconventional work was the worry that it would be seen as narcissistic drivel. Even though the media and many people expressed interest in what I was doing, the demon of self-doubt always lurked in the shadows. I was quite upset, and Anne found that even funnier.

A few days later I met Carl Leggo, one of my academic supervisors, for breakfast. I was still feeling glum that some people obviously thought what I was doing was crap that should not be recognized by the university. Expecting reassurance, I told Carl the story. He was drinking coffee at the time and started laughing so hard I thought coffee would come out his nose. That upset me even more. When he could finally talk he said, "Congratulations! Single-handedly you are destroying the value of every PhD that has been or ever will be awarded by UBC." Ah. I let it go and settled down to eat my pancakes.

During that year, one of my most pervasive feelings was of avoiding the dissertation. No matter how much time I spent with the media, responding to people who emailed me, giving presentations, or working on my website, I recognized that I had not yet begun the real work of telling the deeper more intricate story of my year alone in the wilderness. But eventually the distractions lost their seductive power and I settled down to write. Patti continued to be an invaluable friend and collaborator as I started working through the almost nine hundred pages of the original journal.

Once I finally got started, I worked on the dissertation steadily for almost two years. It was sometimes intense and exciting and other times a boring slog. I often sat in front of the computer for hours before my heart and mind would settle down to work. I began going to the university in the afternoon and staying late into the night when my energy was focused and there was no one else around. I knew I wouldn't be able to explain to my committee what I was trying to do, but would have to create the dissertation without their guidance by following an inner vision I could still only vaguely see. It was a fascinating process.

On February 14, 2004, shortly after a story appeared in the *Globe and Mail* newspaper that described my retreat into solitude, I received the following email: "I have just read your story in the G and M. As with most (90%) PhDs you are either eccentric or nuts. I don't know which, but I think you are *nuts*." It seemed so incisive that I couldn't resist including it in my dissertation. I wrote back to thank him for his note.

In the spring of 2005, I finally showed my committee what I'd written. I had no idea what I would do if they rejected it, since I didn't have the energy to begin again. They loved it, and together we began to polish the text and prepare for the defense.

I defended the following November and earned a PhD in Interdisciplinary Studies on the physical, emotional, psychological, and spiritual effects of deep wilderness solitude. My dissertation was awarded the highest possible mark. The defense was joyful. Patti flew up from Texas, and many others came to support my innovative approach to research — which included my own lived experience and integrated body, heart, and Spirit with mind. We felt we were creating and surfing a swelling wave of academic change.

Some weeks later I met with one of the university examiners to share a beer and discuss some interesting and challenging questions she had posed during the defense. At one point in our conversation I asked her what percentage of the professors at UBC would probably have rejected my dissertation — not because of quality, but simply because it did not match their preconceived idea of what a doctoral dissertation should be. She laughed and said, "Why, it's a bloody miracle you graduated." I guess the wave is still a ripple.

MEMORIES AND REFLECTIONS

What do I see when I reflect back on my year in the wilderness; what insights still seem important? A sense of spaciousness developed during the year, and time expanded. After a while I put away my watch and calendar, and lived with the shifting spill of light on mountains and sea, the changing lengths of day and night, the wax and wane of moon and tide, and the fall of rain and winter snow. Without the interruptions of a social schedule to break my inner rhythms, I often felt a sense of continuity through the hours and the weeks. But I also sent a check-in email on the first of each month, and this punctuated the stream of days. So while I lived more and more in the flow of my inner and outer world, cultural time was still present.

There was an intensity of experience often absent when I'm involved in social activity. My senses became more acute and my perception of beauty more achingly immediate. Sometimes the world and I came vibrantly *alive*. With the freedom to slow down and return over and over to the here and now, my mind settled and opened to perceive a mysterious Presence that I could experience but not define. I, and all else, belong to and am that Presence. In the silence of solitude I remembered that the world is and always has been Sacred.

My interactions with the nonhuman world paralleled my habitual relationships with people. Usually we believe that going into nature is a peaceful respite from the hurly-burly of our social lives, but this is because we seldom stay long enough for our inner conflicts to catch up with us. Once they do, all the stuff we have to deal with in society manifests itself in relation to the nonhuman world: we take ourselves into solitude with us.

This was especially clear in my relationship with Cat. If I had not taken a cat, some other aspect of the world would have triggered my frustration, rage, and guilt. Had there been another person with me, much of what I dumped on Cat would have landed on my partner. But there was more than that. As I reflect back on my time with Cat, I realize he gave me a profound and terrible gift; he showed me a different world. Dogs are fully domesticated creatures, but cats remain half wild. In our friendship, Cat led me to a fierce and untamed place in myself.

My relationship with the wind and rain was different and changed during the year. In the beginning, I felt the wind to be a threat and an adversary that often prevented me from doing what I wanted. Sometimes I sensed active malevolence, rather than simple implacability, and fear filled my solitary mind. When I began to disidentify with my own desires and fears, I could engage more openly with the wind and allow it to shape me in unexpected ways. Slowly the wind became a teacher, and instead of cursing it I bowed in respect. It is sometimes said that when the student is ready the teacher appears. It seems more likely that we are always in the presence of teachers, and at different stages in our development we become open to their teachings.

The wind taught me to surrender, and the rain taught me to love. In the beginning the rain was an annoyance, but over the months I spent hundreds, perhaps thousands, of hours listening to it patter on the porch roof. That and other water sounds became a mantra that deepened my concentration and carried me inward. There was often bliss as I simply sat and listened. I learned that love is as fundamental as awareness; an open heart as vital as an open mind. Without love, clarity is not enough. I learned that relationship is always possible in any circumstance and is never possible to avoid. I can change the quality of my relationships, but without engagement I cease to exist.

The quality of my relationships was an outward manifestation of my inner attitude and orientation. Over and over I interacted with the world and with myself from a position of power and control. I was intent on exerting my will and having things be the way I wanted them to be. Slowly I came to recognize the enormous pain this attitude caused and at times still causes me. I began to relax my demands and to accept the world and myself as we actually are. I began to see through the strange delusion that we are separate from — and so can somehow own — the world and ourselves.

Learning to open myself to the Mysterious Presence I'm always already part of was as important to inner peace as accepting the world as it is. In solitude I slowly began to accept that I could not autonomously do what needed to be done. The movement from control to trust and surrender was and is at the center of my spiritual journey. But behavioral competence is still important because the process I surrender to includes my own activity.

This shift involves working with aversion and desire. I can relax my effort to control the world only when I'm willing to experience aspects of life that are painful and willing to not experience things I desire. This doesn't mean I need to seek out what I dislike (although this can be useful at times) or avoid what I enjoy. But I so habitually avoid what I don't like and actively seek what I do like that to gently decondition this automatic behavior and simply be with whatever comes into my field of experience allows a sense of peace and spaciousness to emerge in my life. Leaning lightly toward what I do not like and lightly away from what I do has begun to slow my frantic addictive activity. Meditation practice was and is an important part of this process.

Living alone for a year in the wilderness and writing about the experience have brought the realization that more and more I know less and less. I've found no sure answers. Because of this I sometimes feel bereft, as though I've failed in my quest. When caught in such doubt, I long for and question why others have found certainty when I have not. But when I relax into trust, I remember that certainty is a conceptual illusion.

Although I came to feel that, finally, All is Mystery, I also sensed some tentative and probably transient answers of the heart that emerged slowly and sometimes unnoticed through daily living. I saw more clearly than ever before that simply understanding something on a conceptual level is not enough. Transformation is more than changing my thoughts.

Even though, in many ways, I remain a mystery to myself, I have gained some sense of my inner rhythms. While I've failed to learn to willfully control shifts of consciousness from small to Big Mind, I have gained insight into why this is so: the small mind entity that desires freedom actually clings more tightly to itself in its efforts to force a shift. By slowing down and accepting the need to surrender, I open myself for the transformation to take place. The experience of joy, peace, and wonder is a gift — not an earned reward. Rather than ordering myself to march in a preconceived formation, I'm slowly learning to dance. This change requires care, humility, and patience.

In the wilderness I imagined I could somehow live continuously with Big Mind awareness, but (experientially) it didn't happen. Perhaps it's possible for some mystics, or even for me in the future, but the actuality was and is that there are cycles that ebb and flow like the tides. Sometimes in some things I strive to maintain control; sometimes in some things I surrender to the flow of the world.

FINDING BALANCE

People sometimes ask if I recommend deep wilderness solitude to others. I do not. It's painful, difficult, and sometimes dangerous. A person needs to be called to it from deep within, and if someone requires external encouragement, he or she is not ready. But I do think many of us can benefit from stepping out of our hectic daily activities to spend some time alone. Often when I ask someone how they are, they reply, "Busy." This seems to refer to an ongoing state of psychological stress as well as to constant physical activity. I suspect this feeling is pervasive in modern culture and I wonder how long we have lived with the sense that we don't have enough time to do what we believe we must do.

We often seem to value activity above all else, but like all beings we need to rest and recuperate. I suspect the widespread occurrence of depression in our culture is linked to our refusal to allow ourselves quiet time. Feeling the need to remain constantly busy — mentally or physically — in socially productive activity can prevent us from turning inward to simply be with ourselves. Such inward turning requires time and might lower productivity and social standing. It is not that all activity is bad, but many of us are far out of balance and our activity does not come from a place of stillness and wisdom.

Many are entranced by an economic worldview in which endless growth is not only possible, but also desirable and necessary. This ignores or denies the fundamental ecological reality that the Earth is an essentially closed system with limits to growth. Much of our activity seems ecologically destructive, and we disagree about what should be done to fix the problems we have created. Many of us think our own plan of action is *the* solution, but it seems possible that excessive human activity — *in and of itself* — is the basic problem.

The Earth needs to heal, and we cannot *make* it happen; frequently our efforts only deepen the wounds. But if we can relax our demand for material goods and reduce our rate of reproduction, the Earth might be able to heal herself. Perhaps we can find fulfillment in nonmaterial terms and learn that what we seek we have always had.

Our culture is so focused on progress that we frequently don't experience our own lives just as they are here and now. But the world will always be exactly as it is in each moment. It's astonishing how much time and energy we expend in trying to deny this simple fact.

This doesn't imply passivity. Our visions and ideals are also part of this moment. Everything changes, no matter how slowly, and we can act to alleviate suffering. Yet if plans for the future are not balanced with acceptance and joy in this moment, just as it is, our lives go unlived. The challenge is to work with our lives as they are rather than imagine that things are different. If we can learn to soften our aversions and desires, our lives might become less frantic and more spacious.

One fundamental difficulty is that we do not directly perceive ourselves to be biological beings in a *living* world. The nonhuman world has become a sort of inanimate backdrop to our human affairs. Theoretically, we know we depend on the physical and biological systems of Earth, but experientially we are alienated from those systems. We treat the Earth as a stranger we *should* protect for pragmatic or ethical reasons, but until we individually begin to actually experience nonhuman creatures as family and the Earth as our home, we are unlikely to relax our demands for comfort and security or make the changes necessary for our survival, joy, and sense of belonging.

Wilderness solitude has the power to catalyze a transformation in consciousness and a shift in perception. The felt experience of belonging to the ecosphere is psychologically and spiritually healing and may have profound implications for changing our destructive patterns of behavior. I believe we need spiritual transformation as well as economic and legislative solutions.

COMING INTO THE PRESENT

It's been six years since I left the island in southern Chile. That sentence could be the first in another long chapter, but this story has been about living for a year alone in the wilderness, and about coming back again. It's time to imagine a boundary line across the endlessly moving sea of experience.

The year following my doctoral defense was difficult. Apparently, the feelings of disorientation that often occur when students graduate are not age-dependent. The same questions can arise no matter how old we are: What should I do with my life? How am I going to earn a living? Where will I live? Not surprisingly, I've found no sure answers.

Patti still lives in east Texas, and I'm currently back in Vancouver, after spending much of last year in a remote corner of northern California. I live in a tiny apartment two blocks from the sea, and teach an online course that weaves together systems thinking, explorations in philosophy, and transformations of consciousness. As usual, finances are tight, and I continue to do home repairs to earn enough to get by while I write.

I still live by myself, but my friendships are deep, and Patti and I remain closely bonded. I often work late into the night and still spend much of my time alone. I'm usually comfortable, even joyful, in my solitude and experience myself to be part of the world, but at times I still struggle with feelings of isolation. In those times, a wall seems to separate me from others; a wall that begins to dissolve when I lean into it and treat myself and those around me with compassion. My life is quiet and peaceful. I'm learning to walk more lightly on the Earth, and to trust Life to take me where I need to go next.

The process of inner transformation continues. Although I know that All is sacred and *alive*, and that Spirit abides in the city — is the city — at times my heart still longs for wilderness solitude. I see trees as more alive than concrete buildings and hear birdsong as more beautiful than electronic beeping. I continue to practice accepting the world as it is and not as I would like it to be. It is enough, and much more than enough.

PATTI'S STORY

My relationship with Bob and with his exploration of solitude is intricate and dedicated. I first met him in 1987 at a spiritual community in New Hampshire. We were both attending a birthday party for the Dharma teacher Deneal Amos, whose teachings have played an important part in our individual lives. That day we shared only a passing conversation, but I recognized Bob as a man who was earnest in establishing his spiritual practice, and I had the solid sense that he and I would be working together sometime in the future.

That future rolled around twelve years later when through casual circumstance I became reconnected with Bob. As I was introduced to his academic work, I was captivated by the issues of solitude and by his proposed research project. In January 1999 he told me he was planning to begin his fieldwork the following September, but the project had a longer gestation period than expected, and September came and went.

By summer 2000, Bob had decided to do his fieldwork in Chile, but I was beginning to wonder if he would ever get out of Vancouver. I still could not see much forward movement in his logistic preparations. Then, in October, he exploded with ideas and frenetic activity, all directed toward gathering supplies and preparing for his voyage to Chile. I was exhausted just watching him tend to all the details, and then suddenly he was gone.

That winter, I continued to order items and send them down to Chile with the hope they would arrive before he left the mainland. I could feel Bob's exhaustion and anxiety. Finally, the last phone call came on February 4, 2001. I would not hear Bob's voice again for more than a year.

I was confident of the email protocol we had devised. As it turned out, in addition to his monthly check-in message, Bob also sent a report each solstice and equinox that described his life in solitude. These were forwarded to many people who were following his adventure. Sometimes people asked if I knew anything more than what was in the reports; I did not. It was difficult at times to keep the spirit of solitude. Like so many good things, we often want just a little bit more.

Bob was always with me. I spent time each day before meditation holding him in my mind and heart and picturing vibrant and healthy energy for him. Each day (except for a time when I was in the hospital) I made an origami figure and inscribed onto it one of the aspects of Infinite Heart. I held the magical belief that if I made a figure every day, Bob would be safe and sound for another twenty-four hours. Since I made different figures of animals and plants and pinned each to the wall after that day had passed, I ended up with a lovely, colorful collage.

When the 9/11 terrorist attacks occurred, I discussed with the network of people who followed Bob whether to tell him about those events, but I decided against it. Looking back, I'm glad I did not.

In July Bob sent me a list of parts he needed to repair his outboard motors, and there followed several back and forth messages with questions and lists of things to buy. It was a difficult task for me, as I had little knowledge of the parts he needed. I also sensed I was on a wild-goose chase. I doubted he actually needed half the things he asked for, and I suspected they would never reach him anyway. My intuition turned out to be correct.

In our emails we were careful not to say anything personal that would break his emotional solitude. We discussed only business, even though I missed his companionship and guidance. Only once did I send a personal note along with the monthly response to his check-in email. He replied in kind, and it helped take the sting out of missing him so acutely. It was the only time we engaged in personal communication during the year.

As medical adviser, I received a few inquiries from Bob, but I kept my answers impersonal. When he wrote that his tooth was abscessed, I told him precisely what to do, gave him a pep talk, and tried to lead him to believe that everyone has pulled a tooth or two. My precise answers to his questions belied my own worry and personal concern for his health and comfort.

Bob and I exchanged promises before he left Vancouver: he not to die, and I that if he ever went to code-red I would go down immediately to participate in a rescue or a burial. I knew Bob to be a man of his word, and so I never really worried about his safety. I didn't realize how much physical pain he experienced during the year until I read his wilderness journal, and I was careful not to tell him about personal difficulties in my own life. I noted in retrospect that we each tried to protect the other from undue anxiety.

Prior to leaving Canada, Bob said he would probably like me to come and stay with him on the island after his year in solitude to help him reorient to people. But he wouldn't know for sure whether he would be able to tolerate company until the year was almost over. I often wondered what the coming year would bring. Then, in October 2001, I decided to purchase a cheap round-trip ticket from Texas to Punta Arenas, Chile. I emailed Bob and told him I was planning a two-month expedition for February-March, but that he was under no pressure to make a decision about wanting visitors or not. If he didn't want to see anyone at the end of solitude, I would have my own grand adventure in South America.

So I prepared myself for something I could not really plan for. I *knew* Bob would need my help at the end of his year, even if he didn't know it. I was a fifty-two-year-old mother of two teenagers with limited finances, and it didn't seem like the best time for me to go, but I was hearing the call of the unknown.

Before leaving Texas, I emailed the Chilean Navy and the major ferry service to arrange transportation out to Bob's island. The navy never responded, and the ferry officials said they would not make an unscheduled stop in the middle of nowhere. It was frustrating, but I knew from previous experience in Latin America that business often doesn't move along unless you are there in person. There was nothing to do but hope I could arrange things once I arrived in Chile. Never having been to South America before, I stepped into the void.

On February 1, 2002, I arrived in Punta Arenas at midnight after thirty-six hours of flights and layovers. There was a remarkable absence of wind, which I had been told never stops blowing. In fact, this would be one of the last windless nights I would experience in a long time. Even after reading Bob's reports, I didn't grasp the fierceness of the weather until I was actually on the island.

In his February check-in email Bob said he was looking forward to seeing me when the year was over, and he sent a list of food to bring to the island. I spent days in Punta Arenas making repeated shopping trips, little by little buying the produce and dry goods Bob had asked for.

During his last month in solitude, Bob went completely out of email communication. Since my arrival in Chile, I had received no personal note about how I was to get to his island, and I was furious with him. I felt abandoned and didn't know exactly what to do. I was completely on my own, but I still had faith in the process.

But I wasn't as alone as I thought. Bob had told me to contact Alejandra Silva, a biologist with the Chilean National Parks Service in Punta Arenas. When I visited her, she reassured me that everything was set with the navy. I still have no idea why they didn't responded to my emails, but when I went to see the commander, he acted as if he had been waiting to hear from me. Having secured transportation, I could finally relax.

My last day in Punta Arenas brought its own serendipity. In the central plaza, a group of young people was drumming and dancing, and they had attracted the attention of a documentary film crew from South Africa. The South Africans were trying, unsuccessfully, to talk with the dancers, so I stepped in to translate. After the dancing ended, I spent some time chatting with the crew and told them why I was in South America and about Bob's fieldwork. They were captivated and told me it was critical to get film documentation of his project.

I balked at the idea since Bob had never talked about videotaping his work. A video camera was expensive, and I might be stuck with it if he didn't want to film his life on the island. Besides, I had never used a video camera. But the South Africans insisted that Bob's work should not be relegated to a PhD dissertation sitting on a dusty shelf somewhere, and they thought a documentary could perhaps be made of his fieldwork. I finally agreed.

By this time it was late in the afternoon, and I rushed to the camera store. It had closed, but I pleaded with the people inside to let me in. Ten minutes later I was back on the street with a camera, an extra battery, twenty film cassettes, and a receipt for over $600 USD. Trust the process indeed! The next morning, my last day in Punta Arenas, I met the filmmakers for an early breakfast, and they gave me a crash course on operating the camera and basic shooting techniques. I spent the next two days in a pension in Puerto Natales, and at dawn on February 15 I boarded the navy patrol boat *La Yagan*. Shortly after casting off, the crew gathered on the captain's deck, made a circle, prayed, and passed out life vests. I was not included in the prayer circle, and they didn't give me a life vest. I wondered if I should be afraid, but decided there was nothing to be done.

En route I tried to imagine what it would be like to see Bob. We had spent a lot of time together camping and fishing in the wilderness, and it had not always been easy to be with him. His perfectionism sometimes spilled out onto me, and we would have to step apart to deal with the discomfort. I never liked it when he was picky with me, but I usually just let it go because I knew he tormented himself more than he ever criticized me. It was just a fact of his way

in the world. He could be a very demanding partner. Would I find it too difficult to be with him after he had had a year all to himself? Would I be comfortable in camp? Would he welcome the camera and the company? Would I
be a real help with the work? I would soon see.

As for the navy crew, they expressed concern that I might find a mad-
man on the island. It had never occurred to me that Bob might have gone insane, and I had no sense that there was anything to be afraid of. I suspect the
navy crew thought I was as mentally unsound as Bob.

Ten hours after leaving Puerto Natales I was sliding from *La Yagan* down
into Bob's inflatable boat. I was delighted to see him but remained fairly quiet.
I had decided that during the first few days on the island, I did not want to
overwhelm him with conversation and information. This taciturn approach
was not necessary. Bob was a chatty magpie from the moment I arrived. He
flooded me with information about the camp and himself. It seemed clear that
he had been lonely and had missed conversation. Bob is a storyteller by nature, and he certainly was ready to unfurl himself. He seemed cheerful and
steady and happy to share details about his life. He looked a bit gaunt, and I
could tell he had lost at least thirty pounds since I had last seen him.

That first night on the island was warm and cozy, and Bob was quite comfortable as the host. I went to sleep listening to the waves lapping the graveled
shore. It was a sound that would lull me to sleep every night for the next month.
It is a sound I can recall at will whenever I am having a restless bedtime.

My first few days on the island were essentially show-and-tell. We took
a boat ride into the mountains. Bob told stories about the cabin and the
weather. I told Bob that Deneal Amos had died the previous spring, and then
I told him about September 11, 2001. He didn't seem unusually upset by this.
He had not witnessed the media overexposure to the tragedy, and he immediately put it in perspective with the other daily tragedies that occur around
the world.

The video camera affected my experience on the island. Our original
plan was to spend a relaxing two weeks before starting to take down camp, but
the leisure time never materialized. The first weeks were spent documenting
various aspects of the camp, daily life, and Bob's stories about his past year.

I was very happy for the opportunity to see Bob's solitude post, and I think
he was glad to have someone to share it with. He was generous in taking care
of my physical and spiritual needs, and he did everything he could to help me
experience as much as possible of this small world he had so intimately inhabited for twelve months. To be correct, what I refer to as a cabin was not really
a cabin, but a beautiful refuge. I noted the elegance of design, the attention to
detail in the carpentry, the stark simplicity in form and function. It was easy

to feel at home and fall into the daily routine of living; everything seemed so graceful.

Experiencing the beauty of the mountains, sea, wildlife, and weather was a peak experience for me. There were moments when I felt profound joy and heard an inner voice saying, "*This* is enough." This shift of consciousness was facilitated by Bob's careful low-impact approach. Everything he had built fit into place and did not interrupt the flow of the island. The camp seemed as natural as the trees and dense underbrush. Bob had clearly been in his element when he made his home, and he had been very respectful of the non-human world around him. It seemed evident that he had made himself a guest of the environment and not a lord of the manse.

I have always been jealous of Bob's fieldwork. While there, I, too, felt the siren song of solitude calling deep to my being, but it was easy for me to forget that I arrived to a comfortable camp. I never would have been able to build a camp with so many amenities, and I would not have been able to sustain myself during the fierce weather, which plagued me and was much nastier than I had expected. I could not have survived as Bob had; I just got a taste of all the best.

Cat took no time at all in becoming comfortable with me even though I was only the second person he had seen since he was a wee kitten. He took to sitting in my lap and rubbing up and down my leg when I was quiet. I don't remember ever hearing him make a sound. Later, back in Texas, I read in Bob's journal about his tempestuous relationship with Cat. It surprised me because I saw no indication of hard feelings between them. They were always affectionate with each other when I was on the island.

Watching Bob *sky fishing* was a treat. He seemed so happy and so unified with his environment when he was out on the point, working the long-tailed kite to keep it from plunging into the sea. It is a rather rare event to see someone *one* with his element, and it brought a deep joy to witness it. Bob seemed so carefree when flying that lovely handmade kite, as if everything in his universe had disappeared, with the exception of man, fishing rod, wind, water, and kite. Bliss indeed!

Deconstruction of camp was as mindful as construction had been. It was also a physical grunt. Truly, dismantling everything and erasing our footprints were formidable tasks. I was physically exhausted by the end of the long days, and every morning I woke up feeling less energetic than the day before. The rain and wind never seemed to stop. The camp became smaller each day as we tore down the cabin and outhouse, bundled the tarp, and burned the wood frame. Bob wanted to leave the island with few traces of his habitation, and I respect him for his commitment to that.

Despite our best efforts, our plan to be completely ready to go when the navy arrived was thrown to the wind when they unexpectedly appeared four hours earlier than expected. There had been fierce storms for the previous two days and the navy was in a hurry to get back to Puerto Natales, so it was a mad slapdash rush to get off the island.

Suddenly we had a major problem. The captain of the patrol boat did not want to haul out our bundles of trash. They insisted that Bob just leave the refuse on the island. This was, of course, against Bob's intent. I witnessed a display of male confrontation as neither Bob nor the captain would come off their stance. At one point Bob told the captain he would not leave without all the waste material, and the only way they could get him off the island would be in handcuffs. We seemed at an impasse.

Then I stepped forward to say that I would leave with the navy, and Bob could remain on the island until I could find some commercial boat to come and get him and the sacks of trash. Of course I had no idea how to do that, but I think my suggestion helped to show the captain that Bob was firm in his decision. As soon as I said we could leave Bob behind, the captain gave in and allowed everything off the island. What a relief! I haven't had much experience with macho displays, and I was happy when the issue was settled.

We quickly ferried all the camp materials out to the navy boat. In a couple of hours our gear was stowed, Cat was crated on board, and Bob and I were on the captain's deck as we shoved off for Puerto Natales. I was sad to leave but physically grateful, as I had reached my limit of sleeping on the hard floor of the tent. I ached all over.

Bob spent several hours alone on the open deck of the patrol boat, bundled up in rain gear and his angora wool cap, looking back toward the island we were leaving behind. Light rain was falling. I wondered what thoughts were playing with him as we left his home of the past thirteen months. His solitude was broken, and there were few traces that he had ever been on the island. It was a quiet, peaceful ride back to Natales, and we arrived in port long after dark.

Cat turned out to be quite an adventurer. Bob asked me to take Cat home with me until he returned to Vancouver and could take him back. We got him immunizations and a health certificate, and Cat accompanied me on the airplane back to Texas. At home, I kept him indoors for about three weeks. He loved lying on my bed and being treated like a small furry prince. He enjoyed the attention and comfort of indoor living and was very affectionate to everyone. After he was established, we decided it was time to let him out to wander. He wasn't meant to be a house cat, and I hoped he would have exciting adventures as he patrolled the Texas hills around me.

I seriously doubted Bob would ever get settled enough to have Cat as a roommate, but I was happy to have the pup. Sadly, after a week of going out to explore and returning to sleep on my bed, Cat did not return one evening. I never saw him again. I searched the roads to see if he had been hit by a car, but found no trace. I live in a rural area where wild hogs and coyote abound, and my theory is that he went out one night, had a seizure, and a coyote got him. I was sorry to lose him.

What are the effects of solitude I perceive in Bob today? I know him probably as well as anyone does, and it's hard to translate my perceptions. Solitude did leave its mark. How could it not? No one could go through a year of solitude and be unchanged. He seems gentled, not so judgmental of himself and of others, more patient, more willing to share his private time. Overall I find Bob to be much less critical and demanding than ever before.

His countenance reveals a man who has experienced both deep joy and pain. His eyes now have a depth of experience that was not visible before. He presents a lighter touch to the universe. He did not find the ultimate answers he sought, but he is now somewhat whimsical about even posing the questions. Bob has always been very generous toward me, and I detect that he now extends that generosity more to others as well. Certainly I experience the changes as positive, but they are merely amplifications of the wisdom and gentleness I always saw within him.

Bob's honesty shines in his work. Rarely do we read accounts of such bare personal truth. His journal offers more than a heroic tale. It is a picture of a man struggling to accept his own humanness. His commitment to remain open and honest to his own process is a strong invitation to each of us to abandon the *likely stories* we tell ourselves about our daily life and to step cleanly and fully into the life that is ours.

When I read Bob's journal, I am transported into his world of solitude and also into my own experience of solitude. I am honored to have had the opportunity to share in his journey. This, too, is enough!

ACKNOWLEDGMENTS

Inner transformation comes as a gift and brings a profound sense of gratitude. It can't be possessed, but drifts out of and into the mists of unknowing. The mountains, the sea, the sky, and the creatures who live where I spent the year all shared themselves generously with me. For this, too, I'm deeply grateful.

One of the unexpected things about spending a year in solitude and writing about it is how many people have accompanied and supported me along the way. Patti Kuchinsky's intellectual and logistic contributions have been invaluable. She was an always reliable contact person, technical assistant and medical adviser during the year, and she has participated enormously in creating this book. Her own journey to spend a month with me on the island in southern Chile was a courageous act of faith, and her presence eased my reentry into the social world. I'm grateful for her love, honesty, and wisdom.

Before and after my year alone, I spent months in Chile preparing and readjusting. The people I met were warm and helpful. My interactions with the government were almost always positive, and you can't ask for more than that.

Thank you to my friend and mentor Christian de Quincey, who generously offered to edit the manuscript and to act as my literary agent. His interest in my experience and his commitment to shaping and sharing the account encouraged me to continue writing. I've been very fortunate to work with New World Library editor Jason Gardner and freelance editor Jeff Campbell. They not only understood why I was writing from rather than about solitude, but they saw aspects of the story I'd missed and made invaluable suggestions on how to improve it.

The relationship between teacher and student is a delicate dance grounded in mutual respect and trust. An important step in earning a doctorate is developing a meaningful relationship with a supervisor and a supervisory committee; this is especially so for a nontraditional project. I'm extremely fortunate and grateful to have worked with David Tait, Lee Gass, Carl Leggo, Karen Meyer, and the late Peter Frost. They always challenged and supported me, and they trusted the process of our collective adventure into the unknown. Lee, especially, never let me get away with sloppy thinking or writing.

It's not easy to openheartedly let someone you love do something potentially dangerous. My mother honored my decision and gave me her blessing. My sisters Nancy and Peggy and their husbands Bill and Bill also supported me, even though they didn't necessarily understand why I wanted to spend a year alone in the wilderness. They worried about my safety but didn't try to talk me out of going. My nephews Greg and Kevin did understand and they thought it an excellent thing to do. Living in Nancy and Bill's northern California cabin while working on this book was a wonderful gift.

Ron Marsh started to read straight through an early draft of the manuscript, but decided he needed more time for reflection. On February 5, 2006, he began the year-long journey with me — one day at a time. He offered plenty of useful and humorous insights along the way. I've enjoyed many delightful conversations with Pille Bunnell, and I'm grateful to her and David Tait for inviting me to live in their home. Janet Beddoes has always been there; she read various drafts of the manuscript and suggested ways to move it forward. Thank you to my sweat lodge brothers and sisters for welcoming me into their circle, and to many distant writers who have shared their words with me.

I also wish to thank the following people and organizations for contributing generously to the project and to my life: Alejandra Silva, Juan-Pablo and Magdalena Cerda, Adriana Cerda, Diane Levings, Paulina Vilches, German Coronado, Barry McBride, Bart van der Kamp, Heather Akai, Marna Nelson, Jason Harrison, Axel Anderson, Michelle Kelly, Madeleine MacIvor, Tim Michel, Marcel Laplante, Robin Clark, the Chilean Navy and National Parks Service, the Canadian Consulate in Santiago, and Forestry, Interdisciplinary and Graduate Studies, MAGIC, and Civil Engineering at the University of British Columbia. The many people along the way who generously offered free technical advice and taught me what I needed to know. And the old woman in Puerto Varas whose eyes I won't forget.

APPENDIX

BOOKS READ OR CONSULTED IN SOLITUDE

• *Apropos of Dolores*	H.G Wells
• *At Home in the Universe*	Stuart Kauffman
• *Basic Writings*	Chuang Tzu
• *Care of the Soul*	Thomas Moore
• *Commentaries on Living*	Jiddu Krishnamurti
• *Desert Solitaire*	Edward Abbey
• *Dream Work*	Mary Oliver
• *Ecopsychology*	Allen D. Kanner et al.
• *Entre el Cielo y el Silencio*	Nicolas Mihovilovic
• *Essential Rumi*	Coleman Barks
• *Family Moskat*	Isaac Singer
• *Flow*	Mihaly Csikszentmihalyi
• *Gaia*	William Thompson
• *Hermits*	Peter France
• *How Right You Are, Jeeves*	P. G. Wodehouse
• I Ching	Richard Wilhelm (trans.)
• *Johnson Service Manual*	OMC
• *Nature, Man and Woman*	Alan Watts
• *A New Science of Life*	Rupert Sheldrake
• *No Boundary*	Ken Wilber
• *Pedagogy of the Oppressed*	Pablo Freire
• *The Perfect Storm*	Sebastian Junger
• *Right Ho, Jeeves*	P. G. Wodehouse
• *Seeking the Heart of Wisdom*	Goldstein and Kornfield
• *Sex, Ecology, Spirituality*	Ken Wilber

- *Solitude: A Philosophical Encounter*   Philip Koch
- *Solitude: A Return to the Self*   Anthony Storr
- *St. John Ambulance Official*
  Wilderness First Aid Guide   Wayne Merry
- *Teaching a Stone to Talk*   Annie Dillard
- *The Experience of Insight*   Joseph Goldstein
- *The Eye of Spirit*   Ken Wilber
- *Thoughts Without a Thinker*   Mark Epstein
- *Where There Is No Doctor*   David Werner

TOOLS

- Hammer, saw, chisels, large square, combination square, pencils, X-Acto knives, snap line, plumb bob, Surform pocket plane, brace and bits, hand drill, socket set, Crescent wrenches, box-end wrenches, Vise-Grips, pliers, sheet-metal shears, side-cutters, tape measure, hacksaw and spare blades, screwdrivers, swede saws and spare blade, machete, ax and spare handle, hatchet, level, Wonder Bar, pry bar, knife, staple gun, flat file, putty knives, sandpaper, come-along and pulleys, chain saw, extra chain, 2 chain files, spare plugs, chain oil, gas and 2-cycle oil, pick, shovel, trowel, slingshot and ball bearings

CONSTRUCTION MATERIALS

- 5 rolls duct tape, 1 roll Teflon tape, 1 roll masking tape, 6 tubes caulking, 4 tubes Shoe Goo/Marine Goop, Krazy Glue, rubber cement, carpenter's glue, 5 Minute Epoxy, paint thinner, acetone, WD-40
- Reinforcing rod: 20′ 1/2″ and 20′ 1/4″
- White heavy-duty woven polyethylene tarps for roof and walls
- Clear plastic: 6 mm × 10′ × 100′ (for extra layer on roof, on outhouse, over wood-piles, over tent, etc.), 4 mm × 10′ × 50′ (to line inside of cabin), plenty of nails of all sizes: 1″ to 4″, 2000 staples: 1/4″ and 3/8″ length, hard plastic strips for backing nails, various gauges of steel wire, snare wire, 4′ × 4′ clear Plexiglas for window, 3′ × 3′ fine mesh screen, 5′ heavy canvas to make reclining chair
- 4 sheets 5′ × 8′ × 5/8″ plywood (floor), 4 sheets 5′ × 8′ × 1/4″ pressboard (roof, door), 1 sheet 5′ × 8′ × 3/8″ plywood (shelves, table, bed; use shipping crates for more shelf material)
- Lumber: 12 1″ × 2″ × 8′ (shelf and table framing, etc.), 16 1″ × 3″ × 8′ (general use), 50 2″ × 2″ × 12′ (rafters, studs, framing), 6 2″ × 4″ × 8′ (corner posts), 20 2″ × 4″ × 10′ (stringers and floor joists), 6 2″ × 4″ × 12′ (misc.)

OUTDOOR GEAR

- Tent, compass, 2 GPS units, marine charts and topographical maps, map tube
- Boat, patch material, glue, transom wheels, rollers for under boat

- 2 outboard motors, gas can with hose, mounting bracket, extension handle
- Replacement parts (plugs, starter rope, prop, shear pins, electronic brain, coil, fuel pump), gear puller, starter rope, siphon hose, funnel
- 2 foot pumps with adapters
- 2 55-gallon drums, 6 5-gallon containers, 140 gallons gasoline
- 3 gallons 2-cycle oil
- 2 anchors, chain, lots of rope, pulleys
- Kayak, 2 paddles, seat, patch material, 3 life vests, chest waders
- Diving mask, fins, snorkel, wetsuit and extra material, gloves, spear gun, goody bag, fishing gear (2 heavy rods and reels, 1 lightweight trout rod and reel, lots of hooks and weights of all sizes, lures and jigs, extra 20-lb test line, net, gaff, fillet knife, needle-nose pliers, hand scale, reel oil, tools, spare rod guides), waterproof gear bags, materials for making crab traps, fishing license

CABIN SUPPLIES

- Airtight wood stove, 12′ chimney, 2 elbows, damper, chimney cap, stove cement
- Propane cookstove, propane light, hose and fittings, 3 100-pound tanks of propane
- Regulator, spare mantles, grill, 6 cigarette lighters, candles, newspaper, 2 fry pans, 2 small pots, 1 large pot, lids, dishpan, tub for bathing and washing clothes
- 2 plastic buckets, 40-gallon plastic drum for rainwater, plastic tubing, collapsible water containers, Tupperware for storing food
- 2 forks, knives, table- and teaspoons, spatula, large spoon, can opener, sharp knife
- 2 plates, bowls, cups (thermal), Thermos
- Soap for dishes and clothes, 4 green scrubbies, metal scrubby, dishrag, towels and rags
- Lots of: plastic food bags, Ziploc baggies, garbage bags, woven plastic produce sacks, aluminum foil
- 40 rolls toilet paper, 6 rolls paper towels
- Water filter and water purification additive
- Chair, broom
- Toilet kit: razors, lather, soap and shampoo, toothpaste, mirror, nail clippers, toothbrushes, dental floss
- Writing paper, 6 notebooks, 12 pens, write-in-the-rain notebooks, ruler, Magic Markers, playing cards, scissors
- Alarm clock, extra watch, Velcro band, thermometer, barometer, rain gauge
- Sewing kit: needles, thread, nylon thread, buttons, zippers, elastic, patch material, leather, rubber
- Lots of nylon cord, plastic twine, string

CLOTHING AND BEDDING

- 6 pairs sturdy pants, 5 long-sleeve flannel shirts, 6 T-shirts
- 6 pairs wool socks, 6 pairs cotton socks

- 2 pairs felt liners, 1 down bootie
- 1 good shirt and pair of pants for polite company
- 2 sweaters, 2 warm shirts, sweatshirt with hood
- 2 pairs long underwear
- Hollofil coat, down parka, thermal snowsuit, Hollofil vest
- 2 neck scarves, neck warmer
- 3 pairs mittens, 2 pairs rubber gloves, 2 pairs cotton work gloves
- 1 broad-brimmed hat, 2 baseball caps, 2 wool toques, rain hood
- Cheap tennis shoes, 2 pairs lightweight hiking boots, 1 pair lightweight rubber boots, 1 pair jungle boots
- Heavy duty rain gear, Gor-tex light rain gear, waterproof spray
- 6 wool stump socks, 6 cotton stump socks, 4 gel liners
- 2 Therm-a-Rest pads, down sleeping bag
- 2 sheets, 2 blankets, 2 pillows, towels

FIRST-AID SUPPLIES

- First-aid books
- Prosthetic leg repair kit: fiberglass cloth and resin, spare foot, spare socket liner, leather, contact cement, spare straps, rivets, Allen wrench
- Topical remedies: alcohol, iodine, antibiotic cream, cortisone cream, hydrogen peroxide, sodium chloride eyewash, anti-fungal cream, anti-fungal mouthwash, Zovirax cream, artificial tears, Vaseline, Vicks VapoRub, sun cream, insect repellent, almond oil, oil-drillers hand cream, bag balm, liniment, capsaicin cream, arthritis cream
- Pain medicine: 1,200 ibuprofen, 400 Tylenol, 100 Tylenol 3, injectable local anesthetic, injectable morphine, Orajel
- Supplements: multivitamins, vitamin C, calcium, iron, potassium, zinc, magnesium
- Other pills: antacids, laxative, Imodium, Benadryl, Claritin, motion sickness pills, Synthroid, oral antibiotics: for cuts, for intestinal tract, for ears and throat
- Wound care: Second Skin, butterfly strips, sterile pads of various sizes, cotton balls, tensor bandages, premade splint Band-Aids, adhesive tape, sterile eye pads
- Tools: scalpel and blades, suture kit, tweezers, magnifying glass, surgeon's gloves
- Miscellaneous: rubber balls for massaging back, pulleys for exercising, hot water bottle, homeopathic remedies

ELECTRONICS AND ELECTRICAL

- Satellite telephone with antenna wire (with prepaid air time)
- 2 laptops (one for sending email, one for journaling)
- Wind generator, 20´ × 2˝ steel pipe for antenna, guy wire, turnbuckles
- 2 solar panels (approximately 50 W each), voltage regulator, 2 12V–110V inverters

- 2 12V deep cycle batteries, 12 AA rechargeable batteries, charger
- Insulated multistrand electric wire: 12 gauge, 14 gauge, 16 gauge
- Fuses, alligator clips, battery-lead connectors, wire connectors, etc.
- Small 12V fluorescent light and 2 extra tubes, 2 12V incandescent lights and extra bulbs
- 2 headlamps and spare bulbs
- Electric hair clippers, flashing bicycle lights (to mark camp for nighttime on the water)
- Tape recorder and tapes

PHOTOGRAPHY AND OPTICS

- Camera, various lenses, lens cleaning solution and tissue, lens hood, cable release
- Strobes, spare light meter, tripod, spare batteries
- 40 or so rolls of color slide and print film (100 and 200 ISO)
- 2 pairs binoculars (1 waterproof 10×, 1 compact 8×), spare glasses

FOOD

Rice	100 kg	Cocoa powder	1.5 kg
Oatmeal	30	Chocolate pudding mix	2
Lentils	10	Potatoes	20
Peas	10	Onions	10
Pinto beans	10	Bacon	7
Black beans	28	Smoked meat	5
Pasta	20	Cheese	8
Flour	20	Garlic	2
Baking powder	1	Instant coffee	1
Sugar	20	Ground coffee	4
Salt	7	Olives	1
Pepper (and other spices)	1	Pickles	1
Popcorn	5	Sauerkraut	1
Dried fruit: raisins, apricots, figs, apples, peaches, prunes	20	Cooking oil	11 liters
		Vinegar	3
Honey	6	Lemon juice	5
Lard	7	Soya sauce	4
Peanut butter	7	Hot sauce	2
Powdered whole milk	13	Liquor	3
Jam	2	Tea	100 bags
Ketchup	1	Herbal tea	120 bags
Tomato paste	5	Dehydrated soup	30 pkgs
Semisweet chocolate	14	Bouillon cubes	12 boxes

TOTAL EXPENSES

(Fairly Close Estimate Rounded Off from Receipts) = $22,720

All amounts in U.S. dollars.

Punta Arenas (P.A.)
Puerto Natales (P.N.)

HARDWARE, ELECTRICAL, FUEL

CANADA

Home Depot: general stuff	$95
Canadian Tire: general stuff	$80
Other hardware	$85
Subtotal	$260

CHILE

General hardware and electrical odds and ends	$425
Batteries	$105
Anchor	$15
Lumber	$260
Gasoline	$300
Oil	$25
Propane	$90
Subtotal	$1,220
Total	$1,480

EQUIPMENT

CANADA

Boat and parts	$2,110
Outboards and parts	$1,275
Outboard repair (Chile)	$270
Kayak	$85
Chain saw	$85
Binoculars	$260
Glasses	$230
Dive mask	$85
Compass	$45
GPS	$160
Satellite telephone	$2,320
Satphone air time	$200
Solar panels	$550
Wind generator	$535
Electrical	$195
Swede saw	$20
Ax, etc.	$20
Wood stove and chimney	$125
Tarps	$60
Used camping gear (rain gear, tent, parka, Therm-a-Rest, sleeping bag, waterproof bags)	$520
Pants, shirts, etc.	$115
Rain boots	$30
Chest waders	$60
Cookstoves	$30
Total	$9,385

GROCERIES

CHILE

Cheese	$30
Flour	$5
Sugar	$10
Rice	$40
Oil	$5
Dried fruit	$75
Cat food	$5
Peanut butter and chocolate	$60
Oatmeal	$30
Beans and lentils	$50
Honey	$15
Cocoa	$5
Lemon juice	$5
Ketchup	$2
Spices, etc.	$15
Dried soup	$20
Lard	$10
Coffee	$30
Powdered milk	$50
Toilet paper	$15
Chocolate pudding	$10
Pasta	$20
Oil and vinegar	$15
Liquor	$55
Smoked meat	$120
Potatoes, onions, garlic	$20
Other	$105
Total	$822

TRAVEL COSTS

ROUTE/DESTINATION

Vancouver–Santiago	$1,200
Santiago–P.A. and return	$110
P.A.–P.N., 3 round trips	$35
Navy ship	$60
NAVIMAG ferry	$25
Santiago–Miami	$435
Miami–Vancouver	$470
Chile visa and entry tax	$415
Dominican Republic visit	$270

SHIPPING AND CUSTOMS

Vancouver–P.A.	$875
P.A.–Vancouver	$1,220
P.A.–P.N.	$145
Total	$5,260

MEDICAL

CANADA

Accident insurance	$245
Shots	$70
First-aid book	$25
Water treatment	$15
Pharmacy/vitamins	$375
Subtotal	$730

CHILE

Pharmacy/vitamins	$23
Toiletries	$24
Physiotherapy	$25
Dentist	$176
Cat	$13
Subtotal	$261
Total	$991

FOOD AND LODGING

LOCATION	ROUGH COST
Room and board:	
P.A.	$10.50/day × 40 = $420
Room:	
P.N.	$4.50/day × 40 = $180
Room:	
Santiago	$10.50/day × 50 = $525
Food/Meals	
P.N.	$4/day × 40 = $160
Santiago	$7/day × 50 = $350
10% for error	$165
Total	$1,800

EMAIL AND TELEPHONE

CHILE

Email: P.A.	$220
Telephone calls: P.A.	$270
Total	$490

MISCELLANEOUS

Travel gift to Patti	$670
Gift for Alenjandra	$35
Notary	$5
2 fishing licenses	$15
4 haircuts	$25
Fishing gear	$10
Marine charts	$65
Total	$825

AUDIOVISUAL

Camera repair	$55
Tripod	$25
Video camera	$300
Videotape	$85
Television	$120
Tape recorder	$55
Audiotapes	$20
Photographic film	$470
Photo processing	$535
Total	$1,665

NOTES

ON JOURNALING AND STORYTELLING

Epigraph: Henri Nouwen, *The Way of the Heart: Desert Spirituality and Contemporary Ministry* (New York: HarperCollins, 1981), p. 48.

1. Mark Epstein, *Thoughts without a Thinker: Psychotherapy from a Buddhist Perspective* (New York: Basic Books, 1995), p. 73.

APRIL 2001

Epigraph: Bob Marley, "Three Little Birds," *Exodus*, produced by Bob Marley and the Wailers (PolyGram Records, 1977).

1. Rumi, *The Essential Rumi*, trans. Coleman Barks with John Moyne, A. J. Arberry, and Reynold Nicholson (San Francisco: HarperSanFrancisco, 1995), p. 109.

METHOD, SOLITUDE, AND MEDITATION

Epigraphs: Albert Einstein, quoted in the *New York Post*, November 28, 1972, p. 12; Jean-Martin Charcot, quoted in Sigmund Freud, *Introductory Lectures on Psychoanalysis* (New York: Norton, 1966), p. 179.

1. Coming from a natural science background, I knew little about qualitative social science approaches when I began to consider studying myself in solitude for my doctoral research. After changing my focus, I worked for two years at UBC in relative isolation before stumbling into an autoethnography workshop led by Carolyn Ellis. (The university community is so fractured that it's very easy to not know about innovative research methods being developed in other disciplines.)

While I was exposed to new ideas at the workshop, the experience was even more valuable because it clarified and validated the direction I'd been moving in on my own. My intuitive orientation to research and writing is very similar to the open-ended and informal approach of autoethnography: pay attention to what is happening and figure out what you need to do to explore and describe the situation.

Autoethnography follows naturally from the insight: "everything that is said is said by an observer" (Maturana 1978). In the domain of cognitive science, Varela, Thompson, and Rosch (1991) extend the work of Merleu Ponty and argue that it's important to study cognition not only from the perspective of an external observer but also from the perspective of lived experience. There's growing recognition in many fields that studying experience from a first-person perspective is a valid and important academic approach.

Autoethnography research is expressly presented as a personal narrative of the researcher. There is no covert assumption that the author speaks with the disembodied "voice of authority" (Ellis 2004; Ellis and Bochner 2000). It's accepted that another observer wouldn't necessarily experience and interpret events in the same way or even frame the same activities in the ongoing flow of life as important "events" to be interpreted. Emotional impact is welcomed and described as a vital aspect of any experience. In writing, the author speaks from his or her heart and mind directly to the heart and mind of the reader. The primary intention is to evoke resonance in the reader through first-person narrative rather than to provide objective description and analysis.

But my research isn't precisely autoethnographic according to Ellis's definition that "Autoethnography refers to writing about the personal and its relationship to culture. It is an autobiographical genre of writing and research that displays multiple layers of consciousness" (Ellis 2004, p. 37). The primary focus of my research is myself in relationship with the nonhuman world rather than with culture. In some sense it's impossible for a human to ever leave the cultural matrix, and seeking solitude is a cultural phenomenon, but my emphasis is on the auto- rather than the ethnographic.

During the year, I not only worked to remain mindful in the present moment, but I also struggled to make sense of my experience. My search for understanding often relied more on intuitive insight than on a logical progression of thought, but there were threads of insight that wound through the year — often disappearing for a while only to reemerge into consciousness — and seemed to deepen and clarify over time. Some of the threads remained tangled and frayed, and those, too, were an important part of the experience.

In her excellent essay "Writing: A Method of Inquiry," Laura Richardson (2000) reflects on why so much academic writing is deadly dull. She argues that instead of attempting to evoke a living experience for the reader, academic writing usually tries to nail down some aspect of the world. Moreover, the process of exploration is divorced from the process of writing: first you do the research, and then you report the results. As an alternative, she encourages us to integrate the two aspects into a single dynamic process so that writing, itself, becomes an active part of the ongoing research. I've found this to be an exciting approach.

As my own research approach became more immediately self-reflexive, my area of interest broadened to embrace more than the fieldwork of living for a year in solitude. That phase remained the focus, but writing the dissertation was also an opportunity to develop mindful awareness; it became part of my exploration of education as spiritual practice (or spiritual practice in the context of education). My drift into circular self-reflexivity became clear to me while I was writing my doctoral qualifying exam essay. I began to use writing the essay as an example of what I was writing about. In doing so, I felt a surge of energy and excitement, and I thought, "Yes, this is it! This is what I've been looking for. This is the most direct way to bring my own life into the academic process."

JUNE 2001

Epigraph: S. N. Goenka, video recording of oral teaching at the December 1998 Vipassana meditation retreat, North Fork, California. Also see the Vipassana Meditation website, www.dhamma.org (accessed May 2, 2008).

A GLANCE AT OTHER SOLITARIES

Epigraph: Henry David Thoreau, *Walden* (Princeton, NJ: Princeton University Press, 1854; reprint, 1971), p. 37.
1. Ibid., p. 308.
2. Richard Byrd, *Alone* (New York: Putnam, 1938), p. 120.

JULY 2001

Epigraph: Catholic Diocese of Machakos's website, www.machakosdiocese.org /uwo/uwo_28.htm (accessed May 2, 2008).

DANCING IN THE HALLOWED HALLS

Epigraphs: Lao Tzu, *Tao Te Ching*, trans. Witter Bynner (London: Lyrebird, 1972), ch. 1; xx, Henry Miller, quoted in *The Book of Positive Quotations*, ed. John Cook (New York: Random House, 1999), p. 46.
1. Joseph Goldstein, *The Experience of Insight: A Natural Unfolding* (Santa Cruz, CA: Unity Press, 1976), p. 40.
2. Michael Polanyi, *Personal Knowledge* (Chicago: University of Chicago Press, 1958), p. 197.
3. Abraham Maslow, *The Psychology of Science* (New York: Harper & Row, 1966), p. 89.
4. Francisco Varela, in *The View from Within: First-person Approaches to the Study of Consciousness*, ed. Francisco Varela and Jonathan Shear (Thorverton, UK: Imprint Academic, 1999), p. 1.

5. Although I still sometimes get caught in dualistic thinking about realism and subjectivism, I'm slowly relinquishing the dream of an objective "God's-Eye View" of the world; I'm rediscovering my physically and culturally embodied existence. I live in an actual world; my own direct experience is neither abstract nor imaginary. It's true for me in this place at this moment, but it's not universally true.

As a concrete example, imagine how a simple object like a table might look to a spider or an infant. It seems evident that they would perceive it quite differently from how we (adult humans) do. We might say, "Yes, but we see it as it 'really' is." Now imagine seeing the table as a physicist might claim it "really" is: electrons whirling through (or electron clouds in) largely empty space around jiggling clusters of protons and neutrons. She might insist that her version is the correct one. We could also imagine the table as we would see it if we were the carpenter who had built it: the surface he had shaped and sanded, the legs he had turned on a lathe, the pieces he had assembled and varnished. We would notice every variation in grain, each small flaw in workmanship, and the nearly invisible bloodstain from a sliced finger. Which is the most accurate representation of how the world "really" is? Or are they all equally valid from distinct points of view? Perhaps the world is not any one way.

As a social example, imagine two people reading this book: one is intrigued by and identifies with the inner explorations portrayed; the other finds them self-indulgent, tedious, and irrelevant to his or her life. Each — via the journal — perceives the author in a certain way. I compare their experiences of who I am to who I experience myself to be. Which of the three views is objectively correct? Who, actually, am I? Is there an ideal, unbiased, correct answer? If so, who could know with any certainty that he or she has that complete and unbiased answer? Or is the person in the journal actually someone different for each of us? Now consider the metaphor of drawing conceptual outlines on a sheet of acetate. Our notion of who we and others are often tends to obscure the constantly changing Suchness of our being.

This is the position I find myself in. I cannot coherently claim to experience the world as it "really" is. First, my perceptions are constrained by my physical structure. My perceptual gear is sensitive to only a narrow band of all that impinges on it, and then my mind constructs an experience based on the neural response that is triggered by the appropriate stimuli. Cultural training strongly affects what I perceive and how I interpret it. Finally, as Freud and Jung showed, my personal history can affect me so strongly that I project preconceived attributes onto the world and then believe I see what exists "out there."

Although this line of reasoning seems logically clear to me, the idea that I'm cut off from the unknowable "real" world and isolated in my own mind is disturbing; it seems solipsistic and lifeless. In my heart I know that I'm part of something larger and that I didn't create myself. I exist not in a vacuum but in an environmental matrix with which I'm physically, biologically, socially, and culturally coupled. When I visualize the processes of evolution working through enormous stretches of time (or the formless presence of God dancing creation into existence), I realize I come from and belong to that something larger. I am That. But is this felt knowledge any more certain than the positivist's dream of objectivity? Here, the wheels begin to spin, and I lose traction.

I return to my own immediate experience of physical embodiment in this time and place. This awareness not only resists the assumption of pure objectivity, but also protects against flights of pure disconnected subjectivity. My experience of the world is real, but it's neither universal nor permanent. I feel my body-mind relax into this middle way — until the next time my mind begins to grasp for certainty and clutch at thoughts in the wind.

6. Ken Wilber's work is very valuable and worth reading, although some of his more recent "pop" books seem less useful than his earlier ones. For an exploration of the personal development of consciousness (and for a useful bibliography), *No Boundary* (1979) is excellent. Wilber's major work is *Sex, Ecology, Spirituality* (1995), in which he develops in detail his four-quadrant developmental model. *The Eye of Spirit* is a useful alternative (or introduction) to *Sex, Ecology, Spirituality*. All these books discuss the development and validity of various modalities of exploring the world. *Up from Eden* (1981) focuses on cultural evolution and the relationship between evolving consciousness and manifestations of culture.

One could argue that in purporting to present an objective developmental model, Wilber smuggles in his own personal and cultural values. Whenever relative value is assigned to different cultural and personal attitudes and behaviors, the assessment must be based on some hierarchical system. It cannot be otherwise. This creates a problem: What value system do we use? What grounds do we have to assume that the particular system we (or our culture) happen to prefer is universally superior? If we don't overtly acknowledge that the system we're using is our own preference, then we must covertly assume that those values are implicitly better.

Wilber points out the internal contradiction of radical relativism when it claims that all cultural mores and values are equally valid; in doing so it implicitly assumes that its own standard (equality and inclusion) is superior to the alternate standard of judging some cultural mores and values to be better than others. But Wilber himself assumes that spiritual development and a deeper and wider embrace of the world is a pre-given "universal good" rather than simply his own (and his culture's) preference.

The only way out of this bind that I can see is to assume neither that all cultural and personal attitudes and behaviors are equally good nor that one's own judgment is universally valid. Each of us needs to take personal responsibility for our values, live by and argue for them, and trust the flow of the universe to sort things out. There's a challenge here. What if someone else's values include killing anyone who holds values different from his; then what do I do?

7. In his excellent and readable book *Radical Nature*, Christian de Quincey describes four philosophical schools of thought that attempt to create internally

consistent worldviews that include the relationship between consciousness and matter: materialism, idealism, dualism, and panpsychism. Materialism and idealism begin by giving either matter or consciousness precedence as the primary "stuff" of the universe and then attempt to show how the other — which is fundamentally different in kind — can arise spontaneously. Such spontaneous arising miraculously creates something from nothing. This is, according to de Quincey, philosophically forbidden. Dualism gives both matter and consciousness equal but separate status and then attempts to demonstrate how they relate to each other. Such a relationship is also philosophically impossible.

De Quincey, himself, argues for panpsychism, which claims that consciousness and matter are not separate at any level of organization. Consciousness, in one form or another, is inherent to matter all the way down from humans to subatomic particles. This does not imply that rocks can think, but only that they, along with all else, have subjectivity: they are not merely objective things. I find it difficult to imagine that a rock has subjectivity, but I can easily imagine that all organic forms do. More important to me is my experience that the whole flowing universe, when not conceptually divided into separate things — organic and nonorganic — is fully *alive*. And when my mind is still and clear, I perceive consciousness to inhere in the whole world, not just in humans and a few other so-called higher animals. Consciousness may be called Spirit, Life, God, or any of many other names; it manifests to me experientially as the Presence of something.

As far as I can tell, there are internal inconsistencies in all conceptual systems, and I imagine that thoughtful materialists, idealists, or dualists who experience the world through one of those lenses can also point out internal inconsistencies in arguments for panpsychism. This doesn't matter to me. What does matter is that panpsychism has a long history and a respectable philosophical reputation. It's not that I believe panpsychism is necessarily *the* correct philosophical position to hold; rather it is one well-crafted story I can relate to that other people have long used to make sense of their lived experience. I am not alone.

AUGUST 2001

Epigraph: Simone Weil, *Waiting on God: Letters and Essays* (London: Fount, 1977), p. 55.

SEPTEMBER 2001

Epigraph: Antonio Machado, "Cantares," 1929. The original Spanish version is available at the *Los Poetas* website, www.los-poetas.com/a/mach.htm (accessed May 2, 2008); this English translation is mine.

THE URGE TO BE ALONE

Epigraphs: Arthur Schopenhauer, quoted in *The Viking Book of Aphorisms*, ed. W. H. Auden and Louis Kronenberger (New York: Viking, 1962; reprint, New

York: Barnes and Noble Books, 1993), p. 134; John Donne, Meditation V. in *The Complete Poetry and Selected Prose of John Donne*, ed. Charles M. Coffin, (New York: Modern Library, 1952), pp. 420–421; Paul Tillich, *The Eternal Now* (New York: Scribner, 1963), p. 11.

1. Anthony Storr, *Solitude: A Return to the Self* (New York: Ballantine, 1988), p. 35.

2. Ibid., p. 85.

3. Henri Nouwen, *Out of Solitude: Three Meditations on the Christian Life* (Notre Dame, IN: Ave Maria Press, 1974), p. 18.

4. Charles Alexander Eastman, quoted in Philip Koch, *Solitude: A Philosophical Encounter* (Peru, IL: Open Court, 1994), p. 284.

5. Koch, *Solitude*, p. 27.

6. David Hume, quoted in Koch, *Solitude*, p. 211.

7. Storr, *Solitude*, p. xiv.

8. Henri Nouwen, quoted in Koch, *Solitude*, p. 244.

9. Henri Nouwen, *The Way of the Heart: Desert Spirituality and Contemporary Ministry* (New York: HarperCollins, 1981), p. 34.

10. Koch, *Solitude*, p. 230.

11. Octavio Paz, *Labyrinth of Solitude*, trans. Lysander Kemp (New York: Grove, 1961), p. 195.

12. Marcel Proust, quoted in Koch, *Solitude*, p. 160.

13. Koch, *Solitude*, pp. 190, 199.

14. Petrarch, quoted in Koch, *Solitude*, p. 209.

15. Thomas Merton, quoted in Koch, *Solitude*, p. 113.

16. Nouwen, *The Way of the Heart*, p. 27.

17. Koch, *Solitude*, p. 216.

18. The data are taken from Robert Greenway, "The Wilderness Effect and Ecopsychology," in Allen Kanner, Theodore Roszak, and Mary Gomes (eds.), *Ecopsychology: Restoring the Earth, Healing the Mind* (San Francisco: Sierra Club Books, 1995), p. 128.

19. Greenway, "On Crossing and Not Crossing the Wilderness Boundary," unpublished manuscript from a talk given at the 5th World Wilderness Conference, Tromso, Norway, 1993, p. 207.

OCTOBER 2001

Epigraph: Zen proverb quoted in Ken Wilber, *The Spectrum of Consciousness* (Wheaton, IL: Theosophical Publishing House, 1977), p. 300.

TECHNOLOGY AND DESIRE

Epigraphs: Arthur C. Clarke, *Profiles of the Future: An Inquiry into the Limits of the Possible* (London: V. Gollancz, 1982) — this aphorism is often referred to as Clarke's Third Law; David Brower, quoted in Jerry Mander, *In the Absence of the Sacred: The Failure of Technology and the Survival of the Indian Nations* (San Francisco: Sierra Club Books, 1991), p. 43; Thoreau, *Walden*, p. 37.

NOVEMBER 2001

Epigraph: Joseph Campbell with Bill Moyers, *The Power of Myth* (New York: Anchor Books, 1991), p. 1.

DECEMBER 2001

Epigraph: Zen saying, attributed to Shunryu Suzuki-roshi, *Workman's Zen Calendar*, entry for June 14, 2005, (New York: Workman, 2005).

SPIRITUAL PRACTICE

Epigraph: The Buddha, Diamond Sutra, in *The Buddha Speaks*, ed. Anne Bancroft (Boston: Shambhala, 2000), p. 83.
1. Ken Wilber, *Sex, Ecology, Spirituality* (Boston: Shambhala, 1995), pp. 347, 530n2.

SMALL MIND/BIG MIND

Epigraphs: Albert Einstein, quoted in the *New York Post*, November 28, 1972; Chögyam Trungpa Rinpoche, *Cutting through Spiritual Materialism* (Boston: Shambhala, 1973), p. 8.
1. Mel Weitsman, from *Dogen's Shobogenzo*. Talk given at Chapel Hill Zen Center, Chapel Hill, NC, November 8, 1997, available at www.intrex.net/chzg/mel10.htm (accessed May 2, 2008).
2. These three quotes are from Jack Kornfield, *A Path with a Heart* (New York: Bantam, 1993), pp. 147, 254, 269.

FEBRUARY 2002

Epigraph: J. Krishnamurti, "Truth Is a Pathless Land," talk delivered August 2, 1929, Ommen, Netherlands, http://www.kfa.org/history-of-krishnamurti.php (accessed May 2, 2008).

REENTRY

Epigraph: D. T. Suzuki, *The Awakening of Zen* (Boston: Shambhala, 1980), p. 111.

EPILOGUE

Epigraphs: Zen saying, *Workman's Zen Calendar*, entry for March 1, 2005 (New York: Workman, 2005); H. L. Mencken, *Minority Report: H.L. Mencken's Notebook*, (Baltimore: Johns Hopkins University Press, 1997), p. 241.

BIBLIOGRAPHY

Abbey, Edward. *Desert Solitaire*. New York: Ballantine, 1968.

Abram, David. *The Spell of the Sensuous*. New York: Vintage, 1996.

Barbour, Ian. *Religion in an Age of Science*. The Gifford Lectures, vol. 1 San Francisco: Harper & Row, 1990.

Barks, Coleman, with John Moyne, A. J. Arberry, and Reynold Nicholson (trans.). *The Essential Rumi*. San Francisco: HarperSanFrancisco, 1995.

Bohm, David. *Wholeness and the Implicate Order*. London: Routledge & Kegan Paul, 1980.

Broyles, William Jr. *Cast Away*. Directed by Robert Zemeckis. Produced by J. Rapke, R. Zemeckis, and S. Starkey. Distributed by 20th Century Fox, 2002.

Byrd, Richard. *Alone*. New York: Putnam and Sons, 1938.

Chuang Tzu. *Basic Writings*. Translated by Burton Watson. New York: Columbia University Press, 1964.

Coffin, Charles, ed. *The Complete Poetry and Selected Prose of John Donne*. New York: Modern Library, 1952.

Couve, Enrique, and Claudio Vidal-Ojeda. *Birds of the Beagle Channel*. Punta Arenas, Chile: Fantástico Sur, 2000.

Csikszentmihalyi, Mihaly. *Flow: The Psychology of Optimal Experience*. New York: Harper & Row, 1990.

Czajkowski, Chris. *Nuk Tessli: The Life of a Wilderness Dweller*. Victoria, BC: Orca, 1999.

Darwin, Charles. *The Origin of Species*. New York: Modern Library, 1959, 1971.

Defoe, Daniel. *Robinson Crusoe*. Oxford: Oxford University Press, 1719, 1998.

De la Peña, Martin, and Maurice Rumboll. *Birds of Southern South America and Antarctica*. Princeton, NJ: Princeton University Press, 2001.

De Quincey, Christian. "Integral Visioning." http://integralvisioning.org/
article.php?story=cdq-truth-wisdom.

———. *Radical Nature*. Montpelier, VT: Invisible Cities Press, 2002.

Dillard, Annie. *Teaching a Stone to Talk*. New York: Harper & Row, 1982.

Ellis, Caroline. *The Ethnographic I*. Walnut Creek, CA: AltaMira, 2004.

Ellis, Caroline, and Arthur Bochner. "Autoethnography, Personal Narrative,
Reflexivity." In Norman Denzin and Yvonna Lincoln (eds.), *Handbook of
Qualitative Research*, Second Edition. Thousand Oaks, CA: Sage, 2000.

Epstein, Mark. *Thoughts without a Thinker: Psychotherapy from a Buddhist
Perspective*. New York: Basic Books, 1995.

France, Peter. *Hermits*. New York: St. Martin's Griffin, 1996.

Freire, Pablo. *Pedagogy of the Oppressed*. Translated by M.B. Ramos. New York:
Seabury Press, 1970.

Freud, Sigmund. *Introductory Lectures on Psychoanalysis*. New York: Norton, 1966.

Goldstein, Joseph. *The Experience of Insight: A Natural Unfolding*. Santa Cruz, CA:
Unity Press, 1976.

Goldstein, Joseph, and Jack Kornfield. *Seeking the Heart of Wisdom*. Boston:
Shambhala, 1987.

Greenway, Robert. "On Crossing and Not Crossing the Wilderness Boundary."
Unpublished manuscript from a talk given at the 5th World Wilderness
Conference. Tromso, Norway, 1993.

———. "The Wilderness Effect and Ecopsychology." In Allen Kanner,
Theodore Roszak, and Mary Gomes (eds.). *Ecopsychology: Restoring the Earth,
Healing the Mind*. San Francisco: Sierra Club Books, 1995.

Harper, Steven. "The Way of Wilderness." In Allen Kanner, Theodore Roszak,
and Mary Gomes (eds.). *Ecopsychology: Restoring the Earth, Healing the Mind*.
San Francisco: Sierra Club Books, 1995.

Harvey, Andrew, and Eryk Hanut. *Perfume of the Desert: Inspirations from Sufi
Wisdom*. Wheaton, IL: Quest, 1999.

I Ching. Translated by Wilhelm, Richard and Cary Baynes. Princeton, NJ:
Princeton University Press, 1950.

Jung, Carl. *Basic Writings*. Violet de Laszlo (ed.), New York: Random House, 1959.

———. *Man and His Symbols*. New York: Dell, 1964.

Junger, Sebastian. *The Perfect Storm: A True Story of Men Against the Sea*, New
York: Norton, 1997.

Kauffman, Stuart. *At Home in the Universe: The Search for Laws of Self-organization
and Complexity*. New York: Oxford University Press, 1995.

Keith, Sam, and Richard Proenneke. *One Man's Wilderness: An Alaskan Odyssey*.
Anchorage: Alaska Northwest Publishing Co., 1973.

Koch, Philip. *Solitude: A Philosophical Encounter*. Peru, IL: Open Court, 1994.

Kornfield, Jack. *A Path with a Heart*. New York: Bantam Books, 1993.

Krishnamurti, J. *Commentaries on Living: First Series*. D. Rajagopal (ed.).
    Wheaton, IL: Quest, 1968.

Lao Tzu. *Tao Te Ching*. Translated by Witter Bynner. London: Lyrebird, 1972.

Margulis, Lynn. Early Life. In William Thompson (ed.). *Gaia: A Way of Knowing*.
    Great Barrington, MA: Lindisfarne Press, 1987.

Maslow, Abraham. *The Psychology of Science*. New York: Harper & Row, 1966.

Maslow, Abraham. *Toward a Psychology of Being*. Second Edition. New York:
    Van Nostrand Reinhold, 1968.

Maturana, Humberto. "Biology of Language: The Epistemology of Reality." In
    *Psychology and Biology of Language and Thought: Essays in Honor of Eric
    Lenneberg*. San Diego: Academic Press, 1978.

Maturana, Humberto R., and Francisco Varela. *The Tree of Knowledge: The Biolog-
    ical Roots of Human Understanding*. Boston: Shambhala, 1987.

Merry, Wayne. *St. John Ambulance Official Wilderness First Aid Guide*. Toronto:
    McClelland & Stewart, 1994.

Merton, Thomas. *New Seeds of Contemplation*. Boston: Shambhala, 1972.

————. *The Wisdom of the Desert*. New York: New Directions, 1960.

Mihovilovic, Nicolás. *Entre el Cielo y el Silencio*. Santiago, Chile: Pineda Libros, 1974.

Moore, Thomas. *Care of the Soul*. New York: HarperCollins, 1992.

Network Innovations website. http://www.networkinv.com.

Nouwen, Henri. *Out of Solitude: Three Meditations on the Christian Life*. Notre
    Dame, IN: Ave Maria Press, 1974.

————. *The Way of the Heart: Desert Spirituality and Contemporary Ministry*. New
    York: HarperCollins, 1981.

Oliver, Mary. *Dream Work*. Boston: Atlantic Monthly Press, 1986.

Outboard Marine Corporation. *Johnson Outboards Service Manual: Models 9.9-30*.
    Waukegan, IL: Outboard Marine Corporation, 1991.

Patterson, Kevin. *The Water in Between: A Journey at Sea*. Toronto: Random
    House Canada, 1999.

Paz, Octavio. *Labyrinth of Solitude*. New York: Grove Press, 1961.

Piaget, Jean. *The Psychology of the Child*. New York: Basic Books, 1969.

Polanyi, Michael. *Personal Knowledge*. Chicago: University of Chicago Press, 1958.

Richardson, Laura. "Writing: A Method of Inquiry." In Norman Denzin and
    Yvonna Lincoln (eds.), *Handbook of Qualitative Research*, Second Edition.
    Thousand Oaks, CA: Sage, 2000.

Severin, Tim. *In Search of Robinson Crusoe*. New York: Basic Books, 2002.

Shekhdar, Jim, and Edward Griffiths. *Bold Man of the Sea*. London: Hodder &
    Stoughton, 2002.

Simon, Alvah. *North to the Night: A Spiritual Odyssey in the Arctic*. Camden, ME:
    International Marine, 1998.

Singer, Isaac. *The Family Moskat*. New York: Farrar, Straus & Giroux, 1950.

Storr, Anthony. *Solitude: A Return to the Self*. New York: Ballantine, 1988.

Suzuki, Shunryu. *Zen Mind, Beginner's Mind*. Edited by Trudi Dixon. New York: Weatherhill, 1970.

Thompson, William, ed. *Gaia: A Way of Knowing*. Great Barrington, MA: Lindisfarne Press, 1987.

Thoreau, Henry David. *Walden*. Princeton, NJ: Princeton University Press, 1854, 1971.

Trungpa, Chögyam. *Cutting Through Spiritual Materialism*. Boston: Shambhala, 1973.

————. *The Myth of Freedom*. Boston: Shambhala, 1976.

Varela, Francisco. Editor's Introduction. In Francisco Varela and Jonathan Shear (eds.). *The View from Within: First-person Approaches to the Study of Consciousness*. Thorverton, UK: Imprint Academic, 1999.

Varela, Francisco, Evan Thompson, and Eleanor Rosch. *The Embodied Mind*. Cambridge, MA: MIT Press, 1991.

Watts, Alan. *Nature, Man and Woman*. New York: Pantheon Books, 1958.

Wells, H. G. *Apropos of Dolores*. London: J. Cape, 1938.

Werner, David. *Where There Is No Doctor: A Village Healthcare Handbook*. Palo Alto, CA: Hesperian Foundation, 1977.

Wilber, Ken. *The Eye of Spirit*. Boston: Shambhala, 1998.

————. *No Boundary*. Boston: Shambhala, 1979.

————. *Sex, Ecology, Spirituality*. Boston: Shambhala, 1995.

————. *Up from Eden*. New York: Doubleday, 1981.

Wodehouse, P. G. *How Right You Are, Jeeves*. New York: Harper & Row, 1960.

————. *Right Ho, Jeeves*. Middlesex, UK: Penguin Books, 1934, 1975.

Puerto Montt

CHILE

A
N
D
E
S

ARGENTINA

Atlantic Ocean

Retreat
Site

Pacific Ocean

Puerto Natales

Strait of Magellan

Punta Arenas

Tierra del
Fuego

N

TIP OF SOUTH AMERICA

0   50   100   150 mi

0   50 100 150 200 250 km

Cape Horn

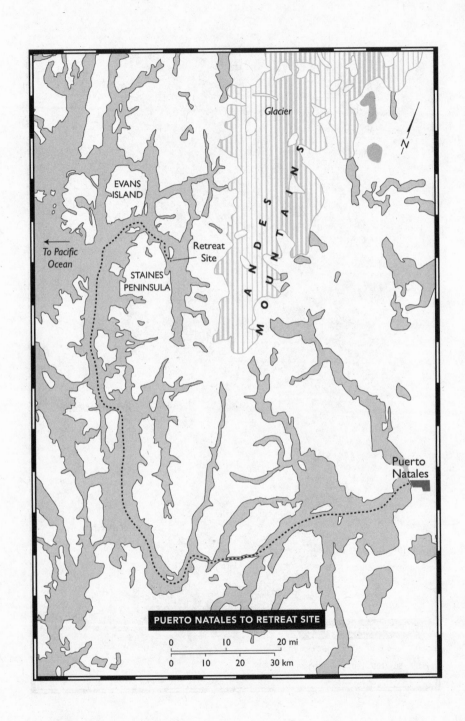

Glacier

EVANS
ISLAND

To Pacific
Ocean

Retreat
Site

STAINES
PENINSULA

A
N
D
E
S

M
O
U
N
T
A
I
N
S

N

Puerto
Natales

PUERTO NATALES TO RETREAT SITE

0   10   20 mi

0   10   20   30 km

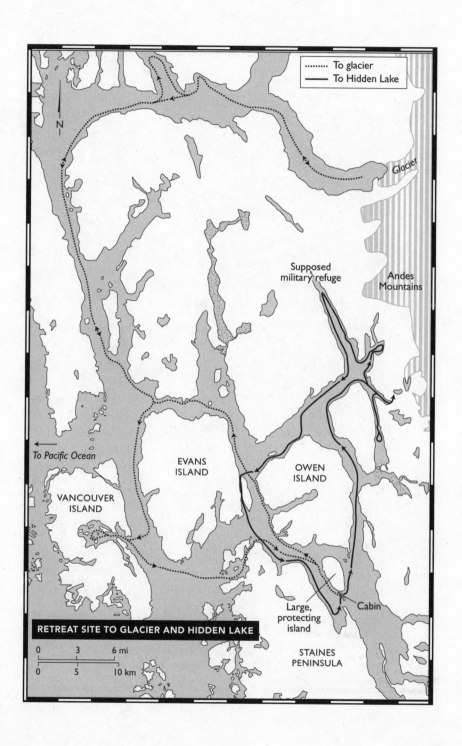

Legend:
- ·········· To glacier
- ———— To Hidden Lake

Glacier

Andes Mountains

Supposed military refuge

To Pacific Ocean

EVANS ISLAND

OWEN ISLAND

VANCOUVER ISLAND

Large, protecting island

Cabin

STAINES PENINSULA

N

RETREAT SITE TO GLACIER AND HIDDEN LAKE

| 0 | 3 | 6 mi |
| 0 | 5 | 10 km |

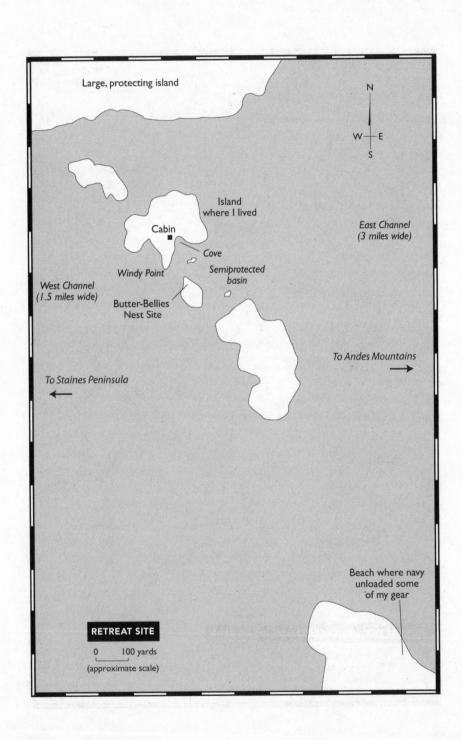

Large, protecting island

N
W — E
S

Island
where I lived

Cabin

East Channel
(3 miles wide)

Cove

Windy Point

Semiprotected
basin

West Channel
(1.5 miles wide)

Butter-Bellies
Nest Site

To Andes Mountains →

← To Staines Peninsula

Beach where navy
unloaded some
of my gear

RETREAT SITE

0   100 yards
(approximate scale)

ABOUT THE AUTHOR

Born in Ventura, California, Robert Kull has spent years wandering North and South America, working as a scuba instructor, travel guide, construction worker, logger, dishwasher, truck driver, bartender, community organic gardening teacher, firefighter, photographer, and professor. In 1985 he lost his lower right leg after a motorcycle crash in the Dominican Republic. He began undergraduate studies at age forty and now holds a PhD from the University of British Columbia. He currently lives in Vancouver, BC. His website is www.bobkull.org.

NEW WORLD LIBRARY is dedicated to publishing books and other media that inspire and challenge us to improve the quality of our lives and the world.

We are a socially and environmentally aware company, and we strive to embody the ideals presented in our publications. We recognize that we have an ethical responsibility to our customers, our staff members, and our planet.

We serve our customers by creating the finest publications possible on personal growth, creativity, spirituality, wellness, and other areas of emerging importance. We serve New World Library employees with generous benefits, significant profit sharing, and constant encouragement to pursue their most expansive dreams.

As a member of the Green Press Initiative, we print an increasing number of books with soy-based ink on 100 percent postconsumer-waste recycled paper. Also, we power our offices with solar energy and contribute to nonprofit organizations working to make the world a better place for us all.

Our products are available
in bookstores everywhere.
For our catalog, please contact:

New World Library
14 Pamaron Way
Novato, California 94949

Phone: 415-884-2100 or 800-972-6657
Catalog requests: Ext. 50
Orders: Ext. 52
Fax: 415-884-2199
Email: escort@newworldlibrary.com

To subscribe to our electronic newsletter, visit
www.newworldlibrary.com